Mutual Fund Investing For Canadians

2nd Edition

by Bryan Borzykowski and Andrew Bell

for dummies®

A Wiley Brand

Mutual Fund Investing For Canadians For Dummies®, 2nd Edition

Published by: **John Wiley & Sons, Inc.**, 111 River Street, Hoboken, NJ 07030-5774, www.wiley.com

Copyright © 2024 by John Wiley & Sons, Inc., Hoboken, New Jersey

Media and software compilation copyright © 2024 by John Wiley & Sons, Inc. All rights reserved.

Published simultaneously in Canada

For general information on our other products and services, please contact our Customer Care Department within the U.S. at 877-762-2974, outside the U.S. at 317-572-3993, or fax 317-572-4002. For technical support, please visit https://hub.wiley.com/community/support/dummies.

Wiley publishes in a variety of print and electronic formats and by print-on-demand. Some material included with standard print versions of this book may not be included in e-books or in print-on-demand. If this book refers to media such as a CD or DVD that is not included in the version you purchased, you may download this material at http://booksupport.wiley.com. For more information about Wiley products, visit www.wiley.com.

Library of Congress Control Number: 2024930164

ISBN 978-1-394-21976-6 (pbk); ISBN 978-1-394-21977-3 (ebk); ISBN 978-1-394-21978-0 (ebk)

SKY10064807_011224

Contents at a Glance

Introduction 1

Part 1: Meet the Mutual Fund 5
CHAPTER 1: Mutual Funds 101 7
CHAPTER 2: Buying and Selling Basics 19
CHAPTER 3: Paperwork and Your Rights 35
CHAPTER 4: Building Your Financial Plan 53
CHAPTER 5: Beyond Mutual Funds 67

Part 2: Buying Options: Looking for a Helping Hand 79
CHAPTER 6: Discount Brokers: Cheap Thrills 81
CHAPTER 7: Banks: The Fast Food of Funds 93
CHAPTER 8: Stockbrokers, Financial Planners, and Advisors Aplenty 103
CHAPTER 9: Buying Direct: Five Independents that Sell to the Public 119

Part 3: The Fund Stuff: Building a Strong Portfolio 135
CHAPTER 10: Equity Funds: The Road to Riches 137
CHAPTER 11: Heirloom Equity Funds: The Dull Stuff that Will Make
You Wealthy 155
CHAPTER 12: Las Vegas–Style Equity Funds: Trips You Don't Need 165
CHAPTER 13: Balanced Funds: Boring Can Be Good 179
CHAPTER 14: Bond Funds: Boring Can Be Sexy, Too 195
CHAPTER 15: Exchange-Traded Funds and Index Funds: The Art of
Owning Everything 211
CHAPTER 16: Dividend and Income Funds: Confusion Galore 227
CHAPTER 17: Money Market Funds: Sleepy but Simple 239
CHAPTER 18: Fund Oddities: Strange Brews Sometimes Worth Tasting 249
CHAPTER 19: Segregated Funds: Investing on Autopilot 257
CHAPTER 20: Fund Packages: One-Stop Shopping 267

**Part 4: The Nuts and Bolts of Keeping
Your Portfolio Going** 277
CHAPTER 21: The Places to Go for Fund Information 279
CHAPTER 22: RRSPs and TFSAs: Fertilizer for Your Mutual Funds 289
CHAPTER 23: Taxes: Timing Is Everything 303

Part 5: The Part of Tens 317

CHAPTER 24: Ten Questions to Ask a Potential Financial Advisor 319

CHAPTER 25: Ten Signs You Need a New Financial Advisor 325

CHAPTER 26: Ten Mistakes Investors Make 331

Index 335

Table of Contents

INTRODUCTION 1
    About This Book. 1
    Foolish Assumptions. 2
    Icons Used in This Book 3
    Beyond the Book. 3
    Where to Go from Here 4

PART 1: MEET THE MUTUAL FUND 5

CHAPTER 1: **Mutual Funds 101**. 7
    Getting the Scoop on Mutual Fund. 8
        Open-and closed-end funds 9
        Returns — What's in it for you? 11
        How funds can make you rich .15
        What mutual funds buy 15
    Finding Your Type (of Funds). 17
    Figuring out Where to Buy. 17

CHAPTER 2: **Buying and Selling Basics**. .19
    Reasons to Buy Funds. 19
        Offering safety in numbers: Public scrutiny and accountability. . .20
        Putting your eggs in many baskets. 23
        Getting good returns from professional management 24
        Making investing convenient. .24
        Investing without breaking the bank 25
        Watching over your investment 26
        Cashing out — Getting your money if you need it 27
    Perils and Pitfalls of Funds. 27
        Excessive costs. 27
        Style drift — When managers get lost in the jungle 28
        When managers blow it 28
        Can't see the forest for the funds 29
        Vague explanations of poor performance. 30
        Prospectuses that don't say enough. 30
    Load versus No-Load — The Great Divide. 31
        Load funds — The comfort zone. 31
        No-load funds — The direct approach. 33

CHAPTER 3: **Paperwork and Your Rights**........................35
Getting Set Up 36
Filling in your account (or RRSP) application form 36
Getting confirmed 40
Dealing with Prospectuses...............................40
You've been warned 41
More charges to look for 43
Introducing the Management Report of Fund Performance 44
Looking at what goes into an MRFP 44
Checking out an MRFP 45
Understanding Your Account Statement.....................49
Reading Annual and Semi-Annual Financial Statements
(Or Annual Reports) 50

CHAPTER 4: **Building Your Financial Plan**.....................53
Looking at Your Long-Term Financial Future 54
Setting Your Financial Priorities...........................55
Understanding What Type of Investor You Are 58
Understanding That Investing Is an Inexact Science 59
Remembering the Importance of Diversification................61
Portfolios for Your Type of Investing 62
A look at index funds 62
A penny earned is a penny saved 64
Balancing act 65
One for the risk-takers 65

CHAPTER 5: **Beyond Mutual Funds** 67
The Good Old GIC: You Know Where You Sleep.................68
Looking at the Types of GICs 68
Finding the best rates.................................70
Checking out the benefits of GICs.......................70
Watching out for inflation 71
Bonds: Stable Securities for Every Portfolio 72
Considering bond alternatives 72
Investing directly in bonds.............................73
Stocks: Thrills, Spills, and Twisted Wreckage.................74
Going with index funds and ETFs 75
Buying individual stocks...............................75
Taking a wilder ride with stock alternatives.................76
Managed Products: A Fee Circus...........................77

PART 2: BUYING OPTIONS: LOOKING FOR A HELPING HAND 79

CHAPTER 6: **Discount Brokers: Cheap Thrills** 81

What Are Discount Brokers? 82
Looking into Canadian discounters 83
Getting set up with a discounter 83
Why Discount Brokers Are a Great Place to Buy Funds 84
Your one-stop shop — Convenience 84
Access to a broad selection of options 85
A wealth of investing information .85
At last — a break on costs 86
A word on commissions 86
How to Pick a Discounter 88
Getting a feel for the service 89
Finding the right discounter for you 90
Considering a mutual fund discount broker 90
What's Wrong with Discount Brokers? 91
Getting seduced and abandoned .91
Knowing when to stay away 91
Relying on robots to manage your money 92

CHAPTER 7: **Banks: The Fast Food of Funds** 93

Buy Where You Bank 94
Providing one-stop shopping 94
Keeping it together 94
Offering appealing options 95
Fighting for the right to serve you .95
Buyer Beware: Shortfalls in Bank Offerings 96
Few options 96
Overworked and underpaid: Not just you, some bankers, too . . .97
Lack of pressure to perform 97
How Banks Pulled Up Their Socks 98
Improving your choice of funds 99
Stretching the rules with bank offerings 99
A Few Gems from the Banks 100

CHAPTER 8: **Stockbrokers, Financial Planners, and Advisors Aplenty** 103

Alphabet Soup: Figuring Out All Those Titles 104
Commissioned advisors 105
Fee-only financial planners 106
Fee-based investment advisors 107
Salaried advisors 107

Deciding Whether to Pay a Fee or a Commission. 109
    Paying fees 109
    Going with a commission-paid advisor 111
    Using a Salesperson to Your Advantage 113
Exploring Important Qualifications. 113
The right way to pick an advisor 115
The wrong way to pick an adviser. 116

CHAPTER 9: **Buying Direct: Five Independents that**
Sell to the Public 119
Getting Started with Direct Sellers 120
    Paying to play. 121
    Considering whether a direct seller is right for you 121
Enjoying the Benefits of Dealing with an Independent
No-Load Company. 122
    Putting more money in your pocket. 123
    Offering advice for grown-ups. 123
    Keeping matters simple 124
    Allowing frequent trades 125
Weighing the Drawbacks of Going Direct .128
    Significant levels of cash required 129
    Lack of choice. 129
Sizing Up the Five Independents. 130
    Beutel Goodman 131
    Pembroke 132
    Leith Wheeler. 132
    Mawer 132
    Steadyhand. 133

PART 3: THE FUND STUFF: BUILDING A STRONG
PORTFOLIO 135

CHAPTER 10: **Equity Funds: The Road to Riches**. 137
Making Investing in Stocks Simple 138
    In for the long haul 140
    A test case for capitalism: Meet Angus and Bronwyn 140
    A real-life example of equity investing. .141
Deciding How Much to Bet on Equity Funds 142
    Knowing your investment style. 143
    Learning from history. 144
    Splitting between index and actively managed funds 146
Knowing What Return to Expect from Your Funds. 147

Picking a Fund: The Basics 147
    Select from all industries 148
    Hold blue-chip winners. 149
    Check out past performance, with caution 149
Avoiding a Lemon 151
    Remembering the importance of diversification 152
    Looking at the big picture and knowing when to bail 152

CHAPTER 11: Heirloom Equity Funds: The Dull Stuff that Will Make You Wealthy 155
How Many Equity Funds Do You Need?. 156
    Ruling out specialty funds 157
    Deciding how much to put into equity funds 157
    Dividing your money between Canadian and foreign
    equity funds 158
    How do you split your money among equity funds? 159
Global Equity Funds: Meet Faraway People and Exploit Them. 160
    Applying the ABC rules to your global equity funds. 161
    Checking out three global equity winners 161
Canadian Equity Funds: Making Maple-Syrup-Flavoured Money. . . .162
    Applying the ABC rules to your Canadian equity funds. 163
    Looking at three winners in Canadian equities. 163

CHAPTER 12: Las Vegas–Style Equity Funds: Trips You Don't Need 165
Small and Mid-Sized Company Funds: Spotty Little Fellows. 166
    Hitting highs and lows 166
    Picking a winning fund 167
    Understanding the disadvantages 168
Regional Equity Funds: Welcome to Bangkok — or Hong Kong? 168
    European funds: Why are all these people so well dressed? 169
    Asian funds: The dream that died. 170
    Japanese, please: Once hot, now not 170
    U.S. equity funds: Going for growth 171
    Emerging markets funds: Fast growing or still struggling? 172
Sector Funds: Limitations Galore 174
    Resource funds: Pouring money down a hole 174
    Science and technology funds: But how will you control it,
    Professor?. 176
    Financial services funds: Buying the banks doesn't
    always pay 177

CHAPTER 13: **Balanced Funds: Boring Can Be Good** 179
    Understanding Balanced Funds 180
        Reviewing the asset mix of balanced funds. 180
        Plodding along profitably. 181
        Retiring with balanced funds. 182
        Steering clear of potholes: Consistently strong returns 182
        Taking a look at one balanced biggie 183
    Reviewing the Problems with Balanced Funds 184
        High fees and expenses 184
        Bewildering brews of assets 185
        Difficulty judging fund manager performance 185
    A Simple Plan for Picking the Right Canadian Balanced Fund 186
        Knowing what to avoid. 187
        Identifying the best funds 187
        Looking at some high-quality balanced funds 187
    Global Balanced Funds — As Good as It Gets? 188
        Going global: A near-perfect investment? 189
        Examining a couple of world-beaters. 190
    Tactical Balanced Funds: Pay Me to Lose Your Money 192
        All flash and no pan: Looking at asset allocation
        returns and management styles. 192
        Who's running this crazy show? 193

CHAPTER 14: **Bond Funds: Boring Can Be Sexy, Too** 195
    Some Great Reasons to Choose Bonds 196
        Offering greater security than equities .196
        Increasing their value against deflation. 197
    How Much Do I Need in Bonds? 198
    How to Pick a Good Bond Fund in 30 Seconds. 200
        Insisting on affordability. 200
        Looking for quality in provincial and federal bonds. 200
        Checking out two beautiful bond funds. 201
    How Inflation Affects Bonds 201
        Rising interest rates, falling bond prices 201
        Falling interest rates, rising bond prices 202
    Index Funds and Bonds: A Match Made in Heaven 203
    Long Bonds: Grabbing the Lion by the Tail .203
        Why you may want to rule out long-term bond funds. 204
        Why you may want to consider long-term bond funds. 204
    Short-Term Bond Funds: Playing It Safe. 204
        Getting to know short-term bond funds 205
        Comparing short-term fixed income funds to money
        market funds 205
        Checking out a couple of short-term bond fund winners 206

High-Yield Bond Funds: Naked Bungee-Jumping 207
    Considering the strikes against high-yield bond funds 207
    Investigating high-yield bond funds in Canada. 208
Bonds Outside Canada 208
    Diversification at a high cost 209
    A couple of recommended global bond funds 209

CHAPTER 15: **Exchange-Traded Funds and Index Funds: The Art of Owning Everything** 211
    Buying the Whole Enchilada: The Ups and Downs of Indexing 212
        Exploring why ETFs and index funds are great for you 212
        Delving into the dark side of ETF and index funds 215
    Fitting ETFs and Index Funds into Your Portfolio 216
    Evaluating Regular Mutual Fund and ETF Performance 218
    Understanding Why Fund Managers Seldom Beat the Market 218
        Balancing wins and losses 219
        Paying for active management 220
    Overcoming Some Salespeople's Dislike of Index
    Funds and ETFs 220
    Buying ETFS and index funds. 221
        Selecting the right index. 221
        Choosing between index funds and ETFs 222
        Knowing where to buy 222
        Considering some winning ETFs and index funds 223
    Straying from the Norm: Specialized Index Funds and ETFs 224
        Tilted funds: Indexing on steroids. 225
        Other ETF options 225

CHAPTER 16: **Dividend and Income Funds: Confusion Galore** . . .227
    What Are Dividend and Income Funds?. 228
        Looking at the upside of dividend funds 228
        Considering the downside 229
        Figuring out why companies pay, or don't pay, dividends 229
    Are Dividend and Income Funds Right for You? 231
    The Appealing Tax Implications of Dividends 232
        Crunching the numbers 233
        Understanding why dividend funds may or may
        not be good for your RRSP. 233
        Digging into why dividend funds may or may not be
        good for your TFSA 234
    How to Select a Winning Dividend Fund 235
        Questions to ask before you buy 235
        Two strong dividend and income funds. 236

The Times Are a'Changin': The Fall of Preferred Shares
and Income Trusts..236
    Preferred shares 237
    Income trust funds 237

CHAPTER 17: **Money Market Funds: Sleepy but Simple** 239
Digging into Money Market Funds 240
Checking Up on Your Money Market Fund 242
Deciding if Money Markets Are All They're Cracked Up to Be......244
    Short-term bond funds can be even better than
    money market funds..244
    HISA funds are hot 245
Selecting Winning Money Market Funds: Pick Only the Plums......245
    Choose from a mix of money market funds 246
    Check out U.S. money market funds 247
    Watch those pesky expenses...............................247
    Get the lowdown on MERs..................................247
    Beware of empty promises 248
    Be curious, George 248

CHAPTER 18: **Fund Oddities: Strange Brews Sometimes
Worth Tasting** 249
Target Date Funds: A Gimmick that May Make Sense 250
    Considering your options..................................250
    Knowing what to look for..................................251
ESG Funds: Once Obscure Securities Have Now Gone
Mainstream 251
Labour-Sponsored Funds: Small Business, Big Tax
Break — for Now...252
Funds with Trendy and Focused Mandates......................254

CHAPTER 19: **Segregated Funds: Investing on Autopilot** 257
Hang On to Your Hats: The Rise of the Segregated Fund 258
    Security with segs 258
    The popularity of segs sag 259
    A fancy fund makeover.....................................259
Seg Fund Essentials...260
    Guaranteeing the return of your initial investment.........260
    Living longer than you may 261
    Enabling you to reset the value of successful funds 261
    Offering asset protection.................................261
    Giving to your heir apparent without the hassle 262
The Cost of Certainty 263
The "Deal" with Segs 264
To Seg or Not to Seg: Are They for You?......................265

CHAPTER 20: **Fund Packages: One-Stop Shopping**.................267

The Flavours Fund Packages Come In 268

Checking out the risk categories.........................268

Sticking with Canada or going global 269

What to Find Out Before You Buy...............................269

How much will this cost me? 270

How do I know how well I'm doing? 271

The Upside of Fund Packages 271

The Downside of Fund Packages 272

Steer Clear of the Hype......................................273

A Look at a Decent Fund Package.............................274

PART 4: THE NUTS AND BOLTS OF KEEPING YOUR
PORTFOLIO GOING 277

CHAPTER 21: **The Places to Go for Fund Information** 279

Independent Sources: Where to Get the Honest Goods..........280

Taking a look at the top two.............................280

Checking out other sites worth a visit 282

The Regulatory Jungle: When You Need Official Stuff 284

The Investment Funds Institute of Canada 284

Get Smarter About Money................................285

Mutual Fund Dealers Association of Canada...............285

The System for Electronic Document Analysis and
Retrieval (SEDAR)......................................285

Fund Company Sites: Useful Information, But Mind
the Context..286

Brokers and Planners: Only the Basics 287

CHAPTER 22: **RRSPs and TFSAs: Fertilizer for Your
Mutual Funds**...289

Pour It in and Watch It Grow: Understanding RRSPs..............290

Figuring out how much you can put in your RRSP 291

Understanding the power of tax deferral 292

Investigating what happens to your RRSP after you retire 293

The Really Tax Free Investment Account: TFSA..................294

Delving into the ins and outs of TFSA contributions 294

Investing in a TFSA......................................296

Deciding whether to use an RRSP or TFSA — or both 296

Where to Buy Your RRSP 297

The Beautiful Garden That Is the Self-Directed RRSP 299

The Most Fragrant Flower: Choosing Funds for Your RRSP 300

Including international investments.........................300

Mixing the right assets 301

CHAPTER 23: **Taxes: Timing Is Everything**..........................303

  The Wacky World of Fund Distributions.....................304
      Paying out distributions to fundholders 304
      Watching out for tax exposure 306
      Determining what distributions your fund has declared 307
  Taxes on Fund Distributions 308
      Enjoying tax breaks on Canadian content..................308
      Getting tax slips..................................309
  Taxes When You Sell or Exchange 309
      Checking out tax-skirting fund structures 310
      Working through capital gain calculations..................310
      Avoiding fund purchases near year-end 312
  Index Funds and ETFs: A Tax-Efficient Investment...............312
  A Few More Ideas for Tax Savings.........................313
      Informal trusts or in-trust accounts 313
      Registered education savings plans 314
      Tax-Free First Home Savings Account 315

PART 5: THE PART OF TENS.................................317

CHAPTER 24: **Ten Questions to Ask a Potential Financial
  Advisor** 319

  How Do You Get Paid? 319
  What Do You Think of My Financial Situation? 320
  Will You Sell Me ETFs, Index Funds, and Low-Cost,
  No-Load Funds?.......................................321
  What Will You Do for Me?................................321
  Can You Help with Income-Splitting and Tax Deferral?..........321
  Can I Talk to Some of Your Clients? 322
  What Do You Think of the Market?.........................322
  What Training Do You Have?.............................323
  How Long Have You Been Doing This?.......................323
  Can I See a Sample Client Statement? 323

CHAPTER 25: **Ten Signs You Need a New Financial Advisor**......325

  Produces Rotten Returns.................................325
  Pesters You to Buy New Products after the Firm Is Taken Over 326
  Switches Firms Frequently...............................326
  Keeps Asking for Power of Attorney or Discretionary Authority 327
  Doesn't Return Your Calls or Emails.........................328
  Won't Let You Invest in ETFs and Index Funds 328

Doesn't Care about Your Overall Financial Plan 328
Suggests "Unregistered" Investments or Other Strange Stuff 329
Keeps Wanting You to Buy and Sell Investments 329
Won't Abandon Pet Theories 330

CHAPTER 26: **Ten Mistakes Investors Make** 331
Diversifying Too Much 331
Diversifying Too Little 332
Procrastinating. 332
Being Apathetic 332
Hanging on to Bad Investments 333
Taking Cash out of Your RRSP 333
Ignoring Expenses 333
Failing to Plan for Taxes 334
Obsessing about Insignificant Fees 334
Waiting until the Market Looks Better 334

INDEX 335

Introduction

Canadians love their mutual funds. They're the most popular investment by far in the country and will likely continue to be for some time. But while you may be holding funds in your portfolio, do you really know the ins and outs of this market? Did you know that a lot of funds come with high fees? That some advisors may have a vested interest in selling you certain kinds of funds over others? That there are a whole bunch of fund categories that typical investors should stay away from? That there may be other options, such as exchange-traded and index funds to consider? If you just buy the funds that are recommended by your bank or advisor, then probably not.

While there will always be a place for mutual funds in your portfolio, it's a good idea to understand what you're investing in before you buy. Whether you're a newbie investor who wants to start saving for retirement or a savvy saver who wants to explore different investment options in greater depth, this book has something for you. It's a great guide to mutual funds — and the investing world in general — for Canada's investors.

About This Book

Tons of investment books are on the market, but many go into strategies or ideas that no regular investor needs to bother themselves with. A lot of writers also take the mutual fund, which has been around for decades, for granted, assuming everyone already knows all there is about this asset. Well, you know what they say about assuming things.

This book breaks down everything you need to know about mutual funds and broader investing into an easy-to-understand way. We cover a wide range of topics, some you may not use, others you'll want to revisit as you go deeper on your investment journey.

Like all *For Dummies* books, ideas are organized in simple-to-follow fashion. We start with the basics and then get more complex as your knowledge expands. You can also flip to a particular section, for example on tax or registered retirement savings plans, if you want to get up to speed on a specific topic.

Here are just a few of the topics we cover in this book:

>> Get a good understanding of mutual basics. Discover how these funds are constructed, how they trade, how to make sure you're getting a good one and more.

>> Find out the difference between discount brokerages, mutual fund firms, and banks, and how advisors or salespeople promote and sell these kinds of securities.

>> Understand the fees associated with mutual funds and how advisors are compensated for selling them. (This part of the book is very important!)

>> Get a handle on the wackier funds out there and other mutual fund alternatives.

>> Figure out how these funds are taxed.

Something else to note: Sidebars (shaded boxes of text) dig into the details of a given topic, but they aren't crucial to understanding it. Feel free to read them or skip them. You can pass over the text accompanied by the Technical Stuff icon, too. The text marked with this icon gives some interesting but nonessential information about mutual funds.

Finally, within this book, you may note that some web addresses break across two lines of text. If you're reading this book in print and want to visit one of these web pages, simply key in the web address exactly as it's noted in the text, pretending as though the line break doesn't exist. If you're reading this as an e-book, you've got it easy. Just click the web address to be taken directly to the web page.

Foolish Assumptions

Despite what we know about assumptions, we have made a few about you and why you're picking up this book:

>> You want to discover more about investing and have heard about mutual funds.

>> You want to expand your knowledge beyond the basics.

>> You want to find ways to grow your assets, while keeping as much money as you can inside of your portfolio and not in the hands of the government or salespeople.

>> You want to know a little more, but not too much, about the way the finance and investment industries work.

>> Ultimately, you want to save money for retirement and the many other goals you want to accomplish throughout your life.

>> You know a thing or two about investing, but want some guidance that cuts to the chase and doesn't include jargon or mumbo-jumbo.

Icons Used in This Book

Throughout this book, icons in the margins highlight certain types of valuable information that call out for your attention. Here are the icons you'll encounter and a brief description of each.

TIP

The Tip icon marks tips and shortcuts that you can use to make finding out about investing easier.

REMEMBER

Remember icons mark the information that's especially important to know. To siphon off the most important information in each chapter, just skim through these icons.

TECHNICAL STUFF

The Technical Stuff icon marks information of a more technical nature that you can normally skip over.

WARNING

The Warning icon tells you to watch out! It marks important information that may save you headaches, and money, in the long run.

Beyond the Book

In addition to the abundance of information and guidance related to mutual funds that we provide in this book, you get access to even more help and information online at Dummies.com. Check out this book's online Cheat Sheet. Just go to www.dummies.com and search for "Mutual Funds for Canadians For Dummies Cheat Sheet."

Where to Go from Here

You don't have to read this book all the way through but go ahead if you like! If you want specific information on, say, bond funds, flip to that chapter. If you want to learn more about index funds, then start there. A lot of great information is here no matter where you begin.

For instance, if you're a beginner, start with Chapter 1, which outlines the mutual fund basics. If you already know about discount brokers and banks, jump to Chapter 10, which looks at equity funds, and continue from there. Want to learn a little more about tax-free savings accounts? Head over to Chapter 22.

After you're done reading this book, you can find plenty of other *For Dummies* tomes that can help deepen your investment knowledge. We recommend *ETFs For Canadians For Dummies*, 2nd Edition (Wiley), which explores low-cost funds in greater depth.

1

Meet the Mutual Fund

Get the gist of the mutual fund world.

Find out why mutual funds may be right for you.

Understand the basic mechanics of buying and selling funds.

Start seeing how mutual funds can make you money.

Look at how mutual funds can fit into your financial plan.

Chapter **1**

Mutual Funds 101

There's a good chance you or someone in your family already owns some mutual funds. They can seem complicated — especially today, given how many options there are on the market, which leads people to buy the first fund their financial planner suggests. All too often, Canadians end up disappointed with their funds' performance, because they've been sold something that's either unsuitable for them or just too expensive.

But not to worry! Building a portfolio of excellent funds is easy if you follow a few simple rules and use your own common sense. This stuff isn't complex — a mutual fund is just a money-management tool that operates under clear rules. Yes, it involves a lot of marketing mumbo-jumbo and jargon, but the basic idea could be written on a postage stamp: In return for a fee, the people running the fund promise to invest your money wisely and give it back to you on demand. The fund industry is competitive and sophisticated, which means plenty of good choices are out there.

In this chapter, we show how funds make you money — especially if you leave your investment in place for several years. We also touch on the different types available, and quickly describe the main places you can go to buy funds. We discuss these topics in greater detail throughout the book, but after you read this first chapter, you'll know the basics.

Getting the Scoop on Mutual Fund

REMEMBER

A *mutual fund* is a pool of money that a company gets from investors like you and me and divides into equally priced *units*. Each unit is a tiny slice of the fund. When you put money into the fund or take it out again, you either buy or sell units.

For example, say a fund has *total assets* — that is, money held in trust for investors — of $10 million and investors have been sold a total of 1 million units. Then each unit is worth $10. If you put money into the fund, you're simply sold units at that day's value. If you take money out, the fund buys units back from you at the same price. (Handling purchase and sale transactions in units makes it far simpler to do the paperwork.) And the system has another huge advantage: As long as you know how many units you own, you can simply check their current price to find out how much your total investment is worth. So, if you hold 475 units of a fund whose current unit price is $15.20, then you know your holding has a value of 475 times $15.20, or $7,220.

Owning units of a mutual fund makes you — you guessed it — a *unitholder*. In fact, you and the other unitholders are the legal owners of the fund. But the fund is run by a company that's legally known as the *fund manager* — the firm that handles the investing and also deals with the fund's administration.

The terminology gets confusing here because the person (usually an employee of the fund manager) who chooses which stocks, bonds, or other investments the fund should buy is also usually called the fund manager. To make details clear, we refer to the company that sells and administers the fund as the *management company* or *fund sponsor*. We use the term *fund manager* for the person who picks the stocks and bonds. Their skill is one of the main benefits you get from a mutual fund. Obviously, the fund manager should be experienced and not too reckless — after all, you're trusting them with your money.

Under professional management, the fund invests in *stocks* (shares in companies) and *bonds* (loans from government and businesses) and potentially other assets depending on the fund. That could include physical infrastructure, like toll roads, airports, and highways, or more recently *bitcoin*, a digital currency that many people use to buy and sell goods (often illicit goods) online increasing the pool of money for the investors and boosting the value of the individual units.

For example, if you bought units at $10 each and the fund manager managed to pick investments that doubled in value, your units would grow to $20. In return, the management company slices off fees and expenses. (In the world of mutual funds, just like almost everywhere else, you don't get something for nothing.) Fees and expenses usually come to between 0.3 percent and 3 percent of the fund's assets each year, depending on how a fund invests. Some specialized funds charge much more.

Mutual fund investing is not as confusing as it may seem. A fund company buys and sells the units to the public at what's called a *net asset value*. You get this number by dividing the total net asset value of the fund or company by the number of shares outstanding. This number is known as the net asset value per share (NAVPS). This value increases or decreases proportionally as the value of the fund's investments rises or falls. Say in January you pay $10 each for 100 units in a fund that invests in technology stocks, such as Microsoft, Apple, and NVIDIA. Now, say, by July, the value of the shares the fund holds has dropped by one-fifth. Then your units are worth just $8 each. So your original $1,000 investment is now worth only $800. But that August, several companies in the fund launch a bunch of game-changing artificial intelligence tools. That sends the value of their shares soaring and lifts the fund's units to $15 each. The value of your investment has now grown to $1,500.

Open-and closed-end funds

Say you've made a profit on that technology fund you held. Where can you go from here? Well, that depends on you. You can hang in there and see if the fund can climb higher, or you can cash out. With most funds, you can simply buy or sell units at that day's net asset value. That flexibility is one of the great beauties of mutual funds. Funds that let you come and go as you please in this way are known as *open-end funds*, as though they had a giant door that's never locked. Think of a rowdy Viking banquet where guests are free to come and go at will because the wall at one end of the dining hall has been removed.

That means most mutual funds are marvelously flexible and convenient. The managers allow you to put money into the fund on any business day by buying units, and you take money out again at will by selling your units back to the fund. In other words, an investment in a mutual fund is a *liquid asset*. A liquid asset is either cash, or it's an investment that can be sold and turned into good old cash at a moment's notice. The idea is that cash and close-to-cash investments, just like water, are adaptable and useful in all sorts of situations. The ability to get your cash back at any time is called *liquidity* in investment jargon, and professionals prize it above all else.

The other type of fund is a *closed-end fund*. Investors in these funds often are sold their units when the fund is launched, but to get their money back they must find another investor to buy the units on the stock market such as a share, often at a loss. The fund usually won't buy the units back or may buy only a portion.

WARNING

You can make money in closed-end funds, but it's very tricky. As craven brokerage analysts sometimes say when they hate a stock but can't pluck up the courage to tell investors to sell it: "Avoid."

THE SOMEWHAT SLEAZY DAWN OF THE MUTUAL FUND

The modern mutual fund evolved in the 1920s in the United States. In 1924, one Edward Leffler started the world's first open-end fund, the Massachusetts Investors Trust. It's still going. Mr. Leffler's fund had to be purchased through a broker, who charged a sales commission, adding to an investor's cost. Four years later, Boston investment manager Scudder Stevens & Clark started First Investment Counsel Corp., the first no-load fund (a fund you buy with no sales commission). The fund was called no-load because instead of purchasing it through a commission-charging broker, investors bought it directly from the company.

Nothing was wrong with those early open-end funds. They were run well and they survived the Great Crash of 1929 and the subsequent Depression, in part because the obligation to buy and sell their shares every day at an accurate value tended to keep managers honest and competent. But closed-end funds were the main game in the 1920s, because, as a Yale paper on the history of investment management regulation says, companies were more focused on selling funds than portfolio construction. (Closed-end funds don't buy back your units on demand, meaning you're locked into the fund until you find another investor to buy your units from you on the open market.) And a crooked game it was. By 1929, investors were paying ridiculous prices for closed-end shares. Brokers charged piratical sales commissions of 10 percent, annual expenses topped 12.5 percent, and funds kept their holdings secret. Needless to say, most collapsed in the Crash and ensuing Depression.

Following that debacle, mutual funds in Canada and the United States were far more tightly regulated, with laws forcing them to disclose their holdings at least twice a year and report costs and fees to investors. Plenty of badly run funds are still out there, not to mention plenty of greedy managers who don't put their unitholders' interests first, but at least now, clear rules exist that protect investors who keep their eyes open.

REMEMBER

With most companies' funds, you're free to come and go as you please, but companies often impose a small levy on investors who sell their units within 90 days of buying them. That's because constant trading raises expenses for the other unitholders and makes the fund manager's job harder. The charge (which should go to the fund, and usually does) is generally one percent of the units sold, but it can be more. Check this out before you invest, especially if you're thinking of moving your cash around shortly after you buy.

Returns — What's in it for you?

The main reason why people buy mutual funds is to earn a *return*. A return is simply the profit you get in exchange for either investing in a business (by buying its shares) or for lending money to a government or company (by buying its bonds). It's money you get as a reward for letting other people use your cash — and for putting your money at risk.

Mutual fund buyers earn the same sorts of profits, but they make them indirectly because they're using a fund manager to pick their investments for them. The fund itself earns the profits, which are either paid out to the unitholders or retained within the fund itself, increasing the value of each of its units.

When you invest money, you nearly always hope to get:

» **Trading profits** or *capital gains* (the two mean nearly the same thing) when the value of your holdings goes up. Capital is just the money you tied up in an investment, and a capital gain is simply an increase in its value. For example, say you buy gold bars at $100 each and their price rises to $150. You earned a capital gain of $50, on paper at least.

» **Income** in the form of interest on a bond or loan, or dividends from a company. *Interest* is the regular fee you get in return for lending your money, and *dividends* are a portion of a company's profits paid out to its shareowners. For example, say you deposit $1,000 at a bank at an annual interest rate of five percent; each year you'll get interest of $50 (or five percent of the money you deposited). Dividends are usually paid out by companies on a per-share basis. Say, for example, you own 10,000 shares and the company's directors decide to pay a dividend of 50 cents per share. You'll get a cheque for $5,000.

You also hope to get the money you originally invest back at the end of the day, which doesn't always happen. That's part of the risk you assume with almost any investment. Companies can lose money, sending the value of their shares tumbling. Or inflation can rise (if you're reading this in 2024, you know all about inflation), which nearly always makes the value of both shares and bonds drop rapidly. That's because inflation eats away at the money's value, which makes it less attractive to have the money tied up in such long-term investments where it's vulnerable to steady erosion.

Capital gains versus dividend income

Here's an example to illustrate the difference between earning capital gains and dividend income. Say you buy 100 shares of a company — a Costa Rican crocodile farm, for example — for $115 each and hold them for an entire year. Also, say you get $50 in dividend income during the year because the company has a policy of paying four quarterly dividends of 12.5 cents, or 50 cents per share, annually (that is, 50 cents times the 100 shares you own — $50 right into your pocket).

Now imagine the price of the stock rises in the open market by $12, from $115 to $127. The value of your 100 shares rises from $11,500 to $12,700, for a total capital gain of $1,200.

Your capital gain is only on paper unless you actually sell your holdings at that price.

Add up your gains and income, and that's your total return — $50 in dividends plus a capital gain of $1,200, for a total of $1,250.

Take a look at another example: Say you bought units of a new mutual fund at $24.77 on the first day of April 2023, and it rose to $25.48 by the end of May. Economic volatility then caused the price to go up and down until October, after which the fund began a prolonged fall to $21.83 by the end of March 2024. That's a loss of 2.9 cents on every unit an investor held.

Say the fund also pays out a quarterly *distribution*, a special or scheduled payment to unitholders, of 14.5 cents per unit at the end of June and September; 15.2 cents at the end of December; and 16.0 cents at the end of March, for a total distribution of 58.7 cents. Distributions are made when a fund has earned capital gains, interest, or dividends from its investments.

So what would be your return during the year? On a per-unit basis, you started with $24.77 and during the following 12 months suffered a capital loss of $2.94. However, thanks to the 58.7 cents of distributions, this loss was trimmed to about $2.44 a unit. That represented about 9.8 percent of the starting figure of $24.77, so the *percentage return*, the amount earned or lost by being invested, was a loss of 9.8 percent.

Calculating the return is actually a little more complicated than that because most investors would have simply reinvested the quarterly distribution in more units immediately after being paid out. In fact, returns for mutual funds always assume that all distributions are reinvested in more units. In that case, the fund's official return for the year ending March 31, 2023, would be a loss of 9.5 percent.

Returns as a percentage

Returns on mutual funds, and nearly all other investments, are usually expressed as a percentage of the capital the investor originally put up. That way you can easily compare returns and work out whether or not you did well.

After all, if you tied up $10 million in an investment to earn only $1,000, you wouldn't be using your cash very smartly. That's why the return on any investment is nearly always stated in percentages by expressing the return as a proportion of the original investment.

In the example of the Costa Rican crocodile farm shares you purchased, the return was $50 in dividends plus $1,200 in *capital appreciation*, which is just a fancy term for an increase in the value of your capital, for a total of $1,250. At the beginning of the year, you put $11,500 into the shares by buying 100 of them at $115 each. To get your percentage return (the amount your money grew expressed as a percentage of your initial investment), divide your total return by the amount you initially invested and then multiply the answer by 100. The return of $1,250 represented 10.9 percent of $11,500, so your percentage return during the year was 10.9 percent.

It's the return produced by an investment over several years, however, that people are usually interested in. Yes, it's often useful to look at the return in each individual year — for example, a loss of 10 percent in Year 1, a gain of 15 percent in Year 2, and so on. But that's a long-winded way of expressing details. It's handy to be able to state the return in just one number that represents the average yearly return over a set period. It makes it much easier, for instance, to compare the performance of two different funds. The math can start getting complex here, but don't worry — we stick to the basic method used by the fund industry.

Fund returns are expressed, in percentages, as an *average annual compound return*. That sounds like a mouthful, but the concept is simple. Say you invested $1,000 in a fund for three years. In the first year, the value of your investment dropped by 10 percent, or one-tenth, leaving you with $900. In Year 2, the fund earned you a return of 20 percent, leaving you with $1,080. And in Year 3, the fund produced a return of 10 percent, leaving you with $1,188. So, over the three years, you earned a total of $188, or 18.8 percent of your initial $1,000 investment.

When mutual fund companies convert that return to an "average annual" number, they invariably express the number as a "compound" figure. That simply means the return in Year 2 is added (or compounded) onto the return in Year 1, and the return in Year 3 is then compounded onto the new higher total, and so on. A return of 18.8 percent over three years works out to an average annual compound return of about 5.9 percent.

As the example demonstrates, the actual value of the investment fluctuated over the three years, but it actually grew steadily at 5.9 percent. After one year, the $1,000 would be worth $1,059. After two years, it would be worth $1,121.48. And after three years, it would be worth $1,187.65. The total differs from $1,188 by a few cents because we rounded off the average annual return to one decimal place, instead of fiddling around with hundredths of a percentage point.

There are a few terms to remember when looking at an average annual compound return. Review these terms — *average*, *annual* and *compound* — and their explanations few times.

>> **Average:** That innocuous-looking average usually levels out some mighty rough periods. Mutual funds can easily lose money for years on end — it happened, for example, when the world economy was hurt by inflation and recession in the 1970s. The COVID-19 pandemic also sent mutual funds and equities into a spiral in 2020, but the markets have recovered from pandemic lows.

>> **Annual:** Obviously, this means per year. And mutual funds should be thought of as long-term holdings to be owned for several years. The general rule in the industry is that you shouldn't buy an equity fund — one that invests in shares — unless you plan to own it for five years. That's because stocks can drop sharply, often for a year or more, and you'd be silly to risk money you may need in the short term (to buy a house, say) in an investment that may be down from its purchase value when you go to cash it in. With money you need in the near future, you're better off to stick to a super-stable, short-term bond or money market fund that will lose little or no money (more about those later).

Mutual fund companies sometimes use the old "long-term investing" mantra as an excuse. If their funds are down, they claim it's a long-term game and that investors should give their miraculous strategy time to work. But if the funds are up, the managers run ads screaming about the short-term returns.

>> **Compound:** This little word, which means "added" or "combined" in this context, is the plutonium trigger at the heart of investing. It's the device that makes the whole concept go. It simply means that to really build your nest egg, you have to leave your profits or interest in place and working for you so you can start earning income on income. After a while, of course, you start earning income on the income you earned, until it becomes a very nicely furnished hall of mirrors.

Here's another example of compounding: Mr. Simple and Ms. Compound each have $1,000 to invest, and the bank's offering 10 percent a year. Now, say Mr. Simple puts his money into the bank, but each year he takes the interest earned and hides it under his mattress. After ten years, he'll have his original $1,000 plus the ten annual interest payments of $100 each under his futon, for a total of $2,000. But canny Ms. Compound leaves her money in the account, so each year the interest is added to the pile and the next year's interest is calculated on the higher amount. In other words, at the end of the first year, the bank adds her $100 in interest to her $1,000 initial deposit and then calculates the 10-percent interest for the following year on the higher base of $1,100, which earns her $110. Depending on how the interest is calculated and timed, she'll end the ten years with about $2,594, or $594 more than Mr. Simple. That extra $594 is interest earned on interest.

How funds can make you rich

The real beauty of mutual funds is the way they can grow your money over many years. "Letting your money ride" in a casino — by just leaving it on the odd numbers in roulette, for example — is a dumb strategy. The house will eventually win it from you because the odds are stacked in the casino operator's favour. But letting your money ride in a mutual fund over a decade or more can make you seriously rich.

An investment in the RBC Select Balanced Portfolio, the largest fund by assets in Canada, from its launch in 1986 through the end of June 2023, produced an annual average compound return of about 6.1 percent. If your granny had been prescient enough to put $10,000 into the fund when it was launched, it would have been worth $87,165 in 2023.

The main reason why Canadians had more than $1.8 trillion in mutual funds at the end of 2022 is that funds let you make money in the stock and bond markets almost effortlessly. By the way, that $1.8 trillion figure doesn't even include billions more sitting in *segregated* funds, which are mutual fund-like products sold by life insurance companies. They're called segregated because they're kept separate from the life insurer's regular assets. (You can read more on segregated funds in Chapter 19.) It also doesn't include billions in exchange-traded funds (ETFs), a mutual-fund-like vehicle that trades on a stock exchange, and is a rapidly growing part of the Canadian market and could one day become even more popular that mutual funds. (You can read more about ETFs in Chapter 15.)

Of course, no law says you have to buy mutual funds in order to invest. You may make more money investing on your own behalf, and lots of people from all walks of life do. But it's tricky and dangerous. So millions of Canadians too busy or scared to learn the ropes themselves have found that funds are a wonderfully handy and reasonably cheap alternative.

TIP

Buying funds is like going out to a restaurant compared with buying food, cooking a meal, and cleaning up afterward. Yes, eating out is expensive, but it sure is nice not to have to face those cold pots in the sink covered in slowly congealing mustard sauce.

What mutual funds buy

Mutual funds and other investors put their money into two main long-term investments:

>> **Stocks and shares:** Tiny slices of companies that trade in a big, sometimes chaotic but reasonably well-run electronic vortex called, yes, the stock market.

>> **Bonds:** Loans made to governments or companies, which are packaged up so that investors can trade them to one another.

Folks' memories run deep, and after ugly stock market meltdowns in the 1920s and 1970s, mutual funds and stocks generally had unhealthy reputations for many years. For generations, Canadians and people worldwide preferred to buy sure things, usually bonds or fixed-term deposits from banks, the beloved guaranteed investment certificate (GIC). But as inflation and interest rates started to come down in the 1990s, it became harder and harder to find a GIC that paid a decent rate of interest — research shows most people are truly happy when they get eight percent.

As Table 1-1 shows, the Canadian mutual fund industry has seen some impressive growth — interest exploded after rates on five-year GICs dropped well below that magic eight percent back in the 1990s. At that point, Canadians decided they were willing to take a risk on equity funds. (Inflation reached record levels in 2022 and 2023 — the impact rising prices might have on mutual funds remains to be seen but at the time I'm writing this, GICs are more attractive than they've been in decades.)

Table 1-1 shows the growth of assets under management in the Canadian mutual fund industry from 2010 to the end of December 2022. Yes, growth did decline in 2022, partly because it was a down year for markets, but also because ETFs have started to eat into mutual funds' popularity, which we explain in Chapter 15.

TABLE 1-1

Growth of the Mutual Fund Industry in Canada

Year	Total Assets $Billions
2012	803
2013	999
2014	1,141
2015	1,231
2016	1,339
2017	1,477
2018	1,423
2019	1,630
2020	1,784
2021	2,083
2022	1,809

Industry statistics provided by the Investment Funds Institute of Canada.

Finding Your Type (of Funds)

Mutual funds fall into four main categories. In Chapters 10 to 20 we go into all kinds of funds, but this is a quick breakdown of the bare facts. The four main types of mutual funds are:

>> **Equity funds:** By far the most popular type of fund on the market, equity funds hold stocks and shares. Stocks are often called "equity" because every share is supposed to entitle its owner to an equal portion of the company. We look at the range of equity funds available to you in Chapters 10, 11, and 12.

>> **Balanced funds:** The next biggest category is balanced funds. They generally hold a mixture of just about everything — from Canadian and foreign stocks to bonds from all around the world, as well as very short-term bonds that are almost as safe as cash. Chapter 13 gives you the scoop on balanced funds.

>> **Bond funds:** These beauties, also referred to as "fixed-income" funds, essentially lend money to governments and big companies, collecting regular interest each year and (nearly always) getting the cash back in the end. We offer the thrilling details about these funds in Chapter 14.

>> **Money market funds:** They hold the least volatile and most stable of all investments — very short-term bonds issued by governments and large companies that usually provide the lowest returns. These funds are basically savings vehicles for money you can't afford to take any risks with. They can also act as the safe little cushion of cash found in nearly all well-run portfolios. Chapter 17 fills you in about these funds.

With so many options, there's bound to be a fund that works for you and your financial goals.

Figuring out Where to Buy

So how do you actually buy a fund? In essence, you hand over your money and a few days later, you get a transaction slip or confirmation slip stating the number of units you bought and what price you paid. Chapter 3 goes into detail about some of the legal and bureaucratic form-filling involved in buying a fund (don't worry, it's not complicated).

You can buy a mutual fund from thousands of people and places across Canada, in one of four basic ways:

>> **Buying from professional advisors:** The most common method of making a fund purchase in Canada is to go to a stockbroker, financial planner, or other type of advisor who offers watery coffee, wisdom, and suggestions on what you should buy. These people will also open an account for you in which to hold your mutual funds. They are often paid a commission on the funds they sell. Find out more in Chapters 2 and 8.

Examples of fund companies that sell through advisors, planners, and stockbrokers are Mackenzie Financial Corp., Fidelity Investments Canada Ltd., CI Fund Management Inc., AGF Management Ltd., and Franklin Templeton, all based in Toronto. Investors Group Inc. of Winnipeg, Canada's biggest fund company, also sells through salespeople, but the sales force is affiliated with the company.

>> **Online purchases:** The simplest way to buy funds these days is online at a banks' website. Banks don't charge sales commissions to investors who buy their funds. The disadvantage to this approach is limited selection, because most bank branches are set up to sell only their company's funds. But the beauty of this approach is that you can have all your money — including your savings and chequing accounts and even your mortgage or car loan — in one place. Learn more in Chapter 7.

>> **Buying direct from fund companies:** For those who like to do more research on their own, excellent "no-load" companies sell their funds directly to investors. They're called no-load funds because they're sold with no sales commissions. No-load funds can avoid levying sales charges because they don't market their wares through salespeople. Because these funds don't have to make payments to the advisors who sell them, they often come with lower expenses. We go into more in Chapter 9.

>> **Buying from discount brokers:** Finally, for the real do-it-yourselfers who like to make just about every decision independently, you can find discount brokers, which operate online. Mostly but not always owned by the big banks, they sell funds – sometimes from other companies, sometimes from their own – usually free of commissions and sales pitches. We talk more about discount brokers in Chapter 6.

Chapter **2**

Buying and Selling Basics

M utual funds were one of the 20th century's great wealth-creating inno-vations. Funds transformed stock and bond markets by giving people of modest means easy access to investments previously limited to the rich. The fund-investing concept is likely to remain popular for years, letting ordinary and not-so-ordinary people build their money in markets that would otherwise intimidate them. That's because the idea of packaging expert money management in a consumer product, which is then bought and sold in the form of units, is so brilliantly simple.

In this chapter, we take another look at funds, assessing their great potential as well as their nasty faults. We wrap up with a chat about the relative merits of no-load and load funds, which refers to two different ways advisors and fund compa-nies get paid when they sell you a mutual fund.

Reasons to Buy Funds

In Chapter 1, we discuss how and why mutual funds work and why they make sense in general. Here we give you some specific, significant reasons to make them a big part of your financial plan.

Offering safety in numbers: Public scrutiny and accountability

Perhaps the best aspect of mutual funds is that their performance is public knowledge. When you own a fund, you're in the same boat as thousands of other unitholders, meaning the fund company is pressured to keep up the performance. If the fund lags its rivals for too long, unitholders will start *redeeming* or cashing in their units, which is the sort of worry that makes a manager stare at the ceiling at 4 a.m., sweat rolling down their grey face.

Fund companies are obliged to let the sun shine into their operations — and sunlight is the best disinfectant — by sending unitholders clear annual *financial statements* of the fund's operations. These statements are tables of figures showing what the fund owns at the end of the year, what expenses and fees it paid to the management company, and how well it performed. Statements are audited (that is, checked) by big accounting firms. The management company is obligated to send you semi-annual statements to keep you informed about performance For more on the financial statements for funds, see Chapter 3.

TIP

You can find a lot of this information online on the mutual fund company's website. One particularly useful document is the Fund Facts, which is either online or in a downloadable PDF that lists some of the fund's holdings, fees, geographic makeup, and more.

Most companies only share their Best 10 Ideas online — if they give away too much of their recipe, others could cook up the same recipe. However, you can get a full list from the annual statement, but it's possible your fund manager has sold out of some positions before those documents get to your door. In any case, you want to examine a fund's holdings because if you bought what you thought was a conservative Canadian stock fund, for example, then you want to make sure it actually is conservative. In that case, you may see lots of bank stocks and other companies you've at least heard of.

REMEMBER

The information in the statements can be hard to understand and not particularly useful, but always check one detail: Look at the fund's top 10 holdings.

Your account statements are personal mailings that show how many units you own, how many you've bought and sold, and how much your holdings are worth. Companies usually send you personal account statements at least twice a year. Some fund sellers, such as banks, send quarterly statements, and discount brokers often mail them monthly. Of course, you can also view your statements online and see how much money is in your account every day. See Chapter 3 for more on account statements.

Don't confuse the *financial statements* — which describe how the fund is doing — with your own individual *account statement*.

The next section helps you decipher price and performance figures. When you know what to look for, you can accurately track your funds' performance. We're not saying your fund manager won't give you the straight story, but getting a second opinion is never a bad plan, especially when it comes to your cash.

Finding and reading fund prices

Time was you could check a mutual fund's unit price, or net asset value per share (NAVPS), the price shares are bought and sold for at the end of each trading day in most daily newspapers. But daily tables — as the price details of a fund are called — are now virtually extinct, at least in printed form. *The Globe and Mail* does publish price summary tables on their website, but only for the larger, more popular funds. You also can look up fund prices on individual fund company websites. Morningstar Canada is also an excellent online resource, with articles on mutual funds and performance stats on almost every Canadian fund. You want to familiarize yourself with these tables so you can get some insight into the price of your fund. We talk more about how to look up fund prices and check performance in Chapter 21.

Most mutual funds calculate and publish a value for their units every day that stock and bond markets are open. Some small or very specialized funds do this only monthly or weekly, and some take a day or two getting the information out. Still, unit prices for the most widely available funds are available the next day on fund information websites. The listing also usually shows the change in unit price from the previous day.

Checking and reading mutual fund performance

Because mutual fund investing is primarily a longer-term undertaking, performance statistics can command more of your attention than daily prices do. How often should you check your fund's performance? Unfortunately, this question has no easy answer. But it's a good idea to look every three months or so to see how your manager is doing. Even if you bought your funds through a financial planner or other salesperson — who's supposed to be looking out for your interests — it never hurts to keep an eye on how well the recommendations are turning out.

Determining how a fund is categorized isn't easy nowadays because data providers, who are members of the Canadian Investment Funds Standards Committee, use more than 40 asset categories. Your first step is to enter the name of a fund in a website's general fund search tool, and then check its category on the page that appears.

What you see appear depends on the page you're on. On Morningstar you can sort by short-term performance, long-term performance, fees, portfolio style, and more.

TIP

Similar information is available on www.theglobeandmail.com/investing/ markets/funds. Go to Chapter 21 for the full story on researching funds online.

Making sense of the numbers

What can you do with this jumble of numbers? The unit price is useful information because by multiplying the price by the number of units you own, you can work out the value of your holdings. You can also make sure the unit price online matches the price shown on your statement to double-check their bookkeeping.

The unit price is also handy if you're hazy on which fund you actually own — a lot of smart people aren't always sure! With more than 3,400 funds (at the end of 2022), versions of funds, and fund-like products available in Canada, it's easy to get confused. (This number doesn't include exchange-traded funds, which we get into in Chapter 15.) Often, several different versions of a particular fund are on sale, depending on how you buy it, such as a front-end or back-end load (with the former, the advisor gets a commission when they sell you the fund, with the latter, they get the commission when you sell) and other factors such as investment guarantees.

If your account statement shows you own a fund with a unit price of $10.95, for instance, you see the same price online, chances are you're talking about the same fund. However, you may have to go so far as to check your statements for the precise name of the fund, including the series or class letter — or even check the fund sales code, which is used by fund salespeople when making transactions.

REMEMBER

The meat of the subject is contained in the performance numbers. These returns are after the fund's fees and expenses have been deducted. Some exceptions to this practice exist in the monthly report — that is, funds that levy extra charges that reduce the performance shown — but the returns for all the biggest companies are after charges. The companies that deduct fees and expenses *after* the returns shown in such tables are generally fund companies that sell funds as part of a comprehensive financial package. Clients get a customized statement that lists their fees separately, instead of lumping in the charges with the fund's overall return. Always check whether the returns you're being shown are before or after the deduction of all charges and costs.

THE DIFFERENCE BETWEEN THE AVERAGE AND THE MEDIAN

Sometimes figuring out whether a fund has done better than other funds in its group is harder than it looks. When you look at a fund report, you come across two terms used to describe the typical fund's performance: The *average* and the *median*. The average and the median are both numbers that attempt to show how funds in a particular category have done. That way, if you're interested in a fund, you can compare its performance with that of its rivals. For example, if you're considering buying your bank's Canadian equity fund, it's a good idea to see how it has done compared with other funds in the Canadian equity category. However, sometimes the average can be distorted upward or downward by a few extreme cases, so the median acts as a middle point, giving a good idea of what the typical return for funds was. Here's how it works:

- The **average** is calculated by simply adding up the return figures for all funds for a particular period and then dividing by the number of funds involved.

- The **median** is the halfway mark. Half of the funds are below that point and half are above.

Normally, the two numbers are similar, but a sprinkling of very high or low returns in the sample can pull them apart. An "average" figure can be a misleading comparative, because it gives equal weight to each and every member of that group — regardless of the significance of each member. To be truly useful, an average must be "weighted" according to, in the case of a fund category, each individual fund's assets.

Putting your eggs in many baskets

Another good reason to buy mutual funds is the fact that they instantly mitigate your risk by letting you own lots of stocks and bonds, ideally in many different markets. *Diversification*, spreading your dollars around, is the cornerstone of successful investing. Diversifying means you won't be slaughtered by a collapse in the price of one or two shares.

WARNING

Some people learn about diversification the hard way. Investors think they've lucked into the next big thing, hand over their entire fortune, and then lose it all in a cruel market correction. Pinning your hopes on just one stock or handful of stocks is never a wise move, so don't let this happen to you.

Mutual funds let ordinary investors buy into faraway markets and assets. It would be difficult and expensive for individual investors to purchase shares in Asia or Europe, or bonds issued by Latin American governments (go easy on those, though), if they couldn't buy them through mutual funds.

Although events of global impact such as natural disasters, a pandemic, or war can have an impact on markets worldwide, some respond positively to developments, and others respond negatively. It's tough to keep track of it all and predict which markets will be affected and by how much. So, we ask: Why even try? History demonstrates that a portfolio with lots of different and varied asset classes tend to suffer fewer speed bumps.

REMEMBER

Most equity mutual funds own shares in at least 50 companies — though some funds are more "concentrated" and hold fewer. Academic research suggests that only seven stocks may be enough to provide adequate diversification for an investor, but seeing dozens of names in a portfolio offers a lot more reassurance.

Getting good returns from professional management

One of the most entertaining and informative books ever written on the subject of investing is *A Fool and His Money: The Odyssey of an Average Investor* by John Rothchild. First published in 1988, the book describes Mr. Rothchild's own abject failure in the market and includes his observation that most amateur investors are less than frank about how they've actually done. Even if they've had their heads handed to them, they tend to claim they ended up "about even." The moral of the story: Even if your relatives and pals claim to have made a fortune in the market, treat their boasts with a goodly dose of skepticism.

Yes, bad funds abound. But chances are you'll do better in a mutual fund than you would investing on your own. At least the people running funds are professionals who readily dump a stock when it turns sour, instead of hanging on like grim death, as we amateurs tend to do. The habit of selling quickly and taking the loss while it's still small is said to be one of the main traits that distinguishes the pro from the amateur.

Making investing convenient

Funds are just so darned handy, no wonder hundreds of millions of people around the world buy them. Yes, you could make your own lip balm. You could gather the ingredients and boil them up in a big copper pot for days. But it's easier just to walk into the drugstore and buy a stick. Likewise, it's a snap to let the fund company deduct cash from your bank account regularly — a lot easier than worrying about the market and finding out the difference between investing in a long-dated strip bond and an exciting, newly listed, artificial intelligence startup with scalable technology.

Critics of funds claim, with some justification, that the industry has brainwashed members of the public into thinking they're too stupid to invest for themselves. And it does seem fund companies want us to believe it's necessary to have someone do the investing for us in return for a fat fee. But the reality is that most people are just too busy, confused, or plain lazy to figure out the investing game. This book will make you an educated fund investor, whether you choose to deal with a pro or go it alone. In Chapter 4, we list a few sample portfolios that are about as easy to buy as a candy bar — and a lot better for you.

Investing without breaking the bank

The typical Canadian stock fund rakes off about two percent of your money each year in fees and costs. That's a hefty charge — and Canada has higher mutual fund fees than most developed countries — but the fund company also relieves you of a lot of drudgery and tiresome paperwork in return. Funds offer a lot of convenience. The fund company keeps your money safe and handles the record-keeping for your savings. It all leaves you free and clear to get on with your first love, samba dancing.

In fact, mutual funds are a positive bargain if you're just starting to invest. Quite a few companies let you put as little as $500 into their funds, and you can often open up a regular investment plan — where the money is simply taken out of your bank account — for next to nothing. That's a pretty good deal when you realize that fund companies actually lose money on small accounts. If an investor has, say, $1,000 in an equity fund with a management expense ratio (MER) of two percent, then the company is collecting only $20 in fees and expenses, barely enough to cover postage and administration costs let alone turn a profit. A growing number of discount brokerages in Canada also let you trade for free or, at most, $10 per trade.

The costs of a mutual fund investment are buried in the MER and the relatively dense statement of operations, but at least you can work them out with a bit of digging. Don't hesitate to ask your broker for a clear explanation of their commission rates. They owe you that!

Watching over your investment

Mutual fund companies are pretty closely watched, not only by overworked provincial securities regulators, but also, believe it or not, by rival companies. Competing companies don't want a rotten peach spoiling the reputation of the whole barrel. The Investment Funds Institute of Canada (IFIC), the industry lobby group, is a mouthpiece for the companies, naturally. But it also generally keeps an eye on things. And Toronto, where most of the industry is based, is a village where everyone knows everyone. You'd be surprised how many industry executives tell reporters about skullduggery *off the record* — always about competing fund sellers, of course.

Yes, greed abounds. Despite some improvements in recent years, fees are still too high, unitholder reports are often difficult to decipher, salespeople are given goodies, and funds are sometimes used as horns of plenty when managers divert their trading, and the resulting flow of commissions to their brokerage buddies. The good news is most companies are simply making too much money to risk it all by running scams.

REMEMBER

The stocks, bonds, and other securities a fund buys with your money don't even stay in the coffers of the fund company: Under provincial securities laws, the actual assets of the fund must be held by a separate "custodian," usually a big bank or similar institution. You're most likely to get swindled by your salesperson, but in Chapter 8 we set out some of the best ways to protect yourself. Just stick with regular mutual funds, those that come with a document called a "simplified prospectus" and are managed by widely known companies, and you should be okay.

Cashing out — Getting your money if you need it

If you decide to move your hard-earned cash out of a fund, your fund company will normally get your money to you within three days. Removing money from a fund effortlessly whenever you like may not seem like a big deal — but in the world of investing, being able to do so whenever you want to, with no hassles or questions, is as good as a fling with Ryan Reynolds or Taylor Swift, your choice.

Don't forget that lots of other investments, including guaranteed investment certificates, hit you with a penalty if you take your cash out early. Selling a stock costs you a brokerage commission invariably with no guarantee you'll get a decent price for your shares. Sell a bond, and you're often at the mercy of your dealer, who can pluck a price out of the air.

Perils and Pitfalls of Funds

If you're convinced funds are the right place to be, now we're going to throw you for a bit of a loop. An informed investor is a wealthy investor, after all, and it's important to realize that funds aren't perfect. None of these disadvantages mean you shouldn't buy mutual funds. But keeping them in mind helps you stay out of overpriced and unsuitable investments.

Excessive costs

When you start amassing serious money in mutual funds, your costs can get out-rageous. For example, if you invest $50,000 in a set of typical equity funds with a management expense ratio of two percent, the fund company is siphoning off $1,000 of your money every year. The math gets truly chilling when you extrapolate the cost of management fees over long periods. Over 20 years, at an MER of two percent, and with an annual return of 6 percent, the fund company will end up with an incredible $401,176 — or about a quarter of the total accumulated capital. (The final investment value would be $1,548,640 — it would have been nearly $2 million without the fees.) How so? Simply by slicing that little two percent off the top each year. (Go to getsmateraboutmoney.com/calculators/fee-calculator to find out how much you could pay in fees.)

In theory, that's what it costs to pay a fund manager to actively invest on your behalf. But if you're content to accept whatever return — good or bad — the overall market can achieve, then you can save a bundle by owning Exchange-traded funds (ETFs) or index funds. Index funds are mutual funds with low expenses that simply track the whole stock or bond market by producing a return in line with a market index, such as the Standard & Poor's/Toronto Stock Exchange composite index of approximately 250 well-known companies. An ETF is similar to an index fund except it trades on a stock exchange. In most cases, ETFs don't have a portfolio manager as they simply own all the stocks in an index. A typical index fund, such as RBC Canadian Index, has expenses of 0.50 percent, and the main Canadian market ETF, iShares S&P/TSX 60 Index ETF, charges just 0.15 percent. See Chapter 15 for more on index funds and ETFs.

Style drift — When managers get lost in the jungle

In the past, some managers would *drift* or depart from the type of investments they told you they'd buy when you signed on, usually because they were chasing hot returns or because they were scared. You can keep tabs on the biggest portfolio holdings in your fund by checking the fund company's website — more on that in Chapter 21 — but your only legal entitlement to a full list of all the portfolio contents is when the company sends you annual and semi-annual financial statements, but these typically do not arrive until three months following the period end.

The most prominent type of drift involves value and growth investing styles. The most glaring example of a value manager holding a growth stock was Nortel Networks in the late 1990s, which value managers held in their portfolios long after its price had multiplied many times. However, style drift has largely been a non-issue in recent years.

WARNING

Style drift or not, as an investor, you do need to monitor your fund investments. Ultimately, it's your responsibility to make sure you're headed in the right direction.

When managers blow it

They may be smart and they may be professionals, but fund managers sure can blow it, leaving behind nothing but a lot of little scraps of grey polyester and a bunch of ugly minus signs in front of their returns.

It's rarely as terrifying as that, though. Companies usually replace managers of big funds after just a couple years of bad performance. Having a decent Canadian equity fund, in particular, is a marquee attraction for a company. It's the fund category carrying the most prestige, partly because it wins the most attention from the media. You can be sure that just about every manager running a large equity or balanced fund, Canadian or global, is working their silk socks off trying to top the performance league. Every so often, companies get in bidding wars for managers with a great reputation. So everyone running a fund is trying to get public notice for earning hot returns, because it increases their market value.

Can't see the forest for the funds

By mid-2023, Canada had more than 4,000 or so mutual funds and exchange-traded funds. That includes different versions with varying sales charges, funds that can trade without racking up taxable capital gains, "market-neutral" funds that are supposed to shake off the effects of a bad stock market, and funds that really didn't seem to have any good reason for existing, to be honest.

This ridiculous profusion of products exists for several reasons:

>> **Fund companies have learned the folly of relying too much on just one or two funds.** The danger, for them, is that if performance goes in the tank then investors head for the door, pulling out tens of millions of dollars. Better to offer many varied funds so that if one turns cold, the others are still cooking.

>> **Like being a superhero, the fund business is, well, glamorous, and everyone wants in.** But unlike pulling on the black tights, running a mutual fund is also profitable. When a fund company can get its assets above $100 million or so, it's difficult to lose money because those 2-percent management fees keep rolling in. And all sorts of newcomers have been coming into the fund industry, including insurance companies and even financial planning chains. But they love to offer their own house-brand funds because they get to keep all the fees instead of splitting the take with a separate name-brand fund company such as Mackenzie Financial Corp. or AGF Management Ltd. Clients are often happier with a name they've heard of, though, so insurance companies have taken to hiring well-known mutual fund companies as their fund managers. However, the fund remains the insurance company's own product — and the insurer gets to keep the lion's share of the management fee.

>> **The investment game, with its hype and image obsession, is essentially a branch of showbiz.** Every year you have something new to keep the salespeople awake and the investors hungry.

>> **In fairness to the industry, some of the new funds are meant to satisfy consumers' demands.** Investors' thirst for income-producing investments in recent years brought a raft of funds that invest in income trusts and other income-generating securities. Although income trusts have lost their tax advantage over dividend-paying stocks, income-producing investments remain a popular tool for many boomer-age and older investors.

Vague explanations of poor performance

No matter how badly a fund did, the analysis given to investors is frequently a languid description of the stock or bond market and a few of the manager's choice reflections on the future of civilization.

What unitholders deserve, but too often are denied, is an honest discussion of whether their fund kept up with the market and its peers. Securities regulators are putting the squeeze on companies to improve their reports, but it'll take time. You shouldn't have to be a detective to discover what went wrong with performance and what the manager plans to do about it.

In the meantime, if your fund lags the market and other funds in the same category, ask your broker or financial planner for a clear explanation if you got advice when buying funds. If you bought a no-load fund, look for a written set of reasons in the company's mailings to unitholders or online.

Another big problem in reporting performance is that all too often it's not at all clear who is actually running your fund and how long they've been doing it. Fund companies don't always print the length of a manager's tenure, and they usually don't warn investors in a timely way if they quit or are fired. Yes, a few veteran managers have been running the same fund for years. And some companies such as Fidelity Investments Canada Ltd. make it reasonably plain who's actually calling the shots. But at many companies, managers come and go with such unpredictable frequency that it's difficult if not impossible to keep track of them.

REMEMBER

Rather than worry about finding a genius to pick your stocks, you're much better off looking at the fund itself. Make your decision about investing with an eye to how the fund has performed and what it currently holds, rather than trying to figure out who is in the top spot.

Prospectuses that don't say enough

It's often hard to tell from a company's website, promotional handouts, and even official reports to unitholders whether the returns from its funds have been any good. That's because most companies, incredibly, still don't show their performance against an appropriate market benchmark, such as the Standard & Poor's/Toronto Stock Exchange composite index (S&P/TSX) for Canadian equity funds or the MSCI World Index for global equity funds. (Many ETFs, we should point out, do compare with benchmarks.)

But things have gotten better since the fund industry began producing *prospectuses* that are fairly easy to understand. A prospectus is the document that must be given to the purchasers of a fund, describing its rules and risks. A prospectus must provide performance numbers that compare a fund to a benchmark, such as the S&P/TSX for Canadian equity funds. Prospectuses also give the fund's returns on a year-by-year calendar basis, which is invaluable for checking whether unitholders have enjoyed steady returns or suffered through insane swings.

On the other hand, prospectuses are still of only limited usefulness because they don't say *why* the fund has lagged or outperformed its benchmark. Fortunately, a fairly new, additional document, the *management report of fund performance*, has taken a big step toward providing useful comparative data and explanations of a fund's recent performance. More on these in Chapter 3.

Load versus No-Load — The Great Divide

You can buy mutual funds in two main ways:

>> **Through a professional seller:** You can get a salesperson such as a broker or financial planner to help. The broker has to earn a living, so you'll almost certainly end up buying load funds — a load is a sales charge or commission that's paid to the broker, either by you or by the fund company.

>> **Going it alone:** You can pick your funds on your own, with perhaps some advice from a bank staffer or mutual fund employee. In that case, you'll often end up buying *no-load* funds, which don't levy a sales commission.

Grey areas abound. You can buy *load* funds on your own and pay no commissions (through a discount broker, which will provide little or no advice). Some brokers will sell you no-load funds or load funds on which they waive commissions. And banks can fall in between the two stools. But those are the two essential methods.

Load funds — The comfort zone

Most mutual funds in Canada are sold to investors by a salesperson who is in turn paid by way of a sales commission. Millions of people love the feeling of having an advocate and advisor who seems to know their way through the jungle of investing. And why not hire a professional? After all, you probably don't fix your plumbing yourself or remove your own appendix (too hard to get the stains out of the kitchen tiles).

Your advisor might work for a stockbroker, a financial planning firm, or an insurance brokerage — or they may be self-employed. But the important point is this: If you buy funds through a salesperson, your primary relationship is with them, not with the fund company.

Any fund company should be able to answer your questions about your account. Always make sure you get a regular account statement from the fund company itself (unless you're with one of the big online brokerage firms, which usually handle all the recordkeeping). Load companies, such as CI Funds and Fidelity Investments Canada, typically don't sell funds directly to consumers. The companies' systems and much of their marketing are designed to deal with advisors, but that is changing. Most fund companies do sell direct through online brokerage accounts and more are marketing direct to consumer.

Seeing which companies sell load funds

Table 2-1 shows Canada's 10 biggest mutual fund companies at the end of August 2023 and the method they use to sell their funds. Many companies sell both load and no-load — if you buy online yourself through a broker, you shouldn't have to pay any commissions.

TABLE 2-1 **Canada's 10 Biggest Fund Companies and How They Sell Their Funds**

	In Billions
RBC Global Asset Management Inc. – No load	298.4
TD Asset Management Inc. – No Load	175.9
Fidelity Investments Canada ULC – Load	171.7
1832 Asset Management L.P. – Load	134.3
CIBC Asset Management Inc. – No load	126.4
CI Global Asset Management – Load	104.8
I.G. Investment Management, Ltd. – Load	103.7
BMO Investments Inc. – No load	93.4
Manulife Investment Management Limited – Load	77.9
Mackenzie Financial Corporation – Load	58.5
Top 10	**1,345.1**

Source: Investment Funds Institute of Canada

Decoding sales commissions

Sales commissions on load funds come in a bewildering number of variations and forms. And discount brokers have dreamed up more ways to make the whole matter even more complicated (see Chapter 6 for details). But when you buy a load fund from a broker or planner, you have three basic options.

You can negotiate and pay an upfront commission — known as a *sales charge* or *front load* — to the salesperson. Savvy investors usually pay two percent or less. That entitles you to sell the fund at any time with no further charges, and it sometimes gets you lower annual expenses.

Alternately, you can buy funds on a "low-load" basis. Some firms refer to this as "no-load," even though you must buy them through an advisor. There's no free lunch, of course, as a low-load fund generally will have higher annual expenses than the front-end version of the same fund.

When this book was first written, you could also buy *back-end load funds*, where the fund company itself paid the commission to the broker — usually five percent in the case of an equity fund or a balanced fund and less for a bond fund. The investor was often on the hook for a "redemption charge" if they sold the fund within a set number of years.

This payment structure, also known as deferred sales charges (DSC), allowed salespeople to garner an upfront payment that wasn't deducted from client contributions. That may seem like a good thing — you wouldn't get charged anything upfront, but where does the fee come from? Higher management expenses ultimately ate into more of the return. The big problem was that many investors were not aware that they were paying a higher fee, while the fee structure was also shown to incentivize advisors who bought these kinds of funds, even if the fund was not in the client's best interest. In 2022, the DSC structure was banned by provincial securities regulators.

No-load funds — The direct approach

The other great branch of the fund industry is the no-load sector — funds that sell directly to the public with no sales commissions. Here, life is much simpler. A no-load shop opens an account for you when you contact them; you do this without the involvement of a broker, planner, or any other kind of advisor. You're not charged to buy or sell a fund, although remember that to discourage in-and-out trading, you often face a penalty of two percent or so if you dump a fund within three months of buying.

The banks dominate the no-load fund business through their vast customer bases, online discount brokerage arms, and branch networks. Until recently, they had difficulty building a strong record and big market share in equity funds. However, the Big Five banks (RBC, CIBC, Scotiabank, BMO, and TD) have made gains in this area through improved performance and marketing through their branch networks, which has helped propel them to the top rungs of the fund-asset rankings.

Because no-load funds usually don't pay sales commissions to brokers — although they sometimes pay trailer fees to persuade advisors to sell their funds — their annual expenses and fees should be much lower than those of load funds. Should be, but aren't. Bankers aren't known for cutting fees where they can get away with keeping them high, and most no-load funds in Canada are only slightly cheaper than broker-sold funds.

TIP

In other words, you can expect to part with around two percent of your assets each year when you invest in most equity or balanced funds, no matter where you buy them. Some bank-run equity funds charge less than two percent — mostly income-oriented dividend funds, which generally are less complicated to manage than more aggressive stock funds.

The banks and a few other no-load fund sellers also are the place to find index funds, which have ultra-low expenses — mostly less than one percent. An index fund costs very little to manage because its portfolio simply tracks the whole market by mimicking an index. These are known as passively managed funds, with no investment decisions necessary on the part of the managers. Because index funds generate such small management fees, load companies can't afford to sell them and also pay commissions to brokers. See Chapter 15 for more about index funds — and even less expensive passive exchange-traded funds, or ETFs.

No-load fund sellers' main bread and butter, such as other fund companies, are actively managed funds — some of which also have relatively low expenses. Actively managed funds, unlike index funds, buy and sell particular stocks in an attempt to beat the market and other managers. However, no-load shops' bargain funds often have relatively high minimum investments in order to keep costs low (servicing tiny accounts isn't profitable, remember). See Chapter 9 for more on dealing directly with no-load companies.

IN THIS CHAPTER

» **Making a fund purchase**

» **Figuring out a prospectus in a few seconds**

» **Getting to know the management report of fund performance**

» **Hearing what your account statement has to say**

» **Checking on how your investment is growing through annual reports**

Chapter **3**

Paperwork and Your Rights

E ver get work done on your house and notice how contractors talk? They use expressions such as "six of one and half a dozen of another" or "you could do that," and they'll pound 'em out in a barrage that leaves you more confused than before. People in the investment business like to drone on in the same way. They produce documents that explain every angle and aspect, but skip the stuff you really want to know: Is this fund any good and how has it done?

Investors hate getting emails and piles upon piles of paper in the mail, but the reports keep coming. To some extent, the verbiage isn't the companies' fault. Securities law obliges those selling investments to disclose trivia their clients couldn't care less about. Still, it's pretty simple to filter out the noise in the emails and papers mailings you get from a fund company — and cut straight to the information that really matters. And the documents from fund companies have improved, especially prospectuses, the all-important fact sheets that tell you about the promise and perils of a fund before you buy it. Industry regulators have gone further, requiring fund companies to provide performance update reports, written in plain English, to unitholders twice a year.

In general, the documents and forms you have to deal with are pretty straightforward. Mutual fund forms are set up to be easy to fill out. Some special questions apply for opening a registered retirement savings plan, or you may need to fill in sections of your tax return to report investment income and gains, but they tend to be simple.

In this chapter, we go over the important documentation to demystify your account statement (the regular report that shows how you're doing) and walk you through a simplified prospectus (the brochure that describes the fund). As always, watch for the costs loaded on your account. We show you where to sniff around.

Getting Set Up

The big issue to decide straight away is whether you're investing inside a registered account — a special tax-sheltered account in which investment returns pile up tax-free — or in an ordinary, taxable account in which your money is subject to taxes (see Chapter 22 for more on how registered retirement savings plans and tax-free savings accounts work). You can expect to fill out two main types of forms when you buy mutual funds:

>> An account application form — which may just be called a "retirement savings plan" form if it's for an RRSP.

>> A form allowing the fund company to take fixed amounts out of your bank account for investment in funds, if you've decided to start a regular investing program. People usually have the money taken out monthly, but some fund companies allow you to use different time frames, such as every pay period.

TIP

Starting a program of regular investments of small amounts into even a conservative mutual fund is one of the best ways of getting rich painlessly. For example, putting just $10,000 into the Royal Bank of Canada's biggest balanced fund — the RBC Select Balanced Portfolio, which holds a relatively stable mixture of stocks and bonds — from mid-2013 to mid-2023 left an investor with about $18,000.

Filling in your account (or RRSP) application form

When you decide to buy a mutual fund, the first detail you are asked to fill out is an "account application" form — which tells the company who you are, what you want to buy, and how much you want to spend. An account is like a little shelf on which all your investments are kept at the broker's or the mutual fund company's office.

The account application is the document that tells the fund company the following:

>> Your name

>> Address

>> Level of investment knowledge

>> The amount of money you want to put into each fund

For investors, this account application is actually one of the most useful and informative documents mutual fund sellers distribute. That's because it contains hard information the fund company needs, so the new account form is free of vagueness and verbosity. For example, in the space where the form asks how much you want to invest in each fund, it nearly always clearly states the minimum investment.

Before you agree to buy anything, have a good look at the application form. And if you have any questions at all, approach your seller for a clear explanation. The form also sometimes discloses what extra fees — such as charges for administration — you're expected to cough up. That's not a sudden attack of candour on the company's part — it's simply that the bureaucrats need to know how you'll be paying: directly or by having it taken out of your account.

The form for opening a new account includes questions, including:

>> How experienced you are as an investor

>> Your annual income

>> Your *net worth* (the value of your personal assets minus your debts)

Be honest when answering these questions. One of the pillars of provincial securities law is a requirement that people selling investments should recommend only securities that are suitable for the customer — a principle referred to in the jargon as *Know Your Client* or KYC. In fact, the account application form is often just referred to as the KYC. The idea is this: An elderly investor on a limited income shouldn't have a big chunk of their portfolio rammed into a cryptocurrency fund or some similarly speculative vehicle.

The KYC can be a useful protection for you if it turns out later that your advisor put you into funds that were too risky for your circumstances, but it also works to the salesperson's advantage. They have an automatic out if you lost money on a volatile fund but you claimed when you opened the account that you knew a fair bit about investing. This is no place to put on a brave face — if you're a complete novice, say so and be proud of it. Pretending to know more than you do can really get you into hot water here if a dispute erupts between you and your investment dealer about an investment that went sour.

In 2021, new KYC reforms came into place. Advisors are now required to collect more information from their clients, including around risk. Before, advisors only had to determine how much risk their client was willing to take on — now they also have to assess *risk capacity*, which is their ability to endure a loss. Some firms have had to completely change their risk profiling process, which is a good thing for their customers.

Another benefit of this change is that client information must now be reviewed at least once a year and any time there's a significant change in a person's situation.

If you're investing with a bank or other no-load, direct fund seller, the application form is issued by the company, and it is clear that your deposit's going straight to them.

But if you're buying funds through a financial advisor or other independent fund salesperson, make sure you fill out an application form issued by the fund company itself.

KNOW YOUR PRODUCT

In 2021, the Canadian Securities Administration introduced a new Know Your Product (KYP) requirement for advisors. It's not a form in the same way the KYC may be, but rather it puts the onus on financial professionals to really know the products they're selling. You may think that would be a given, but with so many products on the market, and different ways to get paid selling those funds, many salespeople end up recommending products they don't fully understand.

As part of the KYP reforms, advisory firms must assess and approve the products they're selling, keep an eye on those products for significant changes and take KYP training. Advisors must also know how to assess costs and ensure they consider a reasonable range of approved products before recommending something. While this is a strong step in the right direction, the rules are prescriptive, giving firms and their advisors leeway in determining how to evaluate a product, so you still want to ask questions to make sure your advisors really do know what they're recommending.

WARNING

For your own security and convenience, it's important that you're recorded as a customer on the books of the fund company, giving you an extra measure of protection if the dealer or financial planner makes an error or even runs into cash-flow or regulatory problems. For example, if you're investing in a Franklin Templeton Investments Corp. fund, see that the form you fill out is a Franklin Templeton form.

When money is held on the books of the mutual fund company itself, the account is said to be *in client name.* In other words, the account bears the name of the individual investor at the head office of the fund company. It's a good arrangement for you because that way, if you ever have a dispute with your broker or you want to move your account elsewhere, your units and your name are in the fund company's records, making it much easier to shift your money.

Nearly every national financial planning company and mutual fund dealer is set up so that mutual fund units are held in client name on the books of the fund company. That means you can expect to get statements at least twice a year from both the dealer and the fund companies you invested with; always check them against each other. However, with traditional stockbrokers such as RBC Dominion Securities Inc., or with discount brokers such as TD Direct Investing, your money may be held only on the broker's books. In that case, the fund company may have no record of your account. Wherever you invest, it usually pays to keep an eye on the securities listed for your account and the transactions shown.

Discount brokers and traditional stockbrokers tend to have sophisticated *back offices* or administration systems because their clients usually own stocks and bonds as well as funds. That means mutual funds are held in the same big pot as other securities, so these brokers don't pass their clients' names on to the mutual fund company.

Unfortunately, that means the fund company may have no record of your investment, and therefore isn't able to send you an annual and semi-annual statement of your personal holdings. That can make it harder to resolve any disputes with your broker over what you bought and how much it's worth. And very early in your investing career, someone is certain to get an order wrong.

REMEMBER

As in any business, mistakes can happen when dealing with discount brokers, mutual fund companies, and fund dealers. The good news is that these are large organizations that have the resources to fix errors. But get everything in writing, retain copies of all the forms you fill out, and keep brief notes of the orders you issue over the phone or online.

TIP

Retain transaction confirmation numbers until you see evidence in your account that a purchase or sale has been conducted properly and according to your wishes.

Getting confirmed

Fund companies are required to send you a *confirmation* or *transaction slip* physically or by email a few days after a transaction. This document confirms you purchased units, for what amount, and whether you bought them with an upfront or "front-end" commission or on a "low-load" basis. (Once common *back-end loads* or deferred sales charges on funds sold with commissions have been phased out in Canada at the behest of regulators.)

REMEMBER

Read the confirmation or transaction slip very carefully, and if you spot any errors, immediately contact the salesperson (or fund company, if you purchased directly) to get the mistake fixed.

Also, when transferring money to pay for your funds, make it payable to the fund company. Or, if it must be made out to your advisor's firm as opposed to the fund company, write "in trust" on the transfer form. That gives you extra protection if the dealer runs into financial problems, potentially tying your money up in bankruptcy proceedings.

REMEMBER

The main detail, after you decide what fund to buy, is keeping a brief note of what you asked for and what you were told. And hang on to copies of everything. If a dispute arises, an investor who can calmly produce notes from their meetings with the advisor, along with copies of documents, will be taken far more seriously.

Dealing with Prospectuses

A mutual fund *prospectus* is the document that must be given to you when you buy a mutual fund. In this key document, the fund company sets out the purpose of the fund, describes the fees, costs, and charges, and warns buyers of the risks involved in investing in the fund. Always ask to see the prospectus before you buy a fund (the salesperson should offer it) and then make sure you read at least these two sections:

>> The investment objectives of the fund — that is, the sort of commodity it invests in.

>> The charges and fees — if they aren't clearly explained, then get your salesperson to help.

Prospectuses traditionally were written using vague language, laden with legalese or with so many technical terms that it was impossible to figure out whether a fund was worth buying. But securities regulators have forced fund companies to produce prospectuses and other documents that are increasingly clear and concise. Nowadays, prospectuses (and their new companions, management reports of fund performance) are summaries that enable investors to put their finger on important information quickly.

The prospectus itself actually comes in two parts. Part A is a very broad, catch-all piece that serves to provide the bulk of the information required to inform you (and, perhaps more importantly, satisfy the lawyers that the regulatory requirements are being met). It covers absolutely every minute detail that could possibly be applied to all funds offered by a company. In some cases, such as when a fund company has various "families" or brands of funds, more than one Part A prospectus exists; be sure to obtain the one that applies to your fund.

A second document — somewhat predictably labelled Part B — provides information specific to your fund. Most fund companies have a list of Part B prospectuses, grouping related funds into individual documents. However, individual funds each have their own sections within this document. This is the part of the prospectus that contains the all-important historical performance and portfolio holdings information.

The third piece of the disclosure puzzle is the management report of fund performance (MRFP), which mercifully is a self-contained piece. (We talk about the MRFP in the next section.)

You've been warned

The mutual fund prospectus is designed to inform you about the nuts and bolts of the fund, but it also serves another purpose, which is to protect the fund salesperson and fund company. Because after it's been given to you, the law assumes you've been adequately warned about the dangers and disadvantages of the fund. No point whining about the losses on funny foreign currencies when you were told of the danger right there on page 137.

Mutual fund prospectuses — which usually cover all or at least several of the funds in a company's lineup under one cover — have always contained the following information:

>> **The name of the fund and its investment objectives:** For example, providing a steady income while preserving capital for a money market fund, or capital gains for a stock fund. Usually it's a bland motherhood statement that tells you little — after all, it would be an odd equity fund that didn't seek capital gains. Perhaps someday they'll invent a fund that tries to *lose* as much money as possible, and also dream up a way to get investors to buy it. We

hope we're still alive to see it: no doubt the wretched thing will find itself stuck with shares that go up like a rocket!

>> **The risks of investing in the fund:** A good prospectus warns of the dangers of losing money in bonds if inflation returns or interest rates turn up. And you can count on seeing a warning that an equity fund is vulnerable if the stock market tanks. Special warnings about the dangers of foreign funds are almost always included, such as the chance of currency losses if the Canadian dollar climbs relative to overseas currencies. And small-capitalization fund prospectuses invariably point to the unpleasant volatility and unique dangers of small-cap stocks. But, once again, the risks section usually consists of stating the bleeding obvious, as our Australian friends would say.

>> **The company's idea of an appropriate investor:** Look for clues as to the sort of investor who should buy the fund and the sort who should avoid it. For example, Franklin Templeton Investments — one of the more conservative fund companies — warns prospective investors in its emerging markets fund of "principal risks," and outlines a whole bunch of scenarios that can go wrong. After reading that, you have no cause to whine if you get beaten up by volatile markets in Brazil or Thailand. Sure enough, although Templeton Emerging Markets has made money for its investors over the years — including returns in excess of 30 percent in 2017 — it also has produced some spectacular losses in other years. Most recently, it tumbled 16 percent in 2022.

>> **The costs and fees imposed on investors:** By law, you find the management fees for a fund and the expenses that have recently been charged to investors. You also see any sales charges or commissions. Along with the charges to investors, the prospectus must also list the commissions, annual fees, and other incentives given to salespeople. In principle, that's a great idea because it tells fund buyers how their advisors may be biased or influenced.

Unfortunately, though, disclosure of commissions is often hedged around with "up to" or "may," leaving most investors no wiser than before. The prospectus also includes a table showing the hypothetical total of expenses and fees an investor in the fund could expect to pay over periods ranging from one to ten years. It's a fairly useful indication as to how much mutual fund investing can cost.

Prospectuses for bank-sold funds also talk vaguely about "incentives" given to their employees, and nearly all mutual fund companies reserve the right to "participate" (as one fund seller delicately puts it) in advertising by brokers and in "conferences" for salespeople. In other words, the fund managers hand over money to help brokers pay for these extras.

However, the good — or bad — old days of flying to Maui for a "seminar" at a fund company's expense are over. The public, media, and regulators just got so tired of the piggery that the fund industry agreed to introduce a sales code, which bans the worst of the excesses.

REMEMBER

A fund company often has two sets of customers: its unitholders (the people who actually own the funds), and the brokers and financial planners who sell its wares. If a broker-sold fund company doesn't keep them sweet, it's in trouble.

More charges to look for

Here are some of the other charges the prospectus must disclose:

>> **Fees for administering Registered Retirement Savings Plans, Tax Free Savings Accounts, Registered Retirement Income Funds, First Home Savings Accounts, and Registered Educational Savings Plans:** These range from zero to upwards of $150 annually. Ask if you can pay them separately — especially where it saves your precious RRSP dollars — but some companies claim that their systems are set up only to take the money directly out of your account (which is handier for them).

>> **Fees for short-term trading:** If you sell a fund within a short period after buying it, usually one to three months, you'll often face a penalty of two percent of the amount you sold. That's because funds are supposed to be a long-term holding, and investors who hop on and off over and over again increase costs for everyone.

PULLING OUT OF THE DEAL

A mutual fund prospectus (the term comes from a Latin word meaning "view") is one of the central pieces of mutual fund regulation. In fact, it's considered so important that in most provinces you have two business days after you get the prospectus to cancel your purchase of a fund *for any reason.* So even if you pull on a clown costume and dance around as you demand your money back, they have to pay up, no matter how silly your explanation.

Interestingly, in many provinces you also have the right to cancel your mutual fund purchase within 48 hours of getting your order confirmation. But don't expect the fund company or broker to welcome your business in the future if you cancel your order without a reasonable justification. The law assumes that until you had a chance to read the prospectus you haven't been properly told about the fund. But after you read it, you're pretty well on your own. Unless you can show that the fund isn't sticking to the promises made in the prospectus, the people selling and running the fund can reasonably argue that all the risks and expenses have been explained to you — and you'll have a tough time cancelling your agreement to buy the fund.

Introducing the Management Report of Fund Performance

In 2005, regulators forced the funds industry to produce annual and semi-annual summaries of fund performance and holdings. These reports, called *management reports of fund performance* (MRFP), also include basic information on the fund's investment mandate and its recent risk experience, and, perhaps most useful of all, a discussion of the fund's recent performance.

Although a fund company must provide you with a copy of a fund's prospectus and its periodic MRFPs, the most recent MRFP is the only document you really need to read to gain a clear picture of a fund's mandate and how the fund's been faring. Most companies now have their MRFPs online, but you can also ask for a copy or find it on SEDAR, the official online depositary of all securities documents filed in Canada. (We discuss SEDAR more in this chapter as well as in Chapter 21, which covers fund research sources.)

Looking at what goes into an MRFP

An MRFP must contain certain information for the specified period and be presented in a prescribed sequence. The format ensures that consistent and up-to-date information will be available for every mutual fund sold in Canada. Here's a summary of the information that must be included in an MRFP:

>> **Investment objectives:** A summary of the fund's fundamental investment objective and strategies.

>> **Risk experience:** How changes to the investment fund over the fiscal year affected the overall level of risk associated with an investment in the investment fund.

>> **Results of operations:** This section covers the fund's performance during the period in question, as compared to its benchmark index. It summarizes noteworthy changes in portfolio holdings, the impact of these changes on the fund's stated objectives, and details of any borrowing in which the fund may have engaged. Portfolio holdings are expressed in terms of individual investments as well as industry sectors, geographic regions, bond investment quality, and currency, as applicable.

>> **Recent developments:** This section includes a discussion of market events and how the fund's overall strategies may have been amended (or not) to respond to the situation. It also must disclose any changes in portfolio managers or in accounting policies.

>> **Related party transactions:** Any transactions involving parties related to the fund must be disclosed. For instance, MD Financial, which is owned by Scotiabank, sells several mutual funds. But the portfolios are managed by 1832 Asset Management, which is also owned by Scotiabank. These relationships are disclosed under the related party transactions in MD's MFRP.

>> **Financial highlights:** These are tables showing a breakdown of the calculation of the net asset value per share (NAVPS), various ratios including the management expense ratio and portfolio turnover ratio.

>> **Management fees:** A breakdown of the services received by the fund that constitute its management fees.

>> **Past performance:** Tables show the fund's rates of return for the past ten calendar years, plus one-, three-, five-, and ten-year compound annual returns.

When securities regulators first unveiled the MRFP concept, fund company executives, investment advisors, and investors all greeted it with groans because they feared it would be yet one more level of tedious and expensive documentation. But, in practice, MRFPs have turned out to be a source of pretty good information, all presented in a document typically less than a dozen pages long.

Checking out an MRFP

Have a look at the 2022 annual MRFP for a large equity income fund, CI Global Income & Growth Fund. Figures 3-1 and 3-2 show some key information about the fund's performance and portfolio holdings:

>> **Year-by-year returns:** These are great for letting you know what kind of swings in value you can expect. These bar charts show returns for four classes of the CI Global Income & Growth fund. The mainstream units, class A, had slightly lower returns than the other classes, which have lower annual expenses because they're sold only by advisors who charge a separate management fee directly to their clients. Regardless of the class, the bars clearly denote the fund's good years and bad.

>> **Annual compound returns:** This shows the rates of return, compounded annually, over one-, three-, five-, and ten-year periods ended March 31, 2023. It also shows the fund's compound annual return since its inception in February 2007, compared with the performance of three benchmark indices, the MSCI ACWI Total Return index, ICE BofA U.S. High Yield Total Return Index, and the J.P. Morgan Global Government Bond Total Return Index. Blended returns of the three indices also are provided.

CI Global Income and Growth Fund
Management Report of Fund Performance for the period/year ended March 31, 2023

PAST PERFORMANCE

This section describes how the Fund has performed in the past. Remember, past returns do not indicate how the Fund will perform in the future. The information shown assumes that distributions made by the Fund in the period(s)/year(s) shown were reinvested in additional units of the Fund or relevant Series/Class of the Fund, as applicable. In addition, the information does not take into account sales, redemption, distribution or other optional charges that would have reduced returns or performance.

Year-by-Year Returns

The following chart/charts shows/show the Fund's annual performance for each of the period(s)/year(s) shown and illustrates/illustrate how the Fund's performance has changed from period/year to period/year. In percentage terms, the chart/charts shows/show how much an investment made on the first day of each financial period/year would have grown or decreased by the last day of each financial period/year, except where noted.

Annual Compound Returns

The following table shows the Fund's annual compound returns for each year indicated, compared to the Blended Index composed of: (60% - MSCI ACWI Total Return Index; 25% - J.P. Morgan Government Bond Total Return Index and 15% - ICE BofA U.S. High Yield Total Return Index (USD)); the MSCI ACWI Total Return Index, the J.P. Morgan Government Bond Total Return Index and the ICE BofA U.S. High Yield Total Return Index (USD).

The J.P. Morgan Global Government Bond Index is an unmanaged index which tracks the performance of actively-traded issues of government bonds worldwide. The Index excludes floating rate notes, perpetuals, bonds targeted at the domestic market for tax purposes and bonds with less than one year remaining to maturity.

The ICE BofA U.S. High Yield Index is an unmanaged index that tracks the performance of below investment grade U.S. dollar-denominated corporate bonds publicly issued in the U.S. domestic market.

The MSCI ACWI Index is a free float-adjusted market capitalization weighted index that is designed to measure the equity market performance of developed and emerging markets. The Index consists of 47 country indices comprising 23 developed and 24 emerging markets. The developed market country indices included are: Australia, Austria, Belgium, Canada, Denmark, Finland, France, Germany, Hong Kong, Ireland, Israel, Italy, Japan, Netherlands, New Zealand, Norway, Portugal, Singapore, Spain, Sweden, Switzerland, the United Kingdom and the United States of America. The emerging market country indices included are: Brazil, Chile, China, Colombia, Czech Republic, Egypt, Greece, Hungary, India, Indonesia, Korea, Kuwait, Malaysia, Mexico, Peru, Philippines, Poland, Qatar, Saudi Arabia, South Africa, Taiwan, Thailand, Turkey and United Arab Emirates.

A discussion of the performance of the Fund as compared to the benchmark is found in the Results of Operations section of this report.

	One Year (%)	Three Years (%)	Five Years (%)	Ten Years (%)	Since Inception (%)
Series A	(4.0)	8.0	4.6	6.5	n/a
Blended Index	(0.7)	7.4	5.1	8.1	n/a
MSCI ACWI Total Return Index	0.1	13.8	7.9	11.2	n/a
ICE BofA U.S. High Yield Total Return Index (USD)	(3.6)	5.8	3.1	4.0	n/a
J.P. Morgan Global Government Bond Total Return Index	(1.6)	(6.6)	(1.1)	2.5	n/a

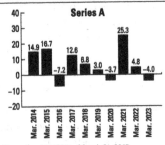

1 2015 return is for the period from December 05, 2014 to March 31, 2015.
2 2018 return is for the period from May 01, 2017 to March 31, 2018.

FIGURE 3-1: Management report of fund performance showing performance information for the CI Global Income & Growth fund.

CI Global Income & Growth Fund

Management Report of Fund Performance for the period/year ended March 31, 2023

SUMMARY OF INVESTMENT PORTFOLIO as at March 31, 2023

Category	% of Net Assets
Country allocation	
U.S.A.	65.7
Canada	7.8
France	3.1
U.K.	3.1
Netherlands	2.3
China	2.3
Short-Term Investment(s)	2.3
Switzerland	1.4
Hong Kong	1.3
Cayman Islands	1.2
Germany	1.2
Singapore	1.1
Chile	0.9
Japan	0.8
South Korea	0.8
Cash & Cash Equivalents	0.8
Mexico	0.7
Bermuda	0.6
Fund(s)	0.5
Zambia	0.4
British Virgin Islands	0.3
Liberia	0.3
Other Net Assets (Liabilities)	0.3
Panama	0.3
Exchange-Traded Fund(s)	0.3
Ireland	0.2
Australia	0.0
Luxembourg	0.0
Foreign Currency Forward Contract(s)	0.0

Category	% of Net Assets
Sector allocation	
Foreign Government Bonds	18.3
Financials	14.3
Information Technology	11.5
Consumer Discretionary	9.8
Health Care	9.2
Consumer Staples	7.2
Industrials	6.4
Energy	6.2
Communication Services	5.7
Materials	3.5
Short-Term Investment(s)	2.3
Real Estate	2.2
Utilities	1.5
Cash & Cash Equivalents	0.8
Fund(s)	0.5
Other Net Assets (Liabilities)	0.3
Exchange-Traded Fund(s)	0.3
Foreign Currency Forward Contract(s)	0.0

Top 25 Holdings	% of Net Assets
United States Treasury Bond, 4.13%, November 15, 2032	5.0
United States Treasury Bond, 4%, November 15, 2052	4.3
United States Treasury Bond, 0.38%, October 31, 2023	3.4
United States Treasury Bond, 1.13%, October 31, 2026	2.8
Microsoft Corp.	2.4
Apple Inc.	2.3
United States Treasury Bill, 4.952%, August 31, 2023	2.1
Advanced Micro Devices Inc.	2.0
Shell PLC	1.8
Eli Lilly and Co.	1.6
Alphabet Inc., Class C	1.4
Safran SA	1.4
Thermo Fisher Scientific Inc.	1.4
US Foods Holding Corp.	1.4
AIA Group Ltd.	1.3
AstraZeneca PLC	1.3
Bank of America Corp.	1.3
UnitedHealth Group Inc.	1.3
AT&T Inc.	1.2
Diageo PLC	1.2
Amazon.com Inc.	1.1
Deutsche Telekom AG, Registered	1.1
Nike Inc., Class B	1.1
STMicroelectronics NV	1.1
Stryker Corp.	1.1
Total Net Assets (in $000's)	**$8,902,025**

© CI Investments

FIGURE 3-2: Management report of fund performance showing portfolio holdings information for the CI Global Income & Growth fund.

>> **Portfolio breakdown:** This table shows in which asset classes, geographies, and sectors the fund invests.

>> **Top-25 holdings:** The big holdings of an equity fund represent the manager's true loves. They're a reliable guide to the personality of the fund. Check 'em out — if they're natural resource producers or small companies you've never heard of, or bonds issued by technology outfits or developing nations, you're in for interesting times, as the old Chinese curse puts it. The top holdings of CI Global Income & Growth are U.S. Treasury Bonds, followed by mega-cap multinationals. Their shares aren't likely to shoot up ten times in value, but they're not likely to go bust either.

The financial section (see Figure 3-3) has some lines of tabular data well worth noting, specifically the following:

>> **Net assets:** Asset growth (or shrinkage) is a key indicator of a fund's health. As you can see, this fund's assets have risen in recent years, due to the strong stock markets as well as in response to investors' thirst for income-producing investments.

>> **Management expense ratio (MER):** This information is useful when you're looking for low-cost funds (and you are). Seeing the figures for five years shows whether the fund company has been able to reduce its MER, particularly if its assets have risen significantly. In mutual funds, economies of scale don't seem to apply.

FIGURE 3-3:
Management
report of fund
performance
showing some of
the financial
information for CI
Global Income &
Growth fund.

CI Global Income & Growth Fund

Management Report of Fund Performance for the period/year ended March 31, 2023

FINANCIAL HIGHLIGHTS

The following table/tables shows/show selected key financial information about the Fund and is/are intended to help you understand the Fund's financial performance for the past five period(s)/year(s), as applicable.

Net Assets per Unit ($) *

	Net assets at the beginning of period/ year $	Total revenue $	Total expenses (excluding distributions) $	Realized gains (losses) for the period/ year $	Unrealized gains (losses) for the period/ year $	Total increase (decrease) from operations	From net investment income (excluding dividends) $	From dividends $	From capital gains $	Return of capital $	Total distributions $	Net assets at the end of the period/ year shown $
Series A												
Commencement of operations February 26, 2007												
Mar. 31, 2023	10.39	0.28	(0.26)	(0.42)	-	(0.40)	(0.07)	-	-	(0.23)	(0.30)	9.66
Mar. 31, 2022	10.26	0.25	(0.26)	0.72	(0.24)	0.47	(0.03)	(0.02)	(0.33)	-	(0.38)	10.39
Mar. 31, 2021	8.56	0.22	(0.24)	0.58	1.53	2.09	(0.04)	-	(0.42)	-	(0.46)	10.26
Mar. 31, 2020	9.23	0.26	(0.23)	0.29	(0.78)	(0.44)	(0.05)	-	-	(0.27)	(0.32)	8.56
Mar. 31, 2019	9.42	0.24	(0.23)	0.32	(0.07)	0.26	(0.07)	-	(0.39)	-	(0.46)	9.23

© CI Investments

>> **Portfolio turnover rate:** This measures the speed at which the manager changes the fund's holdings — a 100-percent turnover rate is high, indicating that trading equivalent to the value of the entire fund took place during the year. High turnover in a fund, of course, means higher transaction costs and greater expenses to the fund. This value has been a staple of U.S. fund reporting for years and was adopted as a Canadian requirement during the recent reporting upgrade.

As for our example, CI Global Income & Growth's turnover rate has been on the high side, no doubt a contributing factor to its MER.

WHAT IS THE S&P/TSX COMPOSITE INDEX?

The S&P/TSX Composite Index is Canada's main stock market barometer, measuring the value of nearly 300 of our most important publicly traded companies, such as Royal Bank of Canada or TC Energy Corp. It's a fine way of checking how good the returns from stocks, in general, have been. For example, the index climbed above 20,000 for the first time in June 2021, in a spectacular recovery from 2020's pandemic crash. But it's hovered around that level ever since reflecting uncertainty around the economy and the impact of rising interest rates.

Every country has benchmarks for measuring returns from its local stock market. The United States has the old-fashioned Dow Jones Industrial Average, a relic of the 1800s that contains 30 giant companies. But the more representative Standard & Poor's index of 500 companies and the technology-heavy Nasdaq Stock Market Composite Index also exist. The wildest index name we've come across is Finland's: The Hex index. (Okay, it's not as wild as it sounds — it stands for the Helsinki Stock Exchange.)

The S&P/TSX Composite Index used to contain a fixed 300 companies — when it was known as the TSE 300 — but the Canadian market turned out to be too small to produce 300 companies large enough for big pension funds and mutual funds to invest in. After persistent criticism that the index was full of little stocks that were hard to trade, the exchange brought in Standard & Poor's Corp. of New York to redesign the market benchmark. The revamped edition was launched in 2002. These days, the index has no fixed number of stocks — as of mid-2023, it contained approximately 240 companies.

Understanding Your Account Statement

Account statements, which show how much your holdings are worth and how much you've bought and sold since the last report from your fund company, are one area where the fund industry still needs to make progress. Investors often have trouble understanding what they actually own and even more difficulty figuring out their rates of return. Every company uses its own system and layout, and jargon such as "book value" isn't much help.

You may get an account statement only twice a year if you invest through a stockbroker or financial planner. The broker or planner and the fund company you use will often both send you statements for the six months ending June 30 and for the year ending December 31. Usually the people who invest through a salesperson aren't interested in monitoring their investments frequently (that's why they hired someone to advise them), so twice-yearly statements are fine. Sometimes, a company can agree to send you statements more frequently — so try asking — but the fund seller's system may not be set up to do this. However, as more brokerages and planning firms have made statement downloading available via their websites, monthly frequency is becoming standard.

If you hold your funds directly with a bank or no-load company, then you'll probably get a statement every quarter. That's because investors who go directly to their bank or to a fund company usually enjoy making their own decisions about investing — so they want to check their holdings more frequently.

Finally, if you invest through a discount broker, your statement often arrives monthly, especially if you've done some buying or selling in your account during the previous month. Discount brokerage customers tend to be very interested in investing, so they insist on regular updates. All companies still send out account statements, but just about every large fund seller also now lets you check your account and recent transactions over the phone or at their Internet site.

Besides your name, address, account number, and the nature of your account (that is, taxable or tax-deferred), your statement almost certainly shows the following:

>> The total value of your investment in each fund you hold, plus a total value for your account.

>> The number of fund units you held and their price or net asset value at the end of the reporting period. Remember to check these against the unit value shown for the fund online — and it's not a bad idea to verify that the number of units matches the number shown in your previous statement, adjusting for any sales or purchases you may have made or for any distributions (in the form of new units) the fund declared.

>> Any purchases or redemptions of units, and at what prices.

Beyond that, statements vary, but many big fund companies also provide the following information:

>> The change in the value of your account, and ideally of your investment in each fund, since your last statement.

>> The book value of your holdings. This technically means the amount you've ever put into the fund, plus reinvested distributions, which is useful for calculating your taxable income in a non-registered account.

Some more service-oriented forms calculate compound rates of return for client portfolios. Although we think this should be a standard service in this era of high technology and regulation, it is an extreme exception to the rule. If your advisor provides this information to you, express how much you appreciate it. On the other hand, if they don't provide portfolio compounded returns, bug them about doing so.

Reading Annual and Semi-Annual Financial Statements (Or Annual Reports)

At least once a year, an emailed pdf or mailed brochure turns up filled with rows of dull-looking figures and dry terms such as "statements of operations" or "net realized gain (loss) on sale of investment (excluding short-term notes)." These are the fund's financial statements, which, like the prospectus (see the earlier section "Dealing with Prospectuses"), usually group several funds into one document. Fund companies produce the statements twice a year. They have to send the report for the fund's financial year-end to all unitholders, but they're generally allowed to send the bi-annual report only to investors who actually request it. There should be a mail-in card for you to do this.

TIP

Unless this stuff really puts you to sleep, ask to have the six-month report mailed to you. You'll be reminding the fund company that you take your money seriously.

As of 2023, all mutual fund dealers and advisors must send two kinds of reports to investors. The first is what we're talking about above — a look at the investment's performance, which also outlines how much money you made or lost over different periods of time.

The second is the annual report on costs and compensation (ARCC), which details the charges and fees you paid to your firm, including operating and transaction charges and any fees related to commissions.

You'll see even more detail starting in 2026, when firms are set to introduce what's called a "total cost of reporting." At that point you'll see all the fees mentioned previously and embedded costs you may not know about today. (This applies to mutual funds and ETFs.) That includes the costs of managing the fund, trading commissions for all stocks that are bought and sold (called the total expense ratio), any trailing commissions paid to compensate dealers and advisors, and more.

Here are some important items to check when reviewing an annual report.

>> The report must show the complete portfolio for the fund, not just the top holdings. It's worth it, and interesting, to glance down the list to see if the manager has any funny-looking stuff that may be an attempt to jazz up performance while taking on more risk. The full portfolio listing also shows how much the fund paid for each stock and bond and what it's worth now: It's always fun to see which investment has proved to be a disaster for the fund, although managers often "window dress" by dumping a turkey so it doesn't show up in the report.

>> The statements often contain a commentary by the manager or fund company on what went right or wrong for the fund. As usual with mutual fund handouts, these tend to be bland and boring descriptions of the market or economic outlook, rather than an honest discussion of the manager's good and bad moves. But look for some important clues. If the portfolio manager has been replaced or if the fund's strategy is being changed in a major way, it may be time to dump it. And keep an eye on the top holdings. If they look riskier than you want, or if they leave out major sectors of the economy, then the fund company may be rolling the dice in order to jack up returns and attract more investors.

DON'T THROW THE BOOK VALUE
AT YOUR MANAGER

Be careful when comparing the book value of your investment in a fund with its market value. The book value is the total sum that's been put into the fund, so in that sense, it represents your total investment. But it also includes the value of any distributions made by the fund in the form of new units, even though they weren't real investments that came out of your pocket. The reinvested distributions have the effect of increasing the book value, and they can make it grow larger than the market value — making it appear the fund has lost you money when it may have been a winner. For example, say you originally invest $10,000 in a fund that produces a return of 20 percent, leaving you with a market value of $12,000. But say the manager is an active trader, and they pay out $4,000 in capital gains distributions along the way. Then your fund could have a book value of $14,000, or $2,000 more than its market value on your statement, even though the manager has done a good job.

IN THIS CHAPTER

» Taking a look at your financial reality

» Setting priorities in your financial life

» Identifying your investor profile

» Checking out the performance of various investments

» Remembering to keep a diversified portfolio

» Getting started — checking out sample portfolios

Chapter **4**

Building Your Financial Plan

Mutual funds, when selected carefully, are great for almost everyone and work best as part of an overall financial plan. But you need to consider some important factors before jumping right in. The most important thing to do is take a frank look at your financial health. Good financial planning isn't rocket science and doesn't have to be scary. It starts with getting your debt under control and buying enough insurance. Once you're ready to save and invest, funds are a powerful ally.

In short, funds are for dealing with your savings, the money you have left over after feeding, housing, and clothing your family and taking care of your own desires. Most people want to do one of three things with their savings, or at least a mixture of these three: Grow a big nest egg for retiring, put money in safekeeping with a reasonable return because they don't know what their ultimate plans will be, or, finally, save money for a short-term purpose such as buying a first home.

In other words, they want funds to grow their money over the long term, for several years or more, to give them a reasonable rate of return while avoiding big losses or to simply hold their money safely with a modest annual payoff.

In this chapter, we walk you through using funds to achieve each of the three goals. We outline the best way to set your objectives, help you identify what kind of investor you are, and show you how to start building a suitable portfolio of funds.

Looking at Your Long-Term Financial Future

Your first step is to relax, grab a giant plate of poutine, and remember you live in the best country in the world. If you're working and paying into the *Canada Pension Plan (CPP)* — and have a reasonable prospect of doing so until you're 65 or so — then you're unlikely to end up in absolute poverty. If you're in a pension plan sponsored by a company, union, or professional association, so much the better. If you can build even some modest savings on top of that — a lump sum equivalent to your final year's income, say — then you really shouldn't have any problems getting by in retirement. But you're no doubt planning to buy something nice near the water or take some agreeable cruises, and, for that stuff, just "getting by" won't cut it. So even if you have a good pension and full government benefits coming your way, you'll need cash to kick-start things. And if you're not in a pension plan, you certainly want to be accumulating your own rainy-day fund.

No clear-cut science exists for determining how much you need to save for retirement, but you don't want to find out that you hugely underestimated your needs.

REMEMBER

Many experts claim that you should try to generate an after-tax income — including all pensions and government benefits — equal to about 70 percent of your present net income.

And the conventional assumption for many planners is that you ignore the value of your home (if you own it, of course) when calculating your wealth in retirement. That's because planners often treat the value of an investor's home as an insurance policy that might be needed for medical expenses and so on.

Mind you, those guidelines are pretty extreme. Many people get by on much less than 70 percent of their former net income after they quit work. And a lot of people will be able to sell their family home for a tidy sum, leaving them with a healthy tax-free profit when they move into something smaller. Still, the rules represent an ideal to aim for.

REMEMBER

Just about everybody in Canada with a paying job, including the self-employed, is covered by the CPP. That's the federal government-sponsored pension plan, which you pay for by making contributions throughout your working life. The very similar Quebec Pension Plan exists for those working in Quebec.

For 2023, the maximum monthly benefit payable under the CPP for those aged 65 was $1,306.57, payable for life and increasing in line with inflation. If you delay payment until you're 70, however, you'll get $1,855.33 per month.

On top of that is Old Age Security, a pension provided to all Canadians over 65 who lived in this country long enough. As of July 2023, it was $691 a month for people between 65 and 74 and $760 per month for people 75 and older. (This benefit is income tested — if you make over $134,626 in 2023 you won't get any OAS payments at all.) Finally, the Guaranteed Income Supplement is for low-income seniors, which is something you won't have to worry about if you heed the advice in this book and become a successful mutual fund investor.

All that said, the best way to ensure you'll be free of financial worries in the years to come is to plan carefully and pay attention to your finances. By using investment options such as mutual funds, you can make your retirement a better experience. You'll feel more flush with cash and be able to travel, shop, and generally relax in high style. Plus, investing isn't all about your day in the sun; sound investments can help you meet many of your life goals, such as educating yourself and your children, buying your dream home, starting your own business, and much, much more.

REMEMBER

Start saving now, today, because the younger you are the more powerful the effect of buying mutual funds. Yes, you'll probably get by in retirement, but starting a regular contribution plan to a fund at an early age can earn you thousands of dollars. Say you put $100 monthly into a mutual fund for five straight years and earn a 6 percent annual rate of return: You end up with more than $7,000. But if you'd started five years earlier you'd be sitting on a lot more — $16,500 or so.

Setting Your Financial Priorities

Pick up any of the piles of unwanted personal finance books in the store, and they all begin by saying the same point, mainly because it's true: Pay your debts.

I GAVE AT THE OFFICE: MAKING A CONTRIBUTION AT WORK

If you're working for a large company or for the government, and they offer a traditional defined benefit plan, it's usually a good idea to sign on for it. These plans usually provide a significant pension income, but they are becoming harder and harder to find as many employers stop offering them in favour of less expensive defined contribution plans and group RRSPs. A defined benefit plan is a pension that promises to pay a percentage of your salary when you leave. A typical generous scheme might offer two percent times years of service times the average of your best (or last) five years of income. So if you worked for 35 years, with the best five years averaging $50,000 each, your annual pension would be two percent times 35 times $50,000, which works out at $35,000 a year. When you're negotiating with a new employer, look for a pension that's at least this good — though again, they're becoming fewer and farther between.

Defined contribution plans are still better than nothing — they're more like RRSPs where payouts relate to market movements. The best part, though, is that many employers will match contributions paid into the account, up to a certain amount. So if you put 5 percent of your salary into an account, then your workplace will also invest 5 percent. Take advantage of that free money.

Whether you're in a defined benefit or defined contribution plan, if you're leaving a job early, it's frequently a good idea to stay in the plan rather than take a lump sum. Pension benefits are often increased in line with inflation, either formally or by way of goodwill payments, and pension schemes also may bring you health benefits.

That's the first step for anyone, and often the most difficult. Remember that if you're shelling out $100 in credit card interest each month and you're in a 50 percent tax and deductions bracket on your uppermost income, then it takes $200 in earnings to pay for that sucker.

Building wealth with debt bleeding you dry is impossible, so — with the exception of your home mortgage — becoming borrowing-free is the first move. That's difficult, but it's the first step toward freedom.

WARNING

Fund salespeople and even banks often suggest you borrow money to buy mutual funds. This tactic is known as leveraging your investment and it works out fine as long as the funds go up in value. But remember that if the funds drop, you'll still be on the hook for every penny you borrowed to buy them. So think long and hard before taking out a loan in order to buy mutual funds that invest in stocks and bonds.

Here, roughly in order, are the priorities to set on your road to fiscal responsibility:

1. **Pay off your debts:** Start with the high-interest and non-tax-deductible kind.

2. **Get life insurance:** Buy enough insurance to provide for your loved ones if they lose you and buy fire and theft coverage for your home and property.

    Get quotes on disability insurance. This insurance will provide at least some income if you can't work. If your job doesn't provide any coverage, then it's a must, especially if your household has only one wage earner.

3. **Set up an emergency fund:** Make sure you have access to some cash if an emergency hits. Traditionally, experts advise six months' income.

4. **Have a will drawn up:** Save everybody a lot of hassle and delay (at a horrible time) by biting the bullet and getting this done. If you have a very straightforward situation, a lawyer (or in Quebec, alternatively, a notary) might be able to prepare a will for about $300 to $1,000.

5. **Hire an accountant or other fee-charging expert:** For a charge that can be as low as $200 or $500, they will look over your tax situation. If you do any kind of freelance work or earn any sort of self-employment income, this step is essential (unless your income is so low you can't afford it).

REMEMBER

Only after you've completed those steps should you think about saving and investing money, including buying mutual funds.

When buying funds, make sure you purchase ones that invest in high-quality stocks and bonds. You will have then found a simple and painless way of taking advantage of the high returns earned by most professional investors. Yes, stock and bond prices drop from time to time, but if you don't need the money for years, you have enough time to ride it out.

Funds are also just the ticket for building your short-term savings in order to make a big purchase, maybe your first home. In that case, you want no risk and a nice steady return. Whatever you're chasing in life, funds are a valuable ally above all for their convenience and ease of recordkeeping — just always keep an eye on your statement.

Funds are perfect for almost any financial plan because they're such a maintenance-free and relatively low-cost way of storing and accumulating wealth. Running your own business or buying real estate properties may produce higher returns and lucrative tax write-offs, but being self-employed represents a 24-hour commitment — and whining tenants who call about the drains at 4 a.m. get annoying after a while. Funds are problem-free and easy to monitor, and they produce excellent returns if you keep management fees and costs down.

Anyone who sells mutual funds for a living has a natural in-built bias. It's also why in Part 2 of this book, where we take a close look at financial planners, we recommend you think strongly about going to a fee-only financial planner or accountant who doesn't get commissions for selling products.

Understanding What Type of Investor You Are

So you decided to build some capital. Mutual funds are the most convenient way to do it. The next question is what you'll need the money for. And here's where you can build funds into your financial plan. After your debts and spending are under control, and you've bought adequate insurance and tax advice, the next step is to set goals. Most people have financial objectives that fall into one of these three groups. Chances are your situation fits one of the following descriptions, or it's a blend of two of them:

>> **Growth investors** are building a portfolio of long-term savings that are supposed to last through retirement or through an extended and far-off period of not working.

In that case, it doesn't really matter if the stock market goes into long slumps — it can even be to your advantage if you're steadily investing all the while, because you get to buy stocks cheaply. The real danger is having your money eroded by inflation. So the goal is maximum growth, and that means lots of equity funds with a relatively small proportion of the portfolio in bonds in order to spread your risk.

Growth investors are the greediest of all: They typically chase annual returns of eight percent or more and are willing to expose their portfolio to danger in order to get it.

>> **Balanced investors** aren't sure what's likely to happen in their life, but it could include buying a home, moving to an exotic locale, or starting a family. But whatever the eventual goal is, it's definitely going to require a few thousand dollars.

In that case, caution is the watchword. You may need the money soon, and it would be awful to have to sell your mutual funds straight after the stock market collapsed, scything into their value. So the best formula is lots of money market funds and bond funds, with a modest equity component if you're comfortable taking on some risk. Balanced investors are generally happy with returns of four to seven percent annually.

>> **Savers** are amassing a pile of money to buy a home or car within the next few years, or building a war-chest so they can stop working for a while or perhaps to go back to school.

If you're one of these people, then you want to keep risk to a minimum, because this is money you'll need very soon. That means no stocks, or hardly any, and lots of short-term bonds and money market securities. Savers traditionally will settle for annual rates of return of three percent or less as long as their money isn't at risk.

For all three investor types, mutual funds are a wonderful tool. They're cheap or free to buy, flexible, and convenient. The fund company handles all the record-keeping, which means funds require little or no thought or attention from the investor (but do check your statement carefully). And funds offer attractive rates of return. So decide which goal matches yours, and then look at the suggested sample portfolios in the later section, "Portfolios for Your Type of Investing" for some ideas.

Understanding That Investing Is an Inexact Science

Okay, so in this section, we give you the straight goods. Even reporting on financial markets daily doesn't shield us from the inevitable hits and misses every investor encounters when they throw their hat in the ring. Andrew Bell, the author of the first edition of this book, who now works at BNN Bloomberg, began his investing career in the mid-1990s, when he opened a self-directed RRSP at Toronto-Dominion's discount brokerage, then called Green Line Investor Services, then TD Waterhouse, and now TD Direct Investing. We'll spare you all the details of his expensive education, but here are a few lowlights:

>> Andrew thought a company called Pallet Pallet — which was trying to consolidate the vibrant and exciting market for wooden warehouse pallets — was a turnaround possibility. The company's stock had plunged to pennies after it tried to grow too fast and ran into soaring costs. Needless to say, the pallet industry turned out to be fragmented into tiny mom-and-pop operations for some very good reasons. (Andrew never really found out what they are, though. He's sure a sitcom is in there somewhere.) And he ended up selling his Pallet Pallet shares at a loss.

>> He decided that flying Canadian Airlines was another recovery candidate — but being the greatest market strategist of the late 20th century, he was too clever to bother with the company's boring common stock. No, he bought *warrants*, a speculative sort of certificate that gains real value only if the underlying shares climb. Climb a lot, that is. They didn't, and he lost more money. The company went bust in 2001.

>> Andrew reckoned Asia was in for a major bounce back from its sell-off of 1994, when the average Asian fund dropped 11 percent. So he plunged into madcap Asian mutual funds. Asian markets promptly went into a four-year slump, culminating in the near economic meltdown of 1998. After a while, he stopped looking at his returns.

Okay, Andrew had a couple of successes in technology stocks that actually popped up like they were supposed to. But he has found that funds are the way to go, for him anyway. For many people in this country, including Andrew when he first wrote this book, Canadian equity funds have proved to be a solid investment.

TIP

U.S. funds, which are exposed to the most diversified market in the world, have also been smart buys over the last decade.

TIP

BORROWING FOR RRSPs

Borrowing to invest can be a good idea if you plan to put the money into your RRSP — that's because contributions to an RRSP can be used to reduce your taxable income, generating lucrative tax savings for you. You can then use the tax refund you get to pay off some of the loan: Banks even have RRSP loan-marketing schemes based on this strategy. And remember that when it's in the RRSP, the money grows tax-free.

Still, even though taking out an RRSP loan offers advantages, experts often advise that you limit your borrowing to an amount you can pay off in one or two years. If you're borrowing money to invest outside an RRSP, then the interest you pay on the loan can be written off as an expense for tax purposes, even if your investments tank. But because the government considers RRSPs to be such a generous tax break, interest you pay on a loan taken out for an RRSP contribution can't be used as a tax deduction. Don't let the tax sweetener blind you to the fact that playing with other people's money in this way, by borrowing money to invest, is a risky strategy: you still have to pay them back. See Chapter 22 for more on RRSPs.

For most people, their portfolio seems to thrive when they ignore them and get on with their life. When people attempt to fiddle, fuss, and apply master strategies, it all goes wrong again. The best investing advice? Check your online statements only periodically, and let the pros get on with their jobs. After all, why hire a plumber and then go around yourself banging on the pipes with a screwdriver? The moral of this story: Prepare yourself for the fact that your best-laid plans, including can't-miss investments, can suddenly go awry. Prepare yourself for this probability, and you'll not only sleep better but also be able to afford a more expensive mattress.

Remembering the Importance of Diversification

Investing over two decades makes the stock market look like a pretty good place to be. But the road to riches looks somewhat smoother with bonds added to the mix. If you ever look at a graph for a balanced portfolio of say, 60 percent equities and 40 percent stocks, it will resemble a gentler hike up Quebec's Laurentians, compared to the Rocky Mountain image presented by stock-only portfolios. So despite the potentially better returns from stocks, your nerves will probably have an easier time of it with a balanced portfolio.

When the first edition of this book was written in 2000 — when the stock market was only beginning to turn bad — the 20-year return on the MSCI World Index was a huge 17.1 percent. Over the last decade, which includes a painful 2022, the MSCI World Index returned 9.89 percent. Stocks may be a great long-term investment, but it depends whose long term we're talking about — in other words, which period you use for measuring. The bottom line is you may get lucky with stocks if you cash out at the right time, when the market is surging. But who's that lucky?

REMEMBER

The sensible course is to own lots of bonds (loans to companies and governments) as well as stocks — that way your portfolio has a chance to produce the steady returns that retirement saving is all about.

Gains from foreign investments can also come from currency changes — and over the last several years the Canadian dollar has fallen in value against the U.S. dollar, producing a bonus for Canadian investors. Here's how that works: On June 30, 2023, $10,000 U.S. dollar equalled $13,200 Canadian dollars. Over the next six months, the U.S. dollar's value climbed against the loonie. On December 6, 2023, that $10,000 was worth $13,600 Canadian dollars. You got $400 for doing nothing!

The opposite, of course, is the case when the loonie surges, like it did in 2011, when its value was on par with the Greenback.

Portfolios for Your Type of Investing

In this section, we look at three suggested mutual fund portfolios that offer a good prospect of achieving the different goals of a short-term saver, a balanced investor, and a growth investor. Are these the very best portfolios that could ever be designed? No, because the future can't be predicted with complete accuracy.

TIP

Distrust any financial professional who says they can tell you what the markets will be up to, or down to, in the years to come.

These portfolios represent a cautious guess as to what the global economy will do, and they amount to a forecast that the world isn't likely to slide into either hyper-inflation or bitter deflation (a prolonged fall in prices).

As you become more knowledgeable about and interested in investing, you may want to start adding to or altering these suggestions. But they're a good place to start when you're adding the power of mutual funds to your financial plan.

A look at index funds

The portfolios we discuss in this chapter include lots of so-called *index funds* — funds that simply track a stock or bond market average or index by essentially buying every stock in the market. For example, most Canadian equity index funds are designed to produce a return in line with the S&P/TSX index. Index funds offer huge advantages to investors, such as low costs (less than one percent of your money each year, compared with well over two percent for traditional equity funds) and the reassurance that your fund won't badly underperform the market. Even better than index funds, though, are exchange-traded funds, or ETFs, which save you even more in annual expenses. We stick to index funds here because we're talking about mutual funds, but you can find out more about ETFs in Bryan's *ETFs For Canadians For Dummies* book, released in 2022.

When it comes to indexes, it's important to remember that a few highly priced stocks — often tech companies — can skew an index's performance. In Canada, that's been Nortel, BlackBerry and more recently Shopify. If one high-flying company does well, the index rises. If it goes bust, as it did in the case of Nortel and later BlackBerry, performance can suffer. Over the last couple of decades, stock index proprietors introduced capped versions of their indices to offset the effect of these dominant stocks, and some fund companies launched capped index funds based on these new barometers. Many BlackRock iShares Canadian equity ETFs track the corresponding S&P/TSX capped indices. However, many index funds remain true to the basic, uncapped indices. Thus, half the stock market money in our portfolios has been allocated to traditional-style, "actively managed" funds, which have managers who attempt to predict which stocks will go up and which will drop. For more on index funds and ETFs, see Chapter 15.

Note that international equity funds usually invest in stocks outside of North America, so the international index funds mentioned here don't track the U.S. market. That's why we also include U.S. index funds. However, global equity funds buy stocks everywhere, including the United States. The actively managed funds in these portfolios are global, so you needn't include separate U.S. equity funds.

Some experts will look at these suggested portfolios and complain that we haven't included any specialized funds that invest in small companies. In the past, shares in small companies have occasionally produced huge returns, and evidence suggests they sometimes do well when big-company stocks are languishing. Traditionally, that has happened in very hot stock markets, when investors are willing to buy risky little stocks in pursuit of big gains.

TIP

In other words, buying shares in lesser-known companies provides something called *diversification* — the strategy of spreading an investor's risk among different investments.

But small-company shares also have a nasty habit of stagnating for years, and their returns tend to be highly volatile — big gains one year and then nothing for several years. So to keep things simple, we've left small-company funds out of these sample portfolios. You may miss out on a percentage point or two of returns every few years, but you'll be avoiding a lot of risk. As you get more comfortable with investing, you may decide to add some small-stock funds to your portfolio. Just make sure you buy at least two, because different types of small stocks tend to thrive at different times. It's frustrating to find yourself stuck with a manager who bought just the wrong sort of small-company shares.

One other detail to note: It's difficult for fund managers to beat their benchmarks after fees are taken into account. These days, many people used index-hugging ETFs for the core part of their portfolio — Canadian equity and U.S. equity for instance — and buy mutual funds for niche areas, such as Chinese equity or even emerging market equity more broadly. That's something to consider, as it'll save you money on fees. However, there are plenty of good Canadian fund managers, too, who are trying to beat their benchmark, so look at everything before buying.

REMEMBER

Part 3 contains chapters on each type of fund, explaining the advantages and drawbacks of each in detail.

A penny earned is a penny saved

The first portfolio, shown in Table 4-1, is ideal for savers. The savers' portfolio consists mostly of Canadian assets (no point speculating on currency changes if you're just saving for a Volvo), so it can be held both within and outside an RRSP, ideally in a tax-free savings account — an account that charges no tax on gains, dividends, or income as you're saving and when you withdraw. It includes small quantities of regular bonds, even though their prices can be volatile, to increase its interest income. And the global bonds provide a small amount of protection against a possible drop in the value of the Canadian dollar because they're bought and sold in foreign currencies.

TABLE 4-1

Suggested Portfolio for Savings (20% Money Market and 80% Bonds)

Fund Type	Percentage of Total Portfolio
Money market fund	20%
Canadian short-term bond or short-term bond index fund	50%
Canadian bond or bond index fund	20%
Global bond or global bond index fund	10%

You could make this portfolio even simpler by just putting half the money into a money market fund and the rest into a short-term bond fund. Money market funds are very unlikely ever to lose money for their unitholders (it would probably take a major financial dislocation before one did). Short-term bond funds are a little more dangerous, but they're also slightly more lucrative to own than money market funds.

TECHNICAL STUFF

Ever since the Great Recession in 2008, bond and money market funds have been difficult investments to be in. That's because interest rates were slashed and stayed low for a long time. That all changed in 2023, when inflation started getting out of control. Central banks around the world increased rates dramatically. While that put pressure on homeowners whose mortgage rates soared, bonds and money market funds started offering much sweeter returns.

At the time of writing, a 3-year Government of Canada benchmark bond yield was at 4.33 percent — far higher than it has been over the last decade. Some money market funds are paying closer to 5 percent.

Balancing act

The next portfolio, Table 4-2, for balanced investors, is truly one you can just buy and forget.

TABLE 4-2

Suggested Portfolio for Balanced Investors (55% Bonds and 45% Stocks)

Fund Type	Percentage of Total Portfolio
Money market fund	5%
Canadian short-term bond or short-term bond index fund	25%
Canadian bond or bond index fund	15%
Global bond or global bond index fund	10%
Canadian equity index fund	8%
Conservative Canadian equity fund A	4%
Conservative Canadian equity fund B	3%
Conservative global equity fund A	7%
Conservative global equity fund B	8%
International equity index fund	10%
U.S. equity index fund	5%

With its large 30-percent proportion of cash and cash-like, short-term bonds, this portfolio is unlikely to lose more than 10 percent in a single year, unless a sharp uptick occurs in inflation, the economy slides into a recession, or some national or global mishap sends the bond market into a downward spiral. Okay, yes, that's exactly what's happened in 2022, but as of late 2023, inflation is coming down and central banks are now pausing on rate hikes. That could change, but bonds are in a much better place today than they were in 2022, when inflation and rate hikes caused the asset class to lose a lot of money.

One for the risk-takers

Then there's the Ferrari of the stock market, for those who relish the cold taste of fear, the brutal snapping, and the terrible slashing. Check out Table 4-3. You could easily make this portfolio more exciting and dangerous by reducing the bond weighting even more, or by buying emerging-markets funds and narrow regional funds that invest in Asia or Europe.

TABLE 4-3

Suggested Portfolio for Growth Investors (25% Bonds and 75% Stocks)

Fund Type	Percentage of Total Portfolio
Canadian bond fund or bond index fund	15%
Global bond fund	10%
Canadian equity index fund	10%
Conservative Canadian equity fund A	5%
Conservative Canadian equity fund B	5%
International index fund	20%
U.S. equity index fund	10%
Conservative global equity fund A	13%
Conservative global equity fund B	12%

Arguably, every aggressive portfolio should contain a small weighting in developing countries (because of their huge growth prospects), but we left out emerging-markets funds to keep the portfolio as simple as possible. In any case, at least one of your conservative global equity funds is certain to own a few companies in emerging nations. You can also step on the gas by going into volatile sector funds that track just one type of company, such as technology outfits or oil and gas producers. However, once again, your index funds and actively managed funds are almost certain to own these companies and industries anyway.

A portfolio like this is certain to do well as long as stock markets stay strong. It's very broadly diversified, and its big index fund component means you'll end up owning lots of huge, well-run companies.

IN THIS CHAPTER

» Checking out old, reliable, guaranteed investment certificates

» Looking at regular bonds and strip bonds

» Taking stock of stocks

» Investigating managed products

Chapter **5**

Beyond Mutual Funds

S o you've got your debt under control and your insurance taken care of. Time to start saving money. But what are you going to do with those vast piles of cash? Think of this chapter as an investment primer, a rundown on the drawbacks and attractions of the different types of financial assets you can buy with your savings. If you're certain by now that funds are the way to go for you, then feel free to skip to Part 2, where we explain where you can go to buy them. But it's useful to know about the other investment choices you have — including guaranteed investment certificates, which can't be bought through mutual funds at all.

Don't worry, though. The decisions you need to make are fairly simple when you come down to it. The investment business is an incredibly conservative industry. For all the dot-com flash and techno-trading systems, your basic investment options are the same as they were in the 1920s or even the 1820s — stocks, bonds, or cash. Here's what's out there: everything from the mundane to the manic.

In this chapter, we take you for a stroll down Risk Road, moving from the very safest choices to the most unpredictable. Along the way, we point out some of the dangers and delights of each investment — so that even if you end up handing your money over to a fund company to manage, you'll at least have an idea of what they're going to do with it.

The Good Old GIC: You Know Where You Sleep

Even in a higher interest rate world, which we saw in 2023, most banks offer miserable rates of interest — 0.5 percent if you're lucky — on money dumped in a "savings" account. Some non-bank institutions, such as Wealthsimple or EQ Bank, offer better rates on their savings accounts, though most people still bank with the banks. You may be able to get more if you keep a very high balance in the account, or if you opt for an account with a higher rate but bigger transaction fees. And some "e-savings" accounts pay a decent rate with low fees if you abide by certain transaction rules. But without getting bogged down in bank-account research, you can do better if you put the cash in a guaranteed investment certificate (GIC) with a bank, insurance company, or trust company for a fixed period.

A *GIC* is a deposit that a financial institution accepts on the understanding that the money, plus a guaranteed amount of interest, will be returned after a set number of years. The interest is calculated on an annual basis and each year's interest is usually added or "compounded" onto the total for the purpose of calculating the next year's interest — so you earn interest on interest. Say you invest $10,000 into a 10-year GIC in 2024 with five percent interest compounded annually. You would have $16,289 by 2034. A drawback is that you may not be able to get the deposit back before the term is up, or, if you can, you may have to forfeit the interest earned. In other words, these deposits aren't as *liquid* — cashable — as you may think. That means GICs are less flexible than money market funds (which we talk about in Chapter 17) or bond funds, which could produce similar (though in the case of bonds, not guaranteed) returns. The great beauty of GICs, though, is that you know exactly where you stand.

For years, generations even, the GIC was Canada's favourite investment. While they fell out of favour between about 2008 and 2022, when interest rates were at the lowest levels they've been in history, they came back with a vengeance in 2023 after the Bank of Canada hiked rates once again. While you're not getting the 12 percent rates of the 1990s, in late 2023 you could find rates above five percent. Banks have to offer those kinds of rates to attract money because inflation has been rising.

Looking at the Types of GICs

GICs come in a sometimes-bewildering range of shapes and flavours, so always make sure you understand all the mechanics before you buy one. Get an employee of the financial institution to write down the value of the deposit when it matures (except in the case of index-linked GICs, whose returns are tied to the stock market).

Here are some common variations above and beyond the traditional non-cashable GIC (even more specific types exist):

» **Cashable GICs:** Traditional GICs tie your money up or at least reduce the interest you get if you cash out early. But cashable GICs let you take all or part of your money out early with no penalty. Expect to get a lower annual rate, though. It can be a full percentage point lower than the return on a normal non-cashable GIC.

» **Index-linked GICs:** These pay you little or no fixed interest but they promise to return your initial investment and pay a return that's linked to the performance of a stock market index — always a bit watered-down, though, in order to pay for the guaranteed return of capital and leave a profit margin for the bank. In other words, your money is safe from loss but your potential return isn't as good as it would have been investing directly in stocks. For example, a typical GIC linked to the Canadian stock market may pay no guaranteed interest but give the investor a return identical to the change in the Standard & Poor's/Toronto Stock Exchange 60 index — subject to some limitations.

Index GICs are popular when interest rates on ordinary GICs are low. The problem with these products is that their rules and terms are so complicated it can be difficult or impossible to know how well you're doing as you go along. Yes, they offer some stock market action for investors who would otherwise be too nervous to go into equities, but most investors can do better with an index fund or ETF and a couple of conservative equity funds, especially if they can ride out downturns in the market over a few years.

At least one bank, CIBC, has a GIC linked to a diversified "portfolio" of market indices. Some of its Market Linked GIC attach the return to performance of the S&P/TSX 60 index, while others follow a global portfolio of 10 blue-chip stocks, such as AT&T, TELUS, and Alphabet (formerly Google).

Some institutions have rolled out GICs linked to the performance of a specific mutual fund. Royal Bank has one linked to its RBC O'Shaughnessy International Equity Fund. Bank of Montreal links one of its "Progressive GICs" to returns of its BMO Dividend Fund.

» **Convertible GICs:** RRSP marketing season is the first 60 days of the calendar year, when money put into your RRSP can be used to reduce taxable income for the previous year. For example, if you earned $50,000 during 2023 but managed to put $5,000 into a plan by February 29, 2024, then you'd have to pay tax on income of only $45,000 for 2023. During that two-month period, institutions offer flexible GICs that let you invest your money at the one-year rate, but then allow you to switch to a longer-term deposit or to the company's mutual funds.

>> **Escalating-rate GICs:** These GICs also don't lock you in. You can cash out without penalty after one or two years, but if you stay on, the interest rate gets higher. The design of these GICs varies among institutions, and some, such as CIBC, offer more than one type. For example, a CIBC Cashable Escalating Rate GIC taken out in late 2023 paid two percent during the first year, three percent in year two, and 4.25 percent in year three, for an effective annual yield of about 3.07 percent. By comparison, a three-and five-year CIBC Bonus Rate GIC at CIBC, which is a standard non-cashable GIC, paid 4.25 percent. Like index-linked GICs, the returns offered by some of these "escalator" GICs are based on some pretty complex formulas.

Finding the best rates

A quick way to find out the various GIC rates on offer from a wide variety of institutions is to check websites such as Ratehub (ratehub.ca), or NerdWallet (nerdwallet.com).

You often can get a higher rate by going to a smaller company, but dealing with the little outfit may be more troublesome because it won't have the same branch network and resources.

Wherever you go, make sure the institution is a member of the Canada Deposit Insurance Corp. See the following section for more on the deposit insurance protection provided by this government agency.

Checking out the benefits of GICs

Don't spurn the humble GIC out of hand. They never lose money. During bad-news years for the stock market when Canadian equity funds can fall by double digits, sticking to one-year GICs keeps you in the black. GICs offer other advantages:

>> **Simplicity:** They're simple and quick to buy, with no extra fees or complicated forms to fill out. Just about any bank, insurance company, or stockbroker can sell you one.

>> **Income generating:** They're a useful planning tool if you need your portfolio to throw off a regular stream of income. That can be done by "laddering" GICs — putting the money into deposits with separate terms, each maturing on a different date to match your spending needs. Even if you don't need the money for income, having your GICs come due at different times is also handy

for reducing "reinvestment risk." That's the problem of getting a pile of money to reinvest from a maturing bond or deposit just as interest rates are low. If the money comes up for re-investment at different times, you can re-invest it at a variety of interest rates.

>> **Safe and secure:** If you buy a GIC from a bank, trust company, or loan company, as long as the GIC's term to maturity doesn't exceed five years, your money is protected by insurance provided by the federal government's Canada Deposit Insurance Corporation. If the financial institution fails, CDIC will cover an individual for up to $100,000 in deposits (including chequing accounts and the like but *not* mutual funds) at that institution. When buying a GIC, always make sure the company you're dealing with has CDIC coverage. Go to www.cdic.ca for more information, including the "CIDC Financial Professional Trivia Challenge" — at last, a fun activity for guests at one of your holiday parties.

Watching out for inflation

WARNING

Before you abandon all thoughts of buying mutual funds and plunge into GICs instead, remember that fixed-rate deposits can be trouble in one important sense. In a low-rate environment, as the world was in between 2008 and 2022, they do little to protect you against inflation. Fortunately, inflation was also nearly non-existent until 2022, so this wasn't as big of an issue, but it was a big deal in 2023. Inflation soared more than it has in decades, which means anyone in a low-rate GIC would have lost big bucks. (In purchasing power, at least.) Now that GIC rates have caught up to rising interest rates, there's less chance of that happening going forward. (At the end of 2023, inflation hadn't gotten under control.)

As Table 5-1 shows, even quite modest rates of inflation eat away alarmingly quickly at the real value of your savings. In 2023, inflation rates hit above eight percent, and while it's come down since, it's not yet at the one percent to three percent range preferred by central banks. Inflation of just three percent a year wipes out about one-fifth of the value of your money in five years.

The curse of inflation means that, as an investor, you're constantly clambering up a slippery, moving staircase covered in rotting mackerel and parts of Scotsmen. Stand still or go forward too slowly, and you end up sliding backward.

TABLE 5-1 ## How Inflation Destroys Money over Time

Time Elapsed	Approx. Value of $10,000 at 3-percent Inflation
Initial amount	$10,000
One year	$9,700
Two years	$9,215
Three years	$8,754
Four years	$8,317
Five years	$7,901
Six years	$7,506
Seven years	$7,130
Eight years	$6,774
Nine years	$6,435
Ten years	$6,113

Bonds: Stable Securities for Every Portfolio

Bonds are loans to governments or corporations that have been packaged into certificates that trade on the open market. They usually pay a fixed rate of interest, often twice a year. And they "mature" or come due after a set number of years, when the holder of the bond gets back the value of the original loan, known as the "principal."

But don't bother buying individual bonds until you've got $10,000 or so to spend, because the cost of buying a cheap bond index mutual fund is so low. Index funds, which just earn a return in line with an entire bond market or index, are particularly suitable for the bond market because normal human managers find it very difficult to earn much more than their rivals without taking risks.

The median Canadian fixed income fund has annual expenses of about 1.8 percent, but many bond funds can be held for less than one percent a year. That's less than $100 out of a $10,000 investment, so you're doing fine.

Considering bond alternatives

If you're comfortable buying and selling on the stock exchange, it's worth thinking about buying a *bond exchange-traded fund* — bond ETFs are units in a simple trust that give you ownership of bonds but trade on the exchange like a share. We talk lots more on exchange-traded funds — which are perhaps the best deal of all for small investors — in Chapter 15. The big advantage to buying a bond ETF is that you save on fees. The biggest domestic bond ETF, iShares Core Canadian Universe Bond Index ETF, charges just 0.1 percent.

You can also consider bond funds, which are purchased in the same way as any mutual fund. The annual fund expenses cut into your yield, yes — but you may just decide the cost is worth it. In Chapter 14, we single out some bond funds that have relatively low expenses — and that have done a good job investing, too, by the way!

REMEMBER

Don't forget, though, that with a bond fund, you are essentially playing the bond market without the backup security of being able to hold a bond to its maturity date, and thus recover your original investment or principal in addition to the periodic interest payments. Bond fund managers buy and sell bonds on the market, and thus you are signing on to a pretty aggressive form of investing. No, you won't exactly be a "master of the universe," as in Tom Wolfe's *The Bonfire of the Vanities*, but you will be participating in a fairly active market.

Investing directly in bonds

You can obtain a far better yield than bond funds by investing directly in bonds. However, the bond market is not always the friendliest place for small investors — it can be difficult to get information or do trades. It's just not a popular product, and profit margins for the dealer are thin. If you really want to buy a bond directly, you can go through a broker or advisor, but there isn't an easy way to track prices. Save the hassle and get a bond fund or ETF.

REMEMBER

The trouble with bonds is that, unlike stocks, they don't trade in a central marketplace where the prices are posted.

If you buy stocks, your broker usually just acts as an "agent" who connects you with the seller's broker, collecting a commission for the service. But your broker generally buys and sells bonds as a "principal" — that is, the firm actually owns the bonds it trades, holding them in "inventory" like a store. That means when you're trading bonds, you generally have to ask your broker what the firm's price quote is for a bond you want to buy or sell. And then you more or less have to accept the price that's offered.

Even bigger problems can occur in buying and selling *strip bonds*, which are bonds that have been modified by brokers to reflect the fact that many long-term buyers who hold bonds until maturity aren't interested in collecting periodic interest payments. In fact, such dribs and drabs of interest are a liability because they must constantly be reinvested. So strip bonds pay no interest until they mature — the interest payments have been "stripped" away. Instead, they're bought at a deep discount to their face value, maturing at full value or "par" like a normal bond.

For example, you may pay your broker 50 cents on the dollar for a strip bond maturing in ten years. That will give you an annual compound yield of about 7.2 percent. In other words, an investment of $5,000 becomes $10,000 after a decade. Because strip bondholders are prepared to wait until they get any of their money back, they're rewarded with a higher yield to maturity. It's often 0.5 to one percentage point of extra yield yearly compared with a regular bond with a similar term to maturity.

WARNING

Strip bonds can be difficult to unload. They're volatile, losing their market value quickly when interest rates rise. That's because higher rates offer better interest-earning opportunities in the here and now, so they rapidly devalue money you don't get for a long time. And strip bonds are all about waiting for a faraway payoff.

Because strip bonds are often sold as a retail product, your broker may be reluctant to buy one back from you at a decent price if the firm has no demand for strips from other clients. So if you're buying a strip, plan on holding it to maturity.

If you have at least $10,000 to play with, buy bonds and hold them to maturity by all means. You know exactly what yield you're getting and how much money you'll have when the bonds mature. With a bond mutual fund, which is constantly rolling over its holdings, you won't have nearly that much certainty.

REMEMBER

If you plan to try trading bonds, remember that making money in this market ("going forward," an annoying expression Bay Street types like to use a dozen times before breakfast) can be tougher in the long run. That's because bond prices usually only go up when interest rates and the rate of inflation fall — if inflation stays unchanged, then all you're likely to get from a bond is its yield to maturity at the time of purchase.

Stocks: Thrills, Spills, and Twisted Wreckage

The stock market is insane. Although you can spot stocks trading at crazy prices and make money buying those individual shares, it's hard — so hard as to be damned near impossible. But don't worry, there are ways to build your nest egg, such as through exchange-traded and index funds.

Going with index funds and ETFs

Unless you plan to spend quite a bit of time tracking stocks and reading the financial press, you're probably best off in equity funds. The easiest strategy of all: Just climb aboard the madness by putting a chunk of your money into stock index funds or ETFs — which track the whole stock market — and you'll be doing what a lot of smart pros do.

The indexes themselves go crazy from time to time, as they did in 2020 when COVID-19 made everyone think the world was about to end. Perhaps the most spectacular example of abrupt stock market activity was in 1999 and 2000, when technology and telecommunications stocks dominated the market benchmarks. It may all seem too much to stomach, but when you look at the long-term record of stock market performance, particularly in North America, it's hard to stay away from the index-investing party. You're only alive three times, after all, and the last two times you come back as something in the sea, so why not have fun now?

If we've whet your appetite with this brief glimpse into the world of index funds, head over to Chapter 15, where we discuss them in greater detail.

Buying individual stocks

Think you can beat the market? Good luck. Picking good stocks consistently is really, really hard. You also need a broker to put through your trades. Your shares get held in the brokerage's computer system under an account in your name. Always check your statement and transaction confirmation slips carefully, because mistakes happen.

If you want to buy individual stocks, you need a bit of money to make it worth the trouble and expense — say, at least $10,000 — unless you're just throwing a few thousand at the market for laughs (and it is enjoyable, so try it when you get a chance). Most trades go through in "board lots" of 100 shares at a time, for efficiency. If you're dealing in blue-chip companies, buying 100 shares can add up — it costs $2,500 for 100 shares trading at $25 each. Buying fewer than 100 shares at a time is generally inefficient because it means dealing in an "odd" or "broken" lot of less than 100. If you deal in odd lots, you often get a lower price when you sell and have to pay more per share after you buy.

And, as usual in investing, you must make a choice between having a salesperson take care of all the humdrum stuff at a cost or doing it yourself at less expense. The price of buying stock through a full-service traditional stockbroker is usually shrouded in black curtains and dry ice. Establishing commission rates can be like bargaining in a grim, sweaty bazaar on the edge of a desert — in other words, full-service brokerage commissions are completely negotiable. A small trade typically may cost four percent of a transaction's value. That's quite a haircut to take when you buy and again when you sell, but most frequent traders could haggle for much less. But don't expect a full-service broker to be too thrilled about your business unless you've got at least $50,000 or even $100,000 to throw into the market because with any less than that, you're more of an annoyance than a revenue stream. And it's not unusual for an experienced and acclaimed broker to accept only "high-net-worth accounts" of $1 million or more.

So investors with modest means are left with a discount broker, which may impose no minimum account size at all but also provides little or no advice or help. Their commission rates vary with some now offering free commission trading, but most charge between $5 and $10. We give you the scoop on discount brokers in Chapter 6.

Buying and selling stocks profitably and reliably is difficult — perhaps impossible — but evidence indicates that ordinary investors can do well by investing in a few well-run, growing companies and simply holding them for years. Mind you, that's emotionally tough to do. Take Shopify Inc., an Ottawa-based tech company that helps small businesses easily set up online storefronts. If you'd bought Shopify shares at the start of 2019, your investment would have increased by a whopping 343 percent in five years. But it would have been a tough buy-and-hold experience, with the share price moving from about $18.50 a share in January 2003 to about $213 in November 2021 because of strong sales during the COVID-19 pandemic, then tumbling to $41 in June 2022 thanks to people getting out more and shopping online less. The stock rallied after some big layoffs, hitting $81 in November 2023.

Taking a wilder ride with stock alternatives

For those who find even stocks too staid — options, warrants, futures, and rights are the wonder drug of investing albeit volatile ways to play or speculate on a share, market, or commodity. They're structured to offer faster price changes than the underlying asset itself. The general principle is that for a little money, you get to "buy risk" from someone who doesn't want it. But the downside is that your wild party has a time limit because the speculative instrument always expires after a set period. That's a huge drawback: Many a market veteran will testify that picking the right investment is tough enough, without having the clock ticking against you. Buy these things only with money you don't care about. For more about options, pick up a copy of *Options Trading For Dummies*.

Managed Products: A Fee Circus

Every year, the investment industry comes up with warehouses full of glittering, new, nougat-flavoured, candy-coloured, "managed" investment products, each holding out the prospect of riches and implying your savings will be exposed to only the barest smidgeon of risk. A lot of these exciting innovations fail to deliver the golden eggs. The problem is that when investments are done up in such fancy packages, somebody has to pay for all the frills and gorgeous ribbons — and it's always the retail buyer. The investment may be called a *unit trust*, a *royalty trust*, a *closed-end fund*, a *partnership*, or an *income trust* — whatever the name and no matter how wonderful the sales spiel, never forget that if someone's trying to sell the thing to you, they are collecting a fee somewhere down the line.

Several complex investment vehicles are best left to sophisticated, experienced investors. Although they can be difficult to understand, it should be noted that some are, however, well managed, underpriced, and lucrative to own. But all carry disadvantages:

>> **Limited partnerships:** These investments are so complicated you need to have a lawyer look them over for you, and even then you're vulnerable. They usually produce tax breaks for the buyers by investing in risky exploits such as movies or natural resources, but unless you have money to burn, don't consider these highly speculative investments.

>> **Hedge funds:** These began as privately run funds for the very rich, but are now sold to the small investor, often through hedge "funds of funds." Hedging is the practice of protecting your investments against loss — by selling borrowed shares at the same time as you buy others, for example. And that's what the rich are mostly interested in when it comes to investing: protecting what they have. Hedge funds are no longer all about avoiding losses, though. Some, although not all, use exotic or risky techniques to chase high returns. Hedge funds used to require a minimum investment of $25,000, but they now can be had for as little as $1,000. But absolutely make sure you get professional advice before putting any serious money into this type of product.

In your investing career, stick to the investments the professionals buy — bonds and stocks and simple mutual funds that invest in bonds and stocks.

Buying a fancy, managed product adds a level of cost and complexity that can only reduce your returns. Buying a stock at the issue price when it's first sold to the public is risky, too, even though you usually get it commission-free. Grab it later after the price has fallen, which it likely will eventually. The issue price has often been inflated to pay for brokerage commissions and other marketing expenses, not to mention general hype — so let some other poor investor pay for all those shiny new Mercedes and BMW automobiles you see parked in Bay Street garages.

2

Buying Options: Looking for a Helping Hand

IN THIS PART . . .

Find out which discount brokers to consider.

Understand the advantages and drawbacks of buying with banks.

Discover what motivates financial planners and advisors to sell you funds.

Get a handle on the few independent fund companies out there.

Chapter **6**

Discount Brokers: Cheap Thrills

D iscount brokers are about the closest you can get, as yet, to investing heaven — they're cheap and simple. A discount brokerage account is a great place to build wealth for the long term because you can put almost any kind of investment into it — including mutual funds, shares, bonds, GICs, or even your own mortgage. Next to the invention of the mutual fund itself, discount brokers have done more than any other financial innovation to open up the stock and bond markets to ordinary people. Best of all, discount brokers are great for keeping costs down, which is one of the most important determinants of investment success.

Discounters are firms set up simply to carry out your buy-and-sell orders — charging low commission rates — and provide an account in which you can hold your investments. They sometimes purport to offer lots of flashy services and information, some of which can actually be useful. But, essentially, a discounter is just a bare-bones, order-taking service.

Picking a discount broker can be tricky. In this chapter, we give you the whole story — how discounters work, how they can save you more of your hard-won cash, how to pick the right one for you, and, finally, a few warnings about problems some discount brokerage customers have run into.

What Are Discount Brokers?

A *discount broker* is a true broker in the sense that it's a firm set up simply to act as an agent. It collects a *commission* — that is, a transaction fee — when you buy or sell stocks, bonds, funds, and other investments. Yes, financial planners, insurance agents, and traditional stockbrokers also take your orders in this way, but they also bill themselves as advisors and experts who get a fee for helping out. Nothing wrong with that as such — but their fees eat into your returns. A Canadian discount brokerage firm is typically an arm of a big bank or a financial technology firm, taking orders over the Internet. A few discount brokers in the United States and Canada offer free trades, though there may be a catch, such as a limited selection of stocks or exchange-traded funds. Virtually all discounters in Canada today execute your transactions for $10 or less, a big improvement from the $30-per-order fees of the 1990s.

TIP

If you're absolutely certain you're going to want personal advice from someone when you pick your funds, then skip this chapter and jump to Chapter 7, where we talk in detail about banks and the services they provide. Discount brokers don't provide much advice, so if you feel you need help picking funds, you won't enjoy using one.

A discounter is like a teller at a horse racing track. They just take your money and place your bet. In the same way, a discount broker offers little or no advice or financial planning. Just a bare-bones account to hold your investments, and rock-bottom fees to buy and sell. Discounters may offer to sell you fancy packages of pre-selected funds but won't provide much personal advice about your situation.

REMEMBER

Discounters, then, essentially offer a commodity. They are largely automated. In return for charging low commissions, discounters hope to attract enough business to turn a profit.

In the past, discounters were subject to the provincial securities rule that obliges brokers to ensure trades are suitable for the client. Like other people in the investment business who accept your money, they were supposed to follow the Know Your Client rule. (See Chapter 3 for more.) However, in recent years, securities regulators in Canada have relaxed the requirement that trades through a discount broker be vetted to see if they fit with the customer's risk tolerance and investment knowledge. That was after lobbying by the discounters, who claimed that having a human being check every trade slowed up the process too much. The message, for those who may have missed it, is this: When investing through a discounter, you're on your own.

Looking into Canadian discounters

Discounters are an industry where you have to be large to make money. That's why the big banks dominate the discount brokerage sector in Canada, because they already have vast customer bases. Each of the big banks has a discount brokerage arm, but they do have at least some competition from fintech outfits such as Wealthsimple, Questrade, Qtrade, CI Direct, and Desjardins, as well as several credit unions across the country.

Getting set up with a discounter

Setting up an account with a discount broker is simplicity itself. You don't have to sit through a sales spiel or show that you have thousands to invest — just go online, complete a few forms, open an account, and put in some money.

You never have to meet anyone face-to-face. The anonymity is relaxing, although be prepared for a long time on hold when problems occur in your account. And you get used to shouting at dazed employees in a harsh barking tone.

Here's more about how to get set up:

1. **Visit the Web site of the discount broker you picked and choose the account type you're looking for: unregistered, RRSP, TFSA, and so on.**

   (Chapter 3 has more details on account set up. Or go to the TD Direct Investing site at www.td.com/ca/en/investing/direct-investing for an example.)

2. **Answer a series of questions.**

   Some of them are a tad sensitive, such as your social insurance number, or intrusive, around your net worth. Dealing with your existing bank is easier because they already have a lot of your information.

3. **After that, just enter your orders by using the firm's website or phone app.**

   Ensure you have fast access to the trade-confirmation slip and check it against the order you placed.

A discounter will pretty well accept your business no matter how poor you are. But you have to have the necessary cash in your account, Jack, before you make the first trade.

Most providers enable you to view and/or download monthly account statements, transaction confirmations, and tax documents via a secure messaging system you can access online or by using a phone app. You can happily ignore all this documentation, but it's worth checking from time to time as mistakes happen.

REMEMBER

Using a discount broker is investing for grownups. No one is around to hold your tiny hand or coo into your tight little rosebud of an ear that "the market always comes back." In return for the low commissions they charge, discounters are geared to provide little or no personal service.

Why Discount Brokers Are a Great Place to Buy Funds

If you're confident about making investment decisions yourself, a discount broker is the best place to buy and hold mutual funds. Discounters let you buy certain mutual funds for no upfront charge when other brokers would demand a commission. They also carry a vast selection of hundreds of mutual funds (more than any broker does), lots of bonds, and just about any stock you care to name. That means you can hold funds from a multitude of different companies — including some low-cost, no-load funds that are hard to buy from a broker or financial planner. And a discount brokerage account also lets you combine funds with your other investments, such as stocks or guaranteed investment certificates, so that all your holdings show up on one convenient statement.

Discounters are the perfect source for mutual funds because the choice is so huge and the charges are so low. Here's a rundown of the other main reasons to strongly consider leaving your money with a discounter.

Your one-stop shop — Convenience

Discount brokers are just extremely convenient. As long as you can get access to the Internet you should be able to sell or buy funds, stocks, and bonds in your discount brokerage account. By contrast, a full-service broker may be out of the office, ill, or busy, creating a delay if the backup person is slow.

Another reason to love discounters: Everything is online, with all letting you look at your account and place orders at any time over the World Wide Web. With a discounter, you are responsible for managing your account. True, no account manager will be pushing a particular stock or fund that may earn them a commission, but the flip side is you won't have a person you can go to with questions, unless you look in the mirror.

Access to a broad selection of options

Wide selection is a powerful reason to go with a discount broker, because discounters sell just about everything. A bank branch or no-load fund company can generally sell you only its own funds, and a broker is likely to have a "select list" of funds with which they are most familiar. But a discount broker lets you select your funds from among hundreds of funds, as well as thousands of stocks and bonds, in North America and often on overseas markets as well. That means you can have the luxury of just one central portfolio that holds all your investments, instead of spreading them all around town.

Discounters have to carry every major fund because otherwise their competitors will beat them on selection. Having every fund available can be very useful for you if you want to leave an underperforming fund. It means you have somewhere to move the money.

Occasionally, for one reason or another, a broker won't offer a particular investment. Some big bank brokerages, for example, currently ban so-called HISA exchange-traded funds because they compete with their own high-interest savings accounts. If selection is important to you, keep that in mind in choosing a broker.

WARNING

Many firms proclaim that they carry hundreds of funds, and in fact they probably do. But you find that some low-cost funds from independent providers come with high minimum purchases of $5,000 and up. Always ask if the fund you're interested in is available and find out about any conditions.

A wealth of investing information

Finally, discount brokers can be useful channels for getting hold of investing information. Check out their websites and you find fee calculators and other useful online tools. Some may have offers of investment newsletters and books at cut-rate prices. A few discounters sell research reports from stock analysts at full-service brokerages — usually the brokerage owned by the discounter's parent.

WARNING

Research shows that most investment advice that analysts publish fails to beat the market over time. And brokerage analysts are notorious for seeing the world through rose-coloured glasses; they rarely say a stock is a Sell because that's certain to enrage the company's management. Angry corporate managers are likely to cut the critical analyst off from information and may even blacklist their firm in the future when it comes to picking brokers to handle a stock issue or other deal.

At last — a break on costs

One of the big pluses with discounters is the fact that most let you buy funds on a *front-load* basis at no initial cost to you. Front-load means that the fund buyer pays an upfront commission directly to the broker or financial planner at the time of purchase — the exact rate is negotiable, but it's usually three percent or less these days, and sometimes as little as one percent. The advantage to the buyer in paying a front-load fee is that they can sell the fund at any time without incurring any more charges.

The discounters aren't being particularly generous with their zero-load offer on front-load funds, mind you. Fund companies love it when their wares are sold front-load because they don't have to pay any commission to the broker.

Some funds used to charge trailer fees on DIY accounts, which is a fee paid by a fund to an advisor for as long as you hold that fund. For years, discount broker-ages sold funds online with those same trailer fees, earning them revenue even though they didn't have anything to do with selling the fund. In 2022, discount brokerages had to stop selling those funds and offer trailer-free (and therefore less expensive) versions instead.

A word on commissions

Table 6-1 lists the major discounters, their websites, and their toll-free telephone numbers. Going online is the best way to check out commissions, which change as discounters jostle for market share. By the time you read this, they'll no doubt have come up with new special offers and dancing kittens in little kilts.

REMEMBER

When looking at these prices, keep a few details in mind:

>> Bank-owned discounters usually levy no fees at all if you're buying or selling funds managed by their parent banks (and most outside funds as well). So, for example, if you're dealing with Royal Bank of Canada's discounter, RBC Direct Investing, you can sell Royal Bank's no-load funds for free.

>> Discounters generally require a $500 to $1,000 minimum investment if you're buying mutual funds. It's a low-margin business, after all, and tiny orders are just more trouble than they're worth for the firm.

>> Higher commission rates often apply if you place your order by talking to a person over the phone. For Internet and automated-telephone orders, the commissions are considerably lower. Note that some brokers have fees for buying and selling certain funds, and fees for short-term trading may also apply.

TABLE 6-1 **How to Contact the Discounters**

Discount Broker	Contact Information
BMO InvestorLine	`www.bmo.com/main/personal/investments/online-investing/investorline/self-directed`
CIBC Investor's Edge	`www.investorsedge.cibc.com`
CI Direct	`www.cifinancial.com/ci-di`
Desjardins Online Brokerage	`www.desjardins.com/ca/personal/savings-investment/disnat-online-brokerage`
National Bank Discount Brokerage	`nbdb.ca`
Qtrade	`www.qtrade.ca`
Questrade	`www.questrade.com`
RBC Direct Investing	`www.rbcdirectinvesting.com`
Scotia iTRADE	`www.scotiabank.com/ca/en/personal/investing/direct-investing`
TD Direct Investing	`www.td.com/ca/en/investing/direct-investing`
Wealthsimple Trade	`www.wealthsimple.com/en-ca/invest/stocks-and-etfs`

>> Since this book was first written, banks have gotten into selling exchange-traded funds (ETFs), which are like mutual funds, only they trade on exchanges like stocks. Many offer free trading of in-house created ETFs, while some sell other ETFs at no commission. For more on ETFs, check out Chapter 15.

In Chapter 2, we discuss the other type of mutual fund sales commission — the *redemption charge*, or *back-end load*. Funds sold on that basis charge you nothing upfront but levy a commission if you sell the fund within six or seven years. Most discounters simply treat back-end loads like regular brokers do.

When a client buys an equity fund on a redemption-charge basis, the broker collects a five percent commission directly from the fund company (not from the client). The firm then extracts any applicable redemption charges from the proceeds if the customer sells the fund early. Some discount brokers have tried "rebating" a portion of that five percent commission back to clients who buy deferred-load funds. It's a nice little bonus, but it also makes the whole exercise more complicated. You do fine without it if you just buy front-load funds.

BACK-END-LOAD REBATES AND BONUSES: AS IF LIFE WASN'T COMPLICATED ENOUGH

We're sorry to keep burdening you with all this commission stuff. And by now you're probably wondering: Why is everyone in the fund industry obsessed with sales charges? Why do they create so many different classes of the same fund, each sold with a different commission, and drape them with confusing conditions, rules, and names? Well, the bottom line is that selling expenses — particularly the cost of paying commissions to brokers and financial planners — are an enormous cost of business for mutual fund companies. Look at this example: Equity-fund salespeople, as a general rule, get one percent of the client's assets each year, either upfront or payable as an annual "trailer" commission. Well, the median Canadian equity fund charges an annual MER of two percent or so, which means about half of the management fee revenue is going to the broker or financial planner who sold the fund.

Getting a bonus straight off the top like that sounds like a great deal, but it hasn't proved popular with discount brokerage customers. That's because with a deferred-load fund, you're "locked in" by the commission you must pay to the fund company if you cash out within about six years. Discount brokerage customers are independent souls who don't like having their hands tied in any way. So they have steered clear of rear-end-load funds carrying rebates, even if the funds looked like a real bargain at first glance.

The bottom line? Sure, take advantage of a rebate if you're certain you want to stay in the fund for several years (until the deferred load no longer applies), but don't lose dollars just to save cents. If you think a possibility exists that you'll want to sell the fund again while the back-end load is still in effect, then go with the front-load version to keep life simple and your investment strategy unencumbered.

How to Pick a Discounter

Don't get in a lather comparing the discounters' commissions and totting up their special offers. Seeing people in the investment business offering to cut their prices is wonderful, but over the long term, saving $100 on a one-off basis doesn't amount to much. If you plan to simply buy and hold high-quality funds and stocks, it doesn't make a lot of difference if you've spent $100 or $200 in commissions building the portfolio. Yes, cheaper is always better, but fast and polite responses to your orders or questions, and investments that suit your needs, are just as important as low rates.

FORGET THE PERSONAL TOUCH

Select a discount broker carefully. Until a few years ago, service at too many of the firms tended to be spotty, with orders and requests sometimes going through incorrectly or after long delays. But those days happily appear to be behind us — and, of course, traditional "full-service" brokers and financial planners can get orders wrong, too.

Nonetheless, if you're worried about getting trades executed on very busy market days, you may be more comfortable with one of the large bank-owned brokers, which are likely to have more people available to handle your calls, and which may have more robust websites for standing up to heavy traffic. They also provide extra liquidity by buying and selling with you from their own accounts.

Generally, when dealing with a discounter, remember that the people answering your queries by email or chat don't know you (unless you're a high roller who's given special attention), so you can forget about getting much personalized help. Yes, some discounters are offering more research and information, but they'll always be the port-of-call for resolute independent souls who want to make all their investing decisions for themselves.

Getting a feel for the service

The important aspect is efficient, accurate, and prompt service — something that, sadly, discounters seem to have had a problem providing in the past. Service levels are better now — although lots of the credit goes to the fact that almost all discount trading happens online nowadays, with no human intervention required.

TIP

If you got the time and energy, you could pick a firm by first opening two or even three separate accounts at different discounters — signing up as a client generally doesn't cost a cent. After a year or so, you'll get a good feel for which discounter is most reliable and the easiest to use, and you can transfer all your assets there. Be sure to ask your family, friends, and work mates about their experience with discounters. If you keep coming across horror stories about a particular firm, then shop elsewhere.

Don't worry too much about picking the right discounter. If you make the wrong choice, you can switch later at the cost of a few weeks' wait and a fee of about $100. It's messy — and watch out for mistakes while they transfer your investments — but you have a right to move.

Finding the right discounter for you

A good source of information on discount brokers (and low-cost investing in general) is the Stingy Investor Web site, at www.stingyinvestor.com. Run by avid number-cruncher Norman Rothery of Toronto, it offers a rundown of discounters' rates. Before deciding to use a particular firm, however, be sure to double-check fees with the brokerages you are considering.

Don't become obsessed with commission rates when choosing a discounter. Some have decided to market themselves as cut-price providers, offering zero commissions in some cases. That's a tremendous deal for investors but remember that if you don't plan to trade stocks frequently, it's only of limited value. Look at the whole picture — including mutual fund commissions, service standards, and special options — before you make your choice.

Try contacting the company a couple of times with questions. If you can't seem to get prompt, decent answers, then consider taking your business somewhere else.

Dealing with your bank's broker makes cash transfers quick and easy, but some experts advise using a discount broker not owned by your usual bank. That way, if a dispute over a trade ever occurs, the broker can't just dip into your bank account and extract money.

Considering a mutual fund discount broker

Apart from the true discount brokers, which are licensed to deal in stocks and bonds as well as funds, investors also can choose from among dozens of "no-load" or "discount" mutual fund dealers that sell only mutual funds. These companies, which are often happy to buy and sell funds over the telephone or internet, usually charge no commission on front-load funds, living off the rich trailer payment instead. Individual stockbrokers and financial planners also frequently offer to sell funds with no load.

Discount fund dealers clearly save you money, and if you're happy with the level of service available and the selection of funds, then go with one. But, once again, don't let cost be the only deciding factor. Saving yourself a one-off expense of two percent is pointless if the dealer subsequently doesn't give you enough advice and choice of products.

REMEMBER

From our perspective, if we were looking to save money, we'd stick to a regular discount broker who's able to sell us shares and bonds as well as funds while also offering low commissions. Call us scaredy-cats, but we'd rather deal with a discounter that's a large multi-billion-dollar organization. That way, we know the systems are in place to administer our accounts properly.

What's Wrong with Discount Brokers?

The major problem with discounters, especially for investors who are just getting going, is that they do not provide advice on your personal financial situation or help you create a financial plan. A discount brokerage is essentially a tool for doing transactions — but buying and selling investments is only part of getting rich. A good planner or full-service stockbroker also provides tips on tax and wealth management — using life insurance, for example — that you won't get from a discounter.

Getting seduced and abandoned

Discounters leave you on your own to make all the decisions, but freedom can bring problems. Some research seems to show that retail investors who work without an advisor don't do well because they're prone to buying high and selling low. That is, they euphorically buy shares and equity funds when the market has soared and then dump them when prices have already crashed. That may be true or just a self-serving myth fostered by the brokerage industry. But a good fund salesperson can impose valuable discipline in two ways: by getting you to save money in the first place and by persuading you to hang on when matters look bleak.

So if you're a nervous or impulsive type, holding your stocks and funds at a discount broker may be a recipe for panic selling and hysterical buying. Perhaps you'd be better off with a planner or old-style broker.

Knowing when to stay away

Although the lure of cheap trades and special offers may be pretty hard to resist, discounters aren't for every Canadian, not even close. Some investors should probably stay away from discounters. For example:

>> Nervous investors who are just starting out may be happier opening a mutual fund account at a bank first. They can get at least some personalized help while they learn the basics of investing before venturing into the discount world.

>> Those who plan to trade frequently in and out of the stock market may be better off going with a competent traditional stockbroker who gives them a break on commissions. Full-service brokers are more expensive, but they can often provide better "execution" of your orders — that is, they can buy and sell stocks at more attractive prices.

Relying on robots to manage your money

If do-it-yourself investing using a discount brokerage sounds intimidating to you, there is another low-cost option that takes the task of picking investments off your hands: the robo advisor. These are services mostly offered by financial technology companies (though BMO and RBC have their own) that essentially run a discount brokerage account for you, populating it with a mix of exchange-traded funds (ETFs) that match your investor profile and goals.

They're called robo-advisors because the process is largely automated. As a result, they can make the service surprisingly cheap. Typically the combined portfolio management fee charged by the advisor and the management expense ratios (MER) on the low-fee index funds they use add up to less than one percent of the value of your funds invested per year. That's a whole lot less than small investors typically pay when they invest with a mutual fund dealer or fund company, not to mention a full-service broker.

A lot of the same institutions that offer discount trading offer robo services, too, including Qtrade, Questrade, Wealthsimple, and CI Direct. However, there are also a handful of dedicated portfolio managers such as Nest Wealth, Modern Advisor, and Justwealth. They all provide a lot of information on their websites that can help you find the right service for you. These providers started appearing in Canada in 2014, and by now have a track record to look back on.

Most publish the returns of their various portfolios going back at least five years; if they don't, request it before investing. When choosing a robo-advisor, compare the returns of similar portfolios with the providers you're considering using. As always, past performance is no guarantee of future performance, but you don't want to get stuck with a laggard. Look at the portfolio breakdowns to ensure you're comfortable with their approach. Then compare the fees they charge. Robo advisors usually have flat minimums, then a fee schedule based on the size of your account. Also consider things like convenience (if your own bank has a robo advisor, transferring funds will be simple) and ease of use.

Chapter **7**

Banks: The Fast Food of Funds

At one time, the banks didn't seem to be able to run a decent equity fund. Those days are long gone. The banks' equity funds have been strong performers in recent years. Plus, they have reduced the costs charged to mutual fund investors, thanks in some part to their lineups of *index funds*, which simply track the entire market (we take a closer look at index funds in Chapter 15). Expenses also have been kept down thanks to internet sales, which are cheap to process.

In most cases, a bank-fund purchase is no further than a mouse-click away from your online bank account statement page. So, perks to keeping your investments where you keep your cash do exist. No meddlesome salespeople are involved.

In this chapter, we explain why banks are a great place to buy mutual funds, especially if you just want a simple option that's also an okay value. This chapter shows why you can just go ahead and use your local bank branch for mutual funds if you want a quick solution. You may not get the best bargain going or make the most money, but it does the job.

Buy Where You Bank

Banks are the very simplest place to buy mutual funds: Just walk in (virtually or to a branch) and put your money into a selection of the house brands. But don't assume they're the best choice. A bank is a great place to start out buying funds, but it's worth taking a long, hard look at what they can and can't offer.

Hey, you're busy, so why not just make things easy on yourself and simply grab your mutual funds at the bank? Mutual fund buyers, especially rookies, can do well at the bank for a number of reasons.

Providing one-stop shopping

Even if you don't have an account with a bank, you can still walk into a branch, hand over a cheque, and sign up for a mutual fund account. Okay, it may take a couple of days to arrange an appointment with a *registered representative*, a bank employee who is licensed to sell funds, but after that, the process should be painless. Most banks have web and telephone services for buying and selling funds after you've opened a fund account, and nearly all let you check your account balance and recent transactions. In fact, most banks let you open a mutual fund investing account online, as part of your banking account access.

REMEMBER

Banks sell their own funds on a no-load basis — no commissions or sales loads. That means all your money goes to work for you right away, and you can cash out at any time with no penalty (although companies impose a short-term trading penalty, typically two percent, on those who sell a fund within 30 to 90 days, depending on the specific fund).

You can set up a fairly decent mutual fund *Registered Retirement Savings Plan* — a tax-sheltered account of retirement money — at a bank in half an hour flat by simply buying one of their pre-selected fund packages. Staff are trained to sell these mixtures, and questionnaires are designed to slot you into the right one so you're likely to get a reasonable fit. See Chapter 20 on fund packages for more about this type of product.

Keeping it together

Most likely you have your mortgage, line of credit, and chequing account at a bank. So buying mutual funds from the company that already holds the mortgage on your house means you can take care of everything in one place, be it a branch, at the bank's website, or on the phone.

Offering to move your mutual fund business to a bank can radically improve your bargaining power when seeking a loan or mortgage. Bank employees get little chocolate soccer balls as rewards when their customers bring their investment portfolios to the branch. Use this to your advantage when looking to extend your credit, take a plunge into the real estate market, or buy a car. In today's competitive banking environment, an investor with a portfolio is a sought-after prize.

Offering appealing options

The employees you deal with at a bank branch or on the telephone are paid wages, so they're not commission-driven jackals. But they usually sell only the house brand. And yes, they receive incentives to attract business, and yes, the banks tend to be vague on exactly what bonuses are paid.

For the most part, you find that banks are happy to sell you *index funds* — low-expense funds that simply track the stock- or bond-market index or benchmark. Index funds are such a good deal they should be part of every investor's arsenal, although we suggest you also have between one-third and one-half of your stock market investments in traditional *actively managed* funds, featuring a person who buys and sells investments in search of trading profits.

Banks, unlike mutual fund companies that market their products through commission-paid salespeople, are able to make money from running index funds because they don't have to pay out those big commissions. Most offer index funds with low expenses — around one percent or less — compared with 2.3 to 2.4 percent on, for example, the median Canadian equity mutual fund. If you were to simply walk into a branch and open up a mutual fund account full of index funds like that, chances are you'd do better than millions of mutual fund investors. For that matter, almost all of the banks' actively managed (non-index-based) mutual funds have expenses that are less than the category medians.

Fighting for the right to serve you

The banks are hungry for your mutual fund business, and they're willing to cut prices and improve service to get it. The fantastic growth of the Canadian mutual fund industry, with assets under management soaring to more than $1.8 trillion by October 2023 from less than $30 billion in 1990, has represented a migration of cash from bank savings accounts and guaranteed investment certificates into funds. The banks have been working very hard to hold on to as much of that money as they can.

Another reason why the banks are fund-mad: Mutual funds are a wonderfully profitable and low-risk business. The management company just keeps raking in those fees no matter how well or badly the fund does. That must be a great comfort to Canadians invested in U.S. equity funds; the average Canadian stock fund lost 5.5 percent during 2022 on an asset-weighted basis.

TECHNICAL STUFF

Lending money, banks' traditional way of making a profit, is more risky than selling mutual funds because borrowers can default and interest rates can jump, leaving the banks stuck with a pile of underpriced loans. So the banks have reinvented themselves as "wealth management" companies, and mutual funds are key players in that ballgame.

Buyer Beware: Shortfalls in Bank Offerings

Nobody's perfect, and buying funds at a bank — online, on the phone, or in person — has its drawbacks. Here, for your viewing pleasure, are the drawbacks of lining the pockets of bean-counters from Quebec and New Brunswick, the sort who become bank chairmen.

Few options

The big problem is lack of choice: The banks have been in no hurry to market other companies' funds because a banker likes sharing fees like a lobster enjoys taking a hot bath. That means customers are often stuck with the bank's line of products, which isn't always the strongest. More and more bank employees have personal finance training, but most aren't specialists in the field. To get a full analysis of your situation, you may still have to go to a planner working for an independent firm.

The narrow selection of funds is the biggest problem with buying from a bank. Most of the big banks offer a full range of funds under their own brand name, but that doesn't necessarily mean that their Canadian equity or global equity funds are any good.

WARNING

Even if you try to build a diversified fund portfolio by buying the bank's index funds and actively managed funds as well, you run a risk that you're leaving too much money with just one investment team.

For example, say a particular group tends to get excited about flashy technology stocks — then you're likely to lose money when other investors get tired of such high-priced, science fiction tales. You can get around this lack of *diversification* — the annoying word for spreading out your investments — by opening an account elsewhere as well, perhaps with another bank. Or you can at least increase your diversification by buying several of the bank's actively managed funds.

Overworked and underpaid: Not just you, some bankers, too

With the rapid growth in online banking and investing, it's getting harder and harder to talk to an actual human being unless you've got a whopping balance in your account. That's a drag, and it's a disadvantage of going to a bank if you'd rather deal with a person than peck at the keyboard of a machine (what's wrong with you, anyway?). Banks may be losing their traditional advantage of owning huge networks of physical branches, because all their competitors are as easily accessed online as they are. Well, almost, because you likely visit your banking website every week anyway.

Lack of pressure to perform

Customers who buy funds from a bank are isolated in the sense that the fund managers don't have brokers and other salespeople breathing in a damp, hot way down their necks, insisting on good returns. If a broker-sold fund's performance goes into the tank, salespeople get angry and embarrassed because they have to face the clients they put into the loser. That's never a fun session. The sales force demands explanations from the manager. So the presence of salespeople probably serves to impose some discipline on fund companies. With bank funds where no brokers are involved, terrible performance used to drag on for years with little publicity or outcry.

Banks now take funds more seriously, meaning that problems get fixed fairly quickly, but bank fund unitholders arguably still don't have anyone looking out for their interests. Yes, nearly all mutual funds have "trustees" who theoretically are on the side of investors, but we've yet to hear of a fund trustee saying a single critical word about a fund's management or expenses. Most unitholders wouldn't know where to look for the trustees' names and no wonder — you have to dig deep into a financial report to find them. However, this search is less onerous now that fund companies are obligated to produce a management report of fund performance twice a year (see Chapter 3 for more on MRFPs). You no longer have to plow through a fund's obscure "annual information form" to identify the trustees.

Another problem with buying funds from your bank is that, well, you're forced to deal with a bank. The Internet has made this a lot easier, but if you need to reach them by phone, your calls may get routed to on-hold hell or voicemail purgatory before they end up in the bottomless pit of general delivery, with Tats in shipping. Increasingly, bank customers are being asked to telephone a central information line (1-800-PLS-HOLD) or use a chatbot (which saves the bank a packet). This is intended to relieve some of the pressure on branch staff, who usually have to deal with all the other services and products the bank delivers and then face the whining, puking, and foot-stamping at home (not to mention the kids). So you may not get the sort of personal attention and time that a good financial planner or even stockbroker delivers.

How Banks Pulled Up Their Socks

Performance of bank-run equity funds has greatly improved during the past decade, although the banks still haven't built much of a record in global equity funds. (Their fixed-income funds have long been okay.) In the past, bank stock funds lagged the competition by a wide margin. They seemed to have difficulty attracting and keeping gifted fund managers (if such a thing as stock-picking talent exists, as opposed to sheer luck). Explanations varied, but one problem seemed to be that hot fund managers demand lavish paycheques and bonuses — but if the banks were to pay such huge amounts to a few individuals, managers elsewhere in their vast dreary bureaucracies would get jealous in a grey, whining way. To some extent, though, the banks seem to have fixed their performance problems, in some cases by spinning off their portfolio management operations into separate companies.

But that has changed. Some bank fund managers have achieved prominence and turned up on portfolio manager roundtables at conferences and in print. More importantly, the funds' numbers are quite strong. Table 7-1 shows the three biggest bank funds in the Canadian equity funds as of mid-2023. As you can see, over five years these giants (with a combined $37 billion in assets) all stacked up reasonably well against the median fund return and the S&P/TSX composite index.

Mutual funds, and increasingly exchange-traded funds (ETFs), have now become such an important business for the banks that it's very unlikely an equity fund would be allowed to drift along with poor numbers for very long before the manager was reassigned . . . to checking mortgage applications . . . in Tuktoyaktuk.

TABLE 7-1

No Longer Laggards: Bank Funds Are Performing Better

Fund Name	Five-Year Return	Ten-Year Return
RBC Canadian Dividend	6.4%	7.5%
TD Dividend Growth	5.9%	7.4%
BMO Dividend	5.5%	7.7%
Median Canadian equity fund	6.1%	6.9%
S&P/TSX	7.8%	8.1%

Improving your choice of funds

Banks branches now have staff who are registered to sell other companies' funds (known in the jargon as *third-party* funds). However, don't expect to be able to buy any fund you want at a bank branch; it seems in-branch reps are most keen on training their staff to talk about funds from companies such as AGF Management Ltd., CI Funds Inc., Fidelity Investments Canada Ltd., Mackenzie Financial Corp., and Franklin Templeton Investments. Those are all honourable companies, but they also happen to be commission-paying fund sponsors that sell their products through brokers and planners — which means that the banks are in line for a gush of commission income in return for selling their wares.

Stretching the rules with bank offerings

You can create a widely diversified portfolio from the funds of just one bank by using a bit of ingenuity. In Chapter 4, we recommend portfolios whose equity portion is made up of a Canadian index fund and an international and U.S. index fund, plus a couple of actively managed Canadian and two global actively managed funds. (Global equity funds buy shares everywhere, but international funds exclude stocks based in the U.S. and Canada.) Achieving that kind of broad mix used to take a good bit of work, but the banks, along with most large fund companies, now offer a wide selection of packaged portfolios. (We explain these "fund packages" in Chapter 20.)

Table 7-2 shows one such package, the Scotia Selected Balanced Income Portfolio (a balanced portfolio consisting of Bank of Nova Scotia and third-party funds) in mid-2023. This is a traditional, cautious mix, with 35 percent of the assets in stocks and 65 percent in fixed income. Two-thirds of the equity exposure is to U.S. and other foreign stocks. (This holdings information was as of July 2023.)

TABLE 7-2   A Conservative Portfolio Using Mostly Scotiabank Funds

Fund Name	Percentage of Portfolio
Dynamic Total Return Bond	19.9%
Scotia Canadian Income	15.9%
Dynamic Canadian Bond	15.9%
Scotia Global Dividend	13.9%
Scotia Wealth Cdn Corporate Bond Pool	9.7%
Scotia Global Equity	8.0%
Scotia Canadian Dividend	5.5%
Dynamic High Yield Bond	3.3%
Scotia Canadian Growth	3.3%
Dynamic Dividend Advantage	2.0%
Scotia Global Small Cap	1.3%
Dynamic Small Business	1.2%

A Few Gems from the Banks

In this section, we discuss three bank funds favoured by Morningstar's fund-analysis team that have produced solid returns in recent years. Will their good performance continue? Impossible to tell. However, Morningstar's analysts like funds with strong management, good long-term performance, and relatively low expenses. (Modest costs always load the dice on the side of the investor.) Check out these three funds:

Renaissance International Equity Currency Neutral

Long term is the name of the game for this CIBC fund, which invests in mostly growth stocks from Europe, the Far East, and the Pacific Rim. The fund is hedged to the Canadian dollar to reduce currency risk. Being a growth-oriented investment, it experienced a significant 16 percent haircut in 2022, but its three-, five- and ten-year total returns all still top eight percent. The same two managers, Roy Leckie and Charles Macquaker of Walter Scott & Partners in Edinburgh, have been running the fund since its outset in 2010. Morningstar gives it a five-star rating with a gold medal.

PH&N Monthly Income

Also earning five stars and a gold medal, PH&N Monthly Income would be a great fund to hold in a Registered Retirement Income Fund. Balanced 64 percent to dividend-paying stocks and 36 percent, fixed income, this all-Canadian fund offered by RBC strives to provide an income stream north of four percent combined with modest capital growth over time. The drawdown during 2022's market correction was a relatively mild five percent. Lead manager Scott Lysakowski has been steering this fund from the start in 2009. It has a very affordable (for active mutual funds) management expense ratio of 0.82.

TD Canadian Small Cap Equity

Since it was launched in 2010, this fund has far outperformed both its peers and its benchmark index, all for a moderate MER around one percent. The outperformance has continued despite significant turnover of its management team. (The fund has been run by Anna Castro, Michael Craig, and Christian Madeiros of Connor, Clark & Lunn Investment Management since the start of 2022.) You should always expect volatility in the small-cap space — best suited to young or well-off investors with a long-time horizon — but the team managed to get through the bear market of 2022 almost unscathed with just a one percent loss. Being focused on Canadian equities, it has a skew to natural resources with a smattering of consumer, industrial, and technology stocks thrown in.

Chapter **8**

Stockbrokers, Financial Planners, and Advisors Aplenty

C ivilization may run out of drinking water, out of brain surgeons, and out of Vancouver Island marmots. But it'll never run out of mutual fund sales-people. More than 100,000 people are licensed to sell financial products in Canada, many of them focused on mutual funds. They come in a bewildering range of guises, from Boss-suited executives in the downtown core of big cities to down-home types wolfing down the free sandwiches at fund company lunches. And they give themselves a galaxy of names: financial consultant, investment counsellor, estate planner, financial advisor, investment executive, personal financial planner. Don't get worked up trying to figure out the differences among them. Financial planning remains a mostly self-regulated industry, although a few national industry groups such as Advocis and FP Canada do exist.

In this chapter, we describe the main types of fund salespeople and tell you about the advantages of using financial planners who charge only an upfront or annual fee, rather than collect commissions on the products they sell you. We also provide some basic tips on the right and wrong ways to pick an advisor.

Alphabet Soup: Figuring Out All Those Titles

You can spend a good month or two crafting a long list of all the elaborate titles financial advisors give themselves. But it wouldn't help people much with their financial planning. So how do you wade through all the options and get down to what's best for you and your money? That's the key — your first challenge should be figuring out exactly what kind of financial planning you want rather than trying to decode their titles. In other words, do you need a fast once-over or a harrowing session of soul-searching?

After you decide you need some help drawing up a financial plan and picking the right mutual funds, ask yourself two questions:

>> **Do I want just a quick solution or a complete financial plan?** If you're reasonably comfortable with your money arrangements as they stand and you just want someone who'll suggest a few funds, then you can keep matters simple by going to a storefront mutual fund dealer, a stockbroker, or a bank. They can recommend a package of funds and set up the account for you. If, however, you want help planning your fiscal future, make sure you deal with someone who has had some formal financial planning training (more on that later) and is also genuinely interested in the subject. And the best choice of all is to go with an unbiased planner who charges you a separate fee for their expertise, instead of selling you mutual funds that pay them a commission.

>> **How much money will I be investing?** Don't expect miracles. If you're planning to put $5,000 a year into your fund portfolio, the chairman of CIBC Wood Gundy won't be asking you out to golf. It can be a good idea to tell the advisor up front how much you think you're likely to save each year. You'll often be able to tell from their reaction whether you're likely to get much in the way of attention or advice.

TIP

Here's a great way to find out if a fund salesperson is likely to be of much use in drawing up a financial plan: Don't just ask about investing. Also bring up subjects such as buying disability and life insurance, estate planning, and minimizing taxes. If the answers are superficial or unsatisfactory, then this person probably isn't the best advisor to help you build a successful plan.

Drawing up a comprehensive financial plan is a complicated process, covering the client's taxes, income, spending, and retirement plans. Choosing investments is only a small part of that, but many advisors are paid just for selling life insurance or mutual funds, so saving and investing become all they want to talk about. In fact, as we outline in Chapter 4, every competent financial planner worth their salt should emphasize getting rid of high-interest debt as your first step toward sound money management. If they don't look at your whole financial picture, look elsewhere for help. So beware of commission-paid salespeople who encourage you to go ahead and buy funds even though you already have big credit card debts. This method is no way to build a sound financial plan or invest for profit.

REMEMBER

Be sure a financial planner is qualified. The Institute of Advanced Financial Planners (IAFP) has some good guidelines at www.iafp.ca. Advocis also has excellent information at www.advocis.ca.

Advisors can be divided into several main groups according to how they earn their living: You find advisors who

» Get paid a commission for selling you investments.

» Charge a one-time fee for producing a financial plan, without specific investment advice.

» Charge you a separate fee for designing an investment portfolio.

» Earn a salary from an organization such as a bank that markets its own line of investments.

Commissioned advisors

The vast majority of Canadians choose to go with a financial advisor who gets paid by a mutual fund company or insurance company for selling investment "products." Unlike many Americans, Canadians seem to prefer having the expense of investing advice hidden from them, buried in the fee of a mutual fund or the cost of insurance. That way, it seems so much less painful than having to cut the advisor a cheque.

An obvious example of a commission-paid salesperson is the traditional stockbroker, who makes money when you buy stocks, bonds, or funds. The broker gets a transaction fee, or commission, each time you put an order through.

» With stocks, the commission is added onto the cost when you buy or is deducted from the proceeds when you sell — and your transaction confirmation should clearly show how much was charged. For example, when you buy or sell $10,000 worth of shares, you can expect to pay a sales commission of up to $300.

» With bonds, the "commission" is normally a profit margin that's hidden in the price, just like buying a pair of jeans at The Gap. That's because brokers usually sell to their clients bonds that they already own themselves. No separate commission is charged or shown on your confirmation slip because the broker has already taken a markup.

>> With funds, details get more complicated. But the essence of the system is that the broker (or financial planner or insurance salesperson) is paid by the fund company. The fund company, remember, charges an annual management fee — which is deducted from the assets of the fund — and pays roughly half of that out to the salesperson.

Commission-paid salespeople also include life insurance salespeople, whether independent or tied to a particular insurance company. In addition to life insurance, these agents are often licensed to sell mutual funds or the insurance industry's version of mutual funds, which are known as *segregated funds*. Segregated funds — so-called because their assets must be kept separate from those of the insurance company — carry guarantees to refund up to 100 percent of an investor's initial outlay. More on those in Chapter 19.

Finally, Canada is home to thousands of *financial planners*, either in franchises, chains of stores, or small independent offices, whose bread and butter is the mutual fund.

Fee-only financial planners

This group is far smaller but represents an excellent choice for those who don't mind signing a cheque to get advice. They're *fee-only* financial planners who aren't interested in selling products. In fact, in some cases they may not even be licensed to sell products. Fee-only planners draw up a financial plan that addresses your entire money situation and sets personal financial goals, both near term and far.

A good financial plan helps you set broad investing goals but does not discuss specific investments, or even market sectors. Rather, it points you in the right investing direction based on your present lifestyle needs, tax situation, insurance needs, and estate planning goals, among other factors. You must go to a licensed investment advisor, commissioned or fee-based, to construct and maintain an investment portfolio. Or do it yourself by using a discount brokerage account.

A properly executed, custom financial plan can cost $2,000 or more, although some acceptable — but less customized — financial plans are available for a few hundred dollars. These plans are created by planners who use off-the-shelf software.

WARNING

A fee-only financial planner may produce a plan and then refer you to a commission-charging dealer — or even collect commissions on funds you buy under the table. First, such practices are illegal. Second, that kind of double-charging adds another layer of complexity and fees, and it may not be the best deal for you. If the advisor is simply putting you into funds that pay commissions to salespeople, then why did you pay a fee for advice?

Fee-based investment advisors

Unlike fee-only financial planners, fee-based investment advisors are licensed investment salespeople who can be affiliated with a traditional stock brokerage, a mutual fund dealer, or a financial planning firm. The drawback of going with a fee-based advisor is the pain of paying the freight, which can be substantial. It may be a fee based on assets under management — a percentage of your investments (typically one or two percent) — or it can be a charge that ranges from $150 an hour to several hundred, depending on the complexity of your affairs.

With a fee-charging planner, you may have to make more choices about the investments you buy and the strategy you adopt. That's because the financial plan produced for each client is different, reflecting individual needs and wants, whereas commission-paid salespeople are often happiest suggesting a predesigned and relatively fixed package of funds that leaves you with few decisions to make.

TIP

Investors with substantial assets — say, approaching $1 million — should strongly consider going with a fee-charging planner. Your accountant or lawyer may offer the service or may be willing to recommend someone. The fee often runs into the thousands of dollars, but that's a bargain compared with the hidden cost of high mutual fund management fees levied by fund companies that sell through commissioned advisors.

Salaried advisors

Thousands of financial advisors are working for banks to handle the "wealth-management" needs of the aging baby boomers and Gen Xers. They're generally on salary — plus bonuses if they can persuade you to put your savings into one of the bank's products, usually mutual funds or some other kind of managed-money program.

As we explain in Chapter 7, these bank employees are often limited in the products they can offer, and their training may not be as thorough as that of brokers or specialized financial planners. That means their advice should always be taken with a pinch of salt: They're employed to push the bank's products or sell funds that pay the bank a fat fee.

Still, especially for investors with relatively simple needs and clear financial goals, the bank can be a great place to start off investing. Compared with the hard-driving world of brokers or financial planners, little sales pressure occurs. The product choices are simple, and having all your money in one place makes for easy record-keeping.

REMEMBER

But don't forget you're doing the bank a favour by handing over your savings. That means you're entitled to a helpful and experienced bank employee, not some rookie. And don't get railroaded into buying one of the fixed arrangements of funds the banks love to pitch (it makes their administration much easier, for one thing). If you feel that none of the pre-selected packages meets your needs, insist on a custom mixture of funds.

In general, the bank is the perfect first stop for starting-out investors who have only a few thousand dollars at their disposal. The banks are equipped to deal with small accounts and they have handy automated systems that enable you to check your account balance and transactions without waiting for someone to get back to you.

And banks' employee training in investment advice is getting better all the time as the wealth-management business becomes vital to their future profit growth. Some banks even have qualified brokers available in the branch who can sell you a range of stocks and bonds or funds from nearly every company.

The blurred distinctions among all these types of commission-paid advisors make the whole business of looking for help confusing. But at least you have one factor going for you: Remember that if you buy mutual funds, your money is reasonably safe because it goes to the fund company instead of staying with the broker or dealer. So if you decide to dump your salesperson and their firm, you can simply shift the account elsewhere, after some whingeing and delays on the part of the old salesperson. Your money is doubly safe because even the fund company itself has to leave the fund's assets with a separate custodian for safekeeping.

REMEMBER

Make sure you'll be receiving a statement at least twice a year from the fund company (ask to see a sample) so you can be certain you're on the fund company's books. And make your payment out to the fund company, not to the salesperson. Get transaction confirmations for your purchases from the company — alternatively, you can call the fund company itself to double-check that they have a record of your investment.

Deciding Whether to Pay a Fee or a Commission

Your first decision when selecting an advisor is this: Do you want to pay a fee to a fee-based advisor, or are you happy with a commission-collecting salesperson? Don't rush your decision and just take the easy way out by refusing to pay a fee up front.

For example, the first time Bryan went to a tax accountant, he agreed to pay a couple of hundred dollars to have the accountant look over his taxes and file his return. He got back a much bigger refund than he would have on his own, and it felt great to have a professional working for him. And because he was paying the accountant a fee, he knew what was motivating him.

Paying fees

The first step in hiring an advisor is to look for fee transparency. A fee-only planner or fee-based advisor charges by the hour or by the project (say, producing a financial plan). A fee-based advisor is licensed and may charge by the hour or by assets under management, and/or earn commission for product sales. A commissioned advisor depends entirely on product sales to cover the cost of doing planning work.

REMEMBER

In any case, insist on an "engagement letter" stating what the advisor will do for you and how you will pay for it. That way, you separate or "unbundle" the advice from the sale of the investment product.

FOLLOW THE MONEY

Here's a breakdown of how you pay the advisor and their firm hundreds of dollars, directly or indirectly, when you buy broker-sold funds.

Say you have a total of $10,000 to invest in a mutual fund. In most situations you have to pay a "front load" or "sales charge." Usually zero to two percent, depending on what you can negotiate, this fee is deducted from your investment and the balance is used to purchase the mutual fund. Under this option, you may sell your mutual fund at any time with no further sales charges.

(continued)

(continued)

In years past, you had the option of buying funds with a "redemption charge," also known as a "deferred sales charge" or "back-end load." The fund company paid the advisor's firm a commission, but no deduction was made from your purchase amount and all your money went into the investment. However, investors had to pay a fee if they sold within a specified period, typically seven years. The size of the redemption fee declined as time went by, and you typically didn't have to pay the fee if you kept your investment within the fund's "family." But regulators came to view the practice as anti-competitive and forced dealers to phase out back-loaded funds. The only funds like this still out there are ones the holders bought several years ago. None are being sold to new clients.

The only alternative to funds with initial sales charges these days are "no load" funds. These are usually sold directly by banks and fund companies to their own clients. They may have higher management expense ratios than competing front-loaded funds, however. One way or another, people want to get paid.

So how much is the advisor paid? If you buy the funds with a front load and pay a one percent upfront commission, the advisor's firm is immediately paid $100. The advisor gets a portion of this, generally 40 to 70 percent. If we assume a 60 percent split, they make $60 on your $10,000 investment. If you bought the fund on a redemption-charge basis (not many of these are still in circulation), the advisor's firm is paid a commission from the fund company — usually five percent of the amount invested, or $500. Again, if the split is 60 percent, your advisor will be paid $300.

The advisor's firm is also paid a "trailer" commission from the fund company, usually one percent per year on equity funds (less on balanced or bond funds) purchased on a front-load basis. The trailer is half that amount if the fund is purchased with a redemption charge. The trailer fee remunerates the advisor for providing ongoing service to you. Assuming a $10,000 investment, the trailer varies from $25 to $100 per year, depending on the fund purchased. The trailer is part of the fund management fee and is based on the market value of your funds. If your fund increases in value, the trailer will be higher; if it decreases, it will be lower. So if you prosper, so does your advisor, and vice versa.

Note that as of June 2022, fund companies are forbidden from paying trailer fees to dealers such as discount brokerages and "order execution only" salespeople who offer no investment advice. The trailer fee is meant to compensate the advisor for advice, so if you're not getting any, your dealer can only offer versions of funds without trailer fees.

With respect to advice, though, be realistic. If you have only a few thousand dollars to invest, the commissions are not going to cover much. If you want planning, you have to pay extra. Competent professionals don't come cheap. Fee-only planners and accountants almost certainly charge a few thousand dollars to produce anything more than a "quickie" plan. Be aware that a fee-only advisor is not licensed to provide specific investment advice, so you still must find someone to help purchase and manage your investments.

Going with a commission-paid advisor

You often indirectly pay hundreds of dollars to invest in mutual funds. Frequently, commissioned advisors are able and willing to provide significant planning in return for your investment business.

Fee-charging advisors who also help with investing are easier to find in Canada than was the case earlier this century, although you have to ask around to find one. Canadians by the millions use commission-paid salespeople. After all, such advisors offer a handy one-stop solution: a financial roadmap of sorts and the glitz and comfort of a mutual fund from a familiar name — all backed up by gorgeous fact sheets and torrents of advertising in social media and on television. Most of them do a reasonable job for clients, putting them into solid (if overpriced) funds and getting them to save money, the first step in wealth accumulation.

Imagine a confusing, tangled jungle where every plant, animal, and weird fungus is grey. Well, that's kind of like the financial planning scene in Canada, where investors are confronted by competing trade associations, duelling regulators, and rival professional qualifications.

Progress has occurred on the self-regulatory front, however. Many financial planners are members of Advocis, a national umbrella group formed in 2002 through the merger of the Canadian Association of Insurance and Financial Advisors (CAIFA) and the Canadian Association of Financial Planners (CAFP). The much smaller Institute of Advanced Financial Planners (IAFP) was formed by a group of financial planners who saw a need to promote the former CAFP's professional designation, the RFP or Registered Financial Planner. Also significant was the creation of the Financial Planners Standards Council (FPSC) in 1995 by Advocis, groups representing the three accounting professions, and the credit unions. The FPSC, now calling itself FP Canada, is the official administrator of the Certified Financial Planner (CFP) designation in Canada. Although not legally required, the CFP is regarded as the minimum qualification for a Canadian financial planner. The IAFP believes its RFP designation is superior, but of course that falls into the category of debate.

Commission-paid salespeople and advisors usually fit into one of these three groups.

Stockbrokers

They often like to be known by more touchy-feely names such as "investment advisor" and are at the top of the food chain. They work for fairly tightly regulated traditional brokerage firms, the biggest of which are owned by the major banks. Examples include RBC Dominion Securities, CIBC Wood Gundy, and BMO Nesbitt Burns. Because brokerage firms generally are geared to dealing with relatively wealthy clients, a broker usually won't give you too much time unless you have $100,000 or so to invest. They may take you on as a client if you have less money than that, but don't expect fawning attention, just a meeting or two per year at most. For those with enough money, brokers can be an excellent choice because they can sell anything — including stocks, bonds, funds, and a range of more exotic investments. Another plus: Their training and in-house support are fairly good.

WARNING

On the negative side, be aware that many brokers are sometimes leaned on to promote stocks and other securities that are underwritten by their firm's investment bankers.

Stock brokerages are self-regulated by the Canadian Investment Regulatory Organization (CIRO) and are members of one or more stock exchanges. Find out more about CIRO, recently created out of the merger of the Investment Industry Regulatory Organization of Canada and the Mutual Fund Dealers Association, online at www.ciro.ca.

Financial planners

They are usually licensed to deal only in mutual funds or guaranteed investment certificates. They may work independently or as part of a large chain, and their quality varies greatly. Some are professional, smart, and dedicated, and some are little more than part-timers who can sell you a fund and that's about it. To deal in funds, they must register with the provincial securities commission, but regulation of the profession has been patchy. The creation of the Mutual Fund Dealers Association of Canada (MFDA) in 2001 has provided a self-regulatory framework for fund dealers. It was set up to catch mutual fund dealers who "fall through the cracks" with no industry-run body to keep an eye on them. The 2023 merger of the MFDA and IIROC to form CIRO brings all mutual fund dealers under the same professional authority. It will admit members, check that they're complying with the rules, and publicly discipline offenders, imposing fines, suspension, or termination of membership.

Insurance agents and brokers

Both can sell you insurance, but a broker usually deals with numerous insurance companies while an agent generally has a relationship with just one. The lines have blurred to an extent between financial institutions, due to ownership of fund companies by insurance companies and other relationships between the two. As a result, some insurance salespeople now are registered to sell mutual funds. Moreover, life insurers, which once had a lock on the retirement planning market, in some cases have launched their own mutual fund families to hang on to customers' money. They've also made their traditional *segregated funds* more innovative and have spruced up their marketing. Seg funds are mutual fund–like products that usually promise to refund your invested capital if you hold them long enough (see Chapter 19). In general, pick an insurance agent or broker to help you with financial planning if they are able to sell mutual funds as well as insurance products. If the salesperson is limited to insurance, you're narrowing your options.

Using a Salesperson to Your Advantage

We've all got hectic lives, so it can be a nice feeling to have someone take us by the hand and deal with our investing dilemmas. The stock and bond markets are confusing, scary places, and millions of people find it reassuring to have an ally looking out for them.

Brokers or planners, especially if they're experienced, will usually know some neat tricks and handy shortcuts when it comes to investing. For example, they may suggest ways of minimizing your tax liability by setting up a simple trust for your children or grandchildren.

A good advisor imposes discipline on their clients by inducing them to save money — and should prevent them from making rash decisions, such as selling after the market turns down sharply. Without an arm's-length person imposing some sort of structure on your finances, it's easy to let debts mount up and your money problems drift.

Exploring Important Qualifications

To fix yourself up with a well-trained and professional planner, make sure they meet one of the following tests:

>> **Membership in Advocis:** This national association and lobby group for financial planners, also known as the Financial Advisors Association of Canada, had 17,000 members as of 2023. To join, a planner must complete some fairly tough planning courses or have a professional designation such as Chartered Professional Accountant. The requirement to take courses probably discourages complete incompetents from becoming members of Advocis. The group has a code of ethics — although no guarantee exists you won't end up with a bad apple — and it imposes follow-up "education" on members each year. Contact Advocis at www.advocis.ca.

- **Membership in the Institute of Advanced Financial Planners:** The IAFP was set up in 2002 by a group of RFPs to promote, as the organization's name suggests, a higher level of financial planning than is promised by the FPSC and its presumably more basic CFP designation. The group claims its requirements for admission (including the RFP exam) and continuing education are more stringent. Contact IAFP at www.iafp.ca.

- **Completion of a recognized industry course:** These include courses that lead to the Certified Financial Planner (CFP) and Registered Financial Planner (RFP) designations. You can confirm that an individual has one of these designations by contacting the FPSC or IAFP, respectively; both organizations' websites have look-up tools.

- **Employment by a chartered bank, stock brokerage, or other fund company that is a member of CIRO:** If the person works for a bank, you can be sure of some supervision, although take nothing for granted. The banks have set up their own personal finance training system, but no guarantee exists that the person you get is particularly knowledgeable. If the broker works for a CIRO-certified brokerage firm you know they have passed the courses required to become an Investment Advisor, the official term that describes a member broker.

  The core CIRO-qualifying course is the Canadian Securities Course, which covers an impressive range of investing and industry-related information. Members of the public are also welcome to take this and other excellent courses offered by CIRO's educational arm, Canadian Securities Institute (CSI). Contact the CSI at www.csi.ca. CIRO is a lobby group and disciplinary body for stockbrokers and mutual fund dealers.

- **In Quebec, membership in the *Institut québécois de planification financière*:** Quebec regulates financial planners based in that province, requiring an exam and offering its own designation, the Financial Planner (F.Pl., or *planificateur financier* in French). A financial planner practising in Quebec also must either have a certificate issued by the *Autorité des marchés* financiers, the Quebec government body that regulates securities markets in that province or hold one of several professional designations. Contact the IQFP at www.iqpf.org.

- **In British Columbia:** A financial planner must be a Certified Financial Planner (CFP) or be licensed by one of a number of professional groups as laid out by the B.C. Securities Commission.

Unfortunately, you can easily come across bad planners, brokers, and advisors who have impressive qualifications or reputable employers. But at least you know that if they've gone to the trouble of getting trained, or they're under some kind of supervision from a large organization, you're less likely to be stuck with a complete turkey.

The right way to pick an advisor

Finding an advisor is like picking a building contractor or nanny: Word of mouth and your own gut instincts are among the best methods to use. So your first move should be to ask friends and relatives what they've done and whether they're happy with their advisors. Then contact several candidates without making a commitment. Apart from qualifications and membership in a professional association (see the preceding section), also check out a few more details, such as their employment history and the kinds of clients they typically work with.

>> **Does the advisor seem curious about you and willing to answer questions frankly?** A good advisor will ask you questions about your income, life history, assets, financial goals, health, marital status, pension, and investment knowledge. If that doesn't happen, you can be dealing with a sales-driven hotshot who's just looking to make commissions quickly. Shop elsewhere. And ask about sales commissions as well as the advisor's experience and training. Vague answers are a bad sign.

>> **Does the advisor work for a firm with an adequate back office for client record-keeping and supervision?** Jargon alert — having an adequate "back office" is just a fancy way of saying they are set up to administer clients' accounts and orders. Ask to see a typical client statement and ensure that the firm has a *compliance officer,* an employee who keeps an eye on the salespeople and the way they treat clients.

>> **Does the advisor sell a broad range of products?** A planner who wants to talk about funds from just one or two companies is probably lazy. Nobody can be familiar with the products from every company, but you want someone with a good idea of what's out there. You also want an advisor who's knowledgeable about life insurance, or who can at least hook you up with an insurance expert.

>> **Are the advisor's office, grooming, and general image professional?** Nobody's looking for Armani or marble halls, but a cluttered office in a sketchy part of town are signs of someone who hasn't been able to attract many clients. Check out Chapter 24 for some tough questions to ask any advisor before hiring them. We talk more about warning signs in Chapter 25, which includes ten sure signs it's time for you and your advisor to part ways.

The wrong way to pick an adviser

Unfortunately, a lot of what passes for investor education is just a giant sales pitch. Don't get caught up in fancy seminars or lured in with a cold calls.

Watch out for:

>> **So-called "seminars" that purport to enlighten you on a particular topic.** They may claim to help you with preparing a will or taking early retirement, but are really just trying to get lots of sales targets into a room. Wandering around a glitzy "exhibition" or "forum" for investors may be fun and even informative, but these events are also a lure for getting "prospects" — potential customers — into a nice, concentrated bunch where they can be picked off easily.

>> **The phone ringing with a broker, advisor, or planner offering to help.** Decline politely and hang up. Such "cold calls" are a time-honoured method of drumming up business for brokers. The salesperson calling may be perfectly legitimate, but responding to a random email or phone call out of the blue is an awful way of picking someone who's supposed to help you manage your money — such an important aspect of your life.

>> **The internet (and now TikTok and X).** The internet is still a favourite tool of those creatures that occasionally crawl out from under the rocks — the salespeople pushing "unlisted" and "over-the-counter" stocks or other "unregistered" investments that promise fantastic returns.

TECHNICAL STUFF

MINDING YOUR ABCS — AND T's

Glance down the mutual fund listings and you notice that quite a few broker-sold fund families market their funds in different *classes* or *series*, often listed as A or B and even C through F. Not to mention I's and T's.

What do these labels mean to you, the potential unitholder? In most cases, the difference is in the management expense ratio (MER) — the fee charged to the fund to cover sales commissions, portfolio management, and other management costs. In most cases, the MER difference is purely due to the type of sales loads. Sometimes it is because investors in that class of units have paid the sales charge themselves or because they bought the fund directly from the company, bypassing the salesperson. The difference in annual expenses is usually between 0.5 percent and one percent per year. We offer a few examples here:

- Invesco has for years sold its funds in two basic versions. Its original funds, such as the Invesco Canadian Fund SC, can be bought only on a front-load or "sales charge" basis (hence the SC). Other versions could once be bought with a back-end load. The back-end load was expensive for the company to finance — because it must dish out the sales commissions to the salespeople itself — so these other classes of funds carry higher expenses.

- Several fund companies, including RBC, have introduced T-class funds, in which the T stands for "tax." These funds pay distributions to unitholders in the form of return of investment capital rather than dividends, interest, or capital gains. The latter remain within your fund investment, while the return on capital is paid out to you tax-free. As part of your original investment capital, it is not taxable income. See Chapter 18 for more on how these funds work.

- Many F-class funds now exist. These have very small MERs, as they are sold only through advisors who charge management fees directly to their clients. In effect, the MER represents only the fund's portfolio management fee.

It's all pretty bewildering but treating investors differently according to how they buy a fund is arguably fair. That's because the front-load buyers have saved the company a lot of money by paying the load themselves, so they deserve a break on the management fee.

If you're buying a fund that comes in more than one class, do everything you can to get the one with the lowest management fee, especially if you plan to invest for a long time. Sometimes even paying a small sales load is a good idea — but remember that with a front-load fund, your advisor often gets a bigger trailer, so don't put up with any whining at the bargaining table. Over the years, a difference of only 0.5 percent in management fees really adds up. For example, say you put $10,000 into a deferred-load fund that produced an average annual compound return of 10 percent over a decade: You'd end up with $25,937. But say the fund was also available in a front-load version with a management fee that was 0.5 percentage points lower. The fund would likely give you an annual return of 10.5 percent instead of 10 percent. If you managed to buy that version of the fund with no sales load, your $10,000 would grow to $27,141 — or $1,200 more! Even if you had to pay an upfront sales load of two percent, reducing your initial investment to only $9,800, you would still end up with $26,598, or $661 more than an investor who chose the rear-load version, which, in part, explains the movement to ban deferred sales charges.

Chapter **9**

Buying Direct: Five Independents that Sell to the Public

You may think that being independent is an admirable trait — footloose and fancy free, with no strings attached, right? Unfortunately, in the mutual fund world, that's not always the case. Canada's mutual fund sellers are often referred to as being either bank-owned or "independents." A second, important form of fund-seller categorization is load or no-load. Banks' products are no-load, for the most part, meaning they don't levy sales charges or *loads* to increase your expenses. The independents, by contrast, almost all sell on a load basis. On the surface, that appears to be a steep price to pay for independence.

Until fairly recently, independent no-load sellers held a reasonable chunk of assets, but bank acquisitions of the two biggest independents in recent years have relegated this fund-sales type to a tiny corner of the fund industry. You no longer have much to choose from among independent no-load funds in Canada.

So why even bother to seek out an independent no-load fund, you may ask, when the banks now have some pretty impressive no-load offerings? (Go to Chapter 7 to see what we mean.) Well, the remaining players in this selling category are respected money managers who run interesting and innovative funds. What's more, dealing directly with an independent is one of the more enjoyable and profitable ways of investing in funds. The company is directly answerable to you when you call or email, and you can pull out your money with no strings attached if the managers don't make the fund go up.

In this chapter, we look at getting rolling with buying direct, go through the pros and cons of this style of investing, and take you through a list of the top no-load players.

TIP

A lot of the advice in this chapter also applies if you're investing in the funds sold by banks or their subsidiaries. In those cases, you also are buying no-load funds directly from the "manufacturer." The missing ingredient — an important one — is independence. The independent no-load sellers mentioned in this chapter are a unique breed of specialized money managers.

Getting Started with Direct Sellers

Whether or not you use an independent fund company that sells directly to investors depends mostly on you. What kind of experience are you looking for? If you want personalized advice from the same person every time, direct sellers probably aren't for you. But if you're comfortable taking more responsibility for your portfolio, these providers offer some of the best-performing, lowest-cost funds out there.

Setting yourself up with an independent no-load company is easy:

1. **Check out the investing philosophy and fund lineups of the independent no-load companies on the Internet.** You can consult both the companies' own websites (which we list in Table 9-1) and third-party information sources such as Globefund.com and Morningstar.ca.

2. **Fill out the company's application forms online to open an account.**

The following list includes the biggest no-load fund companies on the Canadian scene.

>> Beutel Goodman (www.beutelgoodman.com)

>> Pembroke Management (Private.pml.ca)

» Leith Wheeler (www.leithwheeler.com)

» Mawer (www.mawer.com)

» Steadyhand (www.steadyhand.com)

No-load fund managers treat you rather like discount brokers do. They have an accessible telephone-answering staff that handles your orders, but they don't know much about you. All you have to do to invest is open an account online or call their number and transfer some money. You won't face any wheedling, pawing salesperson in the shape of a broker, planner, or insurance agent, which means you needn't worry about any fiddly and costly commissions.

No-load companies are generally fairly big businesses, and they can usually be relied on to send pretty reliable statements of your account. Sounds perfect, doesn't it? It is — except you have to put up with a narrow selection and a higher minimum investment.

Paying to play

Expect to face stiff minimum investments of $5,000 or more with some companies that sell directly to the public. The fees they charge are low, so they can't afford to fool around with tiny accounts. By contrast, most banks and fund companies that sell through advisors let you invest as little as $100.

Direct sellers impose these high minimum purchases because they have pretty small mutual fund operations. Their main business is usually managing money for institutions such as pension funds. These companies are not equipped to deal with thousands of unitholders, so to avoid attracting lots of small and unprofitable accounts, they often impose the required minimum investments.

Take Calgary-based Mawer Investment Management Ltd., for example. It sells its no-load funds directly to the public in several provinces, although they also can be purchased through salespeople such as financial planners. Mawer requires a relatively modest minimum investment of $500 in its funds if acquired through an advisor or if bought directly.

Considering whether a direct seller is right for you

Many Canadians are still in love with their banks and brokers, not independent no-load fund companies. They continue to seek out the reassurance of a salesperson or the comforting embrace of a giant institution. That means no-load direct sellers have yet to really catch on in this country. That said, direct sellers are an excellent choice for investors who like to follow their investments closely or seek out funds with low costs.

If you can belly up to the bar with the minimum required investment and don't mind the lack of a personal touch, take a good look at this chapter to see if you're really a fit with this type of investing. Direct sellers of no-load funds are best suited for:

>> **Investors looking for simplicity:** People who are very keen to get a simple solution, with all their investments on one clear account statement. Direct sellers are easy to deal with because you can simply call up and ask questions or make changes to your account without having to go through a broker or other advisor. The same advantages apply to holding your funds at a bank — but direct sellers are much smaller than banks, so they're easier to talk to.

>> **Savvy market trackers:** People who are interested in investing and want to follow the process closely. Such savvy investors love the low annual expenses and often excellent performance that no-load fund sellers offer. Many choose to leave a portion of their money in an account with a direct seller while investing the rest elsewhere. People who enjoy watching the markets often find that the information given to investors in direct-sold funds is more complete — that's because no-load companies deal directly with the investor and see them as the customer; fund salespeople won't muddy the picture. And the simplicity of a no-load account held at a fund company, instead of through an advisor, makes it easy to move money from fund to fund. Active investors who closely track the markets often do more switching around.

Enjoying the Benefits of Dealing with an Independent No-Load Company

Using a no-load company that sells to the public is halfway between the lonely course of picking your own funds at a discount broker on the one hand and the comfy warm blanket of getting help from a bank employee or a salesperson who earns commissions on the other. When you go to such a salesperson (the option we deal with in Chapter 8) or a bank (see Chapter 7), you get lots of help — but you usually pay for the advice in the form of higher annual costs on your fund. And the selection that a bank or commission-paid salesperson carries is often limited to only a few dozen funds. At a no-load company, the people answering the phone can offer some advice, and the expenses on their funds may be low. But the selection of funds on offer is once again limited to the company's own products, and that may be just a handful of funds. Discount brokers (Chapter 6), whoopee, have lots of funds on their sales lists. They're the amusement park of funds. But you ride that roller coaster alone, because you get hardly any help.

REMEMBER

When you contact any fund company, no matter how it sells its products, ignore all the marketing blather and ask for an application form and prospectus. In many cases, these are available online. Those two documents usually set out the stuff you need to know, such as minimum investment and annual costs.

If you want a hassle-free solution to buying your mutual funds, going with a no-load, direct fund seller offers some important advantages. In this section, we discuss the main ones.

Putting more money in your pocket

The biggest plus of buying from a no-load company is the fact that you cut out the intermediary. No-load companies can charge you lower fees — although they don't always choose to do so. Because they don't have to pay an army of brokers — or cover the expense of running a sprawling network of bank branches — some direct sellers' domestic equity funds have annual expenses of 1.3 percent or less. That's much cheaper than most domestic equity mutual funds, which have total annual costs and fees closer to 2.3 percent. The more expensive fund is taking an extra one percent annually out of your mottled hide — over ten years, that difference adds up to 10 percent of your money.

If you were to invest $10,000 and earn a tax-free average annual return of nine percent for a decade, you'd end up with $23,674. But the same $10,000 invested at a 10-percent rate of return, because the expenses were one percentage point lower, would grow to nearly $26,000 (see Table 9-1). That's why it's better to have a fund with a significantly lower annual expense ratio.

Offering advice for grown-ups

Another advantage of going directly to a fund company is that you're treated like a sentient human being rather than simply as a consumer of the fund product. In other words, the company's website and mailings to investors often are more candid about performance. That's because many of the investors who use no-load companies tend to be independent souls who relish the low costs and are happy with the lower level of advice. They're the sort to demand complete reporting of performance.

TABLE 9-1   **Think One Percent Doesn't Matter? That'll Be $2,263 Please**

Year	Value at 9-Percent Return	Value at 10-Percent Return
Initial investment	$10,000	$10,000
1st	$10,900	$11,000
2nd	$11,881	$12,100
3rd	$12,950	$13,310
4th	$14,116	$14,641
5th	$15,386	$16,105
6th	$16,771	$17,716
7th	$18,280	$19,487
8th	$19,926	$21,436
9th	$21,719	$23,579
10th	$23,674	$25,937

TIP

If you're not satisfied with the performance of your no-load funds, or if you have queries, it's simple to just pick up the phone and call. You may not get the errant fund manager or a senior executive, but the representative who answers the phone can probably give you some answers.

And, best of all, buying no-load doesn't mean you have to give up getting advice altogether. Unlike discount brokerages, for a fee, most direct sellers have staff who can advise you on choosing funds and even help you shape your overall investment strategy.

Keeping matters simple

Dealing with a fund company directly is simpler than buying a fund through a salesperson. You're not forced to relay your order or request via someone else, potentially causing confusion or delay. You can call up the company and buy and sell funds in your account right over the phone, as well as ask for forms or other administrative help. Your relationship as a customer is clearly with the fund seller, not with an intermediary as with a broker. That's great for you because

>> You have just one company to deal with and complain to if a mistake occurs in your account. Or did you say you enjoyed muttering endlessly into voice mail?

>> You get just one annual and quarterly statement of account.

>> If you own several funds, it's handy to be able to check on their performance if they're all included in one company's mailings.

>> You can switch money easily from fund to fund as your needs or assets change.

Allowing frequent trades

Moving your money frequently from fund to fund in an attempt to catch rising stock markets and avoid falling ones is often tempting. Naturally, frequent traders love using no-load companies because they don't charge investors to switch their money in and out. That makes a no-load fund company the perfect choice if you fancy yourself someone with the ability to time movements in stock and bond prices — for example, every time the Canadian stock market goes up 20 percent in a year, you may decide to pull out of stocks. But no-load fund companies don't appreciate it when customers move their money around constantly, because it greatly increases the company's administration costs (all those transfers must be accounted for). So they eventually crack down on you by limiting your trades. And you often get slapped with a charge of two percent of your money if you switch out of a fund within three months of buying it.

Still, if you want to try to outguess the markets and trade some money around every few months (even though it's often a bad idea), then direct and no-load may be the way to go. Here's why:

>> The companies have people on staff to move your money from fund to fund quickly and easily.

>> You won't face any sales charges to complicate the transfer of money or add to your costs.

>> Buying the fund directly from the no-load fund company rather than through a discount broker or commission-paid advisor means your sale orders go directly into the fund company's system instead of through a discount brokerage employee. That speeds up the process and reduces the probability of mistakes in your order.

>> You get an account statement and transaction confirmation slip in the mail directly from the no-load company and not through the discounter. That's simpler and more convenient for investors who are closely tracking their own performance.

WARNING

Switching into and out of no-load funds through a discount broker can in fact cost you commissions because discounters often impose small fees of $25 or more each time you sell a no-load fund. A conventional broker won't welcome your business if you plan to chop and change your portfolio all the time because of all the troublesome paperwork you create. (In fact, if you bring a portfolio containing no-load funds to a full-service broker, expect these funds to be sold fairly quickly because they pay no fees or commissions.)

Heavy and constant trading won't thrill even a no-load fund company. That's because trading raises administrative costs, which have to be paid by other investors. So, with many companies, expect to pay a two percent penalty when you move money out of a fund within three months of buying it. And if you really go over the top, you may be banned from switching your money around or limited to a certain number of trades — say, one a month.

No firm rules constitute what counts as heavy trading, but here are a few guidelines:

>> An investor who moves some of their money from fund to fund twice a year or less would count as a light or infrequent trader.

>> Someone who made between two and 12 trades a year would count as a medium trader.

>> More than a dozen trades a year indicates the investor is a heavy trader who thinks they can outguess the market.

A fund company is unlikely to cut off your buying and selling privileges unless you're trading very frequently — making changes to your portfolio every few days or every week. If you do get cut off and can't resolve the situation, you may have to move your money to a discount broker that allows constant trading. But even if you buy through a discounter, the funds you're buying may well levy that two percent penalty if you sell a holding that was bought fewer than three months ago.

The two percent penalty for trading early seems small, but it reduces your return. Imagine you invest in the Canadian stock market ahead of a jump in the price of gold and other metals. Say you put $10,000 into a no-load company's Canadian *equity fund*, a fund that invests in stocks and shares (which in turn are a tiny slice of ownership of companies). Sudden investor confidence lifts the Canadian market by 10 percent in two weeks and your fund matches the rise in the broad market, boosting your investment to $11,000 — at which point you sell half of your holding in the fund, or $5,500. If the company slaps a two percent fee on investors who leave a fund after less than 90 days, then you'll receive a cheque for just $5,390, which is $5,500 minus two percent. Of course, your other $5,500 is still sitting in the fund.

Knowing when to hold 'em

How many trades are too many? Well, research seems to show that almost any level of chopping and changing reduces overall returns because most investors let emotion distort their judgment, leading them to do trades at the wrong time. People sell when the market has slumped and is about to bounce back. And they buy after it has already shot up and is about to go on the slide.

Be sure not to let emotions drive your decisions. Today's stock market is up-and-down, and excess trading is usually a sign of anxiety. Stick to your plan. (See Chapter 4).

Knowing when to walk away

Moving money out of a fund can be sensible at times, and holding the fund directly at a no-load company makes the process easier. Good times to move money include when

» The fund has gone up so much that it now represents a huge portion of your portfolio. For example, if you've decided to keep just half of your money in shares, but one or more of your equity funds have produced a 100-percent return over the past year, then you probably have too much money riding on equities. Time to sell some of those stock funds.

» You've been foolhardy enough to bet on a *specialty* fund that invests in just one narrow section of the market, such as South Korea or financial-services shares, and were lucky enough to score a big profit. Such one-flavour funds tend to post huge crashes soon after their big wins — as investors go cool on the kind of stocks they hold. So think strongly about selling at least some of your units in a specialty fund as soon as it has a good year. No, don't just think about it: get online and do it immediately.

» Your reason for holding the fund no longer applies. For example, a fund manager you like may have quit, or the fund may have changed its investment style.

TIP

Check your portfolio once or twice a year, and if it's out of line with your ideal mix of investments, then readjust it by moving money from one fund to another.

For example, say you decide you want one-third of your $10,000 mutual fund portfolio in sure-and-steady government bonds — certificates issued by the government that pay interest and can be cashed in again at the issue price after a set number of years. The other two-thirds is in lucrative-but-dangerous stocks, those tiny pieces of ownership in companies. See Chapter 5 for more on bonds and stocks.

So your setup is

$3,300 bond funds	33 percent of portfolio
$6,700 stock funds	67 percent of portfolio
$10,000 total portfolio	100 percent of portfolio

Say the bonds hold their value over the next year, remaining at $3,300, but the stocks rise 30 percent to $8,710, which gives you a mix of:

$3,300 bond funds	27 percent of portfolio
$8,710 stock funds	73 percent of portfolio
$12,010 total portfolio	100 percent of portfolio

This means you have too much riding on the stock market in relation to your original plan — almost three-quarters of the total mix. You can fix it easily by moving $663 out of stock funds and into bond funds, leaving you with a portfolio that looks like this:

$3,963 bond funds	33 percent of portfolio
$8,047 stock funds	67 percent of portfolio
$12,010 total portfolio	100 percent of portfolio

If you hold a super-volatile fund that invests in a narrow sector or region, such as a technology company or Latin America, it's a good strategy to move some money out of the fund if it shoots up in value. That way, you lock some profits before the inevitable crash. Holding such funds forever is of dubious benefit because they're at risk of losing money for long periods, as explained in Chapter 12.

Weighing the Drawbacks of Going Direct

Most no-load mutual fund companies offer too few funds to really give you a diversified portfolio — that means an account with many different types of investment. Here are the main drawbacks to using a direct seller.

Significant levels of cash required

Not everyone can go direct. As attractive as it seems to investors who are serious minimalists in terms of their need for guidance and their interest in paying fees to invest, you need a minimum amount of cash to play — in one case, as much as $1 million. This is obviously not the case with novice investors or those in the process of building their portfolio. Although this type of investing may not be the right choice for you now, it is something to keep an eye on as your investing savvy and your portfolio grow.

Lack of choice

The main problem with direct purchase of funds is the narrow selection. Few direct sellers have more than one or two funds, so if you leave all your money with one company, you're at risk of seeing the market turn against that particular investment style.

A typical no-load fund company sells just a couple of funds of each type. Generally, the company offers the following:

>> One or two stock funds

>> One or two bond funds

>> One or two global equity funds

>> Perhaps a few specialty funds, such as one that buys only U.S. stocks

That's a small selection compared to buying from a broker, insurance salesperson, or financial planner, who can often sell you at least a dozen funds in each category. At a discount broker, you can buy hundreds of each.

TIP

You can avoid this lack-of-choice drawback by buying the direct seller's funds through a discount broker instead if they're available. That lets you use the no-load seller's funds, with their nice low expenses, in combination with index funds or funds from other companies. However, your discount broker may not even carry a low-expense company's funds (because the discounter gets little or nothing in sales commissions).

DOING IT THROUGH A DISCOUNTER

Yes, you can often buy no-load mutual funds through your full-service broker and discount broker, instead of going directly to the fund company. But brokers often hit you with a commission or "transaction fee" to let you buy or sell low-expense, no-load funds.

That's because these funds often don't pay the brokers much of anything in ongoing annual commissions — known as *trailers* in the colourful jargon of the fund world. (Indeed, as of June 2022, the Canadian Securities Administrators banned trailer fees on funds sold through discount brokers on the grounds that the investor isn't receiving advice.) But the low costs and fees charged to unitholders in many no-load funds usually make it worthwhile to buy them despite the small charge imposed by the broker, especially if you plan to hang on to the funds for a few years.

Be warned, though: If you buy the funds through a broker, discount or full-service, the fund company probably won't have any record of your investment, so you lose the advantage of being able to deal directly with the company.

Sizing Up the Five Independents

No-load funds from independent companies are a huge business in the United States, with companies such as Janus Capital, T. Rowe Price, and Vanguard Group attracting tens of billions of dollars. But Canadians have never really fallen in love with the concept.

When Fidelity Investments came to Canada in the 1980s, it eschewed the no-load approach that brought it great success in the U.S. market; in this country, it sells only through advisors.

Two other U.S. no-load giants, Scudder and Charles Schwab, ventured north of the border in the 1990s, but lasted only a few years before crying uncle. Scudder came north in 1995, but dismal sales prompted the company to call it quits in 1999 when it sold its funds to IG Financial (now IG Wealth Management), which soon funneled the funds into the Mackenzie Financial lineup. Apparently undaunted by the failure of its home-market rival, Schwab set up shop here that same year, only to throw in the towel less than four years later when it sold out to Scotiabank.

Vanguard, the U.S., no-load, index-fund powerhouse, has taken heed of our inhospitable climate, reviewing the possibilities in our market from time to time but always deciding against it. (Though it does have a solid exchange-traded funds (ETF) business here.)

The two homegrown no-load independents to have achieved success in terms of amassing significant assets — Phillips, Hager & North, and Altamira — were summarily gobbled up by big banks. The same happened to Saxon Investment Management, McLean Budden, and Sceptre over the past decade — plus, swallowed by rival firms that discontinued their direct fund sales.

Although the remaining independent no-load pickings are slim, they're still well worth a look. This group of five has some interesting funds, many with great performance.

WARNING

The problem with buying from these low-cost, no-load sellers is that they don't offer enough funds to give you a truly diversified portfolio. They may argue the point, but we can't help feeling that just one Canadian equity fund or one global equity fund isn't enough to spread your risk adequately — relying on a single manager, management team, or style of investing means a fund can go into a prolonged and nasty slump.

In this section, we take a look at some of the best-known sales policies and products from direct no-load sellers.

Beutel Goodman

The biggest among our group of five independent no-load sellers, Toronto-based Beutel is a big name in institutional investing. The primary function of its 17 funds, as with most of the five, is to provide portfolio management to its individual clients.

Its flagship Canadian Equity Fund, a consistent top performer, is known to fare better than most during bear markets. Its other big funds, income and balanced, also have been strong long-term performers. And 1.21 percent is about as cheap as it gets for a balanced fund's annual expenses. The other funds are similarly inexpensive, in the 1.3-percent neighbourhood.

The challenge is that getting into Beutel Goodman's private client group, where you purchase your funds directly with the help of an in-house advisor, requires a minimum investment of $1 million. Until your portfolio gets to that level, you have to either buy through a third-party advisor or a discount brokerage, neither of which gives you access to the lowest-fee versions of its funds, though the Class D broker versions come close. And even with these intermediaries, the minimum initial fund purchase is $5,000. So Beutel's not the easiest place for the small investor to get their start.

Pembroke

Pembroke Management acquired fellow Montreal-based GBC in 2020 and with it GBC's suite of mutual funds. Like GBC, the private-client money manager sells its funds to anyone who can handle the $100,000 account minimum. Its 10 funds serve primarily as portfolio building blocks for its high-net-worth private clients, most of whom pay the firm to manage their portfolios. Pembroke/GBC is a specialist in small- to medium-capitalized companies — so if you want big blue-chips, go elsewhere.

The firm has a good reputation for being conservative in the risk-plagued, small/mid-cap market. As a no-load independent, its funds' annual expenses are lower than those of the load firms and the banks, although they tend to be on the higher side when compared with other independent direct sellers.

Leith Wheeler

The vast majority of Leith Wheeler's more than $23 billion in assets are managed privately for pension plans, foundations, and high-net-worth people. In terms of mutual fund assets, this Vancouver-based company is on the small side. Its ten mutual funds have achieved strong returns without taking on undue risk.

Recent markets have not been hospitable to value-style managers such as Leith Wheeler. However, the firm has hung in with its funds, achieving performance close to their category medians. Its largest fund, the $4 billion Canadian Equity, held up relatively well through the bear market of 2022 with a 2.7-percent loss, and still has a decent 7.9-percent return over 10 years. Its MER is among the lowest in its category, at 1.49 percent.

The minimum investment is $5,000. You have to submit a message through the company website to begin the account set-up process.

Mawer

This Calgary-based company's 14 funds are all strong performers. But the big star is its Global Equity Fund, which always shows up at the top of performance lists — and all for annual expenses of 1.3 percent. (The median international equity fund's MER is 2.6 percent.) Mawer's main domestic equity fund has likewise been a good buy for investors, with an index-beating 10-year return of nine percent as of mid-2023.

You can message or call Mawer, which has $89 billion in assets under management, to begin the account set-up process. The minimum investment is $500. Alternatively, you can buy its funds through an advisor or discount brokerage.

Steadyhand

Steadyhand Investment Management Ltd. is a rare "new" entrant in the world of no-load fund sellers, launched in 2006. But it has a long pedigree. Chair and co-founder Tom Bradley was president and CEO of Phillips, Hager & North, a Canadian pioneer of low-fee mutual funds later acquired by RBC.

Steadyhand targets what it calls a "mass affluent" demographic with assets of less than $1 million (to start with, anyway) that its founders felt were being neglected by Canada's increasingly consolidated and exclusive mutual fund industry. It requires a minimum investment of just $10,000. The longer you stay with the company, the lower your fees get — after 10 years, for example, clients get a 14 percent discount. The fees also decrease the larger your portfolio gets. A longtime client with a big portfolio can get their management expense ratio down below one percent as a result. And the firm throws in advice on portfolio construction on top of the deal.

IG WEALTH MANAGEMENT: A SPECIAL CASE

IG Wealth Management of Winnipeg (it used to be called Investors Group) is one of Canada's largest fund companies after RBC. It had a huge $261.7 billion in assets as of August 2023. Most of those assets are held within its Mackenzie Financial Corp. subsidiary, which is run as a separate operation. (Both are owned by IGM Financial, which is part of Power Financial.)

IG got to be that size by giving more than a million investors exactly what they want: An all-in-one solution to their financial planning needs.

The company sells directly to the public, but it does so through dedicated salespeople who work exclusively for IG. That means it is rather like a regular "broker-sold" company, such as Mackenzie or Fidelity Investments Canada Ltd., that markets its funds via advisors. If you buy into an IG fund, you face sales commissions, although they're buried in the management fee charged by the fund.

(continued)

(continued)

The company levies annual costs that are in line with or slightly higher than fund industry averages. For example, the $5-billion Mackenzie Global Dividend Fund has annual costs of 2.52 percent. (Other advisors and investors can buy Mackenzie funds separately as well, outside of the IG advisor structure.)

Investors Group funds are generally decent performers. Mackenzie Global Dividend had a 10 percent, 10-year, compound annual return as of mid-2023.

The company's enormous financial clout and partnership with sister company Canada Life (formerly Great-West Life Assurance, which itself has more than 100 segregated funds) enable it to offer a wide range of non-fund products and services. But dealing with IG is essentially the same as buying funds from other broker-sold fund companies that market through commissioned salespeople — in other words, the expenses on its fund are higher than those imposed by the cheaper independent no-load companies.

3

The Fund Stuff: Building a Strong Portfolio

Get insights on the many different categories of funds available.

Discover the portfolio-friendly types of funds to concentrate on.

Understand the risky, expensive, and confusing funds to avoid.

Separate out the useful features from the gimmicks and hype.

Dig into exchange-traded funds and index funds.

Figure out the ins and outs of dividend and income investing.

Make sense of Money Market funds.

IN THIS CHAPTER

» **Understanding how stocks work**

» **Figuring out how much you should put into equity funds**

» **Deciphering a fund's past performance**

» **Walking through the ABCs of picking a winning equity fund**

» **Steering clear of funds that disappoint**

Chapter **10**

Equity Funds: The Road to Riches

Equity mutual funds, which buy stocks and shares of companies, are perhaps the best route to riches you will ever find. Okay, marrying a 95-year-old, millionaire in poor health might be quicker, but then you have to fend off all those rival heirs. Equity funds are a wonderful invention because they hold shares in a huge variety of (usually) great companies. So wide is the selection of holdings in most equity funds that if some of the businesses fail or stagnate, the fund nearly always has enough winners to pull you through.

Equity funds should be the core of just about anybody's investment portfolio, assuming they are investing for at least five years. Because the economy and well-run companies are almost certain to grow over time, stocks and shares can be the engine of growth for your money. If you want to earn decent returns on your cash over the long term, and you've decided to buy mutual funds, you can't avoid buying equity funds. That's because they're the only type of fund likely to produce big returns, possibly 8 to 10 percent or more annually, over the long haul. And those are the types of returns you need to defy inflation and build a substantial nest egg.

Yes, the stock market and the funds that invest in it can drop sharply, sometimes for years — we provide some scary examples in this chapter. So make sure you have a good chunk of bond funds in your holdings as well. But strong evidence exists that equity markets pretty well always rise over periods of ten years or more, so equity funds are a relatively safe bet for buyers who are sure they can hold on for a long time without needing the money back at short notice.

In this chapter, we give you a crash course on how the stock market works and explain why funds are a great way to profit from it. We show why you're best off buying equity funds that invest in big and stable companies, especially businesses that sell their wares all over the world. We also make clear why it's a good idea to hold six or seven equity funds — three Canadian and three or four global — and we give you simple tips for selecting great funds.

Making Investing in Stocks Simple

Believe it or not, making money in the stock market is easy — in theory. You just buy shares — tiny slices of ownership — in well-managed companies and then hold on to them for years. As the businesses you've invested in thrive, so do their owners, and that includes you as a shareholder. But when you actually try to select wonderful companies, things get complicated. For one thing, it's hard to tell which companies have genuinely bright prospects, because the managers of just about every corporation do a great job of blowing their little brass horns and making everything look wonderful in their garden. And, like everything else, the stock market is subject to the whims of fashion. When investors decide they love a particular company or industry, the shares usually go to fantastic heights. At that point, buying stocks turns into a risky game — no point buying a great business if you pay four times what it's really worth.

Being fallible human beings, we constantly sabotage ourselves in the stock market. When everything is going well and shares are climbing to record highs, we feel all warm, fuzzy, and enthusiastic — and we stumble into the market just in time for the crash. And when the economy or the stock market is slumping, we get all depressed and sell our shares at bargain-basement prices — just when we should be grabbing more. But perhaps the biggest problem with investors is our innate belief that we're smarter than everybody else. Everybody thinks the same thing, which means that lots of us are going to end up losers. Don't let us stop you: You can try to make pots of money buying speculative technology companies or penny mining stocks or companies consolidating the pallet industry (don't laugh, Andrew did), but that's really gambling. True investing in stock markets is simply buying well-established, well-run businesses and holding the shares, ideally for years.

Mutual funds are one of the best and easiest ways to make money from the stock market. That's because they

>> Are run by professionals who are trained in the art of checking out businesses.

>> Are set up to make it easy to put your money in and get it back out.

>> Hold a wide variety of companies, spreading your risk and giving you the chance to benefit from growth in a huge range of industries.

By handing your money over to a mutual fund company, you're saving yourself from yourself — if you aren't making the decisions, then you can't risk your savings on wild bets or crazy dreams.

The real kicker in stock market investing is figuring out whether a company is genuinely good — a quality outfit worth putting money into — and whether the price you're being asked to pay for shares is too high. Unfortunately, though, there may be no such thing as a true value for a company, because the numbers all vary so wildly according to the assumptions you make about the future. In that case, a stock is simply worth what people decide to pay for it on any given day. And that may not be very much: Stocks can dive for no apparent reason. But ordinary people saving for the future should care about the crazy volatile stock market for one reason: Good companies thrive, their profits go up, and their stocks gain value over the long term.

Sometimes selecting a good company to invest in can be almost embarrassingly simple. Take what was once everybody's favourite telecommunications toy — sorry, tool — the BlackBerry. From the day these minuscule but versatile little computers appeared in cellphone company boutiques, they seemed a must-have addition to daily life. Innovation, good design, and clever marketing is no accident — it requires talented people, and they don't stay long with badly run companies. Sure enough, an investor who bought shares of Research In Motion — or RIM, the manufacturer of the BlackBerry — soon after the company first issued shares to the public in 1999, multiplied their money more than twentyfold over the next nine years.

In 2007, though, a new entrant to the smartphone market, Apple's iPhone, appeared on the scene with a better product, and RIM stock plunged. The company is still around and publicly traded (now with the brand name Blackberry) but it doesn't even make smartphones anymore. For investors, the moral of the story is that making money on a stock amounts to knowing when to buy and when to sell, which a trained and experienced fund manager will likely know better than you.

In for the long haul

Based on experience in the past century, you almost always win in the stock market over periods of at least ten years provided you stick to big, high-quality companies and you spread your risk by owning at least a dozen of them in different industries. Most equity mutual funds play it even safer by holding at least 50 different stocks (many hold 100 or more) so they can be sure of buying and selling their holdings easily.

REMEMBER

It's hard to lose money in the stock market as long as you buy well-run, large companies and hold them for long enough.

Studies that looked at every ten-year period in the market during the 20th century found that stocks produced a profit in 99 percent of the periods, although that falls to 86 percent if you take inflation into account. So while 20 to 1 might be a stretch, with diversification and patience 5 to 1 is doable.

TECHNICAL
STUFF

Why do most mutual funds hold so many different stocks? Why doesn't the manager just buy their favourite half-dozen shares and run with that? One reason is that when the market turns sour on a company its stock tends to drop like a rock. So exposing a huge proportion of your fund to a single company is a bad idea. Getting stuck with a stock nobody else wants is a fund manager's most ghastly nightmare. Whenever they offer the shares for sale, rival investment managers make sympathetic faces and gentle cooing noises — and then refuse to buy the garbage at anything but sub-bargain prices. Under provincial securities law, a mutual fund can have a maximum of 10 percent of its assets in a single stock to protect investors. And most funds limit their exposure to single shares to five percent or less.

A test case for capitalism: Meet Angus and Bronwyn

Take an equity fund apart and figure out just what it's made of. The "equity" in equity funds is just a fancy word for stocks and shares — two words that mean the same thing. Just like stocks, shares are tiny portions of ownership of a company, imaginary certificates that represent ownership of the business. (Long gone are the days when investors hoarded elaborately printed stock certificates in their safety-deposit boxes; it's all done electronically now.)

Consider a grossly simplified example to see how the stock market works. Suppose you and your Welsh sister-in-law Bronwyn start a dry cleaning business and you each invest $5,000, while your Scottish boyfriend Angus puts up $10,000. That means the store has three *shareholders*, or owners, and a total of four shares: One each for you and Bronwyn (in return for your $5,000 each), and two shares for Angus, because he put up twice as much. Now, say people's silk blouses get wrecked and the business doesn't do well. Bronwyn realizes that Angus wants to get out of this mess, even if he has to take a loss. So she buys both of his shares at only $3,000 each, giving her ownership of three shares, or three-quarters of the business. The important point here is that the price of the shares has fallen because the prospects of the business are poor. But the fact that Angus sold the shares to Bronwyn has no direct effect on the store itself. People are still coming and going, beefing about their spoiled clothes, while the stock trading takes place entirely separately — behind the scenes, as it were.

A real-life example of equity investing

Now, mutual funds usually aren't allowed to buy dry cleaning stores (don't laugh, we know some wild-eyed fund managers who probably would if they could), because investments in tiny companies are too risky. Instead, they trade stocks on the stock market, a vast organized exchange system.

To see how this works, consider Canada's now-fallen stock market star Nortel Networks Corp., a giant global maker of equipment for sending signals over the Internet, phone lines, and just about anything else you care to name. In late 2000, Nortel had about 3 billion shares — that's 3,000 times 1 million — outstanding (that is, in the hands of investors), and they were trading in Toronto at about $70 each. That means the stock market placed a value on the company of about $210 billion — 210,000 times $1 million.

The significant detail in this snapshot, though, was that Nortel shares had soared more than threefold over the previous year. Does that mean Nortel's real value had increased by $140 billion in just a year? Probably not, but Nortel shares climbed because investors went crazy for technology stocks, sending the stock ever higher. In other words, investors kept *bidding*, or offering high prices for Nortel, and as the mania to own the company's shares grew, the stock price continued to rise. But don't forget that the opposite is true, as Nortel investors discovered to their detriment in 2001 and 2002. If investors turn sour on a company, the stock normally drops like a dead donkey. During the summer and early autumn of 2000, Nortel shares had climbed as high as $122, but they slumped to the $70 range by the fall as investors went cool on the Internet.

You may think Nortel was a great value at that point, with the shares down 40 percent from their peak. Many investors did. Wrong. Nortel just kept dropping as the market for telecommunications gear imploded and fears for the company's very solvency increased. By summer 2002, the shares had collapsed to less than $2, dragging down the whole Canadian stock market with them.

"EQUITY" SOUNDS NICE — BUT WHAT DOES IT MEAN?

The term *equity* means "fairness" or "equal treatment," and it's used as a shorthand for stock to indicate that each share is as good as another (in the real world, controlling shareholders sometimes run companies for their own private benefit, but that's another story). In other words, if a friend owns 100 shares in a company and you own 1,000, then you're supposed to get ten times as much say in choosing the directors and you're also supposed to get ten times as much in dividends — no more and no less. Basically, it comes down to who picks the directors, because they call the shots. "Who cares?" you ask. Well, that little fact — the rule that holders of shares get exactly the same treatment in proportion to how many they own — is one of the great aspects about the stock market. If you hold 100 shares and a mysterious Cayman Islands trust owns one million, you both get exactly the same dividends per share and potential increase in share price. The stock market is often rigged or brutal, but it's also a very democratic and fair place — you either sell or buy, your call, with no sort-ofs or might-dos.

Eventually the insolvent company delisted from the stock exchanges where it traded. Creditors took over the company and sold its assets to competitors. Equity investors who held on until the end got nothing for their shares.

Deciding How Much to Bet on Equity Funds

How many of your loonies are you going to dedicate to equity funds? Finding the right balance here is critical. As we mention elsewhere, stocks, in the form of quality equity funds, are the place for the lion's share of your long-term savings. But not everyone has the time or nerve to be a long-term investor.

REMEMBER

Equity funds are not a good place to hold money that you're going to need in the next couple of years. And stocks and equity funds are not suitable investments when you can't afford to suffer any short-term losses. That's because even though stock markets rise over time as the economy expands, share prices can go into vicious slumps for a year or more.

For example, though the S&P/TSX Composite, the index most representative of the Canadian stock market, was up six percent on the year as of September 1, 2023, it was still almost 10 percent below its all-time high in March 2022. Over an 18-month period, the market had fallen. Because mutual fund returns factor in management fees, the median Canadian equity mutual fund return over that period fared slightly worse.

The *median* return is the midpoint between the highest and lowest values of the members of a group — in this case, a fund category. We refer to median returns in this book instead of average returns because they are regarded as more useful measures of how well a group of funds have performed as a group. A category's *average* return is the sum of the returns for all funds within the category, divided by the number of funds — thus giving equal weighting to each fund, regardless of how big or small it is in terms of assets.

Anyway, back to equity funds. Despite all the diversification provided by an equity mutual fund, you can't count on it being there absolutely whenever you need it. So the money you allocate to equity funds should be cash you can let ride for several years — that way your funds have time to bounce back from one of the market's periodic funks.

Knowing your investment style

In Chapter 4, which is all about using mutual funds in your financial plan, we suggest three basic portfolios, depending on what sort of investor you are. The allocation of stocks and bonds in these packages is based on professional portfolios designed by banks and fund companies, but it's not infallible. That's because nobody knows what will happen to the world economy and interest rates in years to come. For example, since the last edition of this guide was published, the world experienced a global financial crisis and the COVID-19 pandemic. And besides, everybody's different: If you have a fat pension from your job, you can afford to take far more risks with your mutual fund portfolio in search of higher returns. If the funds lose money, at least the regular pension deposit will keep you fed.

By contrast, if your mutual funds have to supply all your retirement income (over and above what Old Age Security and the Canada Pension Plan provide), then risking the whole wad in equity funds would be reckless. For example, the S&P 500, the most commonly used gauge of U.S. stock prices, plunged 19.4 percent in 2022. Its Canadian counterpart, the S&P/TSX Composite, fell 8.7 percent. For someone who had their entire savings tied up in these stock markets, that would have been a hair-raising experience.

Investors can logically be divided into three types, each with a very different need and desire for equity funds. Chances are you don't fit neatly into any of the categories, but you'll almost certainly feel closest to one of them:

>> **Savers** are people for whom investment losses are either unacceptable or unbearable. Typically, a saver is someone who will be using their money to make a major purchase, such as a home, within the next couple of years. So all that savers want is a steady and guaranteed return, even if it's less than

five percent a year. The group also includes people of modest means who will need every penny they've saved to live on, and thus can't afford to take any risks. Investors like this probably shouldn't own any equity funds because the risk of loss is just too great.

>> **Balanced investors** are like most of us — we just want a steady return year after year, without too many stomach-turning drops along the way. After all, life plans change, and we may find it necessary to dip into our savings long before retirement. Avoiding huge losses means owning lots of bonds, which are loans to governments and corporations that have been packaged into tiny slices so investors can trade them. In Chapter 4, we suggest that investors in this balanced group limit equity funds to only 50 percent of their portfolio. Only half in stocks is a very cautious mixture, but remember that as you chase higher returns, your risk of loss climbs.

>> **Growth investors** are the aggressive or "long-term" types who don't mind double-digit losses in their portfolios as long as they, ideally, earn 10 percent or more over the long term. In other words, they're investing for at least five years. In Chapter 4, we suggest a portfolio for growth investors that's 75 percent in stocks. If you have many years to go before you'll need the money in the portfolio — that is, you can tie the money up for a decade or more — then you may be happy putting even more of your money into pure stock funds. But before you decide to roll the dice on equities with complete abandon, remember that nearly all professional investors make sure that in the portfolios they run, they own a good dollop of guaranteed investments, in the form of cash and government bonds.

Learning from history

For most of the second half of the 20th century, no other type of investment performed as well as stocks. Real estate went into big slumps. Cash or bonds were safer, but they generally pay much less, meaning their returns are often wiped out by inflation.

How good have stocks been in the long run? Well, sorry to give you a weasel-like answer, but it depends on what period you want to look at. For example, consider three recent 10-year periods and then a 20-year span:

>> **1987–1997:** U.S. stocks were way ahead of global and Canadian stocks. The S&P 500 composite index rose a cumulative 477 percent over this ten-year period, more than twice as much as the MSCI world stock index, which rose 216 percent. Canadian bonds, measured by the TSX DEX universe bond index, outperformed the S&P/TSX composite, 200 percent versus 184 percent.

>> **1992–2002:** Roll ahead to another ten-year span, and U.S. stocks are still well ahead of the pack, up a cumulative 203 percent compared with around 135 percent for Canadian stocks and Canadian bonds.

>> **1997–2007:** During this time, Canadian stocks, propelled by an explosion in the price of oil, gained 147 percent during this period. A distant second was Canadian bonds, up 84 percent, followed by global stocks, up a so-so 41 percent. U.S. stocks trailed badly at 23 percent — thanks in large part to Wall Street's miserable 2007.

>> **2008–2023:** The start of this period marked the peak of a "commodity supercycle" that benefited the commodity-rich Canadian stock market. Especially after crude oil prices tanked in 2014, the Canadian market has underperformed its developed-market peers. Meanwhile, in the U.S., the era was dominated by technology-driven mega-caps that, despite a couple of market crashes, pushed the S&P 500 up 336 percent, including dividends. Bond yields fared poorly as they hit historical lows, but then started rising in 2022 and 2023 as interest rates, for the first time since the Great Recession, started climbing in earnest again.

>> **1980–2023:** Longer term stocks were the clear winners, with Canadian, U.S. and European stocks all producing cumulative returns in excess of 3,500 percent. The only outlier was Japan's Nikkei index, which returned a relatively paltry 1,400 percent. It still beat Canadian bonds, which rose about 1,000 percent, or 10 times, over the period.

These numbers demonstrate a couple of vital lessons:

>> To get really big growth in your money over many years, you almost certainly have to own at least some stocks — but as the time approaches when you need to dip into your savings, sell your equity funds to protect against a market slump.

>> Despite Bay Street's periodic outperformance, you also have to keep lots of your money outside Canada and in big global companies to realize real long-term growth.

The time period you choose to compare investment returns can make all the difference. Global stock markets made huge gains during the last quarter of the 20th century, although a few serious bumps happened along the way. The 21st century has started out more tentatively, although markets still have made huge gains. There will be years or even strings of years when the markets will lose you money. In fact, stock markets can produce losses over many years, so it's unwise to risk every penny of your retirement savings there.

Investors in the late 1960s and early 1970s saw the entire stock market in the United States and Canada stagnate for a decade as inflation and recession sapped confidence in the future of equity investing itself. The inflation-racked period from then into the 1980s presented the worst possible conditions for stocks because interest rates that soared above 20 percent simply tempted investors to put their money into guaranteed deposits. No mutual fund and practically no type of investment can get through catastrophic inflationary times like those without losing money. However, central bankers seem to have learned more about how to run the economy without slipping into inflationary spirals. Or so it seems.

REMEMBER

The point of all these dire warnings about stock declines is that most of the people who are running and selling mutual funds don't remember the grim 1960s and 1970s either. Many of them hadn't even been born. So they'll often spin you a cheerful yarn along the lines of "the stock market always goes up over the long term." Maybe it does, but they won't be around to refund your money if the market goes into a 1970s-style collapse, either. That said, equity salespeople can still point to solid gains over the past 10 years (to August 2023); the S&P/TSX Composite index's total return exceeds eight percent annualized and the S&P 500, more than 12 percent.

Splitting between index and actively managed funds

The best plan is to take the money you set aside for equity funds and simply buy an index fund, or even better, an exchange-traded fund (ETF), that tracks the Canadian stock market, another that tracks the U.S. market, and yet another that tracks stock markets in the rest of the world. Simpler still, you can buy a global equity ETF that allocates part of its portfolio to all these markets, or even an "asset allocation" fund that apportions some of your money to bonds, too.

Put between one-half and two-thirds of your equity money into those two or three index funds or ETFs. Then, with the rest of your stock market money, buy two high-quality "normal" or "actively managed" Canadian equity funds and two high-quality global stock funds. By normal or actively managed, we mean funds whose managers actually buy and sell stocks in pursuit of extra profits — instead of, as an index fund does, simply buying every stock in the market and giving you returns in line with an index or benchmark, such as the S&P/TSX composite index or the MSCI world index. (We offer tips on selecting the best actively managed funds in the section "The ABCs of Picking a Fund," later in this chapter.)

Knowing What Return to Expect from Your Funds

Should you have confidence in the Canadian stock market to make more than 10 percent consistently in the future? Are U.S. stocks likely to return to their heady days of the 2010s, when double-digit returns were the norm? Can you count on 10-percent-plus returns in the future? No, no, and no. And no again.

If you look for about six to eight percent a year, you may achieve your goal by buying shares in large and stable companies, but you're still stuck with a lot of your money at risk in the ever-choppy stock market. If you settle for a four- to six-percent annual return, you're being pretty conservative, meaning you can afford to hold less volatile investments such as bonds and cash; only a major recession or a triumphant return of the dark forces of inflation are likely to give you major losses.

Picking a Fund: The Basics

If you've been worrying about which equity fund among the 3,000-plus on sale in Canada has the best chance of beating the market, forget it. You're better off looking for UFOs in the evening sky. No point trying to pick a fund that'll beat the market because only a tiny group of managers are likely to do so consistently, based on experience over several decades.

Even if a brochure, ad, or salesperson tells you (or at least implies) a fund is the sure road to riches, always make sure you kick the tires yourself. (We explain just how to kick those tires later in this section.) The people who design and run mutual funds are master marketers, and they often sincerely believe their fund is a magic lamp that will reliably outperform the market. If you go to a broker, financial planner, or insurance agent to buy your funds, they too will trot out the same line.

These are salespeople, and to do a good job, they have almost certainly convinced themselves the fund they're selling you is a world-beater. They use reassuring phrases and labels such as "conservative" or "growth at a reasonable price" to convince you their fund is a way to achieve that impossible dream: Big returns at almost no risk. They even talk about the fund's "black box" (a cynical expression used in the investment industry) in the shape of some impressive-sounding formula or method that purports to maximize returns while reducing the danger of losses. Think of witch doctors brandishing painted bones and you get the idea.

Yes, you may get lucky and seize on a manager who outperforms the pack for a while, but they always fall to earth.

Of all the actively managed Canadian equity funds with a five-year track record as of year-end 2022, only seven percent managed to beat the return from the S&P/TSX index during that period. Nearly half beat the benchmark over the down year in 2022, but only 15 percent managed to outperform over 10 years. It's tough to beat the index, apparently.

So instead of using complicated criteria to choose a fund you hope will be a world-beater, we recommend that you follow three basic rules, what we call the ABCs of selecting a great equity fund:

1. Look for a fund that's full of companies from **A**ll industries — and, in the case of global funds, **A**ll major regions of the world.

2. Insist that your fund holds lots of big, stable, and conservative companies — the type that investors call **B**lue-chip (because the blue chip is traditionally the most valuable in poker).

3. Look for a fund that has a habit of producing **C**onsistent returns over the years that aren't out of line with the market or with its rival funds. Later in this chapter, we show you how to do that.

Select from all industries

A fund should hold companies from all, or nearly all, major industries in order to spread risk — and to give unitholders a chance to profit if investors smell opportunity with a particular type of company and drive their stock prices up. Here is one way to break down the industry groups:

>> Banks and other financial companies, such as Citigroup, Royal Bank of Canada, or Deutsche Bank

>> Natural resource producers, such as Imperial Oil, Barrick Gold, or West Fraser Timber

>> Technology companies, such as Microsoft, Apple, or Shopify

>> Manufacturers of industrial and consumer products, such as drug maker Pfizer or auto parts producer Magna International

>> Dull but steady utility and pipeline companies such as Alberta power generator TransAlta or pipeline system TC Energy; telephone companies such as Telus and AT&T also officially fit into this group

>> Retail and consumer service companies such as Canadian Tire and Wal-Mart

Not every group has to be represented in the top holdings of every fund, but a portfolio without at least one resource stock, financial services giant, or technology player among its biggest ten investments may represent a dangerous gamble. Why? Because of the ever-present chance that share prices in that missing sector will suddenly and unpredictably take off, leaving your fund in the dust. Avoid funds making bets like that.

Hold blue-chip winners

Glossy mutual fund brochures often promise the sun, moon, and stars . . . but just look at the fund's top holdings. Whether the fund is Canadian, U.S., or international, at least two-thirds of its ten biggest investments should be big, blue-chip companies that you or someone you trust has at least heard of. A list of the top stocks in any fund is readily available on the Internet — see Chapter 21 for details of what the data-company websites as well as those of individual fund companies offer. Look in the fund's marketing material or in the reports and documents given to unitholders (see Chapter 3). What you're looking for are big and stable firms, the type that offer the best prospect of increasing their shareholders' wealth over the years.

Talk is cheap and fund managers love to drone on about how conservative they are. But managers of supposedly careful funds can sometimes quietly take risks: They put big portions of the fund into weird stuff such as resource stocks or India to jazz up their returns and attract more investors. The list of top holdings is one of the most valuable pieces of information an investor has about a fund because it can't be faked or fudged (ruling out pure fraudulent reporting).

TIP

If you don't see at least a few giant names — companies like Thomson Reuters, CN Rail, Coca-Cola Corp., Bank of Montreal, New York Times Co., General Motors Corp., GlaxoSmithKline PLC, or Toyota Motor Corp. — in the fund's list of its biggest holdings, then the fund manager may be taking undue risks, fooling around with small or obscure companies.

Check out past performance, with caution

After you've satisfied the first two of these conditions, look at the fund's past performance. Begin by filtering out funds that have been around for fewer than five years, unless it's quite clear someone with a record you can check has been running the money. Then look for consistent returns that aren't too much above or below the market. We all want to make lots of money, so leaving past returns until last may seem crazy and exactly opposite to one's natural inclination. But it's the way sophisticated professionals do it. If the people in charge of a multi-billion-dollar pension fund are interviewing new money-management firms, for example, they'll ask first about the expenses and fees the money managers charge and also about the style and method the firms use to select stocks and bonds (more on that topic later). Only then do the pros examine the past record of the managers — it's just assumed they are near the average.

Measuring past performance is almost as impossible as determining the true value of a company's stock — it depends entirely on complex and varying assumptions and conditions. Here's an example: Legendary money manager Frank Mersch of Altamira Investment Services thrashed his competition for most of the early 1990s, playing resource stocks masterfully. He was a journalist's delight, always returning phone calls and providing pithy quotes. Everybody loved him, especially people with money in his fund. It soared more than 30 percent each year from 1990 through 1992, far ahead of the average Canadian stock fund. Who could blame you for deciding Mersch was good — and for putting money into his fund? But then resource stocks slid when commodity prices fell, and Mersch missed out completely on the climb in financial stocks, which rose more than 50 percent in 1997 and again in 1998. The market and his once-beetle-like rivals left him behind, and by 1999 he had departed as manager of the fund.

What happened? Did Mersch suddenly become dumb, or did the market turn against him through no fault of his own — or was it simply that his luck changed? Such questions probably can't be answered accurately, so let's not bother debating them. But let us repeat, yet again: Betting too heavily on yesterday's hot performers, hoping they'll outrun the pack again tomorrow, is a good way to end up in a dud fund.

Don't get too hung up about hot results in the past. Mutual fund companies like to offer lots of funds so they can have a few big performers to bray about in the ads, but those returns are always partly a result of luck. And mutual funds, incidentally, are managed with a freer hand than pension funds, which have strict risk management policies. The temptation always exists to jack up the risk and returns a little to get the money pouring in.

Find out what a fund's past performance has been and, above all, compare it with that of rival funds and the market as a whole. The leading Internet sites for Canadian mutual fund investors and investment advisors are Morningstar.ca and Globefund.com (which just now just directs you to the *Globe and Mail's* investing section).

You can find much more on how to use the web for fund research in Chapter 21, but for now just remember to stick to funds that have been around for at least five years. Compare a fund's numbers against those of its peers — those within the same category — and also against the median returns for all funds in the category. (Refer to Chapter 2 for more on medians, averages, and other performance measures.)

WHO'S RUNNING YOUR FUND? MANAGERS ON THE MOVE

Equity funds offer endless sources of amusement. One of the fun games you can play with a fund is figuring out who exactly is running it. This search is often so difficult that investors shouldn't get too worried about it when they start buying funds. It's impossible with some companies that use a vague "team" to pick stocks. And remember that a superstar manager is extra likely to go cold because they get too much money run. Remember that what is actually in the portfolio is far more important than any amount of talk of wizards running your money.

If you get more interested in mutual funds, you'll no doubt start wondering: Why not just put my money with people who have been successful in the past? One problem is that managers move around so much. As soon as a stock picker builds a strong reputation, all too often, they jump ship to another fund that offers a fat signing bonus. And remember the warning that we've been repeating endlessly in a smug nasal drone: Star managers invariably fall to earth. Sometimes, they go inside themselves, and sometimes they seem to . . . well, they always go inside themselves. Don't get excited about the past history of the manager running your fund. And pay even less attention to fawning newspaper articles proclaiming them a genius. Just look at the fund's main holdings and its track record. If these meet the ABC tests outlined previously, then it's probably a high-quality fund.

Globefund.com and Morningstar.ca supply the annual compound returns for every fund as well as for the average fund in its category and for the market as a whole. If you're interested in a fund, its compound returns should be above the average for its group, but if they're way above — for example, an annual return of 15 percent over five years while the average fund made less than 10 percent — then the manager is probably a risk-taker.

WARNING

Above all, be wary of funds whose returns over five and ten years are below those of the average fund: Such pooches have a dispiriting habit of continuing to bark and dig holes in the garden. Check whether the fund has been near the top or bottom in each individual calendar year to detect big swings in performance over time.

Avoiding a Lemon

Stocks generally go up over time, as the economy grows and companies become more efficient at creating wealth for their owners (which means the people who own their shares, remember). Does this mean that any equity fund you get your hands on will line your pockets over the long haul? Not so fast — for mutual fund buyers, the problem is that individual funds *can* go into long slumps if the fund manager gets it wrong.

Remembering the importance of diversification

As a mutual fund buyer, you can really miss out on returns if you're stuck with a lemon. We can't emphasize this point enough: Spread your holdings among half a dozen funds — including two or three *index funds* or *ETFs*, funds that track the entire stock market, instead of trying to pick individual shares (and possibly getting it wrong) — to help ensure they don't all rot away in something that never really comes back to life.

At all costs, avoid having more than one-third of your money in any one stock market fund. That way you won't expose too much of your capital to a pig of a fund. Fund companies and planners may tell you differently, but we really can't think of an exception.

Looking at the big picture and knowing when to bail

Fund companies and brokers (with some justification) argue endlessly that buying stocks and shares is a long-term game because the market can drop for no good reason. (Of course, that doesn't prevent them from taking out huge ads trumpeting their short-term numbers, but we'll let that go for the moment.)

In fact, an old joke in investing goes like this: Everybody says he's a long-term investor as soon as his stock goes down.

The fund industry says you should ride out losses and that the market always turns, meaning you should be happy leaving money in an equity fund for at least five years. And the industry advises against selling a fund when it becomes a dog, arguing that it's simply having an off year. Well, perhaps, but a fund can take an awfully long time to recover. And it's impossible to tell whether its slump is temporary or long term.

For example, investors in the old AIC Advantage, a powerhouse fund in the 1990s, did not enjoy the 21st century. The fund had a seemingly inbred approach to investing: It focused on the stocks of mutual fund companies. This approach served investors well during the fund's spectacular 547-percent gain from 1991 through 1997. Returns were uneven after that, however, and investors soon grew tired of AIC's pleas for patience and began leaving the fund in droves. The fund seemed to break out of its funk in 2006, when it produced a 24-percent return, but the bad times resumed. AIC got bought out by Manulife in 2009, and the new owners repurposed the fund into a money-market vehicle nothing like its earlier construction.

In some cases, a brief period of bad returns is not the manager's fault. The market just hates the type of companies the manager likes to buy.

Take a look at the ups and downs at AGF's Global Select Fund. The global equity fund, with a geographic allocation about matching market capitalization (50 percent U.S. stocks, just 2.7 percent Canadian), got off to an inauspicious start in 2000, falling 50 percent in the market downturn two years later. It was walloped again during the market crash of 2008-09. But AGF stuck with it, growing the fund to more than $3.5 billion in assets and beating its benchmark index by five percent annually over the past decade. Its annualized returns over the period top 15 percent.

AGF Global Select achieved this record by concentrating on a relatively small number of stocks that stood out for their innovation, exceptional product development, and corporate leadership. That jelled perfectly with the markets' mood, when investors were willing to pay a huge premium for companies showing evidence of revenue and earnings growth.

A manager with a distinctive style — as long as it isn't too, ahem, weird — is a great person to invest with. That's because they often make lots of money on a violent turnaround in the market when other managers are losing their pricey embroidered shirts. But when the odd stocks that the manager likes fall out of favour themselves, unitholders in the fund miss out.

If possible, try to make sure the funds you buy are run by managers with a clearly stated style or method of picking stocks. Then try to choose managers with different styles. That way, when one manager is doing badly the other could be doing well, smoothing out your returns.

But what if your manager, who was good in the past, keeps posting bad returns year after year? Unfortunately, no quick answer exists for the question of when to dump a good manager. Just follow your gut. And ask a few questions if your salesperson seems all puppyish and keen to do a switch. They can be indirectly getting a cut of five percent of the money you switch to another firm's funds because the new firm pays sales commissions.

Chapter **11**

Heirloom Equity Funds: The Dull Stuff that Will Make You Wealthy

I f you're a long-term investor who's able to commit money to mutual funds for at least five years, this chapter is the most important for you. That's because *equity funds* — funds that buy stocks and shares in companies — are such powerful investing tools, offering the potential to grow your money many times over. If you pick a sensibly varied portfolio of high-quality funds, and this chapter shows you how, then you're almost certain to do well as an investor.

REMEMBER

We refer to these funds as "heirloom" funds because that's what they should be — treasured possessions you can hang on to indefinitely.

This chapter isn't about crazy technology funds that soar 80 percent in a year and then crash just as quickly. And it isn't about finding somewhere safe and predictable to hold the cash you're saving up for a car. It's about the "core" mutual funds that account for most of your long-term money, funds you can buy and hold forever if necessary. Yes, they may have bad years, perhaps several in a row, but over time their top-quality stocks and varied holdings are almost sure to pay off. In Chapter 10, we outline the basic steps you need to take to identify a good equity fund. In this chapter, we provide more details of the facets to check, we suggest some excellent funds, and we show you how to select your own mixture of mutual funds.

How Many Equity Funds Do You Need?

Building a great portfolio of mutual funds is simple. All you have to do is make two decisions:

>> How much risk do you want to take — in other words, how much you want riding on equity funds?

>> How much you do like Canada's long-term economic prospects?

We wish we could tell you to simply buy a single stock market fund, using the techniques we suggest, and forget about it. Some advisors even insist you're safe with a single wonderful fund. But that course is just too dangerous.

WARNING

Putting all your money into just one equity fund, even if it's a great one, can lead to periods of harrowing underperformance if that fund goes into a slump — and nearly all funds do from time to time.

Consider, for example, the fate of investors in Trimark Select Growth Fund, which in mid-2008 was AIM Trimark's biggest fund with $3.7 billion in assets. The fund, which gave investors a glittering return of 8.5 percent annually from its launch in May 1989 to the middle of 2008, might have done even better had it not been for a catastrophic 2007. The fund lost 16 percent, as it was hit harder than many other global equity funds by a rapidly rising Canadian dollar. It was Trimark Select Growth's first negative year since 1990, when the young fund lost 7.2 percent in a year when almost all its peers also were firmly in the red. Following a series of fund consolidations by owner Invesco Canada, the fund no longer exists.

REMEMBER

Own more than one equity fund. That way, if one of your funds sags, you have a shot at doing well with the others.

But how many funds should you buy to ensure you assembled an adequately varied collection? Before we answer that, look at the only two types of funds to consider for your serious long-term money:

>> **Global equity funds:** These buy stocks and shares everywhere, from Taiwan to Tupelo. In practice, they usually end up investing in large companies in the rich economies of the world because, to paraphrase the bank robber, that's where the money is. In other words, giant corporations have proven to be just about the most profitable and most stable investments you can make.

>> **Canadian equity funds:** Not surprisingly, these funds buy Canadian stocks. A number of individual categories exist under the Canadian equity umbrella. Some funds concentrate on the very largest corporations, such as the big

> banks or other blue-chip companies such as communications giant Telus Corp., and others are more specialized, such as *small-cap funds,* which buy only smaller companies with supposedly bigger growth prospects. In practice, Canadian equity funds end up holding pretty well the same companies because the Canadian market offers a limited selection. However, it offers a little more variety among small-cap funds.

You'll likely put most of your money into funds in these categories, but there are other areas to look at as well, depending on your risk tolerance levels and time horizon. Just be careful of putting your hard-earned dollars into something that's too risky for your situation.

Ruling out specialty funds

In Chapter 12, we look at the host of dancing unicorns and dogs in tutus the fund industry has come up with to entice money from investors. By that we mean the "specialty" or "regional" equity funds that hold only a certain type of shares or shares in only some countries, the idea being that a concentrated fund will produce huge profits when share prices in that particular industry or part of the world take off like little rockets.

These riskier funds include technology funds, small-company funds, developing-country funds, resource funds, and Asian funds. Some have produced great returns and many hold excellent stocks. But they all suffer from one big affliction: Because they can invest in only a small section of the world's stock markets, they don't give you the variety and stability your long-term money requires.

REMEMBER

So, the only two types of funds you truly need for the portion of your money you've decided to have in equity funds are global equity funds and Canadian equity/large-cap equity funds. Go ahead and buy some of the risky specialty and regional funds if you must, but limit them to just 10 percent of your total portfolio. No hard-and-fast rule applies here, but that's the advice you get from many pros.

Deciding how much to put into equity funds

In Chapters 4 and 10, which deal with using equity mutual funds in your financial plan, we state that all of us as investors fall into one of these three groups:

>> **Savers:** Those who need to use their money in the next couple of years, shouldn't own many (if any) equity funds. The risk of loss in the short term is too great, so savers should just buy investments that pay regular interest.

>> **Balanced investors:** People who want limited exposure to a drop in the value of their funds in any given year often put 45 percent, or slightly more (up to about 60 percent), into equity funds. With the rest, they buy bond funds, which invest in loans to governments and corporations, leaving a small portion of their money sitting in cash or cash-like investments. Or they buy special balanced funds, which consist of a mixture of stocks and bonds.

>> **Growth investors:** The guys who want the maximum return on their money and plan to let it ride the ups and downs of funds for five years or more, often put about 75 percent of their money into equity funds. If you're investing for periods of ten years or more and definitely don't mind big slumps in the value of your mutual fund portfolio along the way, you may want to put even more into the stock market with its allure of higher returns.

While these are the most common types of investors, people are complicated and don't tend to fit into a single bucket. Some of your money may need to be more growth-oriented or more balanced depending on when you need it. Use these numbers as a guide.

Dividing your money between Canadian and foreign equity funds

Should you be patriotic and keep your money in Canada, or look abroad for your investments? No definite answer exists, but the prevailing advice has been to keep the majority of your stock market money outside Canada. The world offers many wonderful opportunities, and the Canadian stock market represents a tiny fraction of the world's overall stock market value. For example, few Canadian companies have the might of Japan's Sony Corp., Royal Dutch Shell of the Netherlands, or U.S.-based Microsoft Corp.

However, most experts would also advise keeping at least some of your money in Canada if you plan to go on living in this country, because you'll need to have assets in Canadian dollars to pay for your expenses here. Plus you pay lower taxes on capital gains and dividends from Canadian equities than on foreign equities when you hold them in outside of a registered account such as registered retirement savings plan (RRSP), a popular tax-advantaged investment account. But if you're convinced that Canada's economy is in trouble, then you may want to move 80 percent or more of your mutual fund money, including equity funds, into non-Canadian stocks and bonds.

How do you split your money among equity funds?

In Chapter 4, we describe a method of dividing your money among equity funds. Put one-half to two-thirds of your stock market money into *index funds* or *exchange-traded funds (ETFs)*, funds that simply track the entire market at low cost to the investor instead of trying to pick the stocks that will go up the most. For much more on index funds and ETFs, check out Chapter 15. Their reliability and low expenses make them one of the very best deals out there for investors.

Canadian stock market index funds and ETFs track the Standard & Poor's/Toronto Stock Exchange composite index or the S&P/TSX 60 index (a more focused collection of the biggest companies listed on the TSX). Global index funds are rare, so you usually have to buy a combo: a U.S. index fund that gives you the same return each year as a list of giant U.S. companies such as the Standard & Poor's 500-stock index, and an international index fund that tracks all the major global markets except for the United States and Canada. Put a U.S. index fund and an international index fund together, and you've got a pretty good global equity index fund. So all you need to buy is a Canadian, a U.S., and an international index fund.

REMEMBER

Two categories of funds invest broadly in foreign stock markets:

>> Global equity

>> International equity

Here's the difference. *Global equity funds* are free to invest anywhere, including the United States, but *international equity funds* stay outside Canada and the United States. The idea behind international funds is that many investors already have plenty of money in the States by owning stocks or other funds, so some fund companies offer funds that stay out of the U.S. market. That's logical thinking, but in keeping with the ABC rules (explained in Chapter 10 and "Applying the ABC rules to your global equity funds" later in this chapter), we believe that when picking your non-Canadian stock funds, you're better off sticking with a fund that's free to go anywhere the manager anticipates getting the best return.

With the rest of your equity fund money, buy just four equity funds — two global and two Canadian — that have a person or team trying to select winning shares. Those are called *actively managed* funds because they buy and sell holdings in an attempt to beat the market and other fund managers instead of just trying to keep up with a market benchmark. The managers, in other words, are trying to pick the few stocks that go up the most.

Often, though, managers fail. But at least if you buy a few actively managed funds as well as index funds, you have a portfolio that isn't tied to just one market benchmark. It has enough variety to ensure that at least one of your funds is probably doing relatively well, even if the others are sagging — as long as the whole stock market isn't crashing. In the event of a wholesale decline in stocks, just about all equity funds — including Canadian and global — will be losers anyway.

Global Equity Funds: Meet Faraway People and Exploit Them

Global equities offer the best chance of steady, high returns on your savings over many years. They should make up about two-thirds of the money you're putting into the stock market — unless you're convinced the Canadian stock market is due for an extended period of outperformance.

REMEMBER

Global equity funds have earned steady, attractive returns over the years, which makes them the very best type of fund to own.

We recommend putting most of your money in global equity funds because

>> They tend to own multinational blue-chip companies, the best growth asset of all.

>> They invest all over the world, spreading your risk and smoothing out your ups and downs — when one country is up, another is often down.

>> The executives running multinational corporations sometimes foul up (remember "Google+"?), but the companies are usually large enough and sufficiently sophisticated to recover from errors.

>> Your mutual fund company is just one of dozens of big international money managers owning shares in these firms.

TECHNICAL STUFF

Many of Canada's biggest mutual funds fall into the global equity class, and some large ones have produced excellent results over the years. Global equity funds are hugely profitable for the companies that run them, so the managers are intensely motivated not to let the performance slip too much. Most global equity funds hold high-quality, blue-chip companies, and they spread their risk over numerous industries and countries so they also meet our ABC test.

REMEMBER

Buy at least two global equity funds because an individual fund can go into a slump for a year or more. Different managers are hot and cold at different times.

Applying the ABC rules to your global equity funds

When choosing a fund, you should follow three basic rules, what we call the ABCs (see Chapter 10) of selecting a great equity fund:

>> **A:** Make sure the fund invests in **All industries** and **Anywhere** in the world. All the important economic regions (that is, North America, Europe, and Asia) should show up in the top-ten holdings.

>> **B:** Insist on **Blue-chip** companies, some of which you have at least heard of.

>> **C:** Demand **Consistent** performance that isn't wildly out of line with the other funds in the group.

Investors who just go to a bank branch to buy their funds or who deal with another company that sells funds directly to the public will have a problem: The bank or company may offer just one suitable global equity fund. And you may not be able to buy index funds. No easy way around this problem exists. If you can't or don't want to go somewhere with a wider selection of funds, just buy the global fund with half of the money you've earmarked for global stocks and then hedge your bets by putting the rest into one or two narrower funds that invest in a single region, such as Europe or Asia.

REMEMBER

Check any global equity fund you buy to make sure it offers plenty of variety. If the top holdings contain no European stocks, for example, or they seem to be all technology companies, then look elsewhere.

Checking out three global equity winners

Here are three conservative and well-run global equity funds that Morningstar's analysts see as good bets in today's increasingly challenging global marketplace:

>> **Mawer Global Equity** has long been trouncing its benchmarks with an annualized return from its inception in 2009 through the end of 2022 just shy of 12 percent. Mawer Investment Management is a boutique fund company based in Calgary that's known to stray from the herd, picking less than obvious value stocks. The Global Equity team of Christian Deckart and Paul Moroz also takes risk management seriously, which to date has resulted in lower drawdowns in fund value when the markets tank. And if that isn't enough to sway you, the fund has a very affordable management expense ratio, as global funds go, of 1.3 percent.

>> **Dynamic U.S. Strategic Yield** is an equity fund with income-hungry investors (think seniors) in mind. It sticks to the familiar U.S. market, which represents

more than half of global market capitalization, so if you want truly global exposure, look somewhere else. It doesn't shoot out the lights when markets are moving up, but it doesn't collapse when markets take a turn for the worse, either. Its management expense ratio is cheap at just a hair over one percent. Morningstar gives it five stars with a gold medal rating.

>> **AGF Global Select Fund** won Lipper Awards for outstanding performance in its category over three-, five- and ten-year periods in 2022. Portfolio manager Tony Genua targets industry leaders that are growing their market share as well as stocks that stand to benefit from market trends. With an annual turnover rate of 57 percent, this fund is actively managed with a capital A. That makes it a suitable complement to index funds.

There are many others, of course, so do your homework, but these three funds are a good place to start.

Canadian Equity Funds: Making Maple-Syrup-Flavoured Money

Your first move when picking Canadian equity funds for the core of your portfolio is to make sure they're classified in one of the Canadian equity categories. (See Chapter 10 for details.) These include:

>> **Canadian equity:** These funds must have 90 percent of their holdings in Canadian-based companies; the fund's average market capitalization must be more than $10 billion.

>> **Canadian focused equity:** The criteria are identical to the Canadian equity category, except funds need be only 50 percent or more in Canada.

>> **Canadian small/mid-cap equity:** These funds must be 90 percent in Canadian stocks with an average market cap below $10 billion.

>> **Canadian focused small/mid-cap equity:** The same as Canadian small/mid-cap equity, except funds need be only 50 percent or more in Canada.

>> **Canadian dividend and income equity:** These funds must have a stated mandate to invest primarily in income-generating securities, and 90 percent of their equity holdings must be Canadian. The average market cap must be above $10 billion.

TIP

If the company where you hold your mutual fund account offers only one conventional actively managed Canadian stock fund, then use it for half of your Canadian stock money and put the rest into a Canadian index fund. If no index fund is available (and one should be), then open an account elsewhere for at least part of your money.

Keep it simple, and don't worry about which equity fund manager is going to thrash the competition because such an outcome is impossible — or at least very, very difficult — to predict. Canada's tiny stock market, which accounts for less than three percent of the world's publicly traded shares, offers a limited number of companies. In fact, for a big-company fund, only a few suitable names exist outside of the S&P/TSX 60 index. So most Canadian equity funds tend to be pretty similar.

Applying the ABC rules to your Canadian equity funds

Applying the ABC rules when you buy Canadian equity funds is simple:

>> Check that the fund invests in **All of Canada's** major industrial sectors, including technology, natural resources, and financial services.

>> Make sure that most of the top-ten holdings are **Blue-chip** companies that you have at least heard of.

>> Demand **Consistent** performance that doesn't lag or wildly outpace the other Canadian equity funds.

Looking at three winners in Canadian equities

Here are three Canadian equity funds selected by Morningstar analysts on the basis of solid long-term performance and strong fund managers:

>> **Canoe Equity Portfolio Class F** has reliably outperformed both the category average and the S&P/TSX Composite Index since its launch in 2011. Canoe Financial senior vice-president and lead manager Rob Taylor takes the growth-at-a-reasonable-price (GAARP) approach to stock selection, an often rewarding hybrid between growth and value investing. He likes stocks with

"optionality," or the potential for additional value creation outside the core business. Running a focused equity fund gives him the leeway to venture beyond Canada when opportunities present themselves, and with a 54 percent portfolio turnover rate, he's used it. Morningstar gives the fund five stars and a silver medal rating.

» **PH&N Conservative Equity Income Series F** is a low-fee fund — its management expense ratio is just 0.77 percent! — that can be counted on to avoid the worst the market has to offer but still deliver solid returns from dividends and capital gains in the good years. It's only been around since 2018, but it performed among the top 10 percent of Canadian equity funds in both 2021 (a terrific year) and 2022 (a terrible one), which is why Morningstar gives it five stars and a gold medal rating. Fund manager Phillips, Hager & North is part of the massive RBC Financial group, so expect this fund to have some staying power.

» **Fidelity True North Fund** manager Maxime Lemieux has an impressive track record going back to 2009, when he took over stewardship of this fund. Despite the limited selection of stocks in the Canadian large-cap space, he's been able to gain some distance on the S&P/TSX benchmark most years. The fund skews towards large, quality companies with strong fundamentals. It's 10-year average annual return is 8.5 percent, earning it five stars and a silver medal rating from Morningstar.

If you want to find other options, go to Morningstar's website, and look for four or five star–rated Canadian equity funds.

Chapter **12**

Las Vegas–Style Equity Funds: Trips You Don't Need

We know it's boring, but it's also true: Slow and steady really does win the equity fund race. In other words, you almost certainly do best over the long haul with the conservative equity funds we describe in Chapter 11, the ones that buy established companies in all industries and in all parts of the world. But you're only human, and the temptation to chase the really hot returns always exists.

For example, over the first nine months of 2023, funds tracking the technology-heavy NASDAQ 100 gained around 35 percent in Canadian dollars. Well, help yourself — but get ready to be bitten. Those same funds lost 27 percent in 2022. Mutual funds are a wonderfully convenient and relatively cheap way of playing, say, the Chinese market. But with this type of narrow investing, focusing on specific areas such as small/mid-cap stocks, an individual geographic region, or a particular industry sector is essentially gambling. In a nutshell, it's probably a waste of time because of what Nobel Prize–winning economists call "rational expectations."

Crudely put, here's how the theory applies to these specialty funds. By the time you realize something may be a good investment, everyone else — or at least everyone who matters — will have cottoned on to it too. Yes, you may do well in a technology fund — just ask anyone who invested in the legendary ARK Innovations Fund in 2016, an exchange-traded fund (ETF) that invests in disruptive and innovative companies. Investors enjoyed a phenomenal streak, including a 152 percent gain in 2020. But after a couple of money-losing years, including a 67 percent loss in 2022, its five-year compound return is now in the red — 2.32 as of October 2023. (And let's not get started on the fund's 0.75 percent management fee.)

Still, hope springs eternal and all that . . . so here's a roundup of some of the funds to watch out for. In this chapter we refrain from suggesting candidates when it comes to these wild funds because returns from this gang are largely a matter of luck — a manager looks like a genius when their favourite type of company or market is in favour, and a loser when that type of investment goes out of fashion.

Small and Mid-Sized Company Funds: Spotty Little Fellows

Small-cap funds have had a tough go of it since the global financial crisis of 2008. The median Canadian small/mid-cap equity fund returned just 5.5 percent annualized over the past decade, according to S&P Global, in contrast to the double-digit returns of U.S. large-caps. But these funds periodically outperform their large-cap counterparts, providing a handy dose of risk-reducing diversification to your portfolio.

Hitting highs and lows

If you bought the Pender Small Cap Opportunities Fund at its launch in 2009 and still owned it 14 years later, you would be bragging about its 14.2 percent compound annual return. But "if" is the operative term here. You'd have weathered some pretty big swings, including a 29 percent loss in 2022 and a 16 percent drop in 2018, assuaged by a 46 percent gain in 2020. Would you have had the nerve to stick with it amid all the volatility? If your answer is yes, then maybe the Canadian small-cap space is right for you.

Who's to know, though? Had you taken the much, much safer middle ground and invested in large-cap Canadian equity funds, you'd have earned a seven percent annual return over the past decade, which is half as good as Pender's fund. But, and here's the rub, few small-cap funds did as well as PenderFund. The average return for the category underperformed most large-cap funds at 5.5 percent a year over 10 years.

Picking a winning fund

Long before you worry about having the nerve to stick with a winning small-cap fund, the first challenge is to pick that fund in the first place. The problem is similar to what confronts the guy who's investing directly in small-cap stocks. Guessing which ones are going to "pop" — market talk for getting their stocks to go up — is a tough game. But never fear; investors have a willing ally in the executives and main shareholders of a company. In fact, they're sometimes *only too happy* for their share price to shoot up. *Cling!* — is that an option bulb lighting up? (*Options* are shares that company management can buy at a fixed low price — and that become nicer and nicer to have when the market price of the shares goes up.) But what's left in a hot stock for everybody else after the corporate management and the investment bankers have torn off their giant hunk often wouldn't fill a small McDonald's pop cup that's been lying for days on the ground beside a gasoline pump.

First, a vital bit of terminology — a company's *stock market capitalization* is the value in money terms that investors are applying to the business. For example, a company with 50 million shares in the hands of its shareholders and a stock price of $5 has a market value, or "market cap," of only $250 million (or 50 million shares times $5), which still makes it quite a small company.

The three most important details to remember about investing in small and medium-sized companies are that:

» Shares in small companies move in their own strange cycles, sometimes sliding when blue-chip stocks go up, which can make them a sort of insurance policy for a portfolio.

» And yes, when they're hot, small caps can produce rich returns. Of all the wacky fund categories, small-cap funds can best justify their existence. But you don't really need them, either.

» Small-company funds can go into long slumps, leaving you with "dead money" — an investment just stagnates — or, worse, saddles you with heavy losses. Most people are better off putting their savings into regular equity funds that buy big companies, a strategy that offers steadier returns.

Understanding the disadvantages

Small-cap funds can be volatile investments best suited to investors who keep a close eye on their holdings. Unpredictable rallies and collapses are the way small-cap stocks work. Yes, Canadian small/mid-cap funds can put together a string of consecutive gains, but investors often have to wait through lean and hungry years for the good times, and disappointments are all too frequent.

REMEMBER

Small-company funds are marked by moves upward that happen only too rarely, a disadvantage that makes them unsuitable for much of your serious money.

The numbers show that small-cap stocks may have their good long-term record only because of periodic crazy bull markets in small-company shares — typically at the end of a great period in the stock market, when investors feel clever and brave enough to start chasing riskier stuff. Investors in small-cap funds didn't get any compensatory extra return as a reward for taking on the risk of buying into smaller companies.

TIP

If you insist on buying small-company funds, buy at least two or three. That's because the managers of small-cap funds tend to be eccentric individuals who love poring over obscure little businesses and developing their own methods.

Managing small-cap funds is very personality-driven. Even an excellent manager can do terribly if their favourite type of stock is out of fashion. And don't forget that the small-cap sector has plenty of walking dead.

Regional Equity Funds: Welcome to Bangkok — or Hong Kong?

Funds that invest in limited areas of the world may sound like they're a good way to speculate. For instance, over the last decade, India's BSE SENSEX index has risen by 222 percent, pretty good when compared to the S&P 500's 154 percent gain. But single regions can also be extremely volatile, and often underperform — Britian's FTSE 100 Index has eked out a measly 16 percent gain since 2013, for example.

Funds that specialize in a particular area often suffer from the curse of all narrow investments, whether they invest in European, Asian, emerging markets, or in individual countries. These markets usually go into slumps. Japan is a good example — it's underperformed for decades. But then again, The Land of the Rising Sun has been one of the hotter markets of 2023, so you never know.

TIP

If you do want to go regional, you may try European funds with their giant blue-chip companies and then perhaps Asia–Pacific Rim. But you're probably better off with two or three global equity funds that hold assets in countries just about everywhere. Look at the holdings of nearly any big global equity fund and you see European and Asian stocks as well as U.S. names.

The pros aren't infallible, though, and they can easily get the mix of countries wrong. That's why it's important with global equity funds to watch out for managers who make big bets on a particular region or country, such as China or India.

The following is a quick rundown of the main types of regional foreign equity funds. We won't spend too much time on them — although we have to admit these narrow, specialized funds can be lots of fun.

European funds: Why are all these people so well dressed?

European funds invest almost entirely in major companies in big, stable European countries, so they're a sensible choice compared with most specialty funds. However, European stock markets have seriously lagged North America's for a number of years. International equity funds, which are mostly weighted to Europe, have returned just 2.3 percent annualized over the past five years. So think about these funds as a way to diversify away from possibly overpriced American mega-caps than to improve your overall returns.

REMEMBER

Don't bother trying to wager on currencies when you buy mutual funds — stick to rock climbing at night. The individual investor has little chance of predicting foreign exchange movements; even currency trading experts are challenged!

As always, if you do go into Europe, buy more than one fund so that a dog doesn't chew up your portfolio too badly. A simple way to do this is to buy one of the half-dozen European index funds available, as opposed to one of the hundred or so actively managed European equity funds. *Index funds* and ETFs buy every stock in a recognized market index or benchmark so that they earn returns in line with the broad stock market. An *actively managed fund,* which is the most common type of fund, buys and sells stocks in an attempt to select the best ones — but it runs the risk of making the wrong choices. European index funds track either single-country indices, such as the Financial Times Stock Exchange 100 (FTSE) in the United Kingdom or a pan-European index, such as the Euronext 100.

Asian funds: The dream that died

This is it — the biggest rollercoaster at the amusement park. A chart of the Asia–Pacific equity category's calendar-year returns since 1990 is littered with double-digit gains and double-digit losses. Returns have been modest of late; the category's median 10-year compound annual return was 3.8 percent as of late 2023.

On the face of it, Asia, which typically includes Asian countries except Japan, presents a pretty enticing investment pitch. The success of many Asian countries in escaping their post-colonial poverty and building modern economies has been a genuine miracle, one of humanity's greatest achievements. The region has pro-business governments (although often repressive) and an apparently insatiable desire to become as fat and self-satisfied as the West.

The region's main stock markets, including Hong Kong, are sometimes upstaged by the up-and-coming Shanghai exchange. You may have a hard time considering China a "developing" country — but it is still developing as rural people continue to migrate to cities. As a trip to most any North American shopping mall will remind you, China quickly has become a global economic powerhouse.

Economics and politics aside, it's hard to ignore Asia when investing outside Canada. But remember the last time you felt queasy on a rollercoaster? Investing in Asia likely will continue to be a wild ride, so tread lightly when considering an Asian fund investment. Or, again, consider doing so through a diversified global equity or international equity fund.

If you buy into Asia, your first choice is whether you want a fund that includes Japan or treats it as a completely separate market. No right or wrong answer exists here. Asian funds that also hold Japanese stocks represent a sort of handy one-stop-shopping investment in the Far East, much of which is an economic suburb of Japan anyway despite China's recent economic surge. But, arguably, a specialized manager located in Tokyo has a better chance of getting it right in such a distinctive country, as Japan marches to its own Kodo drumbeat.

A handful of "country" funds invest only in China, or India, or even a combination of the two. China's economy, of course, has taken off in recent years, and several China funds are available to Canadian investors. India is essentially a continent in its own right, with a potentially giant stock market that moves to its own rhythm. Likewise a handful of India-focused mutual funds are available in Canada.

Japanese, please: Once hot, now not

At the end of the 1980s, foreign investors in the then-red-hot Tokyo market reckoned that any price they paid for a stock was okay because the Japanese economy had moved to a new way of valuing assets. So, Nippon Telegraph traded at 100 times its profits in 1989, and people weren't worried — a bit like the way U.S. investors argued in early 2000 that they were being all prudent and careful when they paid 50 times earnings for a telephone-company stock because they were getting an "earnings yield" of two percent, which isn't far short of the one-year deposit rate. See "U.S. equity funds: Going for growth" in this chapter for an explanation of earnings yield and similar magic incantations.

But Japan crashed, as insane stock markets always do. By 1992, the Nikkei average of 225 big Japanese stocks had fallen by half from its highs of the late 1980s, and it went nowhere for the rest of the decade. The market made the occasional nice bounce off the bottom, but over the ten years from 1990 to 2000, the median Japanese fund produced a miserable median annual return of 5.3 percent. While matters have not gotten much better since, at the time of writing this chapter the country is looking more attractive than some other locales. In fact, the country's Nikkei 225 index is up 37 percent compared to the S&P 500's 24 percent gain. There are plenty of reasons for the climb: inflation is under control there, companies in the hot semiconductor sector are expanding operations in Japan and China-U.S. tensions are causing investors to look elsewhere in Asia for opportunities. Could this be the start of a new era in Japan? And do you want to make a bet that circumstances are finally turning around?

Think of it this way — Japan still is one of the world's biggest economies, a powerhouse of ingenuity and brilliant design. Everybody should have a small portion of their assets in the great Japanese global companies, such as Sony, Toyota Motor, and Mitsubishi. We suggest you do it by buying a couple of conservative global equity funds. As with other major economic regions of the world, most good global stock funds put at least some of their portfolio in Japan.

U.S. equity funds: Going for growth

U.S. stocks, especially the very large-cap kind, have been the driver of a great many investors' portfolio returns for the past 10 years and more. The performance of tech giants such as Apple, Microsoft, and Amazon — often referred to as the FAANG stocks or the "Magnificent Seven" — have pushed not only the S&P 500 index but most U.S. equity mutual funds ahead of other world markets over five- and 10-year periods. Some market watchers think U.S. stocks are now grossly overpriced and due for a fall. It's worth remembering the S&P 500 returned virtually nothing over the first decade of this century.

Maybe the good times will continue, or maybe U.S. stocks will become the greatest horror show in the history of investing as U.S. shares go on falling listlessly to earth. Unfortunately, you can't tell what will happen. Nonetheless, America is the engine of the world's economy, a magic lamp of creativity and intellect. It also represents more than half of global stock market capitalization. So you must have at least some of your savings there. But you don't have to buy regular U.S. equity funds that try to pick winning American stocks. Any sensible global equity fund owns plenty of U.S. companies, so owning a couple of those gives you American content. Add a U.S. equity index fund or ETF — one that tracks the entire U.S. market, usually by mimicking the famous Standard & Poor's index of 500 giant U.S. stocks — and you'll have collected plenty of Americana.

If you want the most diversification in a U.S. index fund, consider a fund that tracks the Russell 3000 index, a massively broad measure that includes just about every stock that matters in the United States, or an equal-weighted fund that divides your capital roughly equally among the S&P's 500 constituents. The idea is that if a long-term decline occurs in the huge blue-chip stocks, such as Microsoft Corp. and Apple that dominate the S&P 500, then you'll be hedging your bets by owning lots of smaller companies. Speaking of blue-chips, it doesn't get much bluer than the Dow Jones industrial average of 30 industrial stocks — even your aging Aunt Betty in North Bay has heard of "the Dow." If you like the familiarity, you can buy an index fund that tracks it, such as the imaginatively named TD Dow Jones Industrial Average Index fund.

U.S. equity funds are like any type of regional or otherwise overly-focused fund: You don't really have to own them. Any well-run global fund will contain a large number of U.S. stocks because America is just too dynamic to ignore.

Emerging markets funds: Fast growing or still struggling?

At least two-thirds of the world's population live in places such as Ghana and Malaysia, where industrial society and all of its plush comforts have yet to fully take root. But why invest there? The theory is that these economies are growing fast from a low level of activity, as opposed to the "mature" economies of the West. Fast growth means corporate profits that are rising quickly — and that's good for stocks, remember?

So these markets are supposed to give you higher long-term returns, at the cost of bigger price swings because shares in these strange places are relatively unstable and prone to dangers such as currency collapse (which nearly always happens, don't kid yourself).

Unfortunately, emerging markets have underperformed many other markets in recent years. The MSCI Emerging Markets Index has returned 5.4 percent annually after averaged over the past 10 years — index funds in that category are not far off that benchmark.

Bear in mind other complications with emerging markets, too. One minor difficulty: Managers don't agree on what constitutes a developing market. Some funds have a broad definition of what constitutes a developing market. For example, many emerging markets funds invest in Hong Kong–listed stocks — needless to say, a well-developed market — in addition to so-called "frontier markets" in the region such as Thailand and Vietnam. That produces a more conservative mixture of investments that can protect investors from some of the nasty drops in emerging markets. But it also could mean missing out on big rallies.

The big problem for investors in emerging markets funds is the tendency of nervous managers to slavishly buy the same few stocks around the world, often the telecom company, in whatever emerging markets they like. So buying two or even three emerging markets funds may not spread your risk as much as you may think — the portfolios often contain the same stuff. In fairness to managers, they're often forced to stick to one or two big stocks in a lot of developing countries because at least they know some sort of professional supervision of the corporate executives is happening, supplied by the other foreign investment managers who own the stock.

Don't get us wrong — we love emerging markets funds, but only as a form of amusement. We enjoy the potential for huge returns. But the evidence seems to be that as the world's markets become linked ever more closely, shares in developing markets are simply going to track those of rich countries. And most well-run global equity funds hold at least a few big companies in developing markets anyway, which further reduces your need to bother with a specialized emerging markets fund. Sure, put a small portion of your portfolio, at most a few percent, in these funds. But don't go banking on double-digit returns — they come along all too rarely.

WHAT EVER HAPPENED TO LATIN AMERICAN FUNDS?

One obvious emerging markets zone is Latin America. These funds at one time were numerous enough to justify a separate category. But investors were reluctant to put all their emerging markets eggs into one geographic basket. By mid-2002, many Latin American equity funds were showing double-digit losses on a ten-year compound annual basis. Fund companies, tired of the poor sales, began to shut down their Latin funds, rolling them into their existing emerging markets funds.

Sector Funds: Limitations Galore

Funds that buy stocks in just one industry or sector of the economy — for example, technology or resource funds — are bucking broncos, producing wild leaps and sickening plunges. That's because investors have a long-standing habit, as we've seen, of suddenly falling in love with a particular type of stock and then bidding those companies' shares to ridiculous prices.

A subset of sector funds are "thematic" funds that attempt to latch onto an area of rapid innovation or market growth. Currently hot categories include stocks benefiting from the proliferation of artificial intelligence (AI) and those mining or refining so-called critical minerals used in electric batteries essential to the global energy transition. The challenge here is that technology development is unpredictable. You can catch a secular tailwind or end up with the next decade's Betamax.

WARNING

Specialized funds are far more volatile than high-quality diversified equity funds that hold *all industries*, the first of our ABC rules in Chapter 10.

The volatility of these funds means they're essentially a gimmick, and not the place for your serious money. Still, they can be fun. Those who enjoy trading can use no-load sector funds as a cheap vehicle for jumping aboard a trend (or what they fondly hope is a trend). And some of the ideas that fund sellers have come up with are impressive: At the end of this section, we talk about some of the weirder sector and specialty funds.

But investors should consider only two types of sector funds:

>> Resource and precious metals funds may arguably have a place in the portfolios of those who are very worried about inflation.

>> Technology funds may be good long-term holdings because at least the companies they own are doing something new (although all too often lately it's dreaming up new ways to entice money out of investors).

Resource funds: Pouring money down a hole

Resource funds buy companies that used to be the backbone of Canada's economy: macho, doughnut-eating types that sell oil, forest products, minerals, and basic commodities such as aluminum. For complicated reasons to do with supply and demand, the prices for these commodities tend to be extremely volatile, often doubling or falling by half in a matter of months. That means the shares of resource companies are incredibly prone to swings.

Investors in resource companies must get used to living like teenagers in their first week in junior high. One day they're up, everyone loves them and their shares, and profits are rolling in as commodity prices rock. The next day, prices are down and suddenly everyone in the class thinks you're a freak.

Take oil, for example. Periodically since the 1970s, the producers have been able to get together and decide on production cuts or increases together (this is especially true for countries who are part of the Organization of the Petroleum Exporting Countries, which includes many middle eastern nations.) Oil company stocks duly rise accordingly. But it's pretty well a mug's game trying to predict when oil booms will come and go, and oil exploration companies have been abysmal at creating long-term wealth for their shareholders. When their shares rise, they tend to flood new share issues into the hot market to grab as much cash from investors as possible while the going is good — sorry, to raise capital for developing new reserves. Eventually, existing shareholders realize that, thanks a lot, they now must give some of the company's profits and dividends to all those scruffy new shareholders. Then oil prices tank again and, presto, oil stocks collapse.

While natural resource funds were big gainers in the first decade of this century, when there was talk of a "commodity supercycle," the last decade has been mostly a wash. Many Canadian energy companies have yet to regain their highs from before the 2014 oil price crash. Even gold seems to have lost its status as a safe haven in volatile markets and a hedge against inflation.

TIP

When you hear an old acquaintance talk about how the world's financial systems are going down and the need to hold precious metals, take it with a grain of salt.

Very conservative investors may want to put small amounts into a couple of diversified resource funds, perhaps a couple of percent of one's portfolio in each fund, or even a couple of gold funds. That's because resource stocks can act as portfolio insurance — commodity prices move in their own weird cycles, and sometimes in the opposite direction to stocks in general.

Before you rush to buy into resource stocks, or catch the gold bug a little too late, consider a much simpler and somewhat less risky way to invest in these markets: Just buy a Canadian equity fund, large-cap or small (see Chapters 10 and 11). If you do decide to buy resource funds, try to buy two with very different portfolio mixtures of forestry, energy, mining, and other commodities. That way, if one manager crashes and burns, the other may make it. And if you buy into gold funds, make sure you hold at least two, because managers can easily miss out on the very hottest mining stocks that are leading the whole group higher. Remember, with most precious metals funds you are buying mining companies, not bullion.

Science and technology funds: But how will you control it, Professor?

Technology funds can buy virtually anything as long as it has something to do with computers, alternative energy, biotechnology, or research. But they're really just super-high-growth equity funds that hold fancy companies trading at Versace-type prices. Like other sector-specific funds, technology funds get popular in waves. These waves tend to break when stock prices lose touch with fundamental attributes such as sales and earnings growth.

Some people argue that's the case with technology stocks right now. What makes this area a tricky place to invest is that many technology stocks are not yet profitable. You would think at some point investors will want their companies to make money. If that time comes, and these businesses aren't growing as planned, they will fall hard. Don't say we didn't warn you.

TIP

If you decide to buy a straight science and technology fund — and we advise against it for most investors because of the excessive risk — limit your investment to less than five percent of your total fund holdings.

Some people reckon they've got a pretty good nose when it comes to technology, which lets them predict which industries will do best next. In that case, you could select more specialized types of tech funds, such as an AI fund, which gives you "exposure" (money management slang for a chance to profit from something) to the software and semiconductor companies trying to take this tech to another level.

Technology fund managers like to put on statesmanlike, long-term faces and predict that the companies in their portfolios today will be the giant household names of tomorrow. They may have a point, and these companies can have many years of exponential growth ahead of them. So there can be a good case for holding a tech fund if you're investing for long periods of, say, ten years or more. But a few good global and Canadian equity funds, including index funds, own plenty of the big tech stocks that show up in specialized technology funds — so, once again, you are probably well covered by simply sticking with your core equity funds. As with so many other specialty funds, buy these only for fun. And get ready to take some spills along the way.

WARNING

Beware of markets in which people buy for trading, not for owning. They have a nasty habit of collapsing.

Financial services funds: Buying the banks doesn't always pay

Everybody hates the banks — except as investments, it seems. The Canadian financial services sector is dominated by the huge Big Five banks and several mammoth life insurance companies. Indeed, these institutions are almost as big a driver of the Canadian stock market as resource companies. However, most funds in the financial services category invest globally, so you are buying into not just Canadian institutions but U.S. and overseas ones as well. So if you want to buy Canadian financials, stick to the Canadian equity category — which, as we keep preaching, is a better place to be anyway.

Canada's financial sector has basically been flat in 2023, and has produced only modest gains over the past five years, trailing the broad market average. But the sector is a generous payer of dividends. And Canadian funds in this sector have fared better, more or less, than their global and U.S. counterparts, which strengthens the case to buy Canadian in this sector.

If you insist on focusing on the Canadian financials rather than participating in this sector through a diversified Canadian equity fund, you can buy the iShares Canadian Financial Monthly Income ETF. Its 10-year compound annual return as of late 2023 was 6.4 percent.

IN THIS CHAPTER

» Using balanced funds as a wonderfully simple all-in-one solution

» Avoiding excessive prices, confusion, and unnecessary risk

» Picking the right Canadian balanced funds

» Covering your risk with global balanced funds — the perfect investment?

» Taking a flyer on tactical balanced funds

Chapter **13**

Balanced Funds: Boring Can Be Good

E ver have a really good shawarma — a Middle Eastern lunch wrap packed with spices, tasty meat, and fresh veggies? Remember the wonderful numb feeling of fullness afterward? Balanced funds are supposed to be a satisfying all-in-one meal like that. You hand your money over to the fund company or bank, and they make all the decisions. A *balanced fund* is a nice broad mixture of many types of investment — the idea being that it'll never lose too much money. The manager usually invests the fund in a cautious blend of stocks, which are tiny pieces of ownership of companies, and long-term and short-term bonds, which are debts owed by governments and companies.

Balanced funds are investment products you buy when you want nice, steady returns of around four to seven percent per year while avoiding losses as much as possible. They're one of the mutual fund industry's most useful inventions and an excellent place for the nervous beginner to get going.

In this chapter, we introduce you to the main types of balanced funds, explain why they're a great way to start off in investing, and warn you about the problems you may encounter. Because these funds may contain a wide variety of assets, it's important to understand how they are categorized: Canadian or global? Neutral or leaning towards equities or fixed income? And with their broad horizons and discretionary allocations, there is the potential for them to charge high fees. This chapter points out the aspects to look for and kinds of funds to avoid.

Understanding Balanced Funds

Balanced funds are for busy people who want a one-decision product they can buy and forget about. Imagine your family had a trusted lawyer or accountant who took care of all your investing needs — the professional, if they were at all sensible, would end up putting the money into a thoughtful blend of bonds and stocks, with a healthy cushion of cash to further reduce risk. That's the essence of a balanced fund — it includes a little bit of everything so that losses can be kept to a minimum if one type of investment falls in value.

Balanced funds, which have been around since the dawn of the fund industry in the 1920s in one form or another, have attracted billions of dollars in recent years as confused investors decide to let someone else pick the right mix for their savings. In 2022, balanced funds represented just under half of all mutual fund assets in Canada, worth $886 billion. That compares with $651 billion (36 percent) invested in equity funds. (These figures are from the Investment Funds Institute of Canada, which represents most mutual fund sponsors.)

Reviewing the asset mix of balanced funds

For most investors, a balanced fund should be a ready-made cautious investment portfolio. Yes, it may lose money — nothing is absolutely safe in investing — but it's unlikely to drop as much as 10 percent in a year (2022 was an exception!). Just check the fund's mix of assets at the fund company's website or in its handouts. If the fund holds plenty of bonds and cash, it's probably safe enough to buy.

Happily, the knowledgeable and practical folks who supervise the classification of Canadian investment funds into various asset categories, the Canadian Investment Funds Standards Committee, several years ago split the unwieldy Canadian balanced and global balanced categories each into three subsets. The following categories help investors immediately identify a fund's asset mix:

>> **Equity balanced funds** have at least 60 percent of their portfolio in equities.

>> **Fixed-income balanced funds** have no more than 40 percent of their portfolio in equities.

>> **Neutral balanced funds** have between 40 and 60 percent of their portfolio in equities.

To keep matters simple, in this chapter we primarily refer to the middle-of-the-road Canadian neutral balanced category.

An old rule states that your portfolio's weighting in bonds plus cash should equal your age. If we assume the average Canadian balanced fund has 54 percent in stocks and 46 percent in guaranteed investments such as bonds and cash, then most neutral balanced funds are suitable for investors aged about 46.

TIP

If you're younger than 46, look for a slightly more aggressive mix in an equity balanced fund, and if you're older, try to find a fixed income balanced fund that appeals to you.

Plodding along profitably

The good news is that Canadian balanced funds have done a pretty good job of avoiding — or at least limiting — losses. The 2022 calendar year was unique. Both the stock and bond markets experienced a downturn, leading to fund losses virtually across the board. But years like that come along only every 30 years or so. A more common scenario is that of 2018 when stocks lost money, bonds gained slightly, and most balanced funds came close to breaking even. (The median Canadian neutral balanced fund lost 1.85 percent.) Even factoring in 2022, the six balanced fund categories tracked by investment research firm Morningstar saw between four percent and 6.6 percent average annual returns over the 15 years to December 31, 2022.

In terms of a global balanced fund — a type of fund we really like because it provides as much diversification as possible within a single fund — the cushioning effect of bond market exposure is even more noticeable. In 2018, the median global neutral balanced fund declined just 0.41 percent amid much higher losses for equity funds.

Now, we know that, over the years, a few weak balanced funds got lost in the shuffle after they were merged into better funds. The fund industry, always remember, has a habit of quietly folding under performers into its stars, cancelling the dogs' years of terrible returns. For example, Fidelity in the mid-1990s took a weak balanced fund and popped it inside its huge Fidelity Canadian Asset Allocation Fund. The old fund's poor returns vanished forever. It's always possible that you'll find yourself stuck in a similar underperformer. To minimize that risk, the best solution of all is to hold two balanced funds so that your entire portfolio doesn't suffer from weakness in one fund. (Morningstar calculates rates of return that overcome this data weakness — known to data geeks and analysts as *survivorship bias* — with its Morningstar fund indices.)

REMEMBER

Don't worry: Despite the broad licence many fund managers have taken in their definition, balanced funds are all about simplicity. Until you make up your mind about your long-term investing plans, you'll almost certainly do fine over three to five years by simply buying a regular balanced fund, or two for more safety, and then forgetting about them.

Retiring with balanced funds

If you really want to adopt a simple approach, use balanced funds in your Registered Retirement Savings Plan (RRSP) — a special account in which investment gains add up without being taxed until you take them out, usually at retirement (see Chapter 22). Balanced funds are a nice cautious mix, just the factor you want for your life savings. Younger investors can be more aggressive, putting nearly all their money into stocks, but above the age of 35, it's a wise idea to own bonds as well. Nothing is forever. If you decide later that you want something else in your RRSP, maybe because the balanced fund you picked turned out to be a dog, then it should be a simple matter to shift the money to another fund or funds within the same RRSP or to another RRSP account without incurring taxes.

So if you just want a simple investment to buy and forget, go for one or two balanced funds. A balanced fund has a single unit value that's published daily, making the value of your holdings easy to check. Its return appears in fund statements every month and online every day. And the performance is also published clearly by the fund company or should be. As with any regular mutual fund, if you bought a pooch the whole world can see, the fund manager will be under pressure to improve it.

Steering clear of potholes: Consistently strong returns

Balanced fund managers' scaredy-cat caution has served investors well. Balanced funds have generated nice steady returns, just as they're supposed to. But remember that balanced funds — and all other investors who own bonds — had a wind at their backs up until the 2010s, because the drop in inflation made bonds steadily more valuable. (See Chapter 14 for more on bonds.) Then inflation hit in 2022, which led the Bank of Canada to rapidly increase its benchmark interest rate and precipitated a decline in bond values. The Canadian consumer price index jumped to eight percent during the second quarter. For the year, the median Canadian fixed-income fund fell nearly 11 percent, while Canadian Equity funds dropped just over five percent.

If we move into an era of deflation (that is, falling prices), bonds will almost certainly become increasingly more valuable because the value of their steady payouts of cash rises consistently. In that case, which unfortunately can involve a very painful recession, balanced funds can easily outperform stock funds.

REMEMBER

Whatever happens, the point remains: A balanced fund is a safe spot for your money, leaving you to get on with your life.

Taking a look at one balanced biggie

Take a look at the biggest Canadian neutral balanced fund, Royal Bank of Canada's RBC Balanced Fund, to get an idea of how a traditional balanced fund works. In mid-2023, this fund had $4.3 billion in assets. Remember, that's more than a million dollars 4,300 times over — so obviously the bank has been delivering something that Mr. and Ms. Canada want: an attractive rate of return with minimal losses.

Here's a breakdown of the fund's assets:

» 34 percent in Canadian stocks

» 26 percent in shares outside Canada

» 36 percent in bonds

» 2 percent in real estate

» 1.4 percent in cash

The fund has a one-year gain of 5.8 percent as of fall 2023, putting it in the top-performing quartile among Canadian neutral balanced funds. At 4.4 percent, however, its ten-year compound annual return lagged that of the median fund in the category. Overall, though, it was a typical balanced fund: a solid investment that's fine for your portfolio if one of your key objectives is security.

Reviewing the Problems with Balanced Funds

Balanced funds, both Canadian and global, have their problems. Their fees and expenses, though lower than they were before the advent of competing ETFs, are still too lavish, which scythes into investors' already modest returns. Fund companies have come up with their usual bewildering variety of products and combinations of products, waving magic wands and muttering incantations that invoke the gods of portfolio theory and the "efficient frontier." It may all be true, but one thing's for sure: You're paying for it. All balanced products are basically porridge. Returns from their different investments are mixed together in a gooey mess, so judging exactly how well the manager did on which asset is hard.

High fees and expenses

The costs and fees charged to balanced fund unitholders are just too high. Fund companies already run big equity and bond funds, paying the salaries and expenses of the people who manage them, and they usually get those people to help select the stuff in their balanced funds. How much extra work is involved in that? The bond manager basically just does the same job again with their portion of the balanced fund, and the equity manager does the same. Some old geezer decides what the asset mix will be, and you're away to the races. As Table 13-1 shows, the median Canadian neutral balanced fund vacuums up 1.65 percent of its investors' money each year, almost as bad as the 2-percent-plus charged by the average Canadian equity fund.

TABLE 13-1   ## Balanced Fund MERs

Category (Mutual Funds Only)	Median MER
Canadian equity balanced	1.72
Canadian neutral balanced	1.65
Canadian fixed income balanced	1.36
Global equity balanced	1.75
Global neutral balanced	1.64
Global fixed income balanced	1.48

The long-term annual return from balanced funds may be only about six percent, or even less. The long term, incidentally, means the rest of our lives, as economists like to say (it's the only joke they know).

Say inflation and taxes combined take four percent out of your annual six percent — then your real return is down to around two percent. So, for a tax-paying account, most of your real return from a balanced fund such as Royal Bank's giant may go into fund expenses and fees.

Bewildering brews of assets

Fund companies know that many of their customers just want simple solutions they can buy and never look at again. So they've come up with a bewildering array of balanced combinations in which you can buy their wares. See Chapter 20 on fund packages for more. Many of these arrangements, such as AGF's "Elements" wrap accounts, have their own unit values, making them look very much like mutual funds themselves. By Morningstar's count, about 1,000 Canadian and global balanced funds are out there.

Difficulty judging fund manager performance

A big difficulty with balanced funds, or any kind of casserole that you buy from a fund company, is that you may have a hard time knowing just what the manager did right or wrong. They may have blown it in bonds, or struck out in stocks, but you can't work it out from the comfortable-looking (you hope) overall return number that the company publishes. Some fund companies provide a commentary that at least gives you a clue as to what went right and what exploded in the manager's shiny little face. For many customers that's fine, because they couldn't care less what went on inside the fund as long as the return is reasonably good. And that's a perfectly sensible approach to take if you don't have the time or interest to look further into mutual funds. But balanced funds are opaque and mysterious, violating one of the huge virtues of mutual funds — the ability to check on performance easily.

Because checking where balanced funds' profits come from is difficult, picking the right fund is harder than it is to pick funds in other categories. In other words, you won't get a clear answer to this crucial question: How much risk did the manager take? Here's an extreme example of two imaginary funds to help illustrate the point.

Say you're trying to choose between two balanced funds:

>> The Tasmanian Devil Fund, which made an average 11 percent over the past ten years, enough to turn $10,000 into $28,394

>> The Mellow Llama Fund, which made nine percent a year and turned $10,000 into $23,674, or almost $5,000 less than the Tasmanian Devil

What if the Devil Fund made its bigger profits by buying bonds and shares issued by risky little technology companies, whereas the Llama Fund owned shares and bonds from big and stable companies and governments? Most balanced fund investors would choose the second fund, because the danger of it crashing and losing, say, half of its value in a year is so much less.

The Devil Fund, with its volatile but high-profit-potential stocks, may be suitable for an investor who doesn't need the money for years and can afford to take risks now. But it's not the right fund for an investor who may need the money at any time.

A Simple Plan for Picking the Right Canadian Balanced Fund

When selecting a balanced fund, you needn't get all worked up about picking the right one. Like money market and bond funds, many balanced funds resemble one another. They're run cautiously, remember, so you're unlikely to go too far wrong.

WARNING

Too many investors make one classic mistake that has cost millions of dollars: Failing to think twice before buying a balanced fund run by the people who also manage your stock fund. First, it will almost certainly be skewed toward equities. Second, within the fund's equity section, you'll likely be putting too many eggs in one basket within the fund's equity section. Naturally, the managers will tend to select the same shares for both funds, and if they get that wrong, then both of your funds will be poor performers.

We frequently refer to the neutral categories in this chapter because we feel these represent the only true, traditional balanced funds — the type that provide the uninspiring but steady performance making these funds so popular and fundamental to the average Canadian investor.

Knowing what to avoid

Be careful with balanced funds that don't include just about every industry in their list of stock holdings. After all, if they are truly "balanced," the balance should extend across industry sectors (and, in the case of bonds, maturity dates).

Consider the fate of investors in the Mackenzie Ivy Growth and Income Fund — with assets of about $2.3 billion, one of the biggest Canadian balanced funds in mid-2008. The fund was very overweight in consumer staples stocks, which took a beating during the first half of 2008. ("Overweight" refers to its position relative to that of the benchmark index, the S&P/TSX composite, which had just 2.2 percent of its constituent stocks in the consumer staples group as of mid-2008.) As a result, the fund lost four percent during that period, while the median Canadian equity balanced fund slipped 0.4 percent.

Identifying the best funds

Relax: Picking a good-quality Canadian balanced fund is surprisingly easy. Easier, anyway, than getting a cranky, tired child into a snowsuit at seven a.m. Look for the following:

>> **A wide asset mix to reduce the fund's risk of loss:** Under the industry's agreed definition, a middle-of-the-road (that is, neutral) balanced fund should have at least 40 percent of its portfolio anchored in cash or bonds or other liquid short-term securities. (*Liquidity* is a measure of how easy it is to sell an investment without suffering a significant loss.)

>> **Low expenses:** This is important because returns are relatively modest with this type of fund. Try to choose a fund or funds with annual expenses lower than the median 2.3 percent for Canadian neutral balanced funds.

Looking at some high-quality balanced funds

In this section, we list the picks of the litter in Canadian balanced funds. Because being obsessive about costs is essential when buying this type of fund, we limit the sample to funds with modest annual fees and expenses.

Remember, though, if inflation and/or interest rates rise abruptly, then even the most boring of Canadian balanced funds will probably lose money. That's because the value of both their stock and bond portfolios will almost certainly go on the slide at the same time.

Here are a few high-quality Canadian balanced funds, chosen with the help of analysts at Morningstar:

>> **Scotia Canadian Balanced Fund** has been an above-average performer in the Canadian neutral balanced category every one of the last 10 years. Morningstar gives it five stars with a silver medal rating. Marketed by Scotiabank and managed by boutique firm 1832 Asset Management, it has a track record going back all the way to 1990 and a reasonable 1.06 percent management expense ratio. In terms of strategy, the management team led by Don Simpson sticks mostly to the middle of the road, with strong representation by big banks and other financial stocks in the equity portion. The managers have the leeway to adjust the allocation between stocks and bonds according to their outlook. They seek to strike a balance between dividend and interest income and capital growth.

>> **RBC Managed Payout Solution** is a fixed income balanced fund targeted at conservative investors and estate funds, so its historical returns don't impress at first glance. But with a surprisingly low management expense ratio for its category, just 0.74 percent, it's nevertheless managed to outperform its peers in both good markets and bad. Currently managed by RBC vice-president and senior portfolio manager, Investment Solutions Sarah Riopelle, it's designed to generate income for unitholders in a tax-efficient way in unregistered accounts. Morningstar rates the fund gold with five stars. This may be a good, safe fund to complement a more adventurous equity balanced or straight equity fund.

>> **PH&N Monthly Income** is a balanced fund aimed at retirees with an ample income stream exceeding four percent per year. Indeed, it's designed to crank out payouts for its holders every month, if necessary through return of capital. But that is seldom the case. It was a top performer in both 2021 and 2022 — very different years in the markets — which earned it a gold medal rating and five stars from Morningstar. With 64 percent of its assets currently in equities and nearly 10 percent in high-yield bonds, senior portfolio manager Scott Lysakowski, head of RBC's PH&N Canadian equity team, shows he's not afraid to dabble in higher-risk, higher return assets. The fund's annual expenses are just 0.82 percent — about half the 1.65 percent charged by the median fund in the category.

Global Balanced Funds — As Good as It Gets?

Those who want to chase (possibly) higher returns outside Canada while spreading their wealth over a huge range of investments may want to explore *global balanced funds*, which, like Canadian balanced funds, come in three varieties: equity balanced, neutral balanced, and fixed-income balanced. (For definitions of each of those categories, see "Understanding Balanced Funds" in this chapter.)

REMEMBER

As always, check the top holdings in the portfolio of a global balanced fund. If they're not mostly stocks and bonds issued by giant companies that you've already heard of, plus bonds from countries such as the United States, Germany, and Japan, then look elsewhere. Why take a risk on low-quality investments?

Like their Canadian counterparts, global balanced funds pull off the trick of buying a bit of everything, but the fact that they do it globally gives you even more diversification and the potential for higher returns.

TIP

Insisting on low costs is important with any balanced fund, Canadian or global, because so much of the portfolio is made up of steady-but-dull bonds and cash, and that keeps annual gains down. So if you want to be left with a decent return, you can't pay too much.

The median global neutral balanced fund hits its investors for 1.64 percent in expenses each year. That MER works out to $82 annually on a $5,000 investment. Some global balanced funds charge well above that, in excess of two percent. These include funds with fancy features, such as *segregated funds* — funds that provide guarantees to refund some or all your original investment after ten years or to pay at least that much to your heirs, even if the fund has in fact produced a loss. These guaranteed or "segregated" funds may give you enormous satisfaction in knowing your money is protected. For that reason, thousands of people buy them. But, like the overpriced extended warranty that pushy electronics sales-people try to get you to buy, such guarantees are usually not worth paying for on something as stable as a balanced fund, which rarely loses money. (We tell the whole story on segregated funds in Chapter 19.)

REMEMBER

Few funds of any sort lose money over ten years (except for the speculative gamblers' funds we look at in Chapter 12), and that means the guarantee is of limited value. So to keep costs down and returns up, look for a global balanced fund with an MER lower than the median 1.64 percent.

Going global: A near-perfect investment?

If you had to invest money in a single fund without ever moving it or looking at it, some kind of global balanced fund with low expenses would make sense. The global balanced fund has finally caught the imagination of Canadian investors, with the number of these funds nearly tripling in this century's first decade. The majority of these assets, happily, are in the global neutral balanced category.

In some ways, the dull old global balanced fund is the perfect mutual fund. Look at the portfolio of any sophisticated, wealthy investor and it almost certainly contains stocks from all over the world plus bonds, with the safety cushion of a little cash. That's what a global balanced fund provides for the average person. It offers instant access to a professionally chosen mixture of investments that should produce a consistent return on their money while staying clear of market gambles. Nearly every major fund seller sells some sort of global balanced fund, and it's a simple matter of dumping your money in and forgetting about it.

Over the short term — particularly in recent years — relying on a global balanced fund to address all your investing needs may not seem so shrewd. A big risk attached to a global balanced fund, as with any foreign fund, is the possibility that Canada's economy, and with it the loonie, will prosper relative to the United States and other countries. It hasn't happened lately, but for an example, just look back to the aughts (2000 to 2009), a time of stagnation for the all-powerful U.S. stock markets. That's why it's almost certainly a good idea to own Canadian assets, too.

Examining a couple of world-beaters

In this section, we highlight a couple of high-quality investments that are unlikely to lead you far astray. But bear in mind that any fund can go into a slump because the manager made a bad call. And buying a global balanced fund is always a compromise because you cannot know exactly what sort of assets you'll end up owning or how precisely the manager produced their returns. A balanced fund is for investors who just want a quick, instant solution.

Here are a couple of global balanced funds with low MERs favoured by Morningstar:

>> **Fidelity Balanced Portfolio** is an index-beating balanced fund that's also outperformed the category average in eight of the past 10 years (and its underperformance in 2016 and 2021 resembled a rounding error). It has a moderate investment turnover rate of 22 percent per year, which doubtless helps it keep its management expense ratio reasonable at 1.09 percent. If you bought it in 2013 and just let it compound for 10 years, you'd have more than doubled your money. Portfolio managers David Wolf and David Tulk, who both previously worked at the Bank of Canada, make use of derivatives such as currency forwards and tactical asset allocation to manage risk and juice returns. Morningstar gives the fund a silver medal rating and five stars.

>> **Dynamic Global Yield Private Pool** has a very competitive MER at 0.9 percent. Yet it's outperformed both the average among its peers and its benchmark index over three- and five-year periods to autumn 2023. Asset manager Dynamic Funds employs a large management team with expertise in various asset classes and geographies. Veteran team leader David Fingold favours stocks with high free cash flow generation, dividend growth, and strong balance sheets.

WHERE DID ALL THE INCOME BALANCED FUNDS GO?

As inflation and interest rates tumbled in the 1990s and stayed near historic lows for many years, older people who were trying to live off their savings have had to cope with an unpleasant reality. With inflation below three percent, the rates seniors got on their GICs and other accounts were at a subsistence level of no more than two percent — and, as interest income, it's fully taxable. That's one of the drawbacks of low inflation: It leaves those who live on a fixed income high and dry. When inflation rose rapidly in 2022, few deposit rates were yet above four percent. As of 2023, they are higher, prompting a turning of the tide as investors rushed back into interest-bearing accounts, though it's not known for how long.

Regardless, the mutual fund industry has benefited from a huge invasion of "GIC refugees" since the mid-1990s. The companies' little elves figured out a way to deliver one of the gifts these people held dear: a nice regular income deposit. The problem was that mutual funds aren't really designed for producing a predictable spinoff of cash — or, at least, enough cash to satisfy investors, especially when companies take out MERs of up to two percent to pay the managers and provide forage for brokers. Finding top-quality bonds or shares that had a high enough yield to satisfy everyone was hard. All the good stuff had been driven up to such high prices by other investors hungry for a stream of cash.

Thus was born the *income balanced fund,* an odd hybrid that's usually designed not only to throw off plenty of interest and dividends, but also to gain or at least hold its value over the long term. For example, an income balanced fund may try to generate monthly payments of $50, or $600 a year, for an investor who held $10,000 worth of the fund. That's a yield of six percent annually, but some funds chase even higher rates of up to nine or 10 percent. To produce this income while also holding its value in the face of inflation, the fund buys a mixture of bonds, shares, and other sorts of investments that pay out cash. The new fund managers were turned loose like hungry bears to grab and eat anything in the world — animal, vegetable, or mineral — that threw off a decent stream of interest or dividend payments. The shortage of good-quality investments producing a decent yield became so acute that many of these managers have been obliged to move down the food chain. They had to buy *income trusts* as well as *real estate trusts* and similar funds that invest in other stuff. These trusts are sort of like mutual funds themselves, but they hold a narrow collection of properties, such as a few power stations, gas wells, or other relatively dull and predictable businesses.

But as income balanced funds snowballed in number, they eventually needed to be classified in different ways. They're now scattered across several categories, including Canadian dividend and income, Canadian income trusts, and the two fixed income balanced categories. See Chapter 16 for more on dividend and income funds, and income trust funds.

Tactical Balanced Funds: Pay Me to Lose Your Money

Tactical balanced funds, also known as asset allocation funds, are the unruly younger brothers of balanced funds — given the freedom to raise hell by dumping all their bonds or stocks, and to chase hot returns with lopsided portfolios. ("Tactical" simply means that the fund makes short-term bets on moves in the different asset classes every few months. The conventional balanced fund categories, on the other hand, contain funds with *strategic* portfolios, which usually means a manager adheres to a rigid asset-allocation mandate over the years as required by the fund's stated investment mandate.)

These are funds that move between different types of investments and take bigger risks than regular balanced funds, all in an attempt to earn fatter returns. For example, a fund of this type may sell nearly all its bonds and seek big profits with a portfolio that's made up almost entirely of shares. Or it may even move heavily into a volatile area of the stock market such as technology stocks. The idea is that the manager is smart and lucky enough to anticipate big swings in the prices of financial assets — history shows, though, that very few people can pull off that trick consistently.

All flash and no pan: Looking at asset allocation returns and management styles

History has shown that tactical asset allocation funds seldom perform any better than index and balanced funds in general.

A few star performers shine among tactical balanced funds run by managers who have managed to consistently generate returns in the top half of the pack — including the $3.2-billion Fidelity Tactical High Income Fund, which has been a top-quartile performer every year since 2018. Other strong five-year performers include

>> Dynamic Strategic Yield Class funds

>> Canoe Asset Allocation Portfolio Class funds

>> Manulife Tactical Income Fund

Ultimately, these funds basically represent an opportunity to watch someone mess around with your money. That's fine if you trust the company and the warty old wizard or witch mixing up the ingredients in the cauldron, but remember that the less balanced a portfolio, the greater the exposure to loss if the main asset class goes into a slump.

Who's running this crazy show?

Much as we'd love to portray tactical balanced fund managers as rebels loading up their funds with junk bonds and cannabis stocks, in reality, they're pretty similar to balanced fund managers. A major fund seller is unlikely to let an asset allocation fund slide off the road completely because the manager took crazy bets.

In fact, the typical tactical balanced fund's asset allocation isn't that different from what you'd find in a neutral balanced fund. However, the median tactical fund comes with a higher MER than its staid cousin.

REMEMBER

The bottom line on asset allocation funds: Put your money in one if you find regular balanced funds too boring but get ready to pay more in fees — and be prepared to lose if the manager gets it wrong.

IN THIS CHAPTER

» **Understanding why bonds are beneficial**

» **Deciding how much you need to invest in bonds and other fixed-income securities**

» **Picking a quality bond fund**

» **Knowing how inflation and interest rates affect bonds**

» **Avoiding management costs with bond index funds**

» **Being bold with long-term bond funds**

» **Playing it safe with short-term bond funds**

» **Taking a risk on high-yield bond funds**

» **Going global by considering foreign fixed-income funds**

Chapter **14**

Bond Funds: Boring Can Be Sexy, Too

uying a *bond* means you're lending money to the government or company that issued the bond. The word "bond" means promise, indicating the borrowers have given their word they'll be around to pay interest and refund the loan. All you're really entitled to get back are the periodic interest payments plus the return of all your money when the debt comes due.

Dull, huh? Bond funds simply hold a bunch of these loans, collecting the interest cheques and cashing in the bonds when they mature. That means bond funds tend to plod along with modest returns, while stocks fly and crash from year to year. Equity (or stock market) funds, with their promise of apparently limitless growth, just seem so much more exciting. But remember that bonds along with stocks represent the two main financial assets you can invest in for the long term — while a little bit of cash on the side is an essential safety valve for nearly any portfolio.

In this chapter, we explain why it's wise to own at least one bond fund, show you how to pick a good one, and help you work out how much you need to invest in bonds.

Some Great Reasons to Choose Bonds

Almost any sophisticated investor's holdings should include a good leavening of bonds because betting the whole wad on shares is just too risky. That's because it exposes your entire savings to nasty losses if the stock market turns down. Some fund salespeople and diehard stock market players used to strut and boast that "I've never owned a bond," but they miss out on the advantages bonds offer.

Offering greater security than equities

Stocks are generally acknowledged to have better long-term performance than bonds. Between 2013 and 2023, the S&P Canada Aggregate Bond Index posted an average annual total return of just 1.78 percent, compared to a 7.24 percent return for the S&P/TSX Composite, the country's preeminent stock index. However, that time frame, during which bond yields started at historic lows and ended above five percent, was an extraordinarily awful one for bonds. Returns in the future are likely to be higher, as they were in the more distant past.

TECHNICAL STUFF

The S&P Canada Aggregate Bond Index tracks a combination of Canadian bonds, including federal, provincial, municipal, and investment-grade corporate bonds that mature in more than one year. There are other indices of Canadian bonds used by index funds, such as the FTSE Canada Universe Bond Index and the Solactive Broad Canadian TR Index but their price behaviour is similar.

Bonds have done particularly poorly in recent years, beset by rising inflation and interest rates. Depending on the index used, Canadian bonds posted negative total returns for three consecutive calendar years: 2021, 2022, and 2023. But that's a historical anomaly. Historically, fixed income can be counted on to generate positive returns in excess of eight out of every 10 years, and almost always during years when stock markets decline.

But numbers aside, here's why you must own some bonds or bond funds: Lending your money short-term, by popping it into a bank deposit or account, doesn't pay you enough. Okay, so you can invest most of your money in the stock market, but that's a recipe for losing most of your pile if the market goes into a huge dive. So we all should leave a portion on long-term loan to big, secure governments and companies. And the way to do that is to buy their bonds, which are essentially certificates representing interest-paying loans to the corporations or governments that issued the bonds.

Stocks can go into a slump for years. American investors still refer to the first 10 years of the new millennium as a "lost decade." From the start of January 2000 through December 2009, the S&P 500 lost 2.72 percent annually in price terms. Even including dividends, the index lost money — 0.95 percent per year, on average.

It can be worse — remember Japan and the way its market hit a euphoric peak in 1989? The country has never been the same since, producing decent returns only sporadically. (Refer to Chapter 12 for more about Japan's market woes.)

You could also lose your job, have legal troubles, or run into some disaster right in the middle of a periodic stock market slump. It would be ugly to be forced to tap into your serious money just after it's been carved up by a stock sell-off. So own some bonds. They serve as a giant, reassuring outrigger for your canoe, producing steady returns while holding their value.

Increasing their value against deflation

Companies and individuals all over the world are getting smarter and more efficient all the time and are producing goods and services at ever-lower prices. While inflation has been on the rise lately, for a while there was genuine concern that we may enter an era of actual falling prices, or *deflation*. If that happened, bonds and cash would be likely to hold their value or even rise in price because the value of money will be rising (*inflation*, the opposite scenario, simply means that money is losing its purchasing power). In other words, deflation is a weird *Through the Looking Glass* world in which cash under the mattress becomes a solid investment that produces a real return.

Does a world of falling prices sound incredible? It's been happening all around us for years in computers and smartphones, where prices drop and processing power increases every few months. Energy prices slumped in 2014 as so-called "fracking" operations flooded the market with oil and gas from previously inaccessible reserves. Granted, an economy-wide slump in prices hasn't happened since The Great Depression of the 1930s, so nobody knows what it would be like — or what would happen to equity markets. But falling prices squeeze corporate profit margins like a vise, and declining profits are like rat poison for stocks. From September 1929 to July 1932, as the Depression got going, the Dow fell by almost 90 percent. We wish that was a typographical error, but it's not. The Dow dropped to 41 from 381.

To use a more recent example, the Dow lost 52 percent during the global financial crisis between its high in October 2007 and March 2009. The more representative S&P 500, which didn't exist during the Great Depression, fell 48 percent in the six months leading up to March 9, 2009. Canada's S&P/TSX Composite, meanwhile, lost fully half its value between June 2008 and the market bottom the following March. If you want your portfolio to avoid this fate, own some bonds.

How Much Do I Need in Bonds?

Take the old rule — that your weighting in cash and bonds should equal your age — as a starting point. For example, if you are 40 years old, then 40 percent of your savings should be in fixed-income stuff, such as bonds. If you're feeling daring, bring it down to 30 percent, or even 25 percent if you insist. But any lower than that and the volatility of your portfolio — a fancy word for the yearly up-and-down changes in the market value of your holdings — starts going off the scale. In other words, if you own only stocks, you're betting a lot of your wealth on swings in just one asset.

If you haven't lived through a grinding, decade-long bear market in stocks, you may be hazy on the value of a bond and think that stocks will always pull you through. Indeed, between about 2009 and 2022, when bonds paid almost nothing, many financial experts wondered very loudly whether investors needed any fixed income in their portfolio at all. In 2022 and 2023, however, yields climbed and stocks were volatile, making people embrace bonds once again.

Going forward, the risk of a long-term slump in equities means that if you're in your 20s, it's probably safe to hold one-fifth of your portfolio in bonds; in your 30s, hold one-third or less in fixed income; in your 40s, hold 40 percent in bonds; in your 50s, hold half your dough in cash and bonds; and in your 60s go toward two-thirds of your portfolio in bonds. Begin with the age rule and then take the cash-plus-bonds weighting up or down depending on your personality.

If you already have or will have another source of income, such as a company pension fund, then you can afford to be more aggressive with your RRSP or TFSA money because it doesn't represent your only hope.

At the same time, with people living longer and retiring later, you may need to keep some more money in stocks than you would have, say, 20 years ago, to ensure that you have enough money to last you well into retirement. As you can see, rules are a good place to start, but some are made to be broken.

REMEMBER

Bonds are a guaranteed source of income, a mighty comforting port in the gale if equity markets collapse.

If you're a self-employed professional and you definitely have to generate your entire retirement income from your RRSPs and other savings, then the asset mix in your portfolio is of life-or-death importance for you. You almost certainly already have an accountant helping with your taxes, so get them to help you choose the amount of bonds in your portfolio or refer you to another fee-charging professional who's knowledgeable about financial planning (see Chapter 8).

Just about any commission-paid broker or financial planner has an off-the-shelf system or software package to help you choose the amount of bonds to hold. Remember, as always, that the results are only as valid as the assumptions the program makes about inflation, interest rates, and the economy. Professional investors routinely get those conditions wrong, so no reason exists why salespeople or their systems should do any better. But just about everybody will tell you to put a portion of your savings into a bond fund.

DO I NEED ALL THIS BORING BONDS-VERSUS-STOCKS STUFF?

Financial planning and structuring a portfolio are not clear-cut techniques that you can just learn and use. Folks in the investment game make the whole scenario even more confusing. Salespeople must have something to sell, after all. But investment theories can't be proved or disproved, in part because they depend on the future. And the future is always unknowable. So investment "research" is more like folk legend or articles of faith.

That means no "right" proportion of your wealth to have in bonds exists — if stocks surge, then almost any amount will seem too much because you'll miss out on returns. But when stocks sink, you'll get a toasty warm feeling from your bonds. If the inflation rate rises, as it did in 2022 and 2023, then bonds and cash assets will steadily lose their real value. But if the opposite happens, and deflation hits, bonds may be about the only things that go up in price, because money will steadily gain value. Remember to buy a bit of every asset class and buy quality, and you'll be fine.

How to Pick a Good Bond Fund in 30 Seconds

Selecting a superior bond fund boils down to two simple rules: It should hold plenty of high-quality, long-term bonds, and it must have low expenses. And, as always, favour funds with low management expense ratios (MERs), which express the yearly fees associated with the fund as a percentage of the money you have invested in it.

TIP

Own at least two Canadian and two global stock funds because any equity manager can go into a slump for years. But you can almost certainly do fine with just one bond fund as long as it has a low MER and is full of quality bonds. No big fund seller allows its managers to make weird bets with a mainstream bond fund, such as buying 20-year paper issued by a bankrupt tin mine. The backlash from investors, the media, and possibly even regulators would be too great.

Insisting on affordability

In general, look only at bond funds with MERs of one percent or less. The funds with low expenses almost all turn out to be no-load products that you buy directly from a bank or direct-selling fund company. That's because fund companies that sell through brokers, financial planners, and other advisors have to add on extra charges in order to have something left over to pay the salespeople; expect to pay an extra 0.5 to 0.75 percent annually on most broker-sold bond funds.

Looking for quality in provincial and federal bonds

Buy a fund with plenty of high-quality, long-term federal and provincial government bonds. A few super-blue-chip company bonds are okay but remember that with business changing at the speed of Elon Musk's hyperactive mind, today's corporate grande-dame could be tomorrow's bag lady. So go easy on the General Electrics. If you're a bit nervous that inflation may come back, you want a middle-of-the-road solution when it comes to bonds. So just get a bond fund or exchange-traded fund (ETF) that matches a broad bond index, such as the S&P Canada Aggregate or FTSE Canada Universe, that represents the entire Canadian bond market.

TIP

If you want a compromise, buy a plain-vanilla bond fund whose average term to maturity is close to the broad indices, which includes both short- and long-term bonds — typically between six and nine years. Many fund companies and bond investors use an index as the benchmark with which they compare the performance and holdings of their funds.

Checking out two beautiful bond funds

Here are two bond fund picks from Morningstar. Although not quite vanilla, both have high-quality holdings, flexible mandates that may enable them to beat the index, and relatively low expenses:

>> **RBC Monthly Income Bond Fund** is designed to generate monthly income for retirees and others who need it. The fund weathered the "Bondageddon" of 2022-2023 better than most of its peers, which may be why Morningstar gives it a gold medal rating and five stars for past performance. Managers Sarah Riopelle and Dagmara Fijalkowski have discretion to boost their corporate bond allocation in search of higher yields; currently corporates represent half its holdings, with government bonds making up 44.5 percent. The fund's MER is 1.09 percent, just a tad higher than we'd like, but it's still a fund worth considering.

>> **Manulife Canadian Unconstrained Bond Fund** got walloped in 2022 but its long-term returns are top-quartile. While considered a Canadian bond fund, it can invest up to 20 percent of its portfolio outside Canada (currently 13 percent). It can also take advantage of tactical opportunities such as floating-rate bank loans (currently 19.5 percent). Its yield to maturity is a rich 6.1 percent as of September 2023, which will make it hard to lose money in the coming years. Morningstar gives it a silver medal and four stars. Its MER is 0.85 percent.

How Inflation Affects Bonds

Although bonds are generally a stable investment, they do have a pair of mortal enemies: rising inflation and his evil henchman, rising interest rates. Central banks generally raise interest rates when an economy starts to overheat and consumer prices rise too fast. Those higher interest rates tend to cool things off. Unfortunately, they also tend to reduce the value of bonds.

Rising interest rates, falling bond prices

A bond falls in value when interest rates rise, because investors are willing to pay less for it. To take a simple example, say you hold a bond paying a five-percent coupon rate but interest rates increase so that other comparable investments, with the same term to maturity, are yielding six percent. If you try to sell your old five-percent bond, you'll have to cut the price to get anyone interested. For example, you may have to mark it down to 95 cents per $1 of face value (bonds always mature at face value or "par," which is 100 cents on the dollar). When you offer the bond at five percent off, the buyer of your cut-price bond will get the regular five-percent interest payment but they also make an extra kick because they bought it at the five-percent discount. When the bond matures at its full face value of $1 per $1 face value, that'll be enough to bring its annual yield up to six percent.

In 2022, interest rates increased sharply because central banks were worried about inflation, which surpassed eight percent at mid-year. Rising interest rates always reduce the market value of bonds that are out in the hands of investors. Bond funds were thus obliged to mark down the value of their holdings accordingly. That year, Canadian bond funds produced an average loss exceeding 10 percent.

Rising inflation makes bondholders and other lenders very, very afraid because they become petrified of seeing the real value of their money wither away. So they demand higher interest rates and bond yields. That means they refuse to buy bonds without getting big discounts, so bond prices fall, and you make less money on your bond funds.

Falling interest rates, rising bond prices

When interest rates fall, as they did off and on from the early 1980s until 2020, the picture looks brighter for bonds. If rates in the market drop to three percent, then your five-percent bond becomes a hotcake and investors will be willing to buy it from you at a premium.

Interest rates fall when inflation drops because lenders become confident that their money won't lose its value too fast while it's in the hands of the borrowers. So they're prepared to accept lower interest rates. One situation that's likely to send bond prices sharply higher in coming years will be an era of stable prices or at least growing confidence among investors that inflation has returned to central banks' preferred range of one to three percent annually for the foreseeable future. In that case, bond buyers are likely to bid bonds up above their face value.

Lower inflation makes bond buyers and other lenders feel more comfortable about tying up their money for years, so they'll accept lower interest rates and bond yields. Lower rates and yields mean higher bond prices, which mean extra profits for your bond funds.

The bottom line, though, is that predicting changes in interest rates can be a futile exercise. Just buy a good bond fund and view it as an insurance policy for your entire savings.

Index Funds and Bonds: A Match Made in Heaven

A bond fund should be like a holiday in Manitoba. Cheap and dull (but that doesn't mean you still can't have fun). Index funds with their low expenses and dreary habit of tracking the whole market are just the ticket. In the United States, index bond funds and now ETFs that simply match the market are by far the most common method of investing in bonds. Index funds and ETFs, you'll recall, are funds that match a well-known market benchmark. In Canada, index bond funds usually track the S&P Canada Aggregate Bond or FTSE Canada Universe Bond indices. In the United States, index fund giant Vanguard sells funds whose annual expenses go down as low as 0.05 percent — that's only one-twentieth of a percent. The median Canadian fixed income fund, by contrast, charges more than one percent. Alas, a Canadian resident cannot buy U.S. mutual funds, although some investors have been known to open an account from a U.S. address and/or using a U.S. discount broker to do this.

You can, however, buy a low-fee Canadian bond index fund from a bank. Better still, consider iShares' fixed-income ETFs. The iShares Core Canadian Universe Bond Index's MER is just 0.1 percent. The cheapest bank-sponsored bond mutual fund is the TD Canadian Bond E class, at 0.39 percent. See more on exchange-traded and index funds in Chapter 15; also check out www.ishares.com.

Long Bonds: Grabbing the Lion by the Tail

Long-term bonds are those with maturity dates five years or more in the future. They are generally regarded as being more risky than short-term fixed-income securities because of the uncertainty of the future direction of interest rates. In exchange for this risk, they tend to provide a better long-term rate of return.

Unfortunately, no clear rules force managers to disclose to the public how long-term their bond portfolios are, but many companies voluntarily compare their holdings to major indices. Bond managers revel in bizarre formulas, and one of their favourites is "duration," which measures how much a bond or portfolio of bonds can drop when interest rates rise. A duration of six years and higher is generally aggressive, while five and down is conservative. Aggressive bond managers are betting that interest rates will fall or at least stay stable. So if you're really worried that inflation will come back, seek out a fund that holds lots of short bonds.

Why you may want to rule out long-term bond funds

Short-term bonds, those with five or fewer years to run, are less vulnerable to rises in interest rates and inflation. Why? Because the time they have left is so brief that investors don't mind tying up their money in them. An instrument with 30 years left to run on it looks far worse when rates rise. (We look at short-term bond funds in the section "Short-Term Bond Funds: Playing It Safe" in this chapter.)

Managers of bond funds, like their flashier stock-picking colleagues, love to dress up their rather monotonous jobs with fancy-sounding strategies and jargon. But running a bond fund basically involves deciding how much risk you're going to take and then buying the bonds that suit that strategy. Bond managers buy as many long-dated bonds as they dare. Investors who can't handle that kind of risk should turn to short-term bonds with fewer than five years to run before they retire. (Wouldn't it be nice to quit in five years!)

Why you may want to consider long-term bond funds

TIP

Why should you look for long-term bonds? Lending long by buying long-term bonds with ten or more years to run before they mature could prove a more lucrative approach if short-term interest rates fall. In 2023, interest rates reached highs not seen in more than a decade. It's expected that rates could fall — not to the ultra-low levels of the 2010s, but maybe by a percentage point or two. If that happens, the bonds you picked up in 2023 will increase in value as rates fall.

For the serious money portion of your portfolio, avoid risky "high-yield" bond funds or sleepwalking "short-term" bonds (more on those later in this chapter). The rule you apply should be this: Bet long-term as a lender because that's where the yield is. An old saying in the bond market is: *Be long or be wrong.* Longer-term bonds usually pay you more interest, but they also drop the most when interest rates go up, and they gain in price more quickly when interest rates decline.

Short-Term Bond Funds: Playing It Safe

Funds in the short-term fixed income category are the funds to buy with money you'd like to have cruise along, earning steady single-digit returns and not being exposed to too much risk. The short-term fixed income category is defined as including funds that invest in investment-grade bonds and other debt securities with an average duration of 3.5 years or less. Most individual short-term funds' mandates specify they hold only securities with maturity dates no more than five years in the future. To be classified in this category, these funds must have less than 25 percent of their portfolios in high-yield bonds. Some funds in this category hold residential mortgages.

These are the sort of funds a church may buy with money being saved up for a new roof. Nice and stable (the fund, not the old roof), but flexible and offering higher returns than a money market fund at the cost of slightly more risk. (*Money market funds*, the safest type of all, are an excellent place to hold the cash portion of your savings. Usually they hold nothing but very short-term loans to the government and big companies. We offer more about them in Chapter 17.)

Getting to know short-term bond funds

Short-term, fixed-income funds are almost entirely invested in government bonds with fewer than five years left before maturity. Corporate bonds may show up in these funds, but they should be from big-brother companies that you've heard of, such as Bell Canada. The main holdings should all be from the federal government and provinces. But not too much from smaller provinces — they're great places, but they tend to have lower credit ratings. Not that much risk of default exists in bonds to those provinces, but in the bond market, perception is everything. A lower credit rating becomes a leaden factor in itself by dragging a bond down to lower prices.

Funds that focus on residential mortgages have historically been even more stable than short-term bond funds, so they fit in just next to money market funds. They hold huge quantities of mortgages that have been packaged by math nerds working at a bank in downtown Toronto, who then also calculate a fee to help keep the bank in the comfortable style to which it's accustomed. The disadvantage of these funds is that they lack the simplicity of funds that stick to bonds. A fund may not be able to find mortgages to buy at decent yields, but bonds are always for sale.

Comparing short-term fixed income funds to money market funds

Money market funds represented the only major category of mutual funds that saw net inflows in 2022, as investors took shelter from falling stock and bond markets. Historically, however, short-term bond funds have performed slightly better than money market funds.

Mortgage and short-term bond funds are different from money market funds in one important way: Mortgage and short-term bond funds are true mutual funds, meaning that their units can drop below a fixed price — in other words, you can lose money. Money market funds are more like a form of savings account than a real fund because they're pretty much eternally held at their $10 unit price. Your return from a money market fund comes only in the form of cash or extra units, whereas short-term bond funds or mortgage funds both pay out distributions — and mark their units up in value when interest rates fall and mark them down when rates rise.

In reality, though, all three types of funds are pretty stable. Since the late 1980s, short-term fixed income funds have lost money only once over a full calendar year, in 2022, and their loss was much more palatable than the fate of the median Canadian long-term fixed-income fund, which fell more than 12 percent.

Checking out a couple of short-term bond fund winners

Most of the time, long-term bonds pay higher rates of interest than short bonds, as a way of compensating investors for the greater interest rate risk they're taking on. The consequence is that yields on short-term bond funds are rarely lavish (think low single digits). So low fees or, conversely, savvy management are key to generating income from these funds.

Here are two short-term bond funds that Morningstar likes:

>> **iShares Core Canadian Short Term Bond Index** is a passively managed ETF, which means it simply tracks the relevant index, with no active investment decisions made to try to better the index's return. It sports the lowest MER in the Canadian short-term bond category at 0.1 percent. The expected return of this conservative category is not very high, so fees play a much larger role in performance. This low fee makes it a tough option to beat.

>> **PH&N Short Term Bond and Mortgage** is one of the least expensive options (next to the ETF) in the Canadian short-term fixed income category. Its MER is 0.5 percent. The fund also has the backing of Canada's biggest bank, RBC, so you know it'll be around for a while.

High-Yield Bond Funds: Naked Bungee-Jumping

Brokers and investment managers like to call bonds issued by less-than-blue-chip companies in unstable industries such as media or minerals "high yield," because buyers demand fat interest rates before they'll touch them with a kilometre-long pole. "High yield" sounds nice and healthy, doesn't it? Sort of like it's full of fibre, dried fruit, and tasty bits of soy. But American investors have long used the correct term for such concoctions: "junk."

In other words, in the bond market you get what you pay for, and to achieve more yield you have to go down the quality scale. That involves buying riskier bonds from smaller companies — obscure stuff that's often hard to sell at any price if the bond market turns down sharply.

For example, during the global financial panic in 2008, bonds from even the biggest global corporations became difficult to trade as investors fled to the safety of government securities. Finding buyers for your junk bonds was like trying to sell lemon juice to hummingbirds.

Some funds in the junk group also hold safe-as-houses government bonds, but they're included in the high-yields because they're also free to juice their yields by grabbing riskier stuff as well.

This section helps you decide whether the bigger potential returns from high-yield funds compensate for the extra risk is up to you. But keep in mind that even the most fervent advocates of junk probably wouldn't advise you to risk all your bond money in high-yield debt. And your portfolio will do just fine if you shop elsewhere and simply stick to bond funds that hold only top-quality government and corporate bonds.

Considering the strikes against high-yield bond funds

Junk bond funds are vulnerable in times of investor paranoia and economic jitters, when just about everyone seeks out government bonds and shares in big, relatively safe companies — a panicky rush for the exits known as a "flight to quality." When stock markets fall, junk bonds tend to do the same.

In other words, corporate and junk bonds have a habit of suffering just like stocks when recession threatens — unlike government bonds, which tend to go *up* because anxious investors reckon the government guarantee means they'll always get their money back. After all, bad economic times increase the pressure on small or debt-laden companies, making it more likely that they'll be forced to renege on their debts, including the hand-knit cozy junk bonds they issued.

Investigating high-yield bond funds in Canada

In the U.S., hundreds of billions of dollars have been invested in mutual funds that hold junk bonds, with generally good results and attractive returns. But in the U.S., investors can buy from a huge number of junk bonds, making it easy to build diversified funds full of the things. And a diversified fund holding dozens of junk bonds from different issuers spreads the risk of disastrous defaults in any one industry.

In Canada, publicly traded junk bonds are far rarer because our cautious pension funds and other investors usually insist on a high credit rating. In the past, riskier borrowers have been forced to sell their junk south of the border. A few mutual fund companies, though, have launched Canadian and foreign junk funds in recent years.

The advantage of high-yield bond funds is that their high yields can often make up for a lack of capital gains when interest rates stubbornly refuse to drop. As of November 2023, the average high yield fund in Canada posted a total return of 2.74 percent year to date, a substantial step up from the 0.62 percent furnished by the average Canadian fixed income fund, according to Morningstar. (It was still way off the high-yield index return of 7.14 percent, however.) Keep in mind, though, the price of high-yield bonds and funds can fall quickly if investors get concerned about credit risk in choppy markets.

Bonds Outside Canada

We'd love to tell you that your Canadian bond fund will provide the long-term stability and steady returns your portfolio requires, but we'd be wrong. A strong case exists for buying a fund that holds *global bonds* — a category that used to be called "U.S. bonds" because the funds so often end up investing in the almighty greenback. Most of these funds still have one-fifth of their portfolios in U.S.

securities. It stands to reason that you need a U.S. bond fund in case a multi-year scenario occurs in which worldwide stock prices and the Canadian dollar both go down, but bonds hold their value — in that case, foreign bonds will be the thing to own. So, unfortunately, for a complete portfolio, you probably need to add a non-Canadian foreign bond as well. That's why we include them in the suggested portfolios in Chapter 4, but there we limit global bonds to just 10 percent of the total holdings.

TIP

If you're nervous about the prospects for Canada and the Canadian dollar, then switch money from the Canadian bond funds to the global bond funds to increase your insurance coverage. Yes, it's yet another asset class, so adding it to your holdings will reduce overall volatility. But it also adds more complexity, expense, and fiddly stuff to worry about.

Fund sellers sometimes claim you need a foreign bond fund to give you currency diversification and protection against a collapse in the Canadian dollar. But you get the same sort of insurance from your global stock holdings, which, of course, are also priced in foreign currencies. That's why you need invest only a small portion of your portfolio in foreign bonds.

Diversification at a high cost

Holding global bonds instead of global stocks comes at a price, however. The median global fixed income fund sold in Canada has a hefty MER compared with most Canadian fixed income funds. That hefty price tag sometimes causes these funds to underperform their Canadian counterparts.

Stinging losses posted by foreign bond funds in 1999 left the average fund down a spine-chilling 10.4 percent. That wasn't the fault of the managers: It was a lousy year for bonds worldwide as interest rates rose. Meanwhile, a slide in many European currencies relative to the Canadian dollar added to the losses.

A couple of recommended global bond funds

Suffice to say that there are more moving parts involved in running a global bond fund than a domestic one. There are currency risks, different likelihoods of default, different debt vehicles on offer (municipal bonds, for example, are uncommon in Canada). You end up paying somewhat more for managers to understand and navigate these extra variables. At the same time, global exposure can help diversify your portfolio. (Yes, financial catastrophes can happen in Canada too!) The analysts at Morningstar like these two global bond funds with annual expenses below the group average:

>> **RBC Global Bond** has an intriguing mix of foreign government bonds, emerging markets debt, and high-yield securities. Its portfolio managers are free to make sector allocations, geographical shifts, and duration calls in an attempt to add value. They can also make currency overlay trades, but the fund's default policy is to have its foreign currency exposure fully hedged. The performance has been solid, with the exception of a 14.7-percent hit in 2022, and its 1.57 percent MER is below the category median. Morningstar gives it a gold medal rating.

>> **Fidelity Investment Grade Total Bond** slid just six percent during the global bond market shrinkage in 2022, when its benchmark index fared five percentage points worse. It's been a top-quartile performer over three- and five-year periods, in fact. And it does this with a rock bottom (by global fund standards) MER of 0.8 percent. The fund's mandate allows it to hold up to 25 percent junk bonds but it generally sticks to the safe U.S. market and benefits from the giant asset manager's expertise in risk management. Morningstar gives it a gold medal rating with five stars.

IN THIS CHAPTER

» Weighing the pros and cons of index funds and ETFs

» Determining how to fit these funds into your portfolio

» Comparing index funds to mutual funds

» Looking at the life of a fund manager

» Discovering why salespeople don't like index funds

» Figuring out where to buy index funds

» Getting to know a few specialized index funds

Chapter **15**

Exchange-Traded Funds and Index Funds: The Art of Owning Everything

E ver notice how things seem to be getting much larger? Cruise ships have 12 restaurants, movies last for hours, pickup trucks require a stepstool to get in, and concert tickets will set you back a couple of days' pay. Well, one of the most effective and profitable investing techniques to emerge in recent years is also a huge idea. It's *indexing:* buying a little of every single significant stock or bond in the market and just holding it, as opposed to trying to pick which one will go up and which will go down.

The name "index" comes from the fact that portfolios managed using this method aim to track a given market index or benchmark. To do that, they buy each stock or bond in the index. For example, a fund designed to follow the Standard & Poor's/Toronto Stock Exchange composite index buys all (or virtually all) of the shares in Canada's main stock index. Mutual funds that use the technique are called *index funds.*

In this chapter, we look at index funds and exchange-traded funds (ETFs), explaining what they are, why they're a great place to put a lot (but maybe not all) of your mutual fund money, and where to buy them.

Buying the Whole Enchilada: The Ups and Downs of Indexing

The whole idea behind index and exchange-traded funds (ETFs) — giving up on trying to pick the best stocks and just betting on the whole market — runs counter to human nature, of course. We all want to believe in the hero fund manager, the Druid who can peer into the entrails of the market and decide which stocks will thrive. So the fund companies run huge ads, and the news media produce fawning stories about how wonderfully perceptive and accurate these stock wizards are. But it's a myth: Managers who can be relied on to beat the market over many years are as rare as vegetarian leopards. And even if they do exist, determining in advance which ones will succeed is essentially impossible.

Exploring why ETFs and index funds are great for you

People who invest in ETFs or index funds are often passionate about their chosen vehicle and will loudly espouse their many virtues. You don't have to drink the Kool-Aid to appreciate the way they save you money on management fees, making it easier for your wealth to grow. They can also be useful for specific purposes or parts of your investment portfolio, complementing your actively managed mutual funds. This section calls out the key reasons to hold them.

They outperform most actively managed funds

Because few managers fail to beat the market over many years, indexing (we use this word instead of saying "index funds and ETFs" over and over again) is an excellent way to go for ordinary investors. With indexing, you don't have to worry whether you made the right choice of manager because all the fund tries to do is match the market. It doesn't buy and sell stocks or bonds in pursuit of profits, but simply buys the shares or bonds that make up a particular index and holds them forever. A computer could run the thing and, with a little human oversight, generally does. These funds make stock-picking expertise irrelevant. That's great for busy people who don't have the time or knowledge to check a manager's credentials and find out whether their track record was achieved through luck or skill.

REMEMBER

Making money in the stock market is a gamble. But it's a casino in which your long-term chances are excellent because good companies grow their profits and share prices over the years.

You improve your odds by simply buying a fund that tracks the whole market — because these big suckers, the successful companies such as financial combine harvester Power Corp. of Canada or network empire Cisco Systems, actually *become* the whole market. And it's good to know that with an index fund, you own them.

They're low-cost

Index funds and ETFs have another shining virtue: They're cheap for an investor to own. No research is involved in just buying every stock in the market (although to hear some index funds types pontificate, you'd think it was the hardest thing in the world), so most index funds in Canada have a management expense ratio, or MER, of one percent or less. In other words, if you have $10,000 sitting in an index fund, you can expect to pay less than $100 (that is, one percent of your money) in fees and costs each year. If an index fund's MER is any higher than one percent, the concept starts to unravel, because it runs the risk of failing to keep up with the index that gives it its name.

ETFs, the first of which launched in Canada in 1990, are even cheaper. These securities are virtually the same as an index mutual fund except they're traded on a stock exchange rather than bought from and redeemed with a fund company. MERs do have a range, but most funds have fees well under one percent.

For instance, the BMO S&P/TSX Capped Composite Index ETF has a measly 0.06 percent MER, the iShares Core S&P 500 Index ETF comes with a 0.08 percent fee, the iShares Canadian Financial Monthly Income ETF, which tracks domestic financial companies has a 0.65 percent MER — down from one percent the last time this book was published. We talk more about ETFs throughout this chapter, but we also suggest picking up *ETFs For Canadians For Dummies*, 2nd Edition (Wiley, 2022), which Bryan also co-authored.

Normal, non-indexed mutual funds — which do try to select particular stocks and bonds in an effort to turn a profit — are known as *actively managed funds* because their managers are actively choosing which stocks to hold and which not to. They're far more expensive to own. The MER of the median Canadian equity mutual fund (active and "passive" funds that just track an index included) is about 2.3 percent, which means the typical actively managed fund rakes off considerably more in fees and costs than an index fund. And that extra 1.3 percentage points is a lot — over 20 years, it adds up to nearly one-third of your money.

Over the last few years, actively managed ETFs have started to pop up. They're similar to actively managed mutual funds, in that a professional manager chooses the stocks or bonds to go into the ETF. But there are two big differences between these funds and traditional mutual funds: the first is that an actively managed ETF is traded on a stock exchange, so you can buy or sell these funds at any time during trading hours. The second is fees, which are more than index-hugging ETFs, but a lot less than mutual funds. The iShares Diversified Monthly Income ETF, which holds income-producing assets such as stocks, bonds, and REITs, has a 0.55 percent MER, which is much lower than many dividend and income mutual funds.

They're great for taxable accounts

Index funds expose you to very little in taxation until you cash them in, making them a great way to defer taxation.

Nearly all mutual funds pay *distributions* to their unitholders — cash payments that most people choose to take in the form of more units of the fund (so the investment continues to compound and grow). Funds make the distributions when they have trading profits or interest (and dividend) income that the manager wants to pay out to the fund's investors.

Say you hold 1,000 units of a fund at the end of the year and the unit value is $10, for a total investment of $10,000. The fund manager generated $1 of trading profits per unit during the year and pays this out to the unitholders. The value of each unit drops by $1, reflecting the payment that has been made. You now hold your original 1,000 units, which are worth $9 each, for a total of $9,000. But you've also received $1,000 in the distribution, which you can take in cash or new units, bringing you back to $10,000.

REMEMBER

No matter how you receive the units, though, you're liable for tax on the distribution, just as if you had earned it trading stocks on your own. Some funds whose managers trade a lot can make very large distributions.

Note, though, that distributions won't attract tax if you hold the fund in a tax-advantaged account such as a Registered Retirement Savings Plan or Tax Free Savings Account, which lets you delay (in the former's case) or avoid (in the latter's) paying taxes on the money you earn within the account. (We talk more about taxes in Chapter 23 and about RRSPs and TFSAs in Chapter 22.)

Index funds just buy and hold the stocks in the index and they do very little trading. So they tend to pay out very little in the way of distributions. That makes them especially suitable for *taxable* accounts — money that isn't held in an RRSP, TFSA, or other tax-deferred account.

ETFs are also extremely tax-efficient. Like index funds, ETFs tend to hold the stocks and bonds in their portfolios for long periods of time. That means less turnover, which means less capital gains and income taxes to pay. There's another tax advantage, however. If a lot of people want to sell their mutual funds at one time — in a major downturn, for instance — the fund company or manager may have to sell the securities in its portfolio to generate the cash it needs to pay investors back. The sale of those stocks can trigger big capital gains. If investors want to sell out of their ETFs, they'll sell them on the stock market to another buyer. While you may have to pay capital gains on the sale of the ETF (assuming you hold it in a non-registered account), your gain is calculated only on the ETF price, not the sale of any underlying securities.

Delving into the dark side of ETF and index funds

Despite the accolades, ETFs and index funds are not risk-free. The big hazard is that the stock market indexes themselves — those seemingly logical benchmarks that these funds follow — often become dominated by just a few high-priced companies. In turn, that means the funds that track those benchmarks become risky investments because they're tied to the fortunes of just a few companies.

Remember when Canadian stock market indexes were dominated by high-priced growth stocks such as Nortel Networks Corp. or BlackBerry? *Growth stocks* are companies whose sales and profits are expanding rapidly. If investors decide that the companies can go on increasing their revenues and earnings for years, then they'll bid the shares up to high prices. But any sign of a slowdown in a company's growth is likely to make its stock price drop like a rock.

At one point, Nortel represented more than 30 percent of the S&P/TSX composite index. That meant an investor in an S&P/TSX index or ETF had one-third of their portfolio in a single stock — a very risky bet.

In the U.S., many index-following funds are now dominated by big tech stocks, such as Apple, Microsoft, and Amazon. For instance, in the iShares Core S&P 500 ETF, which holds 503 stocks, 26 percent of the fund is made up of seven stocks.

They include the aforementioned companies, but also Tesla, Alphabet (formerly Google), and high-flying semiconductor company NVIDIA. Generally, all tech stocks struggle at the same time (though to varying degrees), so if you're holding a passive fund such as this one, and investor sentiment turns south on tech, you're going to notice. Indeed, in late 2022, when tech fell out of favour, this ETF saw its fortunes fall by more than 15 percent.

Fortunately, you can still get exposure to a broad-based S&P 500 or S&P/TSX Composite Index fund (among other indexes that face this same overexposure problem) without taking on a lot of risk. In 2001, the Nortel debacle prompted the Toronto Stock Exchange to introduce *capped indexes*, which limit the impact of any one stock on an index by restricting a stock's percentage position in an index to 10 percent. One-fifth of a portfolio is not as dominant as one-third, true, but it's still quite a bit.

WARNING

So — no matter how good they may sound — don't put all your stock market money into one index fund or ETF. If the handful of giant stocks that dominate an index turn downward suddenly, your portfolio will take a beating.

REMEMBER

The essence of wise investing is spreading your risk among a wide variety of holdings. Of the money you set aside for equity funds, at most two-thirds should be in pure index funds or ETFs.

Fitting ETFs and Index Funds into Your Portfolio

Since the previous edition of this book was published, index funds, and even more so ETFs, have exploded. While Canada is still far and away a mutual fund nation by assets under management, there have been years where ETFs sales outpaced mutual fund sales. Many people have forgone mutual funds entirely, creating full portfolios out of three or four (or in some cases one) ETFs.

There are now ETFs for everything — and unlike with mutual funds, Canadians can buy ETFs listed on exchanges across the world — and most come with low expense ratios and trading flexibility, at least compared to mutual funds. So why buy mutual funds at all? What is even the point of this book? It is entirely possible that in two decades from now this book's sole purpose will be used to balance tables or to help your future kids build a fort, but for now, there is a case to be made to use both ETFs and mutual funds in your portfolio. (Index funds are still a good option for those with lower dollar amounts to invest or who work with advisors who can't buy ETFs, but it's only a matter of time until they disappear.)

Many financial experts these days suggest covering off the core parts of a portfolio — Canada, U.S, and international exposure — with a handful of ETFs. While there are nuances to the Canadian market that only a trained portfolio manager knows, ultimately, a Canadian equity mutual fund isn't that different from a Canadian equity ETF — except for the fees. The CIBC Canadian Equity Fund, for instance, has an MER of 2.15 percent, while the iShares S&P/TSX 60 Index ETF has an MER of 0.15 percent. Think about how much more money you can make by putting that two percent in the market.

Active managers, though, do have a role to play, especially in complicated to understand areas, such as in emerging markets or niche subsectors. You can buy emerging market ETFs, but you may want to trust an experienced manager who actually talks to CEOs. In that case, you can consider filling out your core ETF portfolio with mutual funds where professional expertise matters.

When it comes to bonds, there are plenty of index-focused funds to choose from. There are also a lot of actively managed funds and ETFs to purchase. It's a similar story here — if you want to own a basket of Canadian bonds, a passive fund is usually fine. If you want to own all sorts of credit — corporate bonds, high-yield fixed income, foreign government bonds — you may want an active manager who knows these areas.

As for what to own more of, stocks or bonds, it depends on all sorts of events, including when you're reading this book. If you're reading it in 2024, you'll know bond yields skyrocketed, while stocks have faltered, making fixed income more attractive than it's been in more than a decade. Right now, there's even a case to be made to hold almost all bonds in your portfolio. That is, ultimately, silly because it's important to be diversified, which means holding both stocks and bonds. Usually, when one asset class declines the other does well, so own both.

TIP

Ideally, bonds and bond funds — including bond index funds — should be held *inside* an RRSP or TFSA (or other tax-deferred account) because they throw off lots of interest income each year. As with an equity fund that pays lots of capital gains distributions, if you have to pay tax on all those interest payouts, your after-tax return can be slashed. Better to let them pile up tax-free inside the RRSP or TFSA. Most Canadian bond index funds simply match the entire bond market by tracking the DEX universe bond index. See Chapter 14 for much more on bond funds.

Evaluating Regular Mutual Fund and ETF Performance

There is plenty of evidence showing that regular mutual funds just can't beat the market. Those clever fund managers with shiny, well-scrubbed faces and expensive degrees can't be simply wasting their time, can they?

The numbers seem to show that many of them are. The 2022 S&P Indices vs Active scorecard — a report that tracks the performance of actively managed funds against their respective category benchmarks — found that 79 percent of fund managers underperformed the S&P 500. It's been a similar story for years.

TECHNICAL STUFF

Unfortunately, it's almost impossible for index fund fans to keep matters simple and just buy a global equity index fund. Fund companies usually already offer a U.S. index fund, so they normally sell an international equity index fund that tracks stocks in countries outside North America. That means you have to buy three stock market index funds: one for Canada, one for the U.S., and one for international stocks. (For the record, several European index funds exist as well, along with a handful of Asian and emerging markets index funds.)

TIP

Want an easy and fast place to buy index funds? Go online and use your bank's index funds. You can hold your *actively managed* funds — which try to buy and sell stocks and bonds instead of tracking the whole market — in another account at a discount broker.

Understanding Why Fund Managers Seldom Beat the Market

Grasping the idea that no human being can develop the skill to consistently beat the stock market is tough. People naturally want to believe they can improve their chances by handing the money over to an expert. History shows, however, that hardly anyone manages to stay ahead of the pack year after year.

Many people don't care about who will be running their money, and they simply put it in the first equity, balanced, and bond funds their salesperson suggests. Weirdly, it's possible these investors do better than those who assiduously hunt out top-performing managers — because the hot managers so often tend to flop the next year as their favourite stocks go out of fashion.

In this section, we explore why it's so difficult for most fund managers to beat the stock market.

Balancing wins and losses

Fund managers don't just trade in the stock market — they *are* the market. For every winner who beats the index and earns a profit, there has to be a loser to supply those profits. Yes, some of the losers may be small retail investors (or so the pros would like us to believe), but the institutional investors that dominate stock trading have their share of losers, too. Economists argue endlessly on this point, but it seems clear that the stock market is ultimately a zero-sum game, or at least resembles one. It's sort of like a bunch of aging, boomers getting together to play poker on a Friday night. If Laurie walks away with $500, then Al or Rob or Justin are going to be down that much.

Money managers, believe it or not, are responsible souls who don't want their unitholders to be dragged over the hot coals unduly. So they often shy away from loading their funds to the gunwales with the extremely hot stocks that are driving the indexes higher. History shows that the public will accept mediocre performance, sometimes for years, but it won't take kindly to losses. Increasingly in recent years, the stock market itself has become an insane place, and managers have had trouble keeping up with the index because they cautiously refused to go along with the madness.

WHY YOUR FUND MANAGER ISN'T A MONKEY PLAYING DARTS

The *Wall Street Journal* runs a famous stock-picking contest in which market experts are invited to compete with each other and against non-experts who randomly throw darts at a list of shares. Folklore has it that the randomly thrown darts usually win, but in fact the *Journal* reports the experts actually have done better than their competitors. How come? We asked Burton Malkiel, the author of *A Random Walk Down Wall Street* and one of the godfathers of indexing. The courtly Professor Malkiel came up with two reasons for non-experts' poor showings. First, the U.S. market contains thousands upon thousands of sad-sack, no-hope, tiny stocks. The haphazardly pitched darts, with no expertise to guide them, often fell on one of those soon-to-be-forgotten losers, whereas the human stock jockeys selected real companies with at least some prospects. His other explanation: When the *Journal* reported that a prominent expert had selected a stock in the contest, that news alone was enough to push the share price higher, giving the experts' stocks a leg up compared with the darts' selections. Incidentally, Professor Malkiel wrote in 1973 that a blindfolded monkey throwing darts at the stock page would do just as well as professional money managers. In its contest, the *Journal* got reporters to throw the darts. The paper considered using real monkeys, but, as reporter Georgette Jasen put it, "various hand-wringers have so far prevailed with concerns about things like liability insurance."

MUTUAL FUNDS STILL RULE CANADA

With the proliferation of inexpensive ETFs, you may think that every Canadian investor would dump their high-priced funds in exchange for, umm, exchange-traded funds. Well, you would be wrong. According to the Investment Funds Institute of Canada, in August 2023, Canadians held $1.9 trillion in assets in mutual funds, while ETF assets totalled $355 billion. While ETFs have gained some significant ground over the years, Canadians still love their mutual funds. (The gap is closing far faster in the U.S.)

So why is the cherished notion of using a talented stock picker, a magician who knows which shares to buy, so hard to shake? Why do Canadians shy away from what seems like such a great investment opportunity? Maybe it's a cultural thing, but Canadians traditionally have been reluctant to pay for investment advice on an annual fee basis or in the form of an hourly fee. They would rather get hand-holding from a commission-paid mutual fund salesperson. But a problem exists right there: Such advisors have a powerful incentive to recommend actively managed funds rather than index funds. That is changing — there are more fee-only advisors who can recommend everything, but Canada is still a mutual fund country.

Paying for active management

With the median Canadian equity mutual fund charging its unitholders around two percent a year in fees and expenses, it's virtually impossible for managers to close the gap between them and the market. That MER is a yawning gap, especially when you're trying to compensate for it every year. That gives a natural advantage to index funds and ETFs, with their MERs of one percent or less.

Mutual funds have another hidden expense that's higher for actively managed funds: brokerage commissions. A fund that's constantly buying and selling stocks is naturally going to end up paying more to brokers.

Overcoming Some Salespeople's Dislike of Index Funds and ETFs

Many brokers and planners don't like indexing because these funds don't pay them much or anything in the way of commissions. It's that simple. Well, that and the fact that an investment advisor traditionally has been expected to actually beat the market, which of course your basic index fund or ETF cannot do.

A guideline in the fund industry for equity and balanced funds is that the *sales channel* — that is, stockbrokers or financial planners — gets one percent of the client's money each year. They may get it through a commission paid by the investor or the fund company at the time of purchase. Or the salesperson may get this commission annually in the form of a regular "trailer fee," an annual sales commission paid by the fund company.

Index funds are an exception because, with their rock-bottom annual expense ratios of one percent or less, they can afford to pay little or nothing in commissions to salespeople. The fees just aren't high enough. So, guess what? Be prepared if an advisor gives you a long speech explaining why index funds or ETFs aren't that great after all. A fund salesperson is more likely to try to sell you on how you'll be better off buying an actively managed fund run by a reassuring-looking person who's known for their saint-like devotion to achieving high returns at low risk. The MER? Oh, never mind about that. It's the return that matters, silly.

Now, we don't want to paint all advisors with the same brush. As time has gone on, many people have taken a liking to ETFs, especially the ones who charge by the hour or another set rate. Investors are also becoming savvier and talking to their advisors about ETFs. If you do want the full breadth of options, make sure to find an advisor who can see how ETFs and mutual funds can play a role in your portfolio.

WARNING

If your broker or financial planner refuses to sell you an index fund or an ETF, then strongly consider moving your account elsewhere. So much evidence suggests these funds are a great deal for retail investors. Any salesperson who refuses to carry them is being unfair to their clients.

Buying ETFS and index funds

Even though index funds supposedly simplify the experience of buying mutual funds, enabling you to skirt selecting the best fund manager, you do have some decisions to make. Which index should you follow? Should you buy an index fund or an ETF? And where should you buy? Read this section, and all will be revealed.

Selecting the right index

The problem of which index an index fund or ETF should use is thorny and difficult. On the one hand, if you start guessing which index is the best one to match, then you're getting close to picking stocks again, and this is the antithesis of passive investing. On the other hand, if you just let things go and blindly match a narrow index such as the S&P/TSX 60, which includes only Canadian stocks with very large market capitalizations, or one that's ruled by a few high-fliers, then your index fund has arguably become an aggressive and volatile fund. However, this problem doesn't have a simple answer: Just follow the advice in this book and don't put all your eggs into one index. That way, if the big stocks in the index turn out to be bubbles that burst painfully, a good chunk of your money will be in other funds as well.

In the U.S. market, the safest policy would be to buy a super-broad index fund, one that tracks the huge FT Wilshire 5000 Index, which contains just about every stock in America that's worth buying. CIBC's U.S. Broad Market Index fund tracks the Wilshire, so it would be a good choice. But it seems pretty certain that the better-known S&P 500, which is dominated by fewer and larger companies, will remain the main yardstick for the U.S. market for years to come. U.S. equity index funds are as cheap as Canadian ones, for the most part.

Most global equity index funds track the venerable MSCI world index, while international equity index funds track the MSCI Europe Australasia Far East (EAFE) index. You'd expect index funds based on overseas indexes to have higher MERs than their North American counterparts, but some in fact have very low MERs, such as TD's offerings.

Choosing between index funds and ETFs

Over the years, ETFs have become the go-to option for most index-seeking investors. But there are still plenty of index fund options, too. ETFs tend to be favoured by investors who want to work with an investment advisor and who have larger portfolios. Do-it-yourselfers favour index funds because they mostly are no-load funds and thus not normally within the advisor's product domain, though many DIYers buy ETFs, too. The reason people with larger portfolios tend to buy ETFs is that these funds are bought and sold like stocks, so commissions are payable on each transaction. Thus, they're less suited than index funds to smaller investors who are building a portfolio and like to make frequent purchases. But the most significant difference between index funds and ETFs, of course, is the latter have lower MERs.

Knowing where to buy

If you want to buy an index fund with a truly low MER, you have to go to the banks. (They are also sold by life insurance companies in the segregated fund format, although many of these charge sales fees and, being seg funds, have higher MERs. We talk more about seg funds in Chapter 19.) Banks sell index funds on a no-load basis directly to the public. Every discount broker should carry at least one family of index funds, with no hassles.

ETFs are available from banks, too, but also from investment dealers. Although their MERs are extremely low, as exchange-traded securities, you must pay to buy and sell them. Many advisors include these transaction costs in an annual advisory fee based on the value of the investor's assets under administration.

REMEMBER

If you're with a financial planner or broker who doesn't offer index funds or ETFs, nothing's stopping you from opening a separate fund account at a bank and holding the rest of your money with your advisor. Each of the big bank-owned discount brokers enables you to purchase index funds and ETFs, the former usually from the bank that owns the firm.

The simplicity and relatively clear account statements offered by discount brokers make them perfect for holding index funds and ETFs, especially if you can avoid the fees that some discounters impose for buying and selling other companies' no-load funds. If the discounter is bank-owned, then the bank's own index funds will be free of fees.

Considering some winning ETFs and index funds

Compared to actively managed mutual funds, there's not much to separate one index fund from another. After all, a great many of them track the same indexes. But there's more to choosing one than finding the lowest management expense ratio. Think about liquidity, for example. Is the fund big enough to fetch you a decent price for your units on the day you sell? And how well does it actually follow the index? Not all index funds literally hold every constituent stock in the right proportion; they achieve the effect of tracking an index with the help of derivatives, tradable contracts that kick in when certain conditions are met. That said, here are three great low-cost funds that invest in Canadian stocks, Canadian bonds, and U.S. equities. They come recommended by analysts at Morningstar:

>> **TD Canadian Index Class E** is one of Toronto-Dominion Bank's E-series low-cost index funds, which you purchase online. With a MER of only 0.22 percent, this is an inexpensive way to track the S&P/TSX Composite Index. Investors should keep in mind that, as with any fund that shadows this index, further diversification is recommended given its high concentration in resources and financials.

>> **iShares Canadian Real Return Bond Index ETF** is an ETF that invests in real return bonds by mimicking the FTSE Canada Real Return Bond Index. It offers a safe and simple way to hedge against rising inflation. Given that the actively managed funds in this space tend to be expensive, investors looking to include this asset class in their portfolios will be well served by owning this ETF with its attractive 0.35 percent MER.

>> **iShares Core S&P 500 Index ETF (CAD-hedged)** is a currency-neutral, exchange-traded fund (ETF) that tracks the S&P 500 composite index. Its crazy low 0.08 percent MER makes this one of the cheapest ways to invest in the U.S. stock market and gives the fund an instant leg up on the competition. Note, however, that even less expensive alternatives are available if you don't mind taking on foreign currency risk. For instance, the fund's U.S.–dollar version, iShares Core S&P 500 Index ETF can be had for a hard-to-believe 0.03 percent fee.

Straying from the Norm: Specialized Index Funds and ETFs

Although index funds and ETFs are most commonly used by investors to track the performance of the market as a whole, some specialized index funds and ETFs do exist. These funds are constructed to invest in certain types of stocks, or to track particular sectors.

Tilted funds: Indexing on steroids

Tilted funds have portfolios that are based on an index but adjusted to favour a certain investment style. Such adjustments are done according to a strict, consistent formula. For example, a tilted equity index fund may skew its portfolio slightly in favour of either growth or value stocks and/or toward either small- or large-cap shares. A tilted bond index fund may favour either debt issues with either short- or long-term maturities and/or a particular credit quality.

Other ETF options

ETFs don't limit you to ownership of a broad market index. In Canada, for example, you can buy iShares funds that track several of the S&P/TSX subindexes — energy, financial, gold, materials, and technology industry sectors — as well as a small-cap fund. All have much lower MERs than the specialized mutual funds that invest in those areas.

On the fixed-income side, several iShares ETFs are based on bond indexes that track various bond markets. Again, MERs are rock-bottom — one of the most popular bond funds, the iShares Core Canadian Universe Bond Index ETF has a 0.09 percent MER.

Although the addition of any new cost-effective fund is welcome, ETFs tend to be bought as an inexpensive, simple means of investing in a broad index, minimizing the number and extent of investment decisions. However, when you buy ETFs that focus on specific sectors, you are in some ways getting into market timing and making bets that stocks in, say, the technology industry — or long-term bonds — are going to do better than other sectors or the market as a whole.

WARNING

Be careful when building an ETF portfolio; you may be better off sticking to those funds that track broad indexes.

IN THIS CHAPTER

» **Investigating dividend and income funds**

» **Deciding whether you need dividend and income funds**

» **Reviewing the tax implications of dividends**

» **Selecting a winning dividend fund**

» **Looking at endangered species: Preferred shares and income trusts**

Chapter **16**

Dividend and Income Funds: Confusion Galore

The basic theory behind dividend funds is a good one — invest in blue-chip companies that pay a steady flow of increasing dividends, and you'll be off to the races.

REMEMBER

Dividends are the quarterly payments a company pays to its owners — the shareholders who own its shares. (Although this fund category includes both income and dividend funds, most of the funds in this group overwhelmingly invest in common stocks that pay dividends.)

Over the long term, buying into good-quality companies and growing rich as the dividends increase annually has been one of the best ways to build wealth. If you hold shares in successful companies for long enough, then your dividends will increase to the point where they represent a meaningful source of income. Seems simple, doesn't it? Don't count your earnings yet. This story has a lot more to it than that.

In this chapter, we demystify the concept of the dividend and income fund, identify who should buy one, review the various types of dividend funds, and wrap up with some valuable tips on picking a winner.

What Are Dividend and Income Funds?

When a company earns a profit, it can do only two things with the money: reinvest it in the business or pay all or part of it out as *dividends,* actual cash paid to those who hold shares in the company. (Well, it can also do a third thing — buy back its own shares, which usually pushes the stock price higher.) That's true for every company — from the dirtiest restaurant in Prince Rupert, B.C. (beware the chicken fricassee) to the swishest financial holding company in the fanciest marble-clad office tower in Toronto. Traditionally, established blue-chip corporations have lined their shareholders' pockets over the years by regularly paying a nice steady dividend.

REMEMBER

A *blue-chip* company is a big and stable business, such as Toronto-Dominion Bank or supermarket giant Loblaw Cos. Ltd. The term *blue chip* comes from poker, where a blue betting chip usually has a high value.

TECHNICAL STUFF

We have some good news for you if you buy into a large blue-chip company. The other shareholders include big and assertive professional investors, people with loud voices who usually keep management focused. So if you hold shares in big businesses, you can usually be sure the companies' managers and directors are under at least some pressure to look out for the interests of you and the other shareholders. By contrast, if you invest in small companies, they may not be big enough to attract professional investors, so management will find it easier to neglect shareholders' interests.

Many mutual fund companies sell conservative dividend and income funds that simply buy shares in a bunch of blue-chip mega-companies such as BCE Inc. or Royal Bank of Canada and then pass the dividends they collect straight through to their unitholders. This is investing in dividend funds at its very best — clean and simple.

Looking at the upside of dividend funds

Many big dividend and income funds perform well, producing a stream of ready cash for their investors. In other words, they collect the dividends from big companies and pay them out to you. Best of all, the money normally comes from the fund to you as a dividend payment for tax purposes that's lightly taxed (more on that under "The Appealing Tax Implications of Dividends").

Considering the downside

Sounds great so far, doesn't it? You're probably wondering why we're so cranky about dividend and income funds. The problem is that sometimes their complexity and lack of transparency (always a bad sign in the world of investing) make them next to impossible to wrap your brain around. In theory they're great; in action they can be confusing.

It can be hard to tell whether a fund will actually pay you very much in the way of dividends, whether the distributions will actually be dividends or interest income, and whether the manager is really seeking dividend income or is in fact chasing stocks that will go up. But don't worry, in this section we show you a simple way to figure out what the flow of dividends from a dividend and income fund is likely to be — just look at the fund's main holdings, and they'll tip you off as to what sort of job the fund will do for you.

WARNING

Some dividend and income funds boost their flow of monthly payments to unitholders by holding riskier assets. That'll increase the payments you get from the fund — but the stream of payments these investments dish out to the fund (and ultimately to you) could get cut drastically when those assets are affected by a business downturn.

Figuring out why companies pay, or don't pay, dividends

Companies pay dividends to their shareholders because that's how the owners of the business are rewarded. A large and well-established business, such as a bank, usually throws off enough profits each year to cover the cost of acquiring new equipment and other assets and still has money left over to pay out as dividends. But some companies — particularly fast-growing technology outfits with huge needs for cash to research and develop new products — don't earn enough cash each year to come up with a dividend. They offer such good prospects for growth in sales and profits over the medium to long term, however, that investors are happy to buy their shares even though little chance exists of getting a dividend for several years.

Slow-growing companies

Traditionally, boring businesses whose earnings grow slowly have had to pay out up to half of their profits each year in dividends to keep investors interested in their shares. Traditionally, this has meant shares of one of the big five banks or utilities, such as gas and electric utility Fortis Inc., which as of late-2023 paid a decent dividend of $0.59 a share. That works out to a fat annual dividend yield of 4.37 percent. In other words, Fortis' common shares traded at around $54 in late-

2023 and the annual dividend per share was $2.36; $2.36 represents 4.37 percent of $54, so the annual yield was 4.37 percent.

Banks can increase their profits faster than utilities, partly because they're expanding in profitable areas such as mutual funds and, for some, exchange-traded funds (ETFs), which can be bought with a brokerage account like a stock. But banks are such big companies already they can't increase their profits as fast as, say, a software company can. So, they occupy a sort of middle ground, made up of companies that are likely to increase their earnings at a respectable but not feverish pace in coming years. Banks also pay out a relatively large proportion of their profits as dividends to shareholders. As of late-2023, most big bank stocks yielded between four and seven percent. That may not sound generous, but it wasn't bad when you consider the stocks in the broad Standard & Poor's/Toronto Stock Exchange as a whole tend to yield less than three percent.

Blue-chip companies are sometimes forced to cut their dividends when their profits fall unexpectedly. In January 2023, for instance, Algonquin Power and Utilities Corp slashed its dividend to 10.85 cents a share, down from 18.08 cents. Investors were not happy — the stock dropped almost immediately by more than 30 percent. Managers know how investors feel when they cut their payouts. It's humiliating for all involved, especially for chief financial officers who take the hard questions during quarterly conference calls. They tend to not set the dividend at a certain level unless they think it's sustainable in the first place. But circumstances sometimes intervene.

TIP

A portfolio that holds at least half a dozen blue-chip stocks — such as the typical dividend and income fund — will spread your risk, reducing the pain if one of them slashes a dividend.

Growth companies

So-called growth companies, whose profits are expected to increase rapidly, can get away with paying little or nothing in dividends, and investors still tend to throw their hat — and their cash — into the ring by buying the companies' shares. Investors are willing to forgo gratification today so the company can use the cash to build its business instead. The idea is that when the dividends do eventually come, they'll be bigger than if the company had paid out the cash to shareholders earlier in the game.

When the stock market bull is raging, dividend yield is the farthest thing from an investor's mind. In the techno-frenzy of the late 1990s and in 2000, you hardly heard a murmur about dividends. Dude, who cared? Don't-Care was made to care, in this case, as the Canadian stock market tumbled nearly 20 percent in 2001 and

2002. But the median dividend and income fund, typically with a heavy larding of stable stocks that pay dividends, managed to break even during that two-year period.

Hold at least some conservative dividend-paying stocks, even within a Registered Retirement Savings Plan (RRSP), a special type of tax-advantaged account. Because as the popping of the tech stock balloon showed, it's nice to own something that doesn't depend on a weedy teenage software genius staying conscious. But don't worry. You don't have to take special vitamin pills if your diet is rich and varied, including plenty of herrings' backsides. And, by analogy, you don't need to worry about buying a special dividend fund if your portfolio includes some high-quality equity funds, such as those we cover in Chapter 11. Those funds are bound to hold several dividend-type stocks — and that covers your daily requirement.

Those seemingly insignificant little quarterly dividend cheques are what capitalism and the stock market are all about. Under the law — in the Anglo-Saxon world, at least (and elsewhere, more and more, as the whole world becomes obsessed with investing in stocks à l'américaine) — dividends are about the only way that shareholders can legally get any money out of their company. Yes, they get a payoff if the company is taken over at a fat price or if they sell the shares after they've gone up or if the company "spins off" an asset to its shareholders in the form of a special restructuring. But receiving a dividend remains the only fundamental way in which you can actually extract cash from a business (apart from when an executive receives a bloated salary or options package). It's the thing that ultimately gives a share any value.

What does this all mean to the mutual fund investor? Just that it's fine to engage in torrid flirtation with a natural resources fund or aggressive growth fund but limit it to a dalliance using just a tiny part of your money.

Your core equity funds should also hold plenty of blue-chip stocks that pay a meaningful and rising dividend. Because when a market crash comes — and they always do — they're the shares that are most likely to fall the least and recover first.

Are Dividend and Income Funds Right for You?

You don't have to have a specific reason for being an income investor. Certain people just feel comforted by dividends and distributions that continue to trickle into their accounts no matter what is happening in the markets. Reinvesting income is a proven way to build wealth, after all. But there are also situations where a dividend or income fund comes in particularly handy. A dividend or income fund suits you best if you meet one or more of the following tests:

- » **You're a long-termer but you need cash now:** You need the long-term growth prospects offered by shares, but you also need to make regular withdrawals from your portfolio of investments. Many dividend funds are designed to accumulate a steady stream of cash, which they pay out regularly.

- » **You're in a high tax bracket:** You face a high rate of tax on the income and profits earned by your investments. That may be because you already have a high income or because your investments are held in a taxable account, not a tax-advantaged plan such as a registered retirement savings plan or a tax-free savings account. Remember that dividends are lightly taxed, which makes them a great way to earn investment income for a taxable investor. That means the payments you get from a dividend fund won't be too badly savaged by the government.

- » **You're not a risk taker:** You're nervous about the stock market and you feel happiest with a stock fund full of conservatively run large companies, the sort that pay lots of dividends.

But dividend funds aren't right for everyone, especially people who don't care if their investments pay out a regular income. Why bother with collecting dividends if it compromises your long-term returns?

If your aim is to build your money over many years, then you'll probably do better in a regular stock fund that's free to buy shares in all sorts of companies, including those that pay hardly anything in dividends. That way, you'll own a balanced mixture of shares that also includes some high-flying technology players and natural resource producers, and not just a portfolio of blue-chip, conservative names.

The Appealing Tax Implications of Dividends

In Chapter 23, we take a close look at how the periodic payments you get from a mutual fund are taxed. Dividend and income funds — assuming they are among the vast majority that hold mostly dividend-paying stocks — get special treatment when it comes to taxes. They can be one of the best ways of earning a stream of income that doesn't get too badly mutilated by the tax collector. To encourage Canadians to buy shares issued by Canadian corporations (to help the economy grow), dividends are taxed lighter than *interest income*, which is the sort of fixed payment you get from a bank account, bond, or fixed-term deposit such as a guaranteed investment certificate.

Crunching the numbers

Taxes are always complicated and figuring out dividend rates is no exception. Start with a simple calculation. Say you received a sweet $1,000 in dividends – $207 of that goes to the taxman, while $793 goes into your pocket. If you earned that same amount in interest — a distribution from a bond, for instance — $400 of that would go to taxes, leaving you with $600. Dividends are *tax-efficient* or *tax-advantaged* investments (though not quite as tax advantageous as capital gains) because this type of investment actually helps you keep more of your hard-earned income.

REMEMBER

You know if any mutual fund you own has paid you distributions in the form of capital gains, dividends, or interest because it is indicated on the T3 or T5 statement of investment income you get from your fund company each year to mail in with your tax return.

The calculation for reporting dividends on your tax form is a little laborious and weird, but you soon get used to it (amazing how the prospect of putting more money in one's pocket tends to fire up the old synapses). Essentially the principle is this: You "gross up" the amount of dividends received by increasing them by 38 percent and you report that amount on your tax form. But you then reduce your tax payable by a "tax credit" amounting to 15 percent of the dividends actually received. Don't fret: The tax form provides a step-by-step guide.

Understanding why dividend funds may or may not be good for your RRSP

Fund salespeople have long preached that collecting dividends within a tax-sheltered account such as a registered retirement savings plan (RRSP) isn't that important. That's for two reasons:

>> Within an RRSP, all the income earned is tax-deferred. All withdrawals from the plan are taxed as regular income. That means the dividend tax break is no use within an RRSP, so dividend funds — which are designed to take advantage of the tax law — arguably aren't a good fit.

>> For your core equity funds in an RRSP, it may be better to buy normal equity funds rather than dividend funds because the managers of regular funds have a freer hand to play the market, rather than trying to maximize their dividend income.

But because many dividend and income funds hold big familiar companies, they can logically be treated as super-conservative equity funds that are well suited for RRSPs. Remember the 2001–2002 experience when dividend and income funds outperformed general Canadian equity funds? The bottom line seems to be this: Check the holdings of a dividend fund, and if it's full of regular shares in big companies — as opposed to choices such as income trusts or other investments that are designed to throw off regular streams of cash — then it can probably be treated as a conservative equity fund.

Digging into why dividend funds may or may not be good for your TFSA

Holding dividends in a Tax-Free Savings Account (TFSA), a special vehicle for avoiding taxation on your investment gains, may be a good idea because all withdrawals from the account are not subject to any tax. So the more you can grow inside of the account, the more money you have when you withdraw.

However, because the Canada Revenue Agency (CRA) doesn't come a knockin' for any dollars, depending on how much contribution room you have, you may want to hold faster growing stocks — which likely don't pay a dividend — in the account before old reliable payers. If you have $6,500 of room in 2023 and want to put your money into a fund that can potentially net you big gains, go that route first. Why? Because if you put into your RRSP, you eventually have to pay income tax on the withdrawal. While capital gains are tax advantaged in a non-registered account, if your investment does go gangbusters, you may still have to fork over a lot of tax.

TECHNICAL STUFF

You may be surprised to discover that not all dividends can avoid taxes in a TFSA. Dividends paid by foreign companies (non-Canadian operations) can be subject to tax by foreign governments. For example, dividends paid by companies based in the U.S. are subject to a 15 percent withholding tax by the Internal Revenue Service. You do not get that money back.

AN INSTANT DIVIDEND-PAYING PORTFOLIO

Index funds are one of our favourite ways to invest (we explain why in Chapter 15). And no better way to do so exists than through an exchange-traded fund (ETF). An *ETF* is a fund that is traded on a stock exchange — as opposed to being sold and redeemed directly by mutual fund companies. Of greater interest is the fact that its portfolio is based on a stock index, such as the Standard & Poor's/Toronto Stock Exchange composite index.

The ETF market has expanded rapidly in recent years to include funds that are based on some of the Toronto Stock Exchange's specific industry groups. One fund provides an instant portfolio of blue-chip TSX dividend-paying stocks.

The iShares Canadian Select Dividend Index ETF holds 30 of the highest yielding dividend-paying companies in the Dow Jones Canadian Select Dividend Index. Analysts at Dow Jones look at a companies' dividend growth, yield, and average payout ratio to determine which stocks make the fund's portfolio. Its three biggest holdings in late-2023 were Canadian Tire, Bank of Montreal, and Royal Bank of Canada.

Like most ETFs, Dow Select Dividend's MER is low, low, low — 0.5 percent, compared with more than two percent for the median Canadian dividend and income fund. As of October 2023, it had a three-year compound annual return of 10.63 percent.

How to Select a Winning Dividend Fund

Don't just grab the first dividend and income fund you're offered. Make sure the fund you buy comes with a reasonable management expense ratio — certainly less than the category's 2.23-percent median value. Ensure its largest holdings include the sort of shares and trust units you want to own: high-quality stocks or units of companies in sectors that are known to provide reliable dividends and other income.

Questions to ask before you buy

Put these questions to your salesperson, no-load fund company, or bank employee. If you can't get a straight answer, then consider shopping elsewhere:

>> What distributions has this fund paid over the past year, and how frequently?

>> Is there a stated monthly distribution, and how much is it?

>> Which distributions over the past year counted as dividends from taxable Canadian corporations, entitling the fund's investors to claim the dividend tax credit?

>> Did any of the distributions include a *return of capital* — a partial refund of the investor's own money — to maintain a stated payout rate? Such returns of capital can be not only potentially misleading, but also horrendous to account for at tax time.

You can find this information easily in a fund's management report of fund performance, or MRFP, which should be available as a download from the fund company's website. The information is only as current as the most recent MRFP, but because these reports come out every six months, that should be current enough to give you a good idea of what you may expect in the way of distribution types and amounts.

Two strong dividend and income funds

Here are a couple of top-quality dividend and income funds recommended by analysts at Morningstar:

>> **TD Monthly Income** has done a remarkable job of giving investors the best of both worlds: high returns with relatively modest risk. Much of the fund's outstanding performance had been driven by exposure to the income trust market. But that market is no longer. (Mostly, 3.6 percent of the fund is in income trust units.)

Even in the post–income trust world, this fund has posted solid returns while paying a modest amount of income. Unlike many income-oriented funds, this fund doesn't have a fixed payout schedule. Each year TD determines how much the fund can reasonably pay out without eroding its capital base. Historically, that number has been in the two to three percent range annually. However, TD does offer different versions (H and T) of this fund that have higher fixed payout amounts of eight percent annually if you're looking for more income.

>> **CIBC Monthly Income** also has achieved strong returns. The fund maintains a considerable exposure to common stocks, which should help it produce high-single-digit returns over the long run.

These funds have reasonable expenses and well-regarded managers but remember to ask plenty of questions before you invest.

The Times Are a'Changin': The Fall of Preferred Shares and Income Trusts

Just as fashion ruthlessly moves forward, making your neon ski jacket an eyesore instead of a prized possession, so too does the investment world, and what was hot on Bay Street one day won't be the next. In this section, we look at two investment equivalents to padded shoulders and double-breasted suits.

Preferred shares

Time was when almost all dividend funds invested in preferred shares. But these funds are far and few between nowadays, as the preferred security is practically on the financial industry's endangered species list.

For the history books, *preferred shares* pay a fixed and usually high dividend, which is nice, but the dividend doesn't grow over time. In other words, preferred shareholders are more like lenders to a company than owners. By contrast, an ordinary or common share in a company pays a lower dividend, but the annual rate tends to increase over the years, providing an investment whose value should increase over time.

Preferred shares suit investors who want predictability but also relish the nice tax break attached to dividends. These shares pay a high fixed stated dividend, which can be reduced or omitted if the company hits turbulence — but in practice rarely is. And preferred shareholders nearly always get their dividends before common shareholders are entitled to receive a cent, hence the name.

In return for that lightly taxed and relatively generous stream of income, preferred shareholders miss out on the chance of prospering if the business booms. Preferreds nearly always stay close to their issue price, dropping a little when interest rates rise and rising when rates fall, just like bonds do. You can spot them in stock listings by their trading symbol, which always has "PR" in it. If a stock has a percentage value as part of its name, then it's a preferred share that was set up to produce that percentage yield for buyers of the stock when it was first issued.

There aren't many funds that hold a significant portion of their portfolios in preferreds. The category is now almost entirely dominated by income-oriented equity funds that derive as much as, if not more, of their returns from market performance. They load up on stocks of banks, utilities, pipelines, blue-chip industrial companies — and sometimes even growth companies that pay hardly any dividends. The manager of today's typical dividend and income fund tries to increase the value of their fund's units as the price of the stocks it holds rises while also paying out at least some dividend income. Still, these funds' holdings are usually so conservative they're less volatile than regular equity funds.

Income trust funds

Until late 2006, these funds were *the* place to be in mutual funds. Everyone was hungry for the tax-efficient income these funds provided, and staid, old, slightly higher taxed dividends just didn't cut it anymore. Publicly traded companies were spinning off parts of their operations as income trusts left right and centre. Entire companies were reinventing themselves as income trusts, seemingly simply to make themselves into income-spewing, investor-friendly investment machines.

But then the federal government, under pressure from proponents of the traditional stock market, put an end to the madness, levelling the taxation playing field so that owning an income trust unit was no more tax-wise than owning a dividend-paying share.

By 2023, the traditional income trust has become mostly extinct. Still, other trust structures exist, including royalty trusts, which are energy and mining companies that don't get taxed at the corporate level, enabling them to pay a hefty payment to shareholders. Dividends, however, are taxed as income. Also, Real Estate Investment Trusts (REITs) are publicly traded companies that hold physical real estate. Most pay out dividends.

Chapter **17**

Money Market Funds: Sleepy but Simple

S ome archaeologists and historians have an interesting theory to explain why the Romans were so successful in war, usually against massive odds (apart from Russell Crowe, that is). Bathrooms. Yes, that's right, bathrooms. The Romans liked their plumbing. Centuries before most of Western Europe had any kind of organized sanitation, the Romans were building bathhouses and sewage systems. Even in the field, they stuck to their clean-living ways. This meant their armies didn't die *en masse* of typhoid, cholera, and other diseases transmitted by, well, patchy hygiene. Money market funds are a bit like the humble throne in the bathroom, the white porcelain god that separates us from 15th-century Bruges with its pungent odours, annoying jesters, and unspeakable ditches down the middle of the street. They're dull, they're predictable, they're almost invisible — and they're one of the mutual fund industry's greatest inventions.

Money market funds are simply a safe parking spot for cash, designed to produce at least some sort of return. Until recently, they generated a modest stream of income. But with the rise in interest rates beginning in 2022, investors have rediscovered these funds, which are now generating attractive yields usually with very little volatility. While equity, bond, and balanced funds all saw net outflows in 2022, money market funds enjoyed a net intake of $7 billion from investors seeking a safe haven in turbulent times.

These funds invest in government treasury bills, very short-term bonds, and other fixed-income securities that usually have less than three months to go before they mature and the issuer pays the holders their money back. Money market funds are different in structure from normal mutual funds, and the way they calculate their returns can be confusing. But just use the same rules to pick one as you do with bond funds: Buy quality and, more than ever, insist on a low management expense ratio (MER) — one percent annually at the very most, but many have ratios of 0.5 percent or less. (The *MER* is the cost of managing a fund, and normally includes fees paid to the fund's portfolio managers, as well as marketing, sales, administration, legal, accounting, and reporting costs. These costs are charged directly to the fund as a percentage of the fund's total assets. The fund's net asset value includes the MER.)

As with all mutual fund investing programs, do more than just insist on low costs when buying a money market fund. Lean across the table at the salesperson and demand a fund that has a very low MER. Otherwise, you may not make much off a money market fund.

In this chapter, we show you why money market funds are a great place to hold your cash while you wait to spend or invest it. We also show you how to spot a good money market fund.

Digging into Money Market Funds

Throughout this book we give you tons of grim warnings about how you can easily lose money in mutual funds because of a drop in their unit price. Well, at the risk of contradicting ourselves, that doesn't apply to the vast majority of money market funds because they are held steady at a fixed value, usually $10.

WARNING

Some money market funds — especially the guaranteed type that promise to refund some or all your money — have unit prices that do increase over time.

Keeping the unit price fixed isn't required by law, but it's the practice among fund companies. In theory, if short-term rates were to shoot up exponentially or the government's credit rating collapsed, the fund company would let the value of your money market units drop. But that, fortunately, has not happened in any significant way in Canada. In other words, woe betide the fund company that lets its money market fund units drop below their fixed value. Investors who buy this type of fund aren't known for their devil-may-care attitude to losses. So money market funds are rather like a guaranteed investment certificate: You're certain of getting your cash back, plus extra units that represent the interest you've earned along the way.

The interest is usually calculated daily, but it's generally added to your account every month or when you sell your units. However, money market funds, like nearly all mutual funds, beat the pants off guaranteed investment certificates (GIC), an ultra-safe investment that guarantees a return, because they're "liquid." That's a bit of investment industry jargon that simply means you can liquidate — turn the investment into ready cash — at a moment's notice. Unlike GICs, money market funds refund your money without penalty, usually at a day's notice.

As a guideline, the return from money market funds tends to be similar to the return from one-year GICs, particularly during shorter terms. In the longer term, GICs have done slightly better. However, that's less than you could have gained from an investment in a balanced fund — normally a pretty cautious mix of stuff from the stock market (which is always volatile) and bonds (which usually work in great slow cycles). As of September 2023, the average neutral global balanced fund available in Canada — the most conservative among the various balanced-fund categories — achieved a six-percent annualized return over the previous 10 years. (For more about balanced funds, refer to Chapter 13.)

The *yield* is just the harvest you get on your money, expressed as a percentage of what you invested. So, a madcap biotech fund may go up 50 percent in a year — at huge risk — turning $1,000 into $1,500 (always assuming you were canny enough to sell out before it crashed). For the typical money market fund, however, assuming a current yield of about five percent, we're talking about a return of 50 bucks for tying up $1,000 for a year.

REMEMBER

With a money market fund, you nearly always buy a set of units at a fixed price, usually $10, and that unit price never changes. Your return comes in the form of extra units paid out to you along the way. You're not going to get wealthy soon with one of these funds. Just like bond funds, they're designed only to earn a steady and fairly predictable return, with none of the flash, risk, and potential for big gains you get with an equity fund.

THE FIX ISN'T ALWAYS IN

The unit value of some money market funds does change, increasing slowly as the fund earns interest income. These are the so-called "segregated fund" or "guaranteed investment fund" versions of money market funds. *Seg* or *guaranteed funds* are funds that promise to refund most or all the holder's original investment, as long as they stick around long enough. Chapter 19 deals with segregated funds.

Mind you, with something as safe as a money market fund, such a guarantee is pretty pointless and almost certainly not worth the higher expenses charged on such funds. Some hit their investors for as much as two percent annually, which leaves little or nothing for unitholders after taxes and inflation are taken into account. For legal reasons to do with insurance contracts (you'd get too excited if we explained them all to you), guaranteed and segregated funds often don't give unitholders their returns in the form of extra units. They simply reinvest all interest, capital gains, and other income so that holders of the fund own units with a steadily increasing value. Yet other examples both increase their unit value and pay distributions, just like normal mutual funds. It's terribly confusing for investors, and your salesperson or bank employee could have trouble keeping up. One simple reason justifies the existence of guaranteed and segregated money market funds: They provide a temporary cash parking spot for investors in a company's other guaranteed and segregated fund families, thus avoiding switch-out fees if they were to seek an external place to temporarily store their money pending a reinvestment decision.

Your statement from the fund company should clearly show what's going on, although that's not always the case. Consider switching to another fund company or broker if you can't get a proper explanation — a clear and simple explanation of how your funds work is your inalienable right as an investor. Even if you're an alien.

You can also go to morningstar.ca or globefund.com and check the latest distributions paid by a fund. This information should give you an idea of what system the fund uses.

Checking Up on Your Money Market Fund

Say you want to buy a money market fund but don't know what the yield over the next year is likely to be. Because most money market funds have constant prices, you need to look for a fund's current yield and effective yield. These values represent rough forecasts of what the fund, with its current portfolio, is likely to earn over the next year. Each yield figure uses a slightly different calculation, which we outline in a moment. But remember, both of these yield numbers are just estimates.

TECHNICAL STUFF

Money market funds are full of short-term stuff that matures in the next few months, so the portfolio manager can't be sure if they will be able to replace those treasury bills (very short-term government debt) and other short-term securities with new investments that will produce the same return. If rates are falling, then it will be almost impossible to do so. Don't worry about the difference between the two types of yield. Each calculation basically boils down to the same number of dollars and cents in your pocket. But just for the record, here's how to tell them apart:

>> **Current yield:** Sometimes called the *indicated yield,* this shows the yield the fund earned over the past seven days, which is then "annualized" to show what the same rate of return would work out to over one whole year.

>> **Effective yield:** The *effective yield* is the same annualized number, but this time it assumes that all distributions are reinvested in more units, thus achieving compounding. Because it assumes the new units are being added to your stockpile during the year, earning that extra bit of interest, the effective yield is usually a fraction of a percentage point higher than the current yield.

TIP

A fund's current yield is easy to find on all fund companies' websites — just look for a link to "Prices and Performance," or similar terminology. For money market funds, you'll find tables showing current yields under the Price/Yield column. Finding the effective yield isn't so easy; only a few of the fund companies' websites provide separate columns for current and effective yields.

TIP

When inflation and interest rates are low, no real gap exists between the two types of yield. For example, in late 2023, the $2.5-billion CIBC Money Market Fund (Class A) quoted a current yield of 4.9 percent and an effective yield of 5.02 percent. In times of high interest rates, when compounding means the new units pile up fast, the gap between current and effective yield tends to be greater than in times of low rates.

When short-term interest rates were high — such as the early 1990s, when the returns on money market funds climbed well above 10 percent — fund companies started making a lot of noise about their "effective yields," which were much higher than the "current yield" (because the money was theoretically going to compound at high rates). But investors became so confused over which yield was which (and who can blame them?) the regulators eventually stepped in. The fund industry agreed to show both figures in its advertisements.

So, how much can you expect to earn from a money market fund over the next year? Here's a good guideline: Check what banks are offering to pay on one-year GICs.

To compare one-year GIC rates from all the major banks and other financial institutions, check a comparison site such as ratehub.ca or highinterestsavings.ca, which list the rates offered by virtually every deposit-taking institution on all sorts of loans and deposits, including GICs.

Deciding if Money Markets Are All They're Cracked Up to Be

Don't just assume a money market fund is the only place to park your cash — you can usually earn a full percentage point or two more annually with a low-risk short-term bond fund that has low expenses of one percent or less. That may be even truer today with bond ETFs — exchange traded funds are similar to mutual funds, but trade on a stock exchange — which charge even lower MERs than mutual funds. Chapter 14 on bond funds suggests a few good candidates. In this section, we tell you about other types of short-term securities you may want to put inside your portfolio.

Short-term bond funds can be even better than money market funds

Canadian short-term fixed-income funds historically have provided slightly higher returns than Canadian money market funds. The drawback, though, was slightly more volatility and the danger of losing money. That's because bond prices fall when interest rates rise, as explained in Chapter 14, although short-term bonds fall the least of all (when interest rates drop, however, they also go up the least). Money market funds, by contrast, are designed never to leave investors with a loss. For example, when interest rates rose suddenly in 2022, the average Canadian bond fund suffered a loss of 11 percent.

Before you go plunging into a short-term bond fund, remember the higher returns for bond funds were supported by generally falling interest rates since the 1980s. Because rates have been rising again, short-term bond funds have had a tougher time beating money market funds. Still, short-term bond funds are among the safest of all investments. A portfolio stuffed full of high-quality, short-term government bonds with less than five years to go before they mature (check a fund's top holdings) will ride out nearly any horror the markets can dole out.

HISA funds are hot

Since interest rates spiked in 2022, the hottest investments among exchange-traded funds in Canada have been high interest saving account (HISA) ETFs. These are a kind of money market fund invested in the latest and greatest (in interest-rate terms) high-interest savings accounts, usually offered by online-only banks. Though less widely hyped, essentially the same concept is available in the mutual fund format from companies such as CI Financial and Purpose Investments. And because there's no brokerage trading fee involved in buying a mutual fund, it may be an even better deal for small investors than HISA ETFs.

Like most money market products, HISA funds do not change much in value. Virtually all their return comes from the interest paid by the various bank accounts they hold. As of fall 2023, that income yield is pretty good, between four and five percent, making HISA funds competitive with other money market products and both short- and long-term bond funds. (A few class F funds denominated in U.S. dollars pay more than five percent.)

Several banks and trust companies try to cut out the middleman by offering their own HISA accounts directly or through third-party mutual fund dealers. The advantage here is that they are insured by the Canada Deposit Insurance Corporation like guaranteed investment certificates. That means that investments under $100,000 are risk-free; even in the highly unlikely event that the issuer goes bankrupt, your money is guaranteed.

Of course, HISA funds' yields and most likely their popularity can easily go down again alongside prevailing interest rates. But as stated elsewhere in this chapter, money market funds are best for short-term money storage anyway. If you're investing for the long term, stick with stocks and bonds.

Selecting Winning Money Market Funds: Pick Only the Plums

Don't stay up all night picking a money market fund, because you've got a busy day ahead — a long day of sliding through sticky mud, trying to get a grip on infuriated ostriches. Money market funds tend to be pretty similar. In other words, chasing a big yield is pointless because to get one, the manager has to take more risk. If you're buying your other mutual funds at a bank or bank-owned discount broker, simply buy the bank's money market fund. Enough competition exists in the industry to make it embarrassing for a bank to have its money market fund turn into a hound.

If you're buying through a broker or other commissioned salesperson, their office is probably set up to put clients into a particular money market fund, probably from the fund company the salesperson's organization does the most business with. Because money market funds are just temporary holding spots for cash — or they constitute the low-risk, low-return "cash" portion of your portfolio — one fund is pretty well as good as another.

Just make sure you can find the money market fund online. That way, you know you can track your holdings and check the accuracy of your account statement.

In the next section we explore how to choose money market funds and what to watch out for when you buy.

Choose from a mix of money market funds

Most money markets are ultrasafe, sticking to government-issued Treasury bills and bonds. Others increase the risk level very slightly and pick up about one-fifth of a percentage point in annual yield. Either choice is fine — it depends on your personality. Here's how to tell the two options apart:

>> **Treasury bill funds:** For their very nervous clients, many fund companies offer super-conservative "T-bill" funds that buy only short-term government bonds and government Treasury bills (a type of bond with just a few months before it matures).

>> **Money market funds:** For those willing to take on more risk in a cash investment, lower-quality funds — usually known simply as money market funds — exist that are allowed to increase their yield by buying things such as corporate "commercial paper;" that is, short-term debt issued by big companies when they need a bit of cash to tide them over. Most of these funds really aren't dangerous at all, because the companies that issue the paper they hold are nearly always blue-chip multinationals or their Canadian subsidiaries.

WARNING

However, the global financial crisis of 2007 to 2009 cast a dark shadow over corporate cash investments, so make sure the money market fund you're considering pretty much sticks to safe and sure T-bills and other guaranteed paper.

It would take quite an economic cataclysm indeed before any major money market fund racked up losses big enough to force the bank to let the fund's unit price drop. Although some money market funds held some defaulting commercial debt assets in 2007, the fund sponsors purchased the assets from the funds in question. The bottom line is that to the typical investor, no significant difference exists between the conservative T-bill funds and the mildly more aggressive ones.

In the end, the extra bit of yield you get from a money market fund compared with a T-bill fund is very small. For example, the RBC Canadian Money Market Fund, which is free to buy corporate securities, generated an annual return of 1.53 percent in the five years ended September 2023 — only slightly higher than the 1.42-percent annual return from the RBC Canadian T-Bill Fund, which must stick to government debt.

Check out U.S. money market funds

A handful of Canadian companies also offer U.S. money market funds, either for investors who want to hold a lot of cash in U.S. dollars or for scaredy-cats who want a low-volatility investment safe from a drop in the Canadian dollar. Nearly all the funds in this group are bought and sold in U.S. dollars. The same rules apply to pick a fund. Look for low expenses if you want to end up with anything. In some cases over the past 20 years, investors paid out more to the fund company than they got back in returns.

Most U.S. money market funds offered by Canadian firms have similar MERs to their Canadian dollar counterparts; again, look for fees below one percent.

TIP

Canadians can't buy U.S.-based mutual funds unless through that company's Canadian subsidiary, which includes money market funds.

Watch those pesky expenses

REMEMBER

Because the returns from money market funds are so thin, the slightest increase in expenses can leave you with nothing after taxes and inflation.

So refuse to pay a sales commission when buying a money market fund. The broker or salesperson should be able to let you have it commission-free, especially if you're simply parking your money in the money market fund temporarily while you decide on a long-term home for it. Check that the money market fund offered by your bank or salesperson has produced acceptable returns. It probably has.

Get the lowdown on MERs

The main aspect to look for in a money market fund is low MERs. That can be hard in Canada because the cheapest funds, those with MERs of around 0.4 percent or less, are often "premium" funds from the banks, needing big investments of $100,000 and up, or are funds available only to certain groups such as professionals. (ETFs, which anyone can buy, come with much lower fees.)

But if you're buying only small quantities of the fund, don't get too worked up about costs. If you have, say, $5,000 in a money market fund, representing five percent of your $100,000 portfolio, then a one-percentage-point reduction in expenses on the money market fund means an extra $50 a year for you. Nice, sure, but not a huge deal. For convenience, you may decide just to stick with your fund company's money market product, even if it has higher expenses, and treat the extra $50 as a sort of fee. But remember that all expenses eat into your return.

Beware of empty promises

REMEMBER

Don't bother searching endlessly for the money market fund that promises to give you a few more bucks of income.

If the performance looks hot, chances are the fund company has doctored the return in some way — no doubt legally but not quite candidly. That's because in the drab world of T-bills and short-term bonds, generating any kind of extra return through fancy trading without taking on more risk is very hard. (Getting anyone to play footsie in the cafeteria with you at lunchtime is very hard, too, but let's save that for another day.) You can be pretty sure that the yield of a high-flying fund will magically revert to the middle of the pack — or worse — straight after you buy it.

Be curious, George

As always, be curious — and cautious — when some kind of "account management" fee or commission is added on to a money market fund's published expenses. If you're thinking about paying such a fee, ask to see a sample statement that at least shows clients how the fee is calculated and charged. Does the statement clearly reveal how much is taken off? Such extra charges may be legitimate and even a good deal, but they make checking on your real return a lot more complicated.

Remember that simplicity is one of the great beauties of regular mutual funds, because they publish returns and unit prices after their fees. You have a right to a clear explanation of every fee.

TIP

If the fund company or salesperson doesn't respect you enough to provide you with an explanation, then shop elsewhere.

Chapter **18**

Fund Oddities: Strange Brews Sometimes Worth Tasting

With more than 3,400 mutual funds in Canada, it isn't a surprise that some of them have pretty specific or unusual investment focuses. The variety is nothing like in the United States, where details can get so specific 65 funds invest only in debt securities issued by municipalities in Minnesota — enough to merit a special category. But the Canadian fund industry has grown enough to accommodate funds that have such specific mandates as investing in companies involved in water-supply infrastructure or funds that build their portfolios around holdings in publicly traded stock exchanges.

In this chapter, we round up a motley crew of fund oddities — funds so unusual they're difficult to compare to more traditional equity, fixed-income, or balanced funds. These also include target date or life-cycle funds as well as the long-established but waning labour-sponsored group. We also attempt to describe the contents of the catch-all "specialty" fund category, a dumping ground for funds so unique they can't be placed in an existing category (and aren't numerous enough to merit their own category).

Target Date Funds: A Gimmick that May Make Sense

Notwithstanding record rates of immigration, Canada's population is aging. Our big challenge is to find a way to stop working, while we can still enjoy vacations and family. Perhaps by owning target date funds we'll be spared a never-ending career and/or an undignified retirement.

A *target date fund* is a balanced fund of funds with an investment mandate focused on an end date — the investor's projected retirement date or, in the case of education savings plans, the date at which your child enters university or trade school. A fund that's close to the stated retirement date will be largely invested in fixed-income and cash, and one that is many years away will hold mostly equities. (Table 18-1 illustrates how portfolios differ, depending on how near retirement is.) Some funds begin paying out cash distributions during the last few years ahead of the maturity date. Essentially, life-cycle funds do what you and/or your advisor should be doing in managing an investment portfolio over the years, assuming your goal is to have all the money available (cashable) when retirement begins.

Considering your options

The longest-standing life-cycle mutual funds are IA Clarington's Target series, launched in early 2005. (Primerica Canada has a series of five life-cycle segregated funds that date back to 1994.) Three of the big five banks (BMO, RBC, and TD) have offerings in this category, as do fund companies including Fidelity, Mackenzie, Manulife, Canada Life, and Sun Life.

To give you a sense of how target date portfolios become more conservative as the date approaches, we compare two Fidelity ClearPath funds, one dated 2030, for those now close to retirement, and one dated 2050, for those still early in their careers. As of late 2023, the 2050 fund can take on higher risk (that is, more equity exposure) in the expectation of earning higher returns because the holders' retirement is not imminent.

TABLE 18-1 **Fidelity ClearPath 2030 and 2050 Portfolios**

	2030	2050
Cash	1.3%	1,2%
Bonds	36.6%	7.5%
Equities	61.7%	90.9%

Knowing what to look for

The life-cycle-fund concept is quite straightforward and serves as a structured and disciplined retirement investment program. Check for annual expenses, though. In some cases, MERs are fairly reasonable, considering the life-cycle portfolio adjustment service that's included. Ideally, a life-cycle fund's MER should reflect the fees of the underlying funds it holds.

For example, BMO's Target Education Portfolios hold the bank's own bond and equity mutual funds and ETFs. The 2030-targeted fund's largest holding is the BMO Core Bond Fund, which has an MER of 1.16 percent. For only 0.4 percentage points more — 1.56 percent — the BMO Target Education 2030 Portfolio takes care of allocating your money among this and about 15 other funds.

The question remains, though: Can a life-cycle fund provide the asset allocation and investment selection best suited to your specific retirement goals? For some, shopping for one-size-fits-all garments works, while others insist on a precise size. You need to decide what's right for you. How? Think about whether you're comfortable investing in a single fund that will guide you into retirement. If you like having more control — say putting more investments in the U.S. than Canada or making changes as the economy evolves, you may want to get more hands on with your portfolio.

ESG Funds: Once Obscure Securities Have Now Gone Mainstream

Back in the early 2000s, not nearly as many people were sounding the alarm on climate change as there are now. It was only in 2015 that the Paris Agreement took place, which saw nearly 200 countries agree to lower carbon emissions by 2050. At the same time, the spotlight started shining brighter on other societal challenges, whether it be boardroom diversity, fair labour practices, financial transparency, and much more.

Soon, more and more people began talking about environmental, social, and governance (ESG) issues, with many wanting to incorporate various ESG and sustainability factors into their investing strategies. If you're interested in investing with ESG in mind, a wide range of mutual funds and ETFs are now at your disposal — find out more by reading *ESG Investing For Dummies* (Wiley, 2021).

Some funds are fairly straightforward — versions of standard Canadian equity funds that use certain ESG criteria to weed out companies that may not be as focused on say diversity or governance as others. Other funds are far more niche, focusing only on the number of women in boardrooms or on companies that have exposure to the water industry.

Investing in ESG doesn't mean excluding energy companies, and in Canada, many ESG funds still do hold oil and gas operations. (Though you can find funds that don't have any exposure to these businesses.) The problem with ESG today is that there is no defined criteria that every fund company follows when creating these portfolios, with some simply creating their own set of standards to follow. A lot of these funds are also new and don't have decades long track records, while others feel like the flavour of the day.

ESG, whether it's a focus on climate change or diversity, is here to stay, and there's nothing wrong with investing in these funds. In fact, companies that pay attention to ESG issues are known to take less risks and are less prone to problems (such as a sweat shop exposé or financial fraud) than eschew these ideas.

WARNING

You need to do a lot of due diligence on ESG funds before you invest. Look at the securities' holdings — how does it compare to a regular equity mutual fund or ETF? Are the fees higher, and are they worth the extra cost? What criteria is the fund company or bank following when creating these products? Does it make sense to you? Be curious, ask questions, and then decide to buy.

Labour-Sponsored Funds: Small Business, Big Tax Break — for Now

A *labour-sponsored fund* is a venture capital fund that invests in little companies, most of which will probably fail or stagnate. Officially known as "labour-sponsored venture capital funds" (and now categorized by fund data firms as "retail venture capital" funds), they must have a formal backing from a labour union and — in theory — favour investments in companies that have unionized workforces. Private companies aren't publicly traded, which means the true market worth of the stocks the funds own is impossible to establish clearly. And labour funds' expenses are often obscene. Their investments usually take years to mature, and you lose a huge chunk of the benefit from most of these funds unless you leave your money sitting there for almost a decade.

So why would Canadians invest in labour-sponsored funds? Two reasons: because, depending on the province you live in, you could get an attractive tax break totalling 30 percent or even more of their investment, and because small investors otherwise don't have access to the venture capital market, where little-known ventures sometimes explode in value.

You need to know three main aspects about these funds:

TIP

>> **You can get a sizeable tax credit.** Up until 2017, the federal government would refund 15 percent of your investment in the form of a tax credit, which is why these funds were attractive to many. Unfortunately, you can no longer get the tax credit for labour-sponsored funds (also called a labour-sponsored venture capital corporation) that are registered federally, but you can still get the credit if you bought a provincially-registered fund that comes with a provincial tax credit. In any case, the maximum annual investment eligible for credits is usually $5,000 — so investing that amount in a labour fund that qualifies for both federal and provincial credits can immediately net you tax refunds of up to $1,500 ($750 from each government).

In other words, you can end up with $5,000 worth of fund units in return for a cash outlay of only $3,500. As with contributions to RRSPs, you can usually make your purchase of a labour fund during the first 60 days of a calendar year and have the money earn tax credits for the previous year.

>> **You must make a long commitment.** To stop people from buying labour funds, grabbing the tax credits, and then simply selling the units back to the fund, the federal government imposes an eight-year "hold period." If you cash out of the fund within that period, you have to repay the federal tax credit. That's up from a previous hold period of only five years. The government does make exceptions for illness and so on but reckon on tying up your money for a long time.

>> **You may find they're not so unified.** Labour funds often have few connections with the union movement — in fact, many unions want nothing to do with them, complaining that they're a sort of squalid financial mushroom thriving on vastly expensive government tax subsidies, with the money ending up in the hands of Bay Street types and non-unionized companies. Labour funds are a "dubious stock promotion scheme," according to Jim Stanford, an economist with the Canadian Auto Workers.

Alas, along with the federal government, some provinces, such as Ontario have been scaling back their tax breaks, too. The funds seem to be still going strong in Quebec, British Columbia, Saskatchewan, and Nova Scotia, however.

If you're undeterred by labour funds' shaky tax status and the considerable investment risks, be cautious and put no more than five percent of your money here.

Funds with Trendy and Focused Mandates

The funds we discuss in this chapter are unusual, but they're numerous and mainstream enough to merit their own fund categories. Things get really wild and woolly in the mutual fund data surveyors' "specialty" category. You can imagine how oddball these funds are when they can't be placed in the more than three dozen categories established by the data providers. If some of these funds didn't include such intriguing names as Kyoto Planet and Criterion U.S. Buyback, they'd be lost in this classification backwater.

Some of the names reflect mandates that are in vogue, such as extreme income orientations or environmentally conscious investing. Other funds simply are so focused on a specific subsector they cannot be classified among equity funds that invest in broader sectors.

The trendy nature of most of these funds means they're fleetingly popular, which suggests these funds may make poor short-term investments. However, if you feel strongly about investing in improving the world's ecological situation or renewing infrastructure, then nothing's wrong with making a "feel good" investment of, say, five percent or even 10 percent of your portfolio. As for funds with ultra-specific mandates, if you're able to understand the concepts behind their investment mandates, go for it — but tread very carefully and limit your investment to no more than five percent.

Here's a sampling of trendy and ultra-focused fund offerings:

>> **Infrastructure funds:** The developing world needs to expand and modernize its infrastructure, and this represents a huge opportunity for the industrial world's construction companies, utilities, and other firms involved in infrastructure design and implementation. Although the stated mandates of funds such as IG Mackenzie Global Infrastructure refer to infrastructure work done in foreign countries — often by North American firms — nothing says this or similar funds couldn't invest in companies engaged in rebuilding our own crumbling bridges, sewer systems, and other outdated public facilities.

>> **Ultra-specific mandates:** Some funds' mandates are uber-specific — so minutely focused on one investment area or strategy they're probably best left alone in their unique little fiefdoms. But, just so you know, you can actually buy a fund that focuses on investing in shares of stock exchanges (Caldwell Exchange Fund), or one that "takes advantage of the current under-valuations in the late private or early public markets" (Marquis Bridge Fund), or even one focused exclusively in floating rate debt instruments (Invesco Floating Rate Income).

>> **Cryptocurrency funds:** Several funds now provide investors exposure to bitcoin, ether, and other digital coins — digital currencies that are not subject to government regulation and help facilitate trade (often illicit) over the internet. Many people are interested in crypto because of how much one coin has climbed in value since the asset was first created in 2008. (As of December 2023, one bitcoin was worth $41,700, up 12,651 percent since 2015. It is volatile — bitcoin's down from $64,400 peak in November 2001.) Buying one or more coins (or fractions of coins) can be challenging — you need to deal with a crypto exchange or possess a digital wallet.

If you're interested in owning some digital coins, consider a crypto fund or a fund that holds crypto alongside other more traditional investments, such as stocks and bonds.

IN THIS CHAPTER

» Exploring the roots of segregated funds

» Understanding segregated fund essentials

» Looking at how seg funds limit their guarantees

» Adding up the extra cost of going the seg route

» Comparing seg funds to regular mutual funds

» Deciding whether seg funds are right for you

Chapter **19**

Segregated Funds: Investing on Autopilot

Segregated funds — also sometimes known as "guaranteed investment funds" — are investment funds that promise to at least refund an investor's original investment as long as the investor stays in the fund for ten years or, well, dies. Fund salespeople who go forth to pitch them to cautious older customers find that the super-safe funds are quite popular — with the investors' kids, who don't want to see their inheritance wiped out because Mom couldn't resist the allure of Brazilian junk-bond funds.

Segregated funds have attracted billions of dollars from customers who just can't bear the thought of losing their investments in the capital markets. In return, they're willing to pay much higher annual costs, as seg funds have management expense ratios that can be more than one percentage point higher than a nearly identical mutual fund. Investors are willing to swallow this extra charge for a guarantee that some observers argue is of dubious worth. The cost of this guarantee is inflated by tough rules that require insurers to set aside a sizeable amount of capital to cover the cost of these funds' guarantees. A sizeable proportion of the fund choices on sale in Canada are seg funds, although they represent a small share of industry assets.

REMEMBER

We use the expression "seg funds" for both segregated funds and guaranteed investment funds (*guaranteed* funds is the term used by Manulife Financial, TD Asset Management, and some other seg-fund sponsors). Both terms mean essentially the same thing: funds that promise to refund most or all an investor's initial outlay, if held for long enough.

In this chapter, we explain the main differences between segregated (or guaranteed funds) and regular mutual funds, set out some of the main advantages and drawbacks of seg funds, and offer a few guidelines to help you decide whether they're right for you.

Hang On to Your Hats: The Rise of the Segregated Fund

Segregated funds: What a steamy, exotic name. Surely only those wacky knockabout jesters in life insurance could have come up with such an exciting term. For years, they sold a sort of grey version of a mutual fund, often wrapped inside impenetrable life insurance policies. The funds' assets were kept separated or "segregated" from those of the life insurance company itself, hence the name.

In principle, seg funds were much the same as mutual funds: Investors looking for growth from stocks or steady returns from bonds pooled their money in a professionally managed fund and were issued units, representing ownership of the pool that was supposed to increase in value. Often these funds were marketed as part of frequently incomprehensible "whole life" or "universal life" insurance policies that were supposed to provide an investment return as well as protection for the customer's family.

Security with segs

Seg funds offer one advantage that their flashier Porsche-driving, model-dating, mutual fund rivals can't match. Regulated as insurance products, not investments, seg funds come with an attractive guarantee to refund at least 75 percent of an investor's money as long as they stay invested in the fund for a set period. This guarantee passes on to the holder's estate in the event of the investor's death. In other words, when the funds are cashed in at the time of the holder's death, the heirs get at least 75 percent of the amount that was originally invested or the market value, whichever was higher.

The popularity of segs sag

The rising popularity of mutual funds in the late 1990s, with their easy-to-understand unit prices and relatively strong returns, left life insurers and their dreary complicated seg funds in the shade. Seg funds are usually managed extremely cautiously, and they are loaded down with heavy expenses. Another big problem was the difficulty in figuring out what exactly you were buying: an investment or life insurance?

Tired of life insurance salespeople, the public listened avidly as a host of financial authors and other gurus told them to "buy term and invest the rest." The theory, which is generally a good one, goes like this: Why buy some complicated life insurance product loaded with weird concepts such as "commuted value" and "vanishing premiums" when you have no real way to be sure you're getting value for money? As for comparing the endlessly complex "whole life" policies from different companies, you may as well try to teach raccoons to play rugby.

So, the experts advise you to protect your loved ones by buying straightforward, cheap, term life insurance for a simple monthly premium and use the savings, which would otherwise have vanished into a whole-life policy, to buy regular mutual funds. That way, you're clear on exactly what you own and what you're paying. As you know, we're keen on simplicity, so we agree with the strategy.

TIP

If you're a self-employed businessperson or if you have complicated tax needs, life insurance still can offer some important tax-sheltering and estate-planning benefits. So a place for "whole life" coverage still exists in some cases. Just make sure, though, that you get help in this area from a fee-paid professional such as an accountant, and don't fall for the blandishments of a commission-collecting sales rep.

A fancy fund makeover

In the late 1990s, two interesting things happened. Life insurance companies started selling seg funds that looked like mutual funds — and mutual fund companies started selling seg-fund versions of their mutual funds. Manulife Financial got the ball rolling by launching funds that essentially took well-known mutual funds from big partners such as AIM Trimark Investments (now Invesco Canada), AGF Management Ltd., and Fidelity Investments Canada Ltd. and wrapped them in a nice cozy "guaranteed investment fund" blanket that pledged to return at least all the investors' original outlay if they died or if they held the funds for ten years.

The fund industry soon struck back with CI Investments Inc. launching segregated versions of its own funds in partnership with a life insurance company. Other mutual fund players followed suit, launching seg versions of their mutual funds on which a life insurance company provided the guarantee. Soon, life insurance companies were scrambling to jazz up their stale seg offerings by forming partnerships with fund companies or hiring fancy managers of their own.

In the old days, seg funds were generally grey collections of blue-chip stocks and bonds. But soon after the millennium, the insurance industry came up with much more exciting products, including seg funds that invest in emerging markets, health sciences, resource companies, the technology-crazed NASDAQ stock market, and Asian stocks. Government regulators noticed and started to wonder whether life insurance companies had enough money to make good on the guarantees they attached to these relatively unpredictable funds. They got so worried, in fact, that they forced companies to set aside extra piles of cash to cover the potential cost of providing these risky guarantees to investors.

Seg Fund Essentials

We outline the main features of seg funds here. Note that most of these funds technically count as insurance contracts, which means they involve a whole new set of jargon and concepts. We introduce some of the new terms as we go along, but remember that this short description can't hope to cover every seg fund from every company.

Guaranteeing the return of your initial investment

The essential point with seg funds is their ten-year guarantee. In insurance lingo, when you buy a seg fund, you bought a "contract" that "matures" in ten years. It doesn't matter how you hold the fund: in a taxable account or a Registered Retirement Savings Plan (or some other kind of tax-sheltered account, such as a tax-free savings account). The guarantee usually states that no matter what happens to the fund or the markets in the decade following your purchase, after ten years you're entitled to get back at least the amount of money you put into the fund or the market value of your units, whichever is greater.

Say, for instance, you bought $10,000 worth of a fund that proceeded to have an awful ten years, slashing the value of your holding to $8,000. After the period, you can go to the fund company and get your $10,000 back. If, by contrast, the fund does reasonably well, doubling the value of your holding to $20,000, then you get the $20,000. Under insurance law, the guarantee must be for at least 75 percent of your investment, but many insurers and fund companies have boosted that to 100 percent for marketing reasons. However, tough rules introduced in 2000 forced many companies to scale the guarantee back to 75 percent again, although a good selection of funds with a 100-percent guarantee is still available.

Living longer than you may

The investment-principal guarantee also applies when the *annuitant* (that is, the person whose life has been insured) named in the contract dies. In that case, the value of the seg fund units is paid to the policy's *beneficiary* (the person selected to get the death benefit). No matter when the policy was bought, the amount paid out to the beneficiary is subject to the guarantee. They get either the original investment or the market value at the time of death, whichever is more.

Note that the so-called guarantee is pretty limited. It applies only after ten years or upon death. If you sell your fund units at any other time, you get only the market value, even if it's less than your purchase price. Whining to the fund company if the value of your units has collapsed after three years is pointless. They'll just make a sympathetic face, give you an attractive key ring, and tell you to come back in seven years.

Enabling you to reset the value of successful funds

A popular seg fund feature is the ability to "reset" the amount covered by the guarantee, often up to twice a year. For example, say you put $10,000 into a technology-based seg fund and saw the value of your investment soar to $13,000 in six months. You could reset the value of your contract at the higher amount, so you're guaranteed to get back at least $13,000 after ten years (or your estate is guaranteed to get back at least $13,000 when you die).

The only drawback: Resetting the contract starts the clock ticking again, so you have to wait a full ten years, not nine and a half, before the contract matures.

Offering asset protection

For self-employed businesspeople or professionals who potentially face lawsuits from creditors, segregated funds can be an excellent way to protect assets. Because they're an insurance contract, seg funds are normally out of the reach of creditors, as long as a spouse, parent, child, or grandchild is named as the beneficiary or the beneficiary has been named "irrevocably" (that is, their written consent must be obtained to name a new beneficiary).

Giving to your heir apparent without the hassle

Seg funds are a great way of passing money on to heirs without hassle or fees (apart from redemption charges if you bought the funds on a deferred-load basis). Again, because they count as life insurance, the proceeds from seg funds are paid directly to your heirs after you die; they do not pass through your estate. That means the money escapes provincial probate fees, a sort of death tax in all provinces except Quebec that can run as high as 1.5 percent. And the money is usually paid out to the beneficiaries immediately, without the holdups that can plague the settlement of estates. Normal bequests are public documents, but seg fund contracts are private, so you can leave money to a charity or individual without Nosey Parker finding out about it.

WARNING

Seg funds avoid probate fees, but they can be less tax-efficient than regular mutual funds when the holder dies. Normally, investment assets pass to a spouse with no taxes payable immediately on capital gains that have been earned. But a seg fund is considered to be a trust for tax purposes, so gains earned in these funds may be taxable. Be sure to talk to a knowledgeable accountant.

Because seg funds are life insurance contracts, you must buy them from an advisor who is licensed to sell life insurance, which means that not every financial planner or broker may be able to help you. However, more and more brokers and planners are taking the necessary courses to qualify to sell insurance, or they refer their clients to a colleague or local insurance agent or broker who can sell seg funds.

TIP

Mutual funds must obtain their unitholders' consent to increase fees, but seg funds are pretty well free to charge what they like. Seg funds are complicated beasts, and their "information folders," the prospectus-like documents that set out their features, are tough to read. You have to buy them through a licensed insurance salesperson, so take your time and find an experienced agent or broker whom you trust. You need an expert on your side to help you figure out the often-horrendous complexities.

The Cost of Certainty

How much extra do you pay for the guarantee? For volatile funds, the difference can be several percentage points of your investment each year — slicing into returns like a giant weighted machete cutting rancid butter — but if you shop aggressively and buy sane, high-quality funds, you may be able to get the coverage at a reasonable cost.

One of the issues that makes insurance companies most nervous is, clearly, foreign stock investing, with its added risk in the form of currency swings — on global equity seg funds, insurers cost almost 0.6 of a percentage point more. For investments closer to home, they get less cagey.

On Canadian balanced funds, normally a fairly stable stew of bonds and stocks, insurers apparently ask less than half of a percentage point in extra MER. They charge roughly the same premium for providing the (limited, remember) pledge on Canadian stocks. Of course, looking at category medians or averages doesn't highlight some examples of seg funds with pretty spectacular MERs. How does 4.65 percent annually on the seg version of a TD's Managed Maximum Equity Growth fund sound? That's nearly half your money in a decade. The mutual version of the same fund charges an MER about one-half as much. This, of course, demonstrates the cost of insuring an investment in a risky investment area such as biotechnology. As for bond funds, charging an annual premium of more than one-half of a percentage point to guarantee against losses may seem exorbitant, given the relatively low volatility of bond portfolios. Then again, in 2022, bonds had their worst year on record after interest rates shot up. (When rates rise, bond prices fall.)

The gap between mutual and seg money market funds is smaller — around a percentage point. Yet this seems severe when you consider the safety of this type of investment. Money market seg funds exist only for the purpose of keeping an investor's money within a particular fund family, thus avoiding switch-out fees for an investor who wants to park their money and later reinvest within that family of seg funds.

The "Deal" with Segs

Many commentators have argued forcefully that those costly guarantees are rip-offs when it comes to bond funds and of dubious benefit for balanced funds, which are supposed to be sedate portfolios that avoid losses. After all, in the 15 calendar years from 2007 through 2022, the median Canadian fixed-income mutual fund lost money only twice. The median Canadian neutral balanced mutual fund had only three losing years in that period, falling 13.6 percent in 2008, 1.9 percent in 2018, and 9.1 percent in 2022.

REMEMBER

Given the long-term tendency of stocks to rise, it's also rare, to find any kind of equity fund that loses money over ten years. That makes it unlikely you'll ever need to collect on the ten-year maturity guarantee (which promises to at least refund your investment if you've held the fund for a decade).

Admittedly, a lot of flea-bitten funds get buried within median and average statistics as a result of the fund industry's habit of quietly folding underperformers into their better-performing sister funds. This "survivorship bias," which results in merged and otherwise discontinued funds — many of them truly awful — vanishing from the record is notorious for casting a rosy glow over the industry's performance past. However, data firm Morningstar calculates indices that wipe out survivorship bias and, equally important, produce a weighted average return for all mutual fund categories. (We take a closer look at the Morningstar Canada Fund Indices in Chapter 21.)

If you decide high-MER seg funds are a scam because mutual funds rarely lose money over a decade, you may be missing the point. Over shorter periods, mutual funds are perfectly capable of losing money, and lots of it. For older investors who are worried about dying just as their funds are going into the tank, taking thousands of dollars off the value of their estate, a segregated fund guarantee is mighty comforting. At least on death, the full value of the original investment goes to the heirs.

REALITY CHECK FOR SEG FUNDS

Check out how one segregated fund has fared against the normal mutual funds it's supposed to track. Manulife Financial launched its MLI Fidelity Canadian Asset Allocation GIF Fund 1 in 1997. The fund was pitched as a conservative way to achieve much the same performance as the Fidelity Canadian Asset Allocation Fund, a fund that switches among stocks, bonds, and cash in an effort to achieve high total returns.

At the cost of a higher MER, currently 3.54 percent compared with 2.23 percent for the Fidelity fund, investors in the GIF got the usual guaranteed return of at least their original investment after ten years or upon death. The Fidelity fund, by contrast, could in theory lose money over ten years, leaving unitholders in the red. The Manulife GIF funds were a huge marketing success: By the end of 1999, Manulife Fidelity Canadian Asset Allocation GIF's assets had ballooned to $750 million, making it Canada's seventh-biggest seg fund at that time.

As of October 2023, an investor who put $10,000 into the GIF on inception (January 1997) was sitting on $34,763, or a cumulative 248-percent return on their investment. The same $10,000 investment in the Fidelity fund grew to $48,110, or 348 percent. In other words, the Manulife fund has done a poor job of tracking the Fidelity fund, with the difference in returns attributable to its extra annual costs of more than a percentage point.

To Seg or Not to Seg: Are They for You?

TIP

The bottom line with seg funds is almost certainly that they're best suited for older or unwell investors who have a reasonable probability of passing away in the next few years. Seg funds' protection from creditors also makes them very attractive to self-employed businesspeople and entrepreneurs.

Here are two examples, adapted from material originally produced by AIM Trimark (now Invesco Canada), of older investors who seem well suited for seg funds.

The first is a 77-year-old woman with four nieces and three nephews to whom she wants to leave money without legal hassles and probate fees. She puts $50,000 into a seg fund. If she dies after five years and the value of her deposit has risen to $85,000, her beneficiaries get $85,000, minus any withdrawals or redemption fees if she bought the funds on a back-end-load basis. But say the market has slumped, and the value of her contract is only $43,000. Then her beneficiaries get the guaranteed amount of $50,000, again minus redemption fees.

The other example is a 61-year-old, self-employed engineer who's two years from retirement. He isn't satisfied with the interest rates available on guaranteed investment certificates, but he doesn't want to put his money at risk just before he retires. So he invests $100,000 in seg funds. If it grows to $230,000 in ten years, when the contract matures, he gets $230,000. But if the value of his fund drops to $80,000 at maturity, he gets his original $100,000, minus any withdrawals.

Then consider the estate-planning advantages of seg funds, especially the relative simplicity of passing on money to a beneficiary by simply putting it in a seg fund. Don't get too excited about saving on probate fees, though, because the higher management fees on seg funds will quickly wipe out that advantage.

REMEMBER

Choosing a seg fund really comes down to the famous "pillow factor." Just how well can you sleep at night knowing your money is in danger? If you're really afraid of losses, then seg funds may well be your thing, despite their higher management expense ratio. The emotional security is sometimes worth the higher MERs.

IN THIS CHAPTER

» Looking at preselected fund packages

» Getting the critical information before you buy

» Highlighting fund packages' best attributes

» Acknowledging the downside of packages

» Watching out for the hype

» Checking out a shining example

Chapter **20**

Fund Packages: One-Stop Shopping

We're always being hassled and badgered to think for ourselves in our workplaces — so isn't it nice to let someone else take the wheel for a while? Well, mutual fund companies and stockbrokers are keen students of human behaviour, and they've noticed that many investors like to be presented with simple one-decision products that they can just buy and forget about.

Hence the emergence of fund packages, also known as *wraps, funds of funds*, and, more recently, *all-in-one funds*. Brokers, bank employees, and financial planners enjoy selling them and, increasingly, investors like to buy them — both in mutual fund and exchange-traded fund (ETF) form. These funds are nice and simple to hold because they come with built-in diversification — you can conceivably own one all-in-one fund, something more and more investors do.

In this chapter, we describe the main types of preselected fund packages and list some of their advantages and disadvantages.

The Flavours Fund Packages Come In

A *fund package* is a group of individual mutual funds selected by a fund company or money manager for the purpose of providing the investor with a diversified fund portfolio in a single product. (A growing number of one-stop-shop ETFs work the same way as packaged mutual funds, but we won't get into them here. We suggest picking up *ETFs For Canadians For Dummies, 2E* to discover more.) It's structured as an individual fund (or "wrap") that has a portfolio made up only of individual mutual funds, usually drawn from the sponsoring firm's fund lineup. Depending on its investment objectives, a package typically holds one or more equity funds, a bond fund, and a money market fund (as the cash component).

Fund companies, banks, stockbrokers, insurance companies, fund managers, and financial planning firms have come up with a wide range of fund combinations that claim to take care of your every need, eliminating the need to pick and choose your own funds. Sometimes these are called *managed accounts*.

Checking out the risk categories

Typically, before you're sold a fund package, you are asked to fill out a questionnaire that establishes how much risk you can stand and what sort of annual return you're demanding. From there, the salesperson, bank employee, or fund company representative simply takes your money and sticks it into a suitable package.

You probably are offered something that falls into one of these three risk categories:

>> **Conservative:** The safest packages of all, they're all about conserving capital while offering a reasonable flow of income from bonds or Treasury bills, and perhaps the chance of some capital gains from stocks. (Remember that "income" in this context refers to the steady interest payments generated by bonds, money that you simply plow back into the same kind of investment.)

  These conservative packages are usually full of funds that invest in *bonds* — which are debts owed by governments and big companies — and *money market* securities — which are short-term borrowings by the government and large corporations.

>> **Moderate:** The next step up on the volatility scale, these packages are pretty similar to the typical balanced fund. They're for investors who don't mind the occasional loss in return for the higher returns that stocks and long-term bonds offer. Generally, their mixture of stocks and bonds are close to one-half each, with a cash anchor of about five percent.

>> **Growth:** These packages own mostly stocks and typically have only a small portion of their assets, usually 25 percent or less, in bond and money market funds, with the rest in equities. You are steered into these mixtures only if you indicate on the questionnaire that you won't be needing to cash in any of the investment for several years. If your "horizon" is long term, the theory goes, you shouldn't be worried by a nasty dip in the value of your holdings in the short term.

The most entertaining growth packages, naturally, are those with "aggressive" in their name. This term simply denotes a mixture that puts as little as 10 percent of your assets into bonds and holds lots of volatile stuff such as emerging markets and technology companies.

Check out Chapter 4, where we help you determine what type of investor you are. If you're a saver, you're best suited for a conservative package. Balanced investors, consider a moderate package. Growth packages, unsurprisingly, are best suited to growth investors.

Sticking with Canada or going global

Whether you stay true to the maple leaf or go global depends partly on what you think will happen to currencies and, of course, on your time horizon. If the Canadian dollar tanks, then it would be better to have your money outside the country. If it goes up, then it's better to keep a lot of your investments Canadian. But it's impossible to know what will happen to foreign exchange rates in advance.

For short-term and medium-term savings, an all-Canadian package of investments is probably fine because you plan to spend the money relatively soon, and you'll be spending it in Canadian dollars. But with long-term equity packages, make sure you get at least some global stock action. It spreads your risk by giving you a more mixed bag of investments, and great companies to invest in exist all around the world. And you also need to protect yourself against a drop in the Canadian dollar.

What to Find Out Before You Buy

Because fund packages are highly complex and all-encompassing vehicles under the hood, you could spend all day quizzing your advisor or fund company on specifics. But what led you to this solution likely means that's exactly what you don't want to be bothered with! So make it simple. There are really just two essential questions you need to ask before buying one of these packages. Be sure to pose these stumpers to anyone who tries to peddle a fund portfolio to you.

How much will this cost me?

With some of these preselected mixtures, you must pay the regular fees and expenses of the funds included in the service plus an extra fee for the package itself that can run as high as one percent annually.

Adding another one percent in yearly costs is a heavy weight to put on your portfolio, especially if some of the equity funds in the package already have management expense ratios (MERs) of more than 2.5 percent. Many brokers and financial planners sell their own private wrap or asset allocation products that use funds that charge low or no management fees. But in this case, the client pays a separate fee — often listed directly on their statement — to cover the asset allocation service.

Not all companies have the MER of these funds listed on their website, though some do. Some even waive the fees associated with the underlying funds. Fidelity Investments has an interesting line under the MER section of its managed portfolios fund facts documents: "This is the total of the Fund's management fee (including the trailing commission), fixed administration fee, and certain operating expenses (fund costs). Fidelity waived some of the Fund's expenses. If it had not done so, the MER would have been higher."

TECHNICAL STUFF

In theory, costs you incur trying to earn investment income are tax-deductible, so you may be able to claim fund management fees against taxes for funds you hold in non-registered accounts. (Costs cannot be deducted for funds held in an RRSP or TFSA.) Some vendors like to make a big song and dance about this advantage. But that applies only to fees that are charged separately to the investor and not simply deducted from the fund. Ordinary mutual fund charges and fees are quietly taken out of the fund's assets by the manager and can't be claimed as a cost. However, though they're not directly deductible, ordinary fees do reduce your taxable capital gains and income by cutting into the return you get from your funds, so the fees are ultimately deductible, too.

Although it's great to see package fees broken down openly on your statement instead of having them buried in the management expense ratio, make sure you understand what you're paying — because it can be confusing.

WARNING

Funds that charge you expenses separately instead of taking them out of your annual return present another problem. Because they ignore expenses and costs when they report those returns, they'll often seem to be doing better than funds that handle fees and costs in the normal way, by extracting them before they report performance.

How do I know how well I'm doing?

Some services don't publish their returns publicly, and even if they do, the names are often so similar it can be hard to remember what you own. Many, though, do list performance on their websites just like they do with other mutual funds. For instance, as of July 31, 2023, CIBC Managed Growth Portfolio has a 10-year annualized return of 6.9 percent, which is higher than the S&P/TSX Composite Index's 4.22 percent annualized return (though before its 2.47 percent fee is taken into account).

The account statement you receive semi-annually, quarterly, or monthly for any service should make your returns absolutely clear, so ask to see a sample before you sign up. Don't be fobbed off by vague excuses.

WARNING

If the salesperson or bank employee can't demonstrate that your returns will be clearly reported, avoid the product.

The Upside of Fund Packages

The idea of simply handing over your cash to let professionals decide the asset mix can be wonderfully attractive. And fund packages offer a few other important advantages:

>> **Dealing with only one fund company:** You don't have to juggle account statements and tax slips from several sellers. Most investors, with their busy lives, loathe getting piles of mail from fund companies.

>> **Automatic rebalancing:** You don't have to rejig your funds if strong returns or big losses throw the asset mix of your portfolio out of whack. Many packages are periodically rebalanced by the company so that clients don't end up with too much of their money riding on just one type of investment.

   For example, say you put $100,000 into a sedate portfolio made up equally of bond funds and stock funds. If the stock market slides by 20 percent but interest rates stay unchanged, your stock funds will probably be worth $40,000, while your bond funds will still be worth $50,000. The portfolio service will redeem about $5,000 worth of bond funds to maintain your 50/50 mix and put the money into stocks instead to restore the equal balance.

>> **Charging reasonable fees:** Because they use regular mutual funds that are subject to public scrutiny and fairly tight securities laws, the widely available fund packages charge fees that are usually reasonable, at least when you compare them to the charges that trust companies or lawyers can levy for looking after assets.

The Downside of Fund Packages

Most people pay someone else to change the oil in their car or paint their house. These tedious tasks that, in a pinch, they could do themselves. So there's no shame in getting a fund company to manage your nest egg. Indeed, it might be a wise choice. But go into it with your eyes open. Letting someone else pick your funds for you does have its drawbacks. Here are a few:

>> **An unexciting way to invest:** It's boring and Big Brotherish. All you get is the same gruel-like return earned by everyone else who buys the same package, with no real clue as to which fund did well and which one barked your money away. Being an informed consumer who can tell that, for example, bonds were up while international equities were down just by looking at your account statement is more interesting.

>> **Extra costs:** If extra costs are levied, they eat into your return, especially when tacked on top of the underlying mutual funds' fees and expenses.

>> **Tax implications of rebalancing:** The regular portfolio rebalancing by the fund company can trigger taxable capital gains distributions for investors holding the package of funds outside a tax-advantaged account such as an RRSP or TFSA. Fund companies maintain that these distributions will generally be small because they're simply readjusting the asset mix rather than turning the fund inside out, but taxable payouts add unpredictability and can cut into your real, after-tax return.

>> **Unreported returns:** Be very wary before you buy into any fund or managed investment whose returns and unit price aren't published on financial websites or phone apps. Remember, sunlight disinfects: If the performance isn't publicly reported alongside that of big regular mutual funds making comparisons simple, then you can never really be sure you're not stuck with a dog.

>> **Constricted by your funds:** If you're in pooled or house-brand funds that are sold only through a particular brokerage or financial planning firm, then moving your money elsewhere can be troublesome because your new broker or planner may be unwilling to add this fund to their product lineup. (A *pooled fund* is similar to a mutual fund, except it is sold on an institutional basis by offering memorandum rather than by prospectus, and requires a high minimum investment, often $300,000 or more.)

>> **Potential confusion:** Working out how you're doing or even what package you own can be tricky, given the confusing multiplicity of products with similar names. Web sites and brochures can be vague on how the systems actually work, and salespeople are hard-pressed to keep up with the flood of new offerings. And a whole bunch of transactions may be reported to you on your

statement, just as though you had ordered them, when the portfolio is automatically rebalanced or a fund is dropped from the mixture. If you're not completely sure you understand what you're buying, better to steer clear.

Just about every fund seller claims that its asset allocation strategies are best, and comparing them is just about impossible. That's because the returns produced by any system tell only half the story. The other half is how much risk the portfolio took on and how violent the swings were. To provide a crude example, a portfolio that made 12 percent a year for five years may look superior to one that generated a return of just six percent annually. But if it turns out that the first portfolio was exclusively invested in super-risky, early-stage biotechnology shares while the second held mostly government bonds, then the second portfolio probably did a better job — earning a good profit relative to the low level of risk it incurred.

TIP

Before buying a fund package from a bank or other seller, try to get the goods on how well it's been doing from a third-party online source such as Morningstar. ca. Before you hand over any money, make sure you can actually find the package at one of these sources. That way, you'll be able to track your returns easily from month to month without relying solely on your account statement from the company.

REMEMBER

Don't worry too much about trying to figure out the difference between one company's Nervous Nellie Never-Lose-a-Penny-of-My-Money Portfolio and another fund seller's Shaky Sue Can't-Stand-the-Slightest-Suspicion-of-Suffering-a-Slump-Asset-Allocation Service. The big thing, as usual, is to look for low costs so you know you're getting reasonable value and clear reporting so you at least know how you're doing.

Steer Clear of the Hype

Packages have become an extremely popular product for financial advisors to sell. They transfer the investment selection decisions to portfolio-management experts within their firm or at a fund company of another third-party firm. The advisor's main role is to help you determine the right asset allocation — the breakdown among equities, fixed income, and cash.

Advisors who pitch fund packages praise the benefits of professional portfolio management and the discipline this brings. They talk about portfolio "rebalancing," which the package's managers take care of at regular intervals — often quarterly — to ensure the asset allocation is correct. Advisors all but guarantee you are much better off in a package as opposed to a collection of individually selected funds. But take all such claims with a big swig of salty vinegar. Investment wizards are infallible only until they blow it, and the explosion can be spectacular. The market and economy have a delightful way of throwing weird curveballs that completely fool the number-crunchers.

REMEMBER

When banks and other fund sellers pitch these packages, they're trying to eliminate the need for you to pick any other fund seller's wares. They'd much rather you stuck to their product line than mix and match funds from different sellers. So they offer their super-simple, off-the-shelf packages that relieve you of the need to choose your mutual funds and that tempt you to go with their stuff.

Some companies even sell packages that also include other companies' funds. Even IG Wealth Management, a bastion of the in-house product approach, has packages that include *third-party funds* and ETFs — funds from other managers. However, you'll notice that third-party funds often come from companies such as Fidelity Investments Canada or AGF Management that pay a sales commission to the people who put the package together. These packages may include good funds, but they also carry the same disadvantages as other pre-mixed fund selections. That is, their costs can be high, and it's hard to know which fund is doing well for you and which is sinking like a lead submarine.

Preselected packages of funds are convenient, but you're not guaranteed that the fund company, bank, or broker has got the mix right. And the packages can make it hard to know how well you're doing or even what exactly you own.

REMEMBER

Buying a varied selection of high-quality, low-cost funds, monitoring the mix yourself, and adjusting it when one asset class either soars or falls out of bed is always better.

A Look at a Decent Fund Package

If all-in-one fund packages are new to you, it's possible that you wouldn't recognize one if you saw it. This section provides an example of a fund package that's worthy of your attention.

Canadian Imperial Bank of Commerce offers packages under the Managed Portfolio nameplate that are among the better buys. They impose no extra fees beyond the charges and costs of the underlying CIBC funds.

Table 20-1 gives a breakdown of how their balanced package invests — 60 percent in growth and 40 percent in income investments, as of August 25, 2023. Going through the list of investments, you should get a better understanding of why these are sometimes called "funds of funds." Just remember the underlying assets here are mostly stocks and bonds, as in any other portfolio.

TABLE 20-1

Anatomy of a Fund Package: CIBC Managed Balanced Portfolio

Fund	Percentage of Package
Income Funds	
CIBC Canadian Bond Fund	13.7%
Renaissance Corporate Bond Fund	7.4%
Renaissance Floating Rate Income Fund	5.1%
Renaissance High-Yield Bond Fund	5.1%
CIBC Canadian Short-Term Bond Index Fund	4.4%
CIBC Global Bond Fund	3.5%
Growth funds	
CIBC U.S. Equity Fund	14.3%
Renaissance Canadian Growth Fund	8.4%
CIBC Canadian Equity Value Fund	8.3%
CIBC U.S. Index Fund	8.3%
CIBC International Equity Fund	8%
CIBC European Equity Fund	4.7%
CIBC Emerging Markets Fund	3.6%
CIBC U.S. Small Companies Fund	2.6%
CIBC Asia Pacific Fund	2.3%
Cash	0.5%

4
The Nuts and Bolts of Keeping Your Portfolio Going

Chapter **21**

The Places to Go for Fund Information

D on't get us wrong. The best place to start your fund familiarization journey is right here, reading this book in your favourite armchair or at the dining table, highlighting away.

But after you're done reading this book and it has taken on the appearance of an old shoe, the pages well-worn from careful reading and notations, you need to roll up your sleeves and start doing some research of your own.

You can find pretty much everything you ever wanted to know about investing online, but be careful; there are plenty of people creating TikToks or producing articles about investing (and especially bitcoin and getting rich quick) who may not actually know much at all about making money.

In this chapter, we point you towards some reliable, trusted sources for information about investing. The sources we recommend include media outlets, investment research firms, regulatory sites, financial industry associations, and the banks and fund companies themselves. Each source of information will have its own point of view, priorities, and interests, so getting informed about investing means paying attention to multiple voices.

Independent Sources: Where to Get the Honest Goods

Third-party mutual fund websites are where to start your search. They're perhaps the most useful places to mine fund information because they don't sell investments; their business is just providing you with information. The major sites let you set up a portfolio of funds — and, in many cases, other investment securities such as stocks, bonds, and exchange-traded funds (ETFs). Fund and securities prices are updated daily, enabling you to track your investments — or any collection of investments you want. In some cases, the sites can produce detailed charts and tables of one or more portfolios.

Taking a look at the top two

Globefund.com, which now takes you to *The Globe and Mail*'s mutual fund page, and Morningstar.ca are the country's leading mutual fund information sites. Although some of you may want to check out other sites (we recommend a few later in this section), if you'd rather not bother, you'll do fine with these two.

The Globe and Mail

You can easily find a fund at www.theglobeandmail.com/investing/markets/funds — or just type in globefund.com, which offers information on many mutual and segregated funds sold in Canada. You can look up an individual fund by typing its name in the Search field, search for funds by category, or by sponsoring company. The site offers a detailed report for each fund showing rates of return over the various periods ranging from one month to 20 years, portfolio asset allocation summaries by overall asset class (stocks, bonds, cash), geographic area and (for stocks) industry group, and the portfolio's top-ten individual holdings. You can create charts of a fund's performance over a variety of time frames and compare it against a benchmark index.

In addition to following mutual funds, *The Globe*'s ETF site tracks Canadian and American exchange-traded funds.

REMEMBER

Because they're traded like stocks, you can buy ETFs in the United States even though you don't live there, unlike mutual funds. (For more on ETFs, refer to Chapter 15.)

For stock and bond information, click over to Globeinvestor.com. If your portfolio includes both funds and individual securities, you can keep an eye on them in one spot using *The Globe* Portfolio system.

The Globe's mutual fund and ETF resources benefits hugely from the extensive resource of *The Globe and Mail*. In addition to having access to a sea of performance and other data, you can access recent articles on funds and investing, notably regular contributions from *The Globe*'s respected personal finance columnist Rob Carrick.

We should say Globefund.com is not what it used to be — there were ratings for each fund back in the day, but no longer. Still, it's a great place to get a lot of solid and trusted information.

Morningstar.ca

The Canadian unit of the longtime U.S. mutual fund tracking giant offers an array of data on the thousands of mutual, segregated, and other investment funds sold in this country. This site is up to date and extremely comprehensive in its presentation.

Enter a fund's name in the Search field and you are treated to an impressively detailed fund report. The Portfolio page provides charts of the fund's overall asset allocation (stocks, bonds, cash, and so on), followed by lists showing allocation among industry sectors and the top-10 individual securities holdings. You can get much of this information from other data providers but go to Morningstar.ca to produce a (free) table comparing the asset allocation of all funds in a specific asset category.

Morningstar also rates funds that have a track record of three years or longer, assigning one to five stars. Funds are rated in relation to their peers — other qualifying funds in their asset category. These categories are the official ones supervised by the Canadian Investment Funds Standards Committee, an independent group made up of database firm executives and other impartial industry observers. The rating is based on a risk-adjusted return, which combines rate of return and a risk measure based on the fund's unit-value volatility.

Morningstar's reports set it apart from the rest of the internet pack. Morningstar is the only independent website operator in Canada to provide analysts' reports on individual funds. These reports are prepared according to a rigorous research framework, which ensures each fund is fairly measured against its peers. After the research has been completed, the analysts don't hold any punches, telling a particular fund's story in sometimes brutal clarity. You won't find reports on all the funds you're interested in, but the choice is pretty impressive — the firm's team of analysts covers several hundred funds. The reports are timely, too; reports remain posted for a year or so and are removed if they're not updated by that time.

Morningstar.ca has other unique article content, including profiles of hundreds of portfolio managers, stories on the mutual fund industry, and category ratings for funds that follow environmental, social, and governance (ESG) factors.

The site is free, although Morningstar.ca has a premium version that gives you even more investing tools, insights, and resources.

Checking out other sites worth a visit

Between *The Globe and Mail* and Morningstar, you're set for independent mutual fund information. But we know some people are information junkies — if you're one of those people, we recommend bookmarking the sites we mention in this section.

MoneySense.ca

We're biased about this publication — Bryan honed most of his personal finance writing chops at MoneySense. The site is a must read for investing and money junkies — there's plenty to chew on, including stories about ETFs, mortgage rates, discount brokerages, and more. While the publication — now owned by mortgage comparison site Ratehub — produces mutual fund content, it has scaled back over the years. It used to have a Best Mutual Funds list, but it hasn't been updated since 2020. It does regularly update its Best ETF List, though, which is worth a look.

Fundlibrary.com

Fund Library, one of the first mutual fund Web sites in Canada, offers a wide range of services. Like many fund information sites, Fund Library has also expanded to offering ETF information. Users can find all kinds of information, including data on thousands of Canadian mutual funds, ETFs, and North American stocks; a daily list of the top 10 mutual fund and ETF performers; articles written by investment experts; interactive charts that track historical fund performance and fund-to-fund and fund-to-index comparison charts.

One key feature is its FundGrade fund ratings, which rate funds based on their objectives and quantitative analysis, while its fund profile pages have plenty of useful information, including historical performance, volatility metrics, ESG scores, asset allocation breakdown, and more.

Fund Library also has plenty of original editorial content, including columns from experts, such as personal finance legend Gordon Pape. You can also find manager interviews, industry news, and even some sponsored personal finance content here.

Lipper Leaders

Lipper Inc., found at `www.lipperleaders.com`, is one of Morningstar's biggest competitors in the United States. It's basic website isn't much to look at, but its Lipper Leaders rating system makes it easy to compare funds against their peers. Lipper Leader ratings are calculated for five different *metrics* or analysis areas: total return, consistent return, preservation, expense, and tax efficiency.

Unlike their competitors' ratings, Lipper Leaders are assigned using an even 20-percent peer-group division. For example, the top 20 percent of funds (ranked by specific criteria) in a category receive a rating of 1.

Other sites worth a look

Hungry for more info on mutual funds? A number of other Canadian websites offer interesting mutual fund content, including the following:

>> **CanadianFundWatch.com:** This sometimes quirky website is run by investor advocate Ken Kivenko and consists almost entirely of his commentaries, which tend to lash out at the fund industry's favourite whipping topics such as high management expense ratios (MERs) and investor protections. The site also features explanatory pieces on such analytical measures as the Sharpe Ratio, a widely used assessment of a fund's return relative to a risk-free cash investment (a government Treasury bill). However, the site is not updated nearly as much as it once was.

>> **Financial Post:** Yes, the *Post* is still kicking, and its financial pages are still worth a read. Like everyone else, their investing coverage is broader than it once was, tackling ETFs, stocks, and more, but they're still holding the fund industry to account. Some good mutual fund-related educational content is at `https://financialpost.com/tag/mutual-funds` that's worth perusing.

WHAT EVER HAPPENED TO PAPER?

Back in the day, a great way to get started in mutual fund investing was to go to your local mega-bookstore, head for the business section, browse for an hour or so, and pick a couple of volumes with the right content and tone to buy. A month or so (and a few colour highlighter pens) later, you'd be knowledgeable enough about fund investing to call a broker or financial planner — or, if you were really on top of the topic, a discount broker or other direct seller.

(continued)

(continued)

Although we still recommend including a bookseller in your fund-research pilgrimage — after all, you're reading this book — bookstore shelves have almost nothing left for the Canadian fund investor. Sure, the business section is as vast as ever, but most of those books are about the stock market, portfolio management, financial planning, or other money-related topics. You'll come across plenty of mutual fund books, too, but almost all of these are of real use only to American investors. They contain interesting stuff on portfolio diversification and the benefits of long-term investing, but these books constantly refer to U.S. fund products you can't buy unless you're a U.S. resident.

The news media remain a useful source of mutual fund information, with *The Globe and Mail*, the *Financial Post*, and other large newspapers, including a beefed up *Toronto Star* business section, frequently publishing stories on the risks (and sometimes the benefits) of all kinds of investing. Monthly fund performance reports, however, are only online.

The Regulatory Jungle: When You Need Official Stuff

Sometimes going to the government or an official industry organization for information is unavoidable. At least in this case, you don't have to take a number and line up.

The Investment Funds Institute of Canada

The website of the Investment Funds Institute of Canada (IFIC), the trade group that represents mutual fund companies, is a great place for data junkies who want to know how much money is invested in a particular fund category, or which fund companies are the biggest (or the smallest, or the fastest-growing). The site has a useful Investor Resource Centre, which contains articles on mutual fund taxation, RRSPs, and other personal finance and investing topics. You can also check out a detailed member directory, where you can find contact information and website addresses.

TECHNICAL STUFF

Not every fund company is an IFIC member. Excluded are insurance companies (which operate segregated funds and are members of the Canadian Life and Health Insurance Association), as well as a few mutual fund companies, big and small, which for one reason or another have chosen not to be members. (By "big," we mean really big — like CI Financial.)

Get Smarter About Money

Some good (Ontario) government money went into building the Ontario Security Commission's Get Smarter About Money website (getsmarteraboutmoney.ca), which has a lengthy section on mutual funds and segregated funds. Get Smarter About Money was born out of the OSC's Investor Education Fund, which morphed into what's called the Investor Office, to broaden investor education.

Of particular interest is the Mutual Fund Fee Calculator, accessed from the site's home page under calculators and tools. This tool works out how big a bite sales loads and MERs will take out of an individual fund investment. Usually, these costs are expressed only as percentages; this calculator shows the actual dollars gobbled up by the various fees charged on a typical fund investment over time.

Mutual Fund Dealers Association of Canada

The Mutual Fund Dealers Association of Canada website (MFDA) may be of use — but unlikely of interest. The self-regulatory organization regulates brokerage and financial planning firms licensed to sell mutual funds, as opposed to investment securities in general. You want to go here only if you need information on an MFDA-member firm or about the MFDA Investor Protection Corporation, which is a sort of insurance policy that protects you, the investor, should your broker or planner go broke (don't laugh — it happens). On January 1, 2023, the organization merged with Investment Industry Regulatory Organization of Canada, a self-regulatory organization that oversees all investment dealers and trading activity on Canada's debt and equity markets. The new entity is currently known as the Canadian Investment Regulatory Organization (CIRO). At some point, the MFDA site may find itself under a new CIRO website.

The System for Electronic Document Analysis and Retrieval (SEDAR)

SEDAR has nothing to do with trees or any related earthy analogies about branching out and growing your investments. In fact, it's the address of a website (www.sedar.com) that is about as dull and lifeless as they come. However, its content is extremely important, if not exciting. SEDAR is run by the Canadian Securities Administrators (which represents provincial securities commissions) and contains every public document, report, and filing a fund manager (or any publicly traded company) produces.

SEDAR is a little cumbersome to use at first, but after you get the hang of it, you can find most anything that's ever been filed with a securities commission in Canada. That includes prospectuses, financial statements, annual information forms, and those valuable new documents, management reports of fund performance. You can search by date range, company name, or type of document. When you unearth what you need, you can download it as a PDF file.

Fund Company Sites: Useful Information, But Mind the Context

When the previous edition of this book was published, a lot of fund companies had fairly rudimentary websites — at least by today's standards. Some websites can still use a makeover, but they're now loaded with useful information about personal finance, investing, ETFs and, of course, mutual funds. Besides articles, podcasts, and videos, you also find fund fact sheets and other important information about the mutual funds you own.

On a typical big-company website, you find:

>> **Forms:** Many company websites offer downloadable forms for new account applications, account transfers, pre-authorized chequing (PAC) schemes, and systematic withdrawal plans (SWP). Some may also offer forms that you can simply fill out online instead of downloading. You may still need the help of a fund company official or your advisor to figure out how to complete them!

>> **Marketing-oriented material:** In addition to the expected promotional material, many companies offer detailed profiles on individual funds and portfolio managers. Of even greater use are records (both recent and longer term) of daily fund prices, distributions, and performance.

>> **Information above and beyond the call:** Some companies go to the unusual extent of revealing information that's normally left buried in various legal documents. AGF Investments, for instance, provides a table on the history of the firm's fund mergers, closings, and acquisitions, making it easy for investors to understand the genesis of the company's funds.

>> **Personal finance information:** Many firms' websites also offer articles on financial planning topics, such as basic investing principles, RRSPs, ETFs, education savings plans, and taxation. You also come across calculators (to compute RRSP contributions, say, or the power of compound interest) and other financial-planning tools.

WARNING

Sometimes the personal finance information that fund companies provide is objective, but occasionally the content is skewed toward their products.

Regulatory documents: The twice-a-year management reports of fund performance (MRFPs) are very useful pieces of information. (See Chapter 3 for more.) You find them more easily on a company site than on SEDAR, the government site we look at in the previous section. You still have to dig around a little to find the MRFPs, though. Too bad everyone can't present these via straightforward links, such as BMO's "Prospectuses, Reports & Other Information" link or the Scotiabank's "Investment Documents" page. In many cases, you have to sleuth through smokescreens to locate MRFP downloads.

Brokers and Planners: Only the Basics

You find only basic information on mutual fund investing at most full-service investment dealers' websites, and even less today in some cases, given the rising popularity of ETFs. But discount brokerages, which want you to operate on your own and simply buy and sell products through them (see Chapter 6), offer a wealth of fund information. The following discount brokerages offer Morningstar research tools on their websites (in some cases only to their registered clients) and many other tools, too.

>> BMO InvestorLine

>> RBC Direct Investing

>> TD Direct Investing (td.com/ca/en/investing/direct-investing)

>> Questrade (questrade.com)

>> Q Trade (qtrade.ca)

INVESTING WITHOUT THE NET?

You should always do some online research when buying funds — if you spend hours researching a new TV, you should at least spend some time understanding the vehicles you're putting your money into. But research doesn't guarantee you'll make money from your portfolio. The same old rules of buying quality funds with low expenses and conservative holdings still apply. So don't worry if you're not doing weeks of studying before you invest. You can build an excellent portfolio of funds without ever firing up a browser. In fact, as we all know, the Internet has given birth to a whole new generation of scam artists. And it's certainly created a tidal wave of confusing marketing clutter. So before you buy, make sure you're getting information from a reputable source and, as good journalists know, two sources are better than one.

IN THIS CHAPTER

» Getting to know registered retirement savings plans (RRSPs)

» Delving into tax-free savings accounts (TFSAs)

» Figuring out where to buy an RRSP and TFSA

» Falling in love with self-directed RRSPs and TFSAs

» Deciding which funds should go in your RRSP and TFSAs

Chapter **22**

RRSPs and TFSAs: Fertilizer for Your Mutual Funds

A vocado and toast, summer days and a cozy cottage, tattoos and piercings — some things just go together. And mutual funds are a powerful combination with Canada's beloved *Registered Retirement Savings Plan* (RRSP), a tax-deferred account in which your investments pile up without harassment from the government.

In this chapter, we explain why it's a great idea to fill up your RRSP as a first step when buying funds, and we also look at the sort of funds you should put into your plan. We also dive into tax-free savings accounts (TFSAs), a stellar investment account for both short-term and long-term savings. The chapter also offers a brief rundown of the rules of RRSPs and TFSAs. They can seem complex, but in essence, they're simple — just stick your money in, buy top-quality funds, and watch your nest egg grow and grow.

Pour It in and Watch It Grow: Understanding RRSPs

An RRSP is like a warehouse for investments and assets in which they can accumulate *tax-free* until you take the money out and spend it. At that stage, you have to treat the withdrawals as income and pay taxes on them. But the idea is that you won't care about having to share some of the loot with Ottawa at that stage because the money will have grown tax-free to such a huge pile and also because you'll be in a nice low tax bracket (because your income will be lower in retirement).

So an RRSP isn't an investment in itself — you don't "buy" an RRSP — but rather a tax-privileged account in which you hold investments and assets. Don't even think about it too much. Just go ahead and open an RRSP account. It's one of the great tax breaks Canadians get, for two reasons:

» **The money you put in comes off your income for tax purposes:** The government's attitude is that money you put into an RRSP is cash you've diverted from your income for the moment — or *deferred*, in the jargon — so you don't have to pay tax on it. That's why taxpayers who've contributed to their RRSPs the previous year are likely to get back tax *refunds*, or returns of taxes they already paid.

» **Your investments accumulate tax-free within the plan:** This is the real reason why RRSPs are so powerful. The dollars in there are supercharged because the interest, dividends, and capital gains they attract are free of tax. Added to the pile, those earnings go on to earn their own cute little baby earnings, which in turn produce their own offspring, and so it goes. And tax-free compounding of investment returns is a wonder of the modern world.

Claiming a tax refund for the cash you put into a plan is wonderfully simple and perhaps the most enjoyable aspect about an RRSP (although watching your balance climb steadily is also fun). And the refund can be a fair amount of money. If your top tax bracket is 50 percent (that is, the government takes away 40 percent of the uppermost portion of your income), then a $5,000 RRSP contribution can earn you a refund of $2,500.

Even the saddest and least organized financial planner in Canada can open an RRSP for you and handle your contributions. Ottawa makes it simple. Your tax return clearly asks if you've contributed to an RRSP and then invites you to deduct the amount from your income. And, helpfully, the government mails you a slip along with your tax refund or tax bill each spring showing exactly how much you can contribute for the current year.

Figuring out how much you can put in your RRSP

Actually, it's a good thing the tax authorities tell you how much *room* — or maximum possible contribution — you have. That's because for people who are in a pension scheme at work, the RRSP contribution limits are complicated to calculate. If you're in a pension plan, you're already getting tax relief on the money you contribute to that scheme, and your employer may also be helping out, so policymakers count those contributions against the amount you can plow into your RRSP.

REMEMBER

If you're not in a pension plan, the maximum contribution is up to 18 percent of the income you earned the previous year. However, regardless of that figure, an annual dollar limit applies, which is $30,780 for the 2023 taxation year and $31,560 for 2024. Thereafter, it's supposed to be *indexed* to inflation — that is, the maximum contribution will increase each year in line with the general rise in prices. (The "great thereafter" is never actually reached because, fortunately for tax-break-starved Canadians, the government tends to come back and increase the RRSP limits every few years or so.)

If you're in a pension scheme, then your maximum contribution is reduced by something called the *pension adjustment*, which is the value the tax authorities assign to the value of the pension benefit you build up each year — and it's then used to reduce your maximum RRSP contribution. Your pension adjustment is reported to you each year on the T4 tax slip you get from your employer. The T4 shows the income you earned and the amount of tax paid in that respective year.

TECHNICAL STUFF

If your income is roughly $171,000 or more, you're entitled to contribute the full $30,780 for 2023 — as long as you're not in a pension plan. But if you are, and the tax people decide that the value of the pension benefit you build up during the year is, say, $5,000, then your maximum contribution is reduced by that amount, to $25,780. Still, that's not too shabby. If you can't afford to contribute that much, you needn't waste the unused amount. The government lets you "bank" the amount you can't afford to contribute to use in a future year. So if you could muster only $10,000 for 2023, you add the unused amount — $15,0780 if you were in the pension situation described previously, otherwise $10,000 — to your contribution limit in 2024 or a future year. In effect, you can create a balance of unused contribution room that can be used as an additional RRSP contribution above and beyond your limit in any future year.

You have even a little more RRSP contribution leeway. The Canada Revenue Agency (CRA) lets you put in an extra $2,000 over your lifetime without being required to withdraw that amount and pay a penalty (the taxpayer's version of a fine).

The deadline for making an RRSP contribution that is tax-deductible for a particular year is 60 days following the end of the year in question — normally March 1. So most people make a 2023 RRSP contribution during 2024. Being procrastinators, millions of people leave their RRSP contribution until those two months, and that's why you see a hysterical flood of RRSP advertising and hype in January and February.

It all sounds a bit daunting, but don't worry. You can find out how much you're allowed to contribute to your RRSP for a particular year simply by checking the Notice of Tax Assessment the government sends you a month or so after you file your income tax return or, better yet, on the CRA website. For example, your 2022 assessment includes a section that tells you how much you can contribute for 2023 — that is, by the February 29, 2024, deadline. So take note of this information before you file away that nasty little document.

Understanding the power of tax deferral

Getting a tax refund for contributing to your RRSP is nice, but the even more powerful attraction of RRSPs is the way that income earned within the plan is also *tax-deferred*. It piles up year after year without the Canada Revenue Agency sticking its claws in along the way.

Investment income such as interest and dividends, as well as *capital gains* — a fancy name for trading profits — can pile up tax-free inside an RRSP, which makes an RRSP the ideal place to put your mutual funds. That's because funds throw off their income and capital gains to unitholders each year in the form of distributions. *Distributions* are payments your fund makes to you. You can take them as a cheque or as more units. Most people take the payouts in the form of new units, but it doesn't matter; the distributions are taxable just the same — unless they're earned in a tax-deferred plan such as an RRSP. (See Chapter 23.)

You can be sure that a bond or other income-oriented fund will generate a steady stream of distributions (that's what they're designed to do), and equity funds have a habit of suddenly producing big capital gains for their investors — which can be painful if you don't hold the fund in a tax-deferred account.

Given long enough, money that compounds tax-free grows at a frightening pace. But it's a good sort of scary, if you know what we mean. For example, as shown in Figure 22-1:

>> For example, say you invested $6,000 each year in an ordinary account that earned five percent annually, but you also had to pay 40 percent of the return each year in tax. The money would grow to about $231,000 in 25 years.

>> If you invested that $6,000 in an RRSP at the same rate of return, where it built up tax-free, then you'd have nearly $307,000 after 25 years.

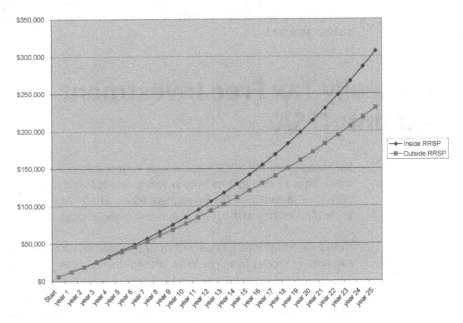

FIGURE 22-1:
$6,000 invested at five percent for 25 years, untaxed and taxed values.

Now, the $231,000 in the taxable account is not too shabby, and the example is a little misleading. You see, the money in the tax-paying account is free and clear — you're at liberty to do whatever you want with every cent because the tax is already paid. By contrast, money in an RRSP isn't really normal capital — in legal terms, it's more like deferred income that you haven't yet declared for tax purposes.

Investigating what happens to your RRSP after you retire

At 71, everyone has to convert their RRSP into something called a *registered retirement income fund* (RRIF). An RRIF is similar to an RRSP in that investments grow tax-free, and you can also hold the same range of assets in an RRIF. But one crucial difference applies: You can't make regular contributions to an RRIF, and you have to steadily withdraw the money that's there according to a specified timetable. And as the money comes out, year after year, the government gets to take a bite out of it.

So, after you take the money out of that whopping quarter-million-dollar RRSP, you want to avoid having to pay tax on every penny of it. The idea, of course, is that by that stage you will have quit working, so you're in a lower tax bracket. But always remember that while the magic of tax-free compounding within an RRSP does produce wonderful growth, the dollars inside the plan have annoying little strings attached.

The Really Tax Free Investment Account: TFSA

For many years the RRSP was the only retirement-related investment account in town. That all changed in 2009, when a new kid — the tax-free savings account (TFSA) — moved onto the investment block. The TFSA was created to help people grow their money without having to worry about taxes at all.

Unlike the RRSP, which taxes withdrawals based on your current income level, you can remove money from the TFSA without incurring any tax penalties at all. Have $50,000 in your account and need $25,000 to buy a car? Go ahead and remove that dough from your account — and put it all towards that sweet Subaru you've been eying. The downside is that you don't get a tax refund when you contribute to the account, but that's also why you don't have to pay anything in the end — you're adding already taxed dollars into the account.

The TFSA is fairly straight forward, but there are some key details you need to understand before using it, which we explain throughout this section.

Delving into the ins and outs of TFSA contributions

When the TFSA was first introduced in 2009, Canadians could only save $5,000 a year in the account. That didn't make it very useful for long-term savings. Over time, though, that contribution room has climbed to the point where if you were 18 in 2009, and never contributed to the account at all, then you'd have $95,000 to use as of 2024. Ideal for a nice lump sum, retirement-focused investment.

In any case, contribution limits are well below the maximum amount you can put in an RRSP, but you can still put away a good chunk of change. Table 22-1 shows what the limits have been since 2009 — it's worth knowing in case you haven't contributed before and want to see how much room you have to use.

TABLE 22-1

TFSA Contribution Limits

Year	Maximum contribution
2009	$5,000
2010	$5,000
2011	$5,000
2012	$5,000
2013	$5,500
2014	$5,500
2015	$10,000
2016	$5,500
2017	$5,500
2019	$6,000
2020	$6,000
2021	$6,000
2022	$6,000
2023	$6,500
2024	$7,000

TECHNICAL
STUFF

As you can see, the contribution amounts are a bit wonky. What happened in 2015, you ask? Well, that was an election year, and in an attempt to woo voters, the Conservative government doubled the limit. It didn't help — Justin Trudeau's Liberal party won the election, and soon after they took power, they put the limit back to essentially where it was before.

The limits are indexed to inflation. After the out-of-control price increases we saw in 2022 and 2023, room has risen once again — to $7,000 in 2024.

Anyone 18 and over can open and start investing in a TFSA. With an RRSP, room only accumulates if you're working — with a TFSA, you start building room the moment you become of age, whether you're paying taxes or not.

Investing in a TFSA

The beauty of the TFSA is that it's another registered account, where gains, dividends, and income can grow tax-free. You can invest in almost anything, just you like you can in an RRSP. That includes:

>> Guaranteed investment certificates (GICs)

>> Government and corporate bonds

>> Mutual funds and exchange-traded funds

>> Securities listed on designated stock exchanges (which would include all the major stock exchanges).

Like with an RRSP, mutual funds are at home inside a TFSA. You can purchase a full range of options and tailor your investments based on your savings needs.

Because you pay no taxes at all when you withdraw, TFSA can be an ideal place for growing your investments — like a high-flying technology mutual fund — where you can keep every cent of those gains. The same goes for bond funds, which issue distributions that would be taxed as income in a non-registered account.

Deciding whether to use an RRSP or TFSA — or both

Figuring out whether to use an RRSP or a TFSA can be confusing but remember that they each have different objectives.

>> **RRSP/Retirement savings:** The RRSP is specifically for retirement savings. If you withdraw in your working years, you can end up with a huge tax bill. The government set it up this way to deter people from liquidating their account before they need the money in retirement. Conversely, Canada's progressive tax system means RRSPs can create major income tax savings during your working years, even bumping you down into a lower tax bracket. So if you're saving for retirement, then use the RRSP.

>> **TFSA/Everything else savings:** Because of the way the TFSA is taxed — or not taxed in this case — this account is far more flexible than the RRSP. (But the flipside of that is you can, potentially, contribute much more to an RRSP.) Many people use the account to save for a car, a vacation, a large-screen TV, and even a down payment on a house, though there are better options, such as the brand new Tax-Free First-Time Homebuyers Account, for housing-related savings.

Most advisors recommend trying to max out the RRSP first and then put savings into a TFSA. However, if you know you're going to need your money sooner than later then the TFSA is a better option.

TIP

You have other TFSA and RRSP strategies, especially when it comes to withdrawing money in retirement, so it can be a good idea to talk to a professional to see how you can best use both.

As straightforward as TFSAs may seem, it is possible to run afoul of the rules — and if you do, the CRA will come calling.

REMEMBER

Here's a key rule you need to know and another critical difference between the TFSA and the RRSP. With the latter, money removed from the account can never be recontributed. Take $10,000 out, and you lose $10,000 in room. With the former, you can remove funds without losing room, but here's the catch: You cannot recontribute what you've taken out until January 1 of the year after you withdraw.

Here's how that might look: If you've contributed every year since 2009, you have used up $95,000 in contribution room. Say you remove $10,000 from the account on December 1 — you cannot put that money back into the account until January 1. If you do recontribute before the New Year, you will be charged a tax equal to 1 percent of the highest additional TFSA amount for each month that the excess stays in your account.

Another scenario: Say you only used $80,000 of your $95,000 of room. You remove $10,000 to take a trip to Mexico to escape the cold Winnipeg winters. Because you haven't reached the limit, you can put funds back into the account, but now you only have $15,000 to work with until January 1, when you get back the $10,000 of room you removed. (Annual room also accumulates, so you get back your $10,000 plus the $7,000 maximum contribution for 2024.)

TIP

It's not as complicated as it sounds — just don't put back whatever you take out until the ball drops in Times Square. You can also find out how much room you have by checking your CRA account online.

Where to Buy Your RRSP

This section focuses on RRSPs but much of it applies to TFSAs, too. Buying an RRSP is simple because banks, brokers, and fund companies just love them. With an RRSP, the money tends to be long-term retirement savings that won't be withdrawn for years, so it sits there producing a stream of fees for the lucky firm that gets to hold it. (Many people hold TFSA dollars for a while, too.)

The RRSP industry, specifically, is massive: Statistics Canada reports Canadians have about $1.4 trillion dollars sitting in RRSPs. However, not enough people are using them — about 22.4 percent of tax filers contributed to their RRSP in 2021. The median contribution in 2021 was $3,890. Contributions in 2021 topped $56.2 billion, up 12 percent from 2020. However, with only a quarter of people using RRSPs, there's billions of more dollars in unused room for Canadians to take advantage of.

You have three basic choices when setting up an RRSP. Here's the triple play:

>> **Basic banking:** You can stumble into a bank, trust company, or credit union and ask for a basic RRSP account that holds that particular institution's mutual funds and other offerings, usually guaranteed investment certificates (refer to Chapter 5).

A limited choice of investments is the problem with doing this, but the simplicity and convenience make it ideal for investors who are just starting out. So if you're looking for convenience, fire ahead and open up a simple plan at a bank. As you discover more and your assets grow, it's pretty easy to move the holdings later into another RRSP at a full-service broker or discount broker plan for a small fee.

Banks offer a wide selection of *index funds and ETFs* that track the entire market at low cost to the unitholders; an RRSP full of index funds with a smaller portion of ordinary actively managed funds is a wise choice for nearly any investor. Bank funds are *no-load* — they sell directly to investors and do not charge a sales commission. No-load funds also are sold by a handful of independent companies. They, too, are happy to set up an RRSP on their books for you.

>> **From your planner:** If you go to a commission-paid financial planner, they may put your investment into a fund company's RRSP. That's an RRSP set up on the books of the fund company, which almost always holds just that company's funds. It's an easy option for the salesperson because the fund manager handles all the administration and registration of the plan with the government. Once again, though, limited choice is a problem from your point of view. But a fund company RRSP is handy for investors who don't want to fiddle around too much with their portfolios because the fund company does all the bookkeeping.

However, not all planners will limit you to a fund company sponsored RRSP. Many have arrangements with an outside trust company or other service provider that lets them offer independent RRSPs and normal taxable accounts that can hold funds from a variety of fund companies. Fee-only planners are more likely to utilize a range of options, because they don't get paid commissions from any fund company.

Self-directed: The final and increasingly popular way to do it is to start up a self-directed RRSP at a discount brokerage company. This is the very finest type of RRSP because you're free to hold virtually anything instead of limiting your portfolio to the wares of just one company. Check out the next section for more. (Same goes for the TFSA.)

The Beautiful Garden That Is the Self-Directed RRSP

Just about everyone should have a self-directed RRSP because, well, these things are marvelous. The traditional RRSP offered by a bank or fund manager is basically a vehicle for holding just their stuff. But with a self-directed plan, you're free to roam the world. A self-directed RRSP is a plan in which you're free to hold just about anything. It's an easy way to own stocks or bonds within an RRSP and to load up on funds from a multiplicity of companies.

Setting up a self-directed RRSP is easy — remember that brokers welcome this type of business because it tends to represent long-term money that'll be on their books for decades. And the term *self-directed* often doesn't apply because many investors have a full-service broker who helps them pick what should go into their plan. However, self-directed RRSPs are ideally suited for discount brokerages because discounters tend to have a large selection of funds available for low or no sales commissions. See Chapter 6 for more on discounters.

WARNING

You can be charged fees associated with setting up a plan, and there may also be trading fees when buying or selling an investment. Most people typically don't actively trade in an RRSP (or a TFSA, though some are more active inside the latter), so the fees shouldn't amount to much, but it's a good idea to double-check those costs before opening an account.

Don't worry that opening a self-directed plan means you have to become a stock market wizard. Stick to the rules for fund selection in this book (which we cover in Chapter 10), and you'll almost certainly do okay. You don't have to start playing stocks directly: Lots of investors hold nothing but conservative mutual funds in their self-directed plans.

And don't be shy about transferring assets from other plans into your self-directed plan. It's your right! The old brokerage firm or bank that's seeing your money depart its coffers will sometimes drag its feet on the paperwork, but the change over will happen.

REMEMBER

If you're moving assets from an existing plan over to the self-directed RRSP, the new brokerage firm may tell you that its systems won't accommodate some or all your old funds. In that case, you may have to sell the funds in the old account and just move the cash proceeds over. That's a hassle, but it shouldn't cost you anything in taxes because the transaction is taking place within an RRSP, shielding any capital gains. (Refer to the previous section "Pour It in and Watch It Grow: Understanding RRSPs" for more about RRSPs and taxes.)

The Most Fragrant Flower: Choosing Funds for Your RRSP

The overriding rule for investments inside your RRSP should be *Insist on Quality* — leave the wacky speculative stuff for the money that's not earmarked to support you in your dotage. That means buying conservative equity and bond funds, and going easy on emerging markets funds, volatile single-industry funds, and small-company funds, which could be better suited to a TFSA.

The dollars inside your plan should be treated as sacrosanct — all incense and white cloth — because they're irreplaceable. Because you are restricted in how much you can contribute to an RRSP over the years, when a magical compounding RRSP dollar has been lost on a slump in the Brazilian market, it can't be restored. Chapter 4 offers two suggested RRSP portfolios, and just about any bank or mutual fund now has a proprietary system for suggesting the asset mix in your plan. (Beware of fund packages, however, which we discuss in Chapter 20.)

REMEMBER

With this type of long-term investing, the costs and fees charged by the funds and fund mixtures assume ever-greater importance. So own at least some index funds or ETFs in your plan, even if you need to convince your broker or fund manager.

Including international investments

Once a time, long, long ago, investing money in an RRSP was severely handicapped by an evil restriction known as the foreign content limit. This meant your RRSP could contain a maximum of 30 percent foreign investments. Cloaked in patriotic reason, in fact this served as a prop for the Canadian stock market and put severe restrictions on how Canadians could use one of the few tax breaks available. But the government washed the foreign content rules away in one fell swoop in its 2006 budget, opening the door completely to investing in foreign stocks and other worldwide markets.

Many people, however, still hold way too much Canadian stock, in part because that's what they're used to doing. If you want a well-diversified portfolio, you can't be afraid to buy U.S. and European-focused funds, or more broad-based emerging market funds.

Some non-geographic restrictions remain in place: An eligible stock must be listed on an exchange approved by the Canada Revenue Agency, you can't put any gold or silver or other precious metals inside of one, no bitcoin or any shares in a private business — the same goes for TFSAs. That shouldn't be a problem in any case. As we said, putting speculative crypto into an RRSP goes against the account's purpose.

Mixing the right assets

As with other forms of investing, your asset mix is almost certain to get more cautious as you get older and closer to taking money out of your plan rather than putting it in. For nearly everyone, that means more bonds and cash and fewer stocks.

Many experts say you should put your bond funds into your RRSP if you're a long-term investor, and the numbers seem to indicate that they're right. That's because bond funds earn and throw off a constant stream of interest, which attracts murderous rates of tax.

Funds usually pay distributions in the form in which they receive the money from their investments. So interest earned by a bond fund is paid as a distribution that's taxable as interest in the investor's hands. Capital gains — the polite term for trading profits — are paid out as *capital gain distributions*, and dividends earned by a fund are paid out as *dividend distributions to the investor*.

Equity funds are mainly about buying and selling stocks so they generate capital gains distributions — and only one-half of a capital gain is taxed in the hands of the investor. Equity funds also produce dividends from Canadian companies — payouts of the company's profits to shareholders — which are also lightly taxed. So, funds that produce distributions in the form of dividends or capital gains are reasonably *tax-efficient*, or lightly taxed, making them more suitable than bond funds for an *open* or taxable account. (Tax efficiency is a value computed by fund data firms that captures the percentage of the pre-tax return that is retained by a hypothetical investor after accounting for taxes on distributions. See Chapter 23 for more on this.) In other words, equity funds are often better than bond funds when it comes to investing outside your RRSP.

Now every rule has its exceptions, and quadruply so when it comes to taxes and investing. An equity fund that pays big distributions year after year, while producing solid returns as well, may be an excellent candidate for your RRSP because you are shielding those payouts from tax. You can get an idea whether the fund manager is in the habit of paying out lots of capital gains by looking at one of the new fund prospectuses or by checking with your advisor.

REMEMBER

But don't get all bogged down in theories: Remember to put top-quality stuff into your RRSP and you'll likely do fine, whether it's bonds or stocks. The market has an old saying that you should never let tax strategies close your eyes to the merits or faults of an investment. Nobody's ever regretted holding a well-managed equity fund in an RRSP over many years, no matter how small the distributions.

IN THIS CHAPTER

» **Understanding fund distributions**

» **Paying taxes on distributions from your fund**

» **Paying taxes when you sell your fund**

» **Figuring out why ETFs and index funds are tax efficient**

» **Considering a few other tax-saving investment options**

Chapter **23**

Taxes: Timing Is Everything

A lot of investment writing and theorizing seems to take place in an airy-fairy world in which everybody is beautifully dressed and articulate, all decisions are perfectly rational, and nobody ever has to pay taxes. In fact, the stock and bond markets are places driven by parties whose interests seldom align perfectly with our own. And taxes do ultimately end up eating into our returns. Unless mutual fund unitholders are investing through a tax-deferred plan — or don't make any money on their investments — the government will go after their share.

In this chapter, we outline how you pay taxes on distributions and other investment gains and how to count and report your taxes payable. Then we look at a couple of methods of reducing the pain by allocating your investment funds tax-efficiently and using vehicles such as trusts and registered accounts.

The Wacky World of Fund Distributions

Now this stuff gets a little complicated, but bear with us because it's worth knowing, and we should be able to cut through it pretty quickly. Mutual funds hold all kinds of company shares, bonds, and cash — and sometimes *derivatives*, those strange financial deals based on *options* and *futures*, which are promises to buy or sell something at a certain price.

All the time, cash is piling up in the fund from three main sources:

» Every year, the stocks pay *dividends* to the fund — which are payouts to the shareholders of a portion of the company's profit.

» Meanwhile, the bonds and cash, which are loans to government and big companies, keep earning interest income.

» The fund also earns *capital gains* — which are essentially trading profits generated by buying low and selling high — when it sells stocks, bonds, and derivatives.

In general, no fund hangs on to these streams of income and capital gains because, if it did, the fund itself would have to pay tax on them, reducing its total return. So just about all mutual funds pay out the interest and dividend income and capital gains to their unitholders in the form of so-called distributions, letting them deal with the tax.

The investors have to pay tax on the income and gains at their own personal rate. It's more sensible to have the unitholders, rather than the fund, pay the tax because many of the unitholders may not even be taxable personally. Those investors can collect the distributions and not owe a penny to Ottawa. And investors who hold the fund in a registered retirement savings plan (RRSP) — a tax-deferred holding tank in which investments can grow tax-free — don't have to pay tax on the distributions immediately, so it would be a waste of money for the fund to pay taxes on their behalf. Other unitholders may have low incomes, meaning that their tax rates are low or zero. And those holding funds in a tax-free savings account (TFSA) never have to pay any tax at all.

Paying out distributions to fundholders

REMEMBER

After a fund pays out a distribution, it reduces the cash value of each of its own units.

Say a fund has total assets of $100 million and 10 million units *outstanding*, or in the hands of investors. Then each unit has a *net asset value* per unit — or price —

of $10 ($100 million divided by 10 million). Now say the manager pays out $20 million in capital gains to the unitholders. That's $2 for every unit ($20 million divided by 10 million units outstanding). If all of them took the payout in cash, then the value of the fund's assets would drop to $80 million. It still has 10 million units outstanding, though, so the value of each unit falls to $8 ($80 million divided by 8 million), because $2 for each unit has been paid.

Table 23-1 shows what happens to your cash if you're a unitholder in the fund and you have 100 units.

TABLE 23-1 ## What If You Take the Distribution in Cash?

Units Held	Unit Price	Value of Units Held	Cash in Hand	Total Holding
Before Distribution				
100	$10	$1,000	Zero	$1,000
After Distribution				
100	$8	$800	$200	$1,000

In other words, you start out owning 100 units, which are worth $10 each, for a total holding of $1,000. The fund declares a distribution of $2 a unit, which you elect to hold in your portfolio in cash. You then still hold 100 units, but the value of each has dropped by $2 to $8, which leaves you with $800 worth of units. But you also have the $200 in cash ($2 for each of your units), which means you still have a total holding of $1,000.

But most people just put the money back into the fund. One of the great advantages of mutual funds is the fact that you can automatically reinvest your income and capital gains in more units, which go to bolster your account and earn even higher streams of income and gains in the future. It's a no-brainer, as we like to say in frontal-lobe surgery. That's what long-term investors do — take their distributions in the form of more units.

So, say you follow that course. You don't get cash but more units. Their value has dropped by $2 each, but that's fine because the investor now owns more of them. This scenario is shown in Table 23-2.

You get an extra 25 units valued at $8 each, which increases your unit total to 125. The units are now worth just $8 each, though, so you still have a total holding of $1,000. As you can see, a distribution isn't really a windfall or a payout to you. It reduces the value of each unit you hold, so it's more like a reshuffling of your investment in the fund.

TABLE 23-2 **What If You Reinvest the Distribution?**

Units Held	Unit Price	Value of Units Held	Cash in Hand	Total Holding
Before Distribution				
100	$10	$1,000	Zero	$1,000
After Distribution				
125	$8	$1,000	Zero	$1,000

Note that if you hold funds in a discount brokerage account, you may have an alarming experience when you get your statement for December 31. Your fund units may have fallen sharply, reflecting the value of a distribution, but there may be no sign of any extra units in your account to make up for it. So it sometimes looks as though the value of your investment has slumped.

TECHNICAL STUFF

That's actually just an administrative glitch: The lines of communication aren't always very good between discount brokers and the fund companies at the end of the year when the fund industry is scrambling to calculate the distributions. Your broker's system may not record the distributions until mid-January or so, after you've gotten your December statement. However, the error should be fixed by the time you get your statement for January 31.

A fund can easily lose money during a calendar year (because its unit price dropped) but also pay out distributions to unitholders because the fund manager earned interest or dividend income or made some capital gains by selling a stock or bond. Taxable unitholders find themselves in the galling position of having to pay taxes on their investment in a fund, even though it lost them money. Gee, thanks.

Watching out for tax exposure

Many equity and balanced funds pay out their capital gains distributions in December, and bond funds and other income funds usually pay out interest income quarterly or even monthly. Funds that seek bond interest, dividends, and other regular income nearly always pay it straight out to unitholders. So, bond, dividend, and other income funds by their nature pay a lot of distributions every year, exposing investors to tax on that income. Unless you need the regular payment, a tax-reducing strategy is to hold investments inside a tax-sheltered plan. See Chapter 22 for information on RRSPs and TFSAs.

By contrast, equity funds can go years without paying any distributions at all because the manager hasn't generated enough trading profits. That can be for a number of good reasons, though. The fund may have simply bought a bunch of good companies and hung on to them without selling the shares, nicely increasing its value per unit.

Fund companies often make a song and dance about the fact that a fund hasn't paid much in distributions in recent years — reducing the tax bill for unitholders — because its manager tends to hold stocks for long periods. Instead of selling shares and earning trading profits that must be paid out in big distributions, some managers try to simply hold good stocks for long periods, increasing the fund's unit value. But always be wary: A takeover bid or drastic change in a company's fortunes may force the manager to sell the stock, forcing the fund to pay out a big distribution.

Fund companies say the lack of annual payouts helps you to defer paying taxes until you sell the fund's units. That may be true, but taxation shouldn't be the first detail you consider when making an investment — the fund should be suitable in other ways, too. However, if you're deciding which fund to hold in a taxable account — that is, an account that isn't an RRSP, TFSA, or some other tax-deferred plan — then a fund that doesn't do much trading is often the best choice. If the fund uses a definite buy-and-hold style, the fund company's literature will usually say so. And as we explain in Chapter 15, equity index funds — funds that simply track the whole stock market — are a great buy-and-hold investment.

REMEMBER

So if you're trying to decide which funds you should put *into* your RRSP or TFSA, the income fund is often the best choice because the distributions can just pile up in there tax-free until you take the money out.

Because a big capital gains distribution produces an apparent abrupt fall in a fund's unit price at the end of the year, mutual fund investors sometimes get a fright. Every year, fund companies get worried phone calls from investors asking why their fund's units seem to have plunged. However, they needn't worry: Yes, the unit price has fallen, but the investor has received more units.

Determining what distributions your fund has declared

TIP

Finding out what distributions your fund has declared is easy. On Morningstar.ca, follow these steps:

1. Type the fund's name in the search field and press enter.

2. On the fund's performance page, click on Distributions, which is located next to Returns. You easily see what's been paid out — and whether it's in the form of interest, foreign income, capital gains, Canadian dividends, or return of capital — for the last five years.

TIP

You can also go to the fund company's website. Mackenzie Financial, for example, provides a handy "Distribution history" button on its fund pages.

Taxes on Fund Distributions

Here's the rub. No matter whether the investor takes the distributions in the form of cash or reinvests them in more units, they're taxable just the same — as long as the fund is held in an *open* (that is, taxable) account and not a tax-deferred plan such as an RRSP or a tax-free plan, as in a TFSA. Always remember that with an RRSP, the distributions are ultimately taxable after you start taking money out of the plan. At that stage, any money you withdraw is taxed as income, just as though you earned it at your normal job.

Enjoying tax breaks on Canadian content

The fact that RRSP withdrawals are taxed like normal income can be a disadvantage because the money gets no special treatment, even if it was originally earned as capital gains or dividends from a Canadian company. That's a pity, because dividends from Canadian corporations and capital gains are eligible, when held inside of a non-registered account, for special tax breaks.

Canadian dividends received by investors get the "federal dividend tax credit," essentially a reduction of the tax you pay to encourage investment in Canadian companies and to reflect the fact that corporations have already been taxed. The formula is confusing because you can also get a provincial dividend tax credit, and you also have something called a gross-up rate (38 percent in 2023), which accounts for any taxes the corporation has already paid on your dividend income.

Check out the example in Table 23-3, provided by RBC Wealth Management, of someone who received $1,000 in eligible dividends and is in the top marginal tax bracket with a combined federal and provincial tax rate of 44 percent.

As for capital gains, half of the gain must be included in your taxable income. What you'll get dinged depends on the tax bracket you're in. For instance, say you're on the hook to pay a gain of $1,000. Only $500 of that income is taxable. If, like in the last example, you have to hand over 44 percent of your money to the government, you'd have to pay a total of $220 on that the $1,000 gain.

While we always recommend holding investments inside of a registered account, thanks to the special capital gains tax treatment in Canada, if you maxed out your RRSP and TFSA, consider holding funds with big capital gain distributions in a registered account first. We go deeper in capital gains in the coming section, "Taxes When You Sell or Exchange."

TABLE 23-3

After tax eligible dividend income

Eligible dividend income	$1,000
Gross-up (38%)	380
Taxable amount	$1,380
Federal tax ($1,380 x 29%)	$400
Less: dividend tax credit ($1,380 x 15%)	(207)
Net federal tax	$193
Provincial tax ($1,380 x 15%)	$207
Less: provincial dividend tax credit ($1,380 x 10%)	(138)
Net provincial tax	$69
Combined tax ($193 + $69)	$262
After-tax amount ($1,000 - $262)	$ 738

Getting tax slips

Don't worry: Your fund company sends you tax slips each year showing how much in interest income, dividends, and capital gains distributions you should report in the appropriate place on your tax form.

If you hold the fund in an RRSP or other tax-deferred plan, you don't get tax slips because you don't pay tax on the distributions.

REMEMBER

You may get two types of tax slips:

» A T3 if the fund you hold is a mutual fund trust, which most funds are, an exchange-traded fund, or a segregated fund. If you hold several funds with one company, you'll probably get just one consolidated T3, but it should have a breakdown on the back showing which fund paid you which sort of distribution.

» A T5 if your fund is itself a corporation issuing shares instead of units. That's a less flexible type of structure, and most funds are trusts.

Taxes When You Sell or Exchange

If you sell or *redeem* some of your fund units at a higher price than you paid, and the fund is held in a taxable account, then you're liable for capital gains tax on the profit you made. The same applies even if you just do an *exchange* or switch — moving money from one fund to another. As far as the Canada Revenue Agency (CRA) is concerned, an exchange is the same as selling Fund A and then buying Fund B. What you do with the proceeds of the sale is irrelevant — if selling the first fund generates a capital gain, then you have to pay taxes on it.

Checking out tax-skirting fund structures

A few companies, such as CI Fund Management Inc., Mackenzie, and AGF Management Ltd., have set up funds that are organized in "classes" or versions that are designed to let you switch from fund to fund without generating capital gains for tax purposes. Technically, they're actually units of the same fund, although one is the Canadian equity class, the next is the bond class, and so on, each with its own cute baby unit price. You can use this fund structure and jump from fund to fund, avoiding taxes on any capital gains along the way. After all, a capital gain is produced when a fund has gone up — and that's why you bought it in the first place.

Many fund marketers have jumped on the tax-free switching bandwagon. But they've gone much further than that, bringing out ever more complicated products.

For example, Fidelity Investments Canada, Mackenzie, and Franklin Templeton Investments started selling classes of existing funds that make a steady payout to investors who want to gradually withdraw their money from their funds — but a lot of the distribution is in the form of *return of capital* or a refund of the investor's own money. That means no tax is payable right then — but it's added to the investor's profit for capital gains purposes when the units are sold. In Chapter 13, we talk about balanced funds designed to distribute income to unitholders that also use this technique.

WARNING

These new tax-managing structures may turn out to be great deals for investors, but they add a level of complexity. Make sure you understand before you buy — or at least get an advisor who you're sure knows which number goes where.

Working through capital gain calculations

So how much tax do you face when you sell units of a mutual fund in a "taxable" account that's not an RRSP or similar tax-deferred plan? Look at the example of the investor who holds 100 units of a fund — say they paid $8 a unit. If they sell half of those units for $10 each, then their account will look something like this:

Purchase   100 units at $8 for total investment of $800

And six months later:

Sell	50 units at $10 for total proceeds of $500
Hold	50 units at $10 for total holding of $500

The units sold for $500 cost the investor $400 originally, so they have to report a capital gain of $100, only half of which must be included in taxable income for the year. The investor also still holds another 50 units.

When the investor was working out the capital gain on the sales, it was necessary to establish the *cost base* or original cost of the units. That was simple to do because it represented just half of the initial investment. But when you've made more than one purchase of the fund, matters become more complex, and you have to work out an *adjusted cost base (ACB)*. Here's an example:

Purchase	100 units at $8 for an investment of $800
Purchase	Another 100 units at $10 for investment of $1,000

The investor now holds 200 units, which cost a total of $1,800, so their ACB is $1,800, or $9 per unit ($1,800 divided by 200).

Sale	100 units at $13 for proceeds of $1,300

The 100 units that were sold at $13 have an ACB of $9 each. That means they were sold for a profit of $4 each, so the investor has generated a capital gain of $400. And the investor also still holds 100 units, whose ACB base remains at $9 per unit.

WARNING

If you get distributions and reinvest them in more units, then that represents yet another purchase of the fund — so you add the value of the distribution to your cost base. And always make sure that you do increase the ACB by the value of reinvested distributions, because if you don't you could face double taxation.

One more complication: Say the investor incurs a "back-end" commission when they sell the fund — that's a sales charge levied on the proceeds of the sale or redemption of the fund.

Sale	50 units at $13 for proceeds of $650, incurring a 5-percent redemption charge

The investor's proceeds from the sale have been reduced by 5 percent, to $617.50. That means, for tax purposes, they've received only $12.35 per unit.

Always keep full records of any reinvested distributions or purchases or sales.

Matters can get horrendously complex if you have a regular purchase plan, which involves buying units at different prices at different times, or if you've done a lot of switching around. But the basic principle remains: The cost of your units is any money you spent to buy them, plus the value of reinvested distributions. And selling some of your units doesn't affect the ACB per unit of the ones that remain.

Several fund companies offer excellent general information on mutual fund taxation. For example, you can download the Mackenzie Mutual Fund Tax Guide from Mackenzie Financial's Web site (go to the tax and estate planning tab on mackenzieinvestments.com). Fidelity (fidelity.ca) also has a lot of useful tax information on its Investor Education pages.

Avoiding fund purchases near year-end

If you're tempted to celebrate the holidays by throwing a few thousand into an equity mutual fund in a taxable account, it may be a good idea to hold off until early January. That's because many funds pay out big capital gains distributions at the end of the year. Even if you buy the fund just before the distribution, you're on the hook for capital gains tax on that distribution. Here's an exaggerated example:

Purchase 100 units at $8 for total investment of $800 on December 10.

Receive distribution: If the fund pays out $2 a unit a few days later, its unit price will drop to about $6. If you reinvest the distribution, you'll end up with 133 units. But you'll also have incurred $200 in taxable capital gains.

In a sense, you're simply paying the tax early because the reinvested distribution is added on to your ACB, which reduces your eventual capital gain after you sell. But most people would rather defer paying tax, thank you very much, so it would have been better to wait until after the distribution was made and then buy the fund. That way, your $800 would have gotten you the same 133 units, but you wouldn't have faced that annoying capital gains bill.

Index Funds and ETFs: A Tax-Efficient Investment

One type of fund that's virtually guaranteed to produce very little in the way of distributions is the equity index fund (bond index funds throw off piles of income, just like regular bond funds). Index funds — and their lower-cost cousins, exchange-traded funds (ETFs) — don't try to buy and sell stocks in pursuit of capital gains; they just hold every stock in the index. (See Chapter 15 for more on index funds and ETFs.) So their stream of capital gains distributions is usually small or non-existent. Yes, they may flow through some of the dividend income they receive, and they may have to declare capital distributions if a major company in the index is taken over or dropped from the benchmark, forcing the index fund to sell it and book a gain. But just like buying good stocks and holding them for years, putting index funds in your non-RRSP portfolio is a highly tax-efficient strategy.

REMEMBER

Taxes are a blind spot for the fund industry. Most investors probably find it virtually impossible to calculate the ACB of the units accurately. And the performance published for funds invariably shows only the returns earned by a non-taxable investor. Both problems may be insoluble because everybody's tax situation is different; however, once again, buying an index fund solves a lot of your problems. The other solution is to find the advisor from heaven: one who goes to the trouble of calculating ACBs for you.

A Few More Ideas for Tax Savings

For the average Canadian, the RRSP is the Rolls-Royce of tax planning, while the TFSA is the Bentley. With an RRSP not only does money grow tax-free within the plan, but you also get to write off each year's contributions against your taxable income. The write-off is known as a *deduction*. With the TFSA, you don't get a deduction, but as a result, you don't have to pay any tax after you withdraw. (We look at RRSPs and TFSAs in greater detail in Chapter 22.)

You can shield your investments, including mutual funds, from taxes through a few other simple methods. Two of the most popular are used to build capital for a child — often to go to college or university — so they're useful for parents and grandparents: Trusts and registered education savings accounts. The tax-free First Home Savings Account is also a great tool to consider.

Informal trusts or in-trust accounts

Informal trusts or *in-trust accounts* are investment accounts set up for the benefit of a child or *beneficiary*. The person who supplies the money is called the *donor*. Income earned by the account, such as dividends, is still taxable in the donor's hands. But capital gains can be taxable in the child's hands, and the child presumably has such a low income that they pay hardly any tax.

The fact that capital gains are taxable in the child's hands makes in-trust accounts ideal homes for equity mutual funds because they usually produce capital gains distributions rather than interest income or lots of dividends. (See "The Wacky World of Fund Distributions" in this chapter for more information.) Contributing money to the account doesn't give you a tax deduction. When the child reaches 18 or 19 (depending on the province), they are free to do anything with the money.

WARNING

Brokers and mutual fund companies have offered informal trusts for years. When setting them up, be careful to make sure the "trustee" — the person overseeing the account on behalf of the beneficiary, often a family member, lawyer, or a financial company itself — is not the same as the donor. Otherwise, the CRA may refuse to have the capital gains taxable in the child's hands. And don't forget that money put into the in-trust account belongs to the child forever: You can't get it back. That means the kid might just choose to squander it at 18 or 19. By law, you can't do anything about it.

Registered education savings plans

Registered education savings plans (RESPs) are more formal government-registered schemes (with, you guessed it, ridiculously complicated rules) in which investment income and capital gains add up tax-free. As with informal trusts, no deduction applies for contributions. While no annual limit on contributions exists, you can contribute only up to $50,000 per child in a lifetime. Contributions may be made for up to 31 years from the date the plan was first set up, and the deadline for terminating a plan is 35 years from the set-up date.

The federal government offers a major plus for RESP investors in the form of its *Canada Education Savings Grant* (CESG), which Ottawa adds to the RESP. The grant is 20 percent of the first $2,500 contributed per child annually, so it's a maximum of $500 per year. The maximum grant for each kid is $7,200. Some provinces provide additional grants.

REMEMBER

The rules for RESPs have been changed a number of times, so keep an eye on federal and provincial budgets and other government announcements for any future amendments.

Three basic types of RESP exist:

>> A so-called scholarship trust where your money is pooled with that of other parents by a money manager. The fees, complicated rules, and super-conservative investments (mostly bonds) of these trusts mean that we would avoid them.

- » RESP accounts offered by mutual fund companies, aimed at getting you to buy their funds. They're fine, but the investment selection is limited.

- » Self-directed RESPs offered at brokers and discount brokers, which can buy stocks, bonds, and cash. Because of flexibility we would go with the self-directed option, but investors who want simplicity often stick to a fund company RESP.

With an RESP, if the child doesn't go to university or college, you can get back your contributions but you must refund any CESG grants. You then pay tax on any accumulated investment income, but you can move $50,000 of it into your RRSP if you still have the contribution room. Contribution room is the limited amount you can put into an RRSP each year, and any quota you don't use can be made up in a subsequent year. For much more on RRSPs, see Chapter 22.

Tax-Free First Home Savings Account

In 2023, the federal government introduced a brand new registered account, the tax-free first home savings account (FHSA) specifically to help people save for a home. This account combines the best of the RRSP and TFSA. It's almost too-good-to-be-true — you get a tax deduction when you contribute and yet you don't have to pay a dime of tax after you withdraw. In this case, you can potentially get a tax refund that you can then invest back into the FHSA.

If only you can do this with retirement savings! But you can't — the government has been desperately trying to find ways to make housing affordable, and while this is probably not the trick, it can help people who have money to earmark their dollars for a home.

Some details to note: You can only save up to $8,000 per year up to a lifetime limit of $40,000. You have 15 years to use the money inside the account from the day you open it. Keep that in mind — if you're 18 and open one, can you be sure you'll own a home by 33? Maybe, but if not, then give it a couple more years before opening the account. If you haven't bought a home in time, you can transfer the funds into your RRSP tax-free.

5

The Part of Tens

Discover the top 10 questions you should ask your advisor.

Find out whether you need a new financial professional in your life.

Read about the 10 investing blunders everyone makes (so you don't make them, too).

Chapter **24**

Ten Questions to Ask a Potential Financial Advisor

L ots of us are uncomfortable with haggling and being assertive with salespeople. Hey, we're polite Canadians, after all. But you need to get some things straight before you hand over a penny to an investment adviser. Ask each of these ten questions and jot down notes to look over later. If the answers you receive are hazy or otherwise unsatisfactory, then look for somebody else.

How Do You Get Paid?

This is the first detail to find out from an advisor because it usually dictates where you'll hold your account and what kind of investment they'll suggest. If the advisor is paid by the hour or offers a flat fee for their services – called a fee-only advisor – then their advice should be reasonably impartial, and you will have at least an idea of how much you'll be paying. And your advisor will probably be happy to help set up an account at a discount broker to hold your investments.

You find many more fee-only advisors than there used to be in Canada, but there are still many who make a living earning sales commissions — usually from a mutual fund company. While this isn't inherently a bad way to make money, it means you need to ask more questions about the ways in which they choose products for their clients. After all, getting you to buy funds is their bottom line. Many commission-based advisors can buy funds from any mutual fund company, but some can get you to move your money over to their firm or to a mutual fund company account where the firm earns commissions — that's known as *asset capture*.

Some commission-paid advisors won't want to discuss the subject of how they get paid. It's not that they're being dishonest. It's because skilled brokers often avoid depressing topics (such as commissions) and confusing statistics (such as rates of return) until they believe they have won your trust. They first sell you on the concept of the fund — investing in big, stable, undervalued companies, for example — and then get down to the mechanics of how to buy it. The same concept happens on the car dealer's lot — the salesperson tries to dodge the issue of price until you pick out a car you like. But don't fall for the line. If you don't get a straight answer on commissions, then go elsewhere.

What Do You Think of My Financial Situation?

Many advisors now talk about holistic wealth planning, which is a fancy way to say they look at your entire financial situation instead of just your investments. This approach is key today — you want your professional to have an understanding of how, say, your lifestyle or future goals, such as sending a kid to an Ivy League American school or one day buying a vacation home, may impact your savings. Ask the advisor you're interviewing for a quick version of the sort of financial strategy they may recommend for you. Listen carefully to the way they express ideas.

Even after a brief interview in which the advisor should outline the way they're paid, how much communication they'll have with you, and how they plan on addressing everything from taxes to investing, an experienced advisor should have a reasonable notion of your financial health and priorities and should be able to make a couple of sensible suggestions. Clearly, the advisor can't give you a definitive financial prescription without knowing your goals, assets, income potential, and liabilities. But the sort of questions that they ask — like how you're using your registered retirement pension plan (RRSP) and what financial goals you might have — and the interest shown in your problems, will tell you whether the planner is comfortable with you as a client.

Will You Sell Me ETFs, Index Funds, and Low-Cost, No-Load Funds?

This question is one of the most important questions you can ask because funds with low expenses are the very best way to accumulate wealth. Unfortunately, too many professionals aren't keen on selling them because the bargain-priced funds don't pay enough in commissions. That's not necessarily because the salespeople are greedy: They have to make a living. But a good planner or broker should be prepared to fix you up with a mixture of low-expense, no-load funds and regular load or commission-charging funds.

Some advisors who are regulated by the Mutual Funds Dealers Association of Canada (MFDA) won't sell ETFs (as opposed to ones who are licensed by the Investment Industry Regulatory Organization of Canada — IIROC). That's because ETFs, at least in the eyes of the MFDA, are more stocks than mutual funds. That's not to say they can't sell them. MFDA advisors who take an ETF competency course from the Canadian ETF Association are free to sell these low-cost funds.

Ask your advisor about the course and if they can buy ETFs. You want your professional to have the full range of products at their disposal — and if they don't, try someone else.

What Will You Do for Me?

"Financial planning" is such a nebulous but complex topic that the term means something different to everyone. Get a clear idea of what your planner or advisor can do for you and how many times a year you can expect to meet. Ideally, there'll be an organized calendar so that tasks such as making a registered retirement savings plan contribution and reviewing your portfolio are dealt with in a predictable way. If you go away from the initial meeting with the impression that all this person wants to do is sell you a few mutual funds, then that's probably all you'll get.

Can You Help with Income-Splitting and Tax Deferral?

Canadians pay a lot of tax, but many opportunities to lessen the burden exist through simple tax deferral and income-splitting devices, such as spousal registered retirement savings plans. An advisor who's not a tax enthusiast isn't worth hiring. Tax deferral is postponing payment of taxes usually by diverting income into a tax-sheltered account such as an RRSP. Income-splitting usually involves shifting income to a spouse or child who's in a low tax bracket.

Make sure the advisor is able to set up a registered education savings plan (RESP), and understands other accounts, such as the new tax-free first home savings account (FHSA) for those who want to buy a first home, and is happy talking about tax-avoidance methods in detail.

REMEMBER

Avoidance is the legal practice of minimizing the tax you pay, but *evasion* is illegal tax-dodging.

Can I Talk to Some of Your Clients?

The best reference is from someone you know, but asking to talk to satisfied customers never hurts. Confidentiality rules will probably prevent an advisor from giving out names, but they should be able to get someone to call you. If the advisor can't think of a single customer (known in the trade as an *account*) who'd be willing to do that, then how much loyalty do they inspire?

What Do You Think of the Market?

Believe it or not, the ideal answer to this question is: "I don't know." You're hiring someone to help manage your savings here, not to accompany you to Las Vegas. One good thing about mutual funds is that they enable brokers and advisors to do what they're good at — selling investments to people — while relieving them of the need to pretend they know how to pick stocks. After all, why should they? It's far more honest for an advisor to admit they can't beat the market and then sell you a "managed money" product run by someone who is trained to do the job.

All right, nothing's wrong with a potential advisor having an opinion on share prices or the economy, and enjoying talking about the market isn't a crime. But if you get a stream of investing theories and stock tips, then you're talking to a frustrated portfolio manager and not someone who's necessarily going to help build your financial future.

What Training Do You Have?

Financial planning is complex, so insist on some kind of specialized training. All mutual fund salespeople have to pass a basic funds course to obtain the license, but that's fairly bare-bones. Also check that the planner has obtained a specific financial planning qualification — the most popular one being the certified financial planner designation. An under-qualified planner or advisor could miss out on some tax-deferral or wealth-building techniques they haven't heard of.

If the salesperson doesn't have much in the way of training, they could try to bamboozle you with bewildering talk of designations and obscure trade associations — "Oh, you have to have your associated affiliated estate-planning-wealth-building-pigeon-shooting certificate before they'll let you join." Unfortunately, you can't do much about that. But if a planner isn't a member of Advocis or the Institute of Advanced Financial Planners, two financial advisor associations, then ask why.

How Long Have You Been Doing This?

While there's nothing wrong with giving a beginner their big break — someone has to do it after all — it may be better to go with a veteran who has at least a few years of experience. Someone who has seen different market cycles and conditions (i.e., The Great Recession in 2008 and the more recent inflation increases) may have more ideas on how to keep your portfolio afloat in tough times and how to take advantage of the upswings.

Can I See a Sample Client Statement?

If you're buying through a financial planner or mutual fund dealer, then expect to get a twice-yearly account statement from the mutual fund companies you're dealing with. It's the best way to ensure your investment is correctly recorded on the fund companies' books. But the advisor's firm should also give you a consolidated account statement showing all your holdings. Check that it's professionally produced and easy to read. Many aren't.

If you invest with a traditional stockbroker, then you may just get a statement from the brokerage firm and not the fund company. Ask to see an example of a statement.

Chapter 25

Ten Signs You Need a New Financial Advisor

Maybe they just say this to fool us into thinking they're human, but senior executives often claim that firing someone is the hardest thing they have to do. And for an investor, switching advisors is also tough. A salesperson's ego and livelihood are tied up in getting and keeping clients, so losing your account can feel like a punch in the stomach.

The circumstances are rarely cut-and-dried. Most investment advisors are a mixture of good and bad, just like the rest of us. But some clear signs indicate that it's time to move on, and this chapter offers ten classics. These signs apply mostly to commission-paid salespeople — because they have the greatest potential for conflict of interest — but drop a fee-only advisor if they develop any of these bad habits.

Produces Rotten Returns

We're amazed at how many clients hang on with a broker or planner through years of poor investment performance, often languishing in mutual funds that consistently lag the market and rival funds. Yes, measuring performance is tricky, especially if you've been sold a confusing package of funds that can't be compared with other investments. Your funds should show up fairly consistently in the middle of the pack or higher.

One year of poor performance is acceptable because good managers often hold stocks that are out of fashion. But develop itchy feet if it happens again. Fund managers can be left behind by the times, after all. Hot funds may fall to the bottom of the league — but bad funds stay that way.

REMEMBER

If you have an awful year in which most or all your funds are near the back of the pack, then ask for a clear explanation from your advisor. If none is forthcoming, consider moving your account.

Pesters You to Buy New Products after the Firm Is Taken Over

Be wary if your advisor's firm changes hands and your salesperson suddenly starts pushing a new line of funds, possibly an "in-house" brand or other limited-distribution product. These funds may be excellent — and you can be sure there'll be a fancy sales pitch — but the firm's new owners may be pressuring your advisor to switch as many clients as possible to the new lineup. You may pay extra costs.

REMEMBER

It's always better to have more choices.

In general, stick with widely available mutual funds that can be transferred later to a new brokerage or financial planner if you decide to change. Alternatively, the new funds may be available everywhere, but the firm's new management may have struck a special distribution deal. Remember, if you switch, you'll probably be on the hook for commissions.

TECHNICAL STUFF

A growing worry in the Canadian investment world is that more companies, especially banks and their advisors, are forcing their clients to buy only their products. However, many other firms allow clients to buy a wide variety of funds not just those in-house only funds.

Switches Firms Frequently

An advisor who doesn't stay put is usually someone with whom employers aren't happy — and that's a sure indication of trouble. The problem may be fairly innocent — poor recordkeeping, for instance — or it could be as serious as putting clients into unsuitable investments. Whatever it is, by the advisor's second or third move, you should probably part company.

Financial planners and stockbrokers are independent businesspeople with their own book of clients. They join a brokerage firm or mutual fund dealership because it provides an office, administrative support, and credibility. So your advisor will almost certainly try to take you and your account along if a move happens. But don't follow blindly. Talk to the firm's office manager to see if another broker or planner suits you and your investing style.

WARNING

Affairs can get tangled when you pit your advisor against their firm. The firm will also want to hang on to your business, so the salesperson's old boss may falsely imply that there was something not quite right with the departing employee.

Investors often find themselves in a tug-of-greed, with both parties battling over "who owns the assets" — yes, that's the industry phrase, even though we're really talking about *your* money here. We're afraid you just have to use your judgment. If the advisor has provided excellent service, then move your money to their new firm. Good advisors are hard to find.

Keeps Asking for Power of Attorney or Discretionary Authority

Be very wary if an advisor seems excessively keen to get *power of attorney* or *discretionary authority* over your money — legal terms that denote giving them the ability to make decisions without consulting you. Even if you find the whole investing process overwhelming, giving the job of choosing and selling securities to a trusted friend, relative, or even your lawyer is usually preferable.

WARNING

Cases of fraud, exploitation, and deception by brokers almost always involve abuse of discretionary authority over clients' accounts. In fact, it's questionable whether you should ever give such sweeping powers to a salesperson.

But advisors who just don't want to hear from you are all too common. If you feel your advisor isn't listening to you, then they probably aren't. Time to find someone who will.

Doesn't Return Your Calls or Emails

Communication is key in the advisor-client relationship, yet too many people have trouble getting hold of their planner, even in our always-connected world. Brokers and planners are salespeople, remember, which means that they're fueled by new conquests. According to some astute observers, people who go into sales are in fact approval junkies: Every time they get a prospect to say yes, it represents validation of them and not the product.

Junkies are annoying, though. Brokers and planners often neglect their former clients, perhaps because the accounts are too small to generate much in the way of commissions and perhaps because the thrill of the chase is gone. But you deserve better! If you can't get hold of your advisor easily, then look for someone else.

Won't Let You Invest in ETFs and Index Funds

While this is becoming less of an issue, some advisors are still averse to selling index products. Advisors who are licensed to sell products by the Mutual Fund Dealer's Association (MFDA), a self-regulatory organization, can't sell exchange-traded funds (ETFs) at all. Ideally, you want to work with someone who can tap into a wide range of products and build the best portfolio for your situation. Mutual funds are great in many cases, but not all, and you want to make sure you're getting access to the best ETFs, too.

Doesn't Care about Your Overall Financial Plan

There was a time when all an advisor did was invest for their clients. That's no longer the case, especially with fee-only professionals. Since the previous edition of this book was published, the advisor community has started talking about holistic planning — financial advice that includes investments, but also budgeting, estate planning, taxes, and more.

If your advisor says they can't help you create a budget to follow or doesn't know any tax experts to help you minimize what you pay the Canada Revenue Agency, you should look elsewhere for help. Investing, as many people now recognize, is only one part of an overall financial plan.

Suggests "Unregistered" Investments or Other Strange Stuff

If your advisor recommends some unregistered investments, head for the hills. If a fund doesn't come with a regular simplified *prospectus* — the legal document setting out the dangers and potential of the fund — and isn't supported by annual and semi-annual management reports of fund performance, then you're probably going into the deal unprotected. If the investment is offered by an insurance company, however, it should be from a company you've heard of and it should come with a prospectus-like document called an *information folder*.

A few "high net worth" funds for the rich generally require a minimum investment of up to $150,000. These are sold more like stocks, with the risks and terms set out in a document called an offering memorandum. They may be good investments, but always check with an accountant or a lawyer. A professional's fee of a few hundred dollars can save you lots of grief.

One of the most common frauds involves offering unlisted stocks, usually with the promise that they'll soon be trading on a proper exchange and that the price will shoot up after that happens. Or an unscrupulous broker will offer "notes" that purport to carry lavish rates of interest. The scam nearly always contains the implication that you're being let in on the deal in a slightly seedy way — "I shouldn't be telling you this, but . . ."

TIP

An old saying exists among fraud artists: "You can't cheat an honest man." So if your salesperson even hints that buying into a deal involves bending the rules, then move your money immediately.

Keeps Wanting You to Buy and Sell Investments

Excessive trading — known as churning in the investment industry — is a classic sign of a greedy salesperson who views you as a lucrative source of commissions rather than as a long-term customer. If your advisor moves your money to a new fund company, and if you buy the funds on a back-end-load basis — incurring a sales commission that applies only if you sell within a set number of years — then the salesperson can get up to five percent of your investment. That's $1,000 if you move $20,000. So always ask why when the advisor suggests you sell. You can be less suspicious about moves between funds sold by the same company because they don't usually generate a commission for the advisor, although some fund salespeople charge a "switch fee" of two percent. Such transfer fees aren't justifiable, so refuse to pay them.

REMEMBER

Funds are supposed to be long-term holdings — at least five years for an equity fund. That's because the stock market often dips for extended periods and because a good money manager's investment style can easily stop working for a year or longer.

Perhaps your advisor can present a compelling reason to sell — a loss of a fund manager or a drastic change in a fund's holdings, for example. In that case, it may be wise to go along with the suggestion. The advisor's knowledge is what you're paying for, after all. But keep in mind that when you move money to a new fund company or buy a new stock, it's payday for your advisor.

Won't Abandon Pet Theories

Some investment advisors are gold fanatics, some are bond nuts ("I don't like to see anything in a registered retirement savings plan (RRSP), but fixed-income securities"), and some think they're all-knowing about the stock market.

TIP

If your salesperson keeps repeating the same mantra no matter what's happening to your portfolio, then consider a change.

The history of the market is littered with those who hung on for dear life, insisting that their particular stocks or ideas "will come back." Advisors and brokers become incredibly attached to these beliefs, even at the cost of losing clients. If you think your advisor has a one-track mind, then get off at the next station.

Chapter 26

Ten Mistakes Investors Make

We've made many investment mistakes in our lives, so that you don't have to (we like to tell ourselves that, at least). Investing is hard because you have to conquer not only inflation, endless sneaky expenses, and taxes, but also your own innate fear and greed. Here are ten warning signs your personal demons are sabotaging your quest for wealth.

Diversifying Too Much

Buying 20 different funds and assuming you can't lose because you've covered all the bases is pointless. Sure, you're certain to own something that's going up — but a chaotic portfolio like that is also bound to contain lots of funds that hold very similar investments. And the more funds you own, the closer your returns will be to the index or market in general — so why not just buy an exchange-traded fund (ETF), a mutual fund-like security that you can buy and sell on a stock exchange, and be done with it?

Keep matters simple by limiting yourself to a few mutual funds (one Canadian, one U.S., and one international) plus a few conservative equity funds. Depending on the fees of the funds, you may also want to consider buying a few ETFs (again, Canadian, U.S., and international) and then purchasing funds where a stock-picking pro can add value, such as an emerging market-focused fund or a niche sector fund. Ultimately, you don't want to pay multiple management fees to everyone and his beagle in return for mediocre returns that track the market, minus expenses.

Diversifying Too Little

Betting the whole lot on one pony can be tempting. But look at what the professionals do, and you'll notice they always own lots of different stuff. If your portfolio isn't a broad mixture of top-quality bonds and stocks, then you're probably going to fall off at the first fence.

TIP

An old investing rule is that you should own your age in bonds and cash.

According to the old saying, a 40-year-old should have just 60 percent of their money in stocks. That seems overly conservative to many people in our go-go age, where retirees can look forward to 25 years or more after quitting work. But if you don't own at least some bonds, then you're walking a tightrope. Why? Because bonds help with diversification — their prices tend to rise when stocks fall and vice versa — and offer a little extra income in the form of distributions.

Procrastinating

Invest $200 a month for 20 years at an 8-percent annual rate of return, and you'll end up with more than $113,000. But wait five years before starting, and you're looking at less than $69,000. Why the difference? Because of the power of compounding, which is when returns grow on top of the previous year's returns. So get going now. Ten years hence, you don't want to be looking back at today . . . and regretting you didn't just put at least some money into your investment account.

Being Apathetic

Allowing your portfolio to slide into mediocrity is so easy — you might ignore your awful funds, perhaps, or let the cash component build up too high. Personal finances aren't exactly a blast, so we're all tempted to leave details to the forces of continental drift. But just a few dull hours of work once or twice a year can make all the difference between a well-adjusted, balanced portfolio and a neglected mess.

Hanging on to Bad Investments

Refusing to sell a bad fund or stock is the true mark of the hopeless amateur. Unfortunately, no green light comes on when it's time to get out. But one thing's for sure — the price you paid is completely irrelevant. Waiting "until it's back where I bought it" is one of the most damaging actions you can do to your wealth. Sell it, absorb the lesson, and move on.

Taking Cash out of Your RRSP

When contribution room to an Registered Retirement Savings Plan (RRSP) has been used up, it can't be replaced. So think long and hard about cashing in any of those supercharged dollars nestling within your plan. You not only pay taxes, and high ones at that, on the withdrawal, but also give up years of tax-free growth.

Withdrawing money for a down payment on a house under the Home Buyers' Plan is a little less harmful because Ottawa lets you put the cash back in. But you're still probably giving up years of tax-sheltered income within the RRSP because the money isn't there to earn it.

TIP

If you think you're going to need money sooner than retirement, make use of a tax-free savings account, another type of tax-advantaged investment account. If you are saving for a home, consider the First-Time Home Savings Account, which was designed specifically for those who want to save up to buy their first abode.

Ignoring Expenses

Those extra one or two percentage points in mutual fund fees and costs seem so unimportant — but they ultimately represent a huge chunk of your retirement savings. Remember that over 20 years, an extra one percentage point in annual expenses eats up one-fifth of the total accumulated capital. Do yourself a favour and go with some low-cost managers — look for a maximum expense ratio of about 1.5 percent on equity funds. Most ETFs have even lower expenses, so you may also want to consider those first.

Failing to Plan for Taxes

Remember that the mutual fund returns that appear online were earned in a magical tax-free land of hugs, kisses, and happy pixies. In the real world, people have to pay taxes. So beware of holding bonds, bond funds, and other income-paying investments in a taxable account. To minimize the taxes you pay, opt for professional advice unless your finances are extremely straightforward.

Tax accountants know perfectly legal tricks that you don't.

Obsessing about Insignificant Fees

If you're happy with an advisor or fund company, then don't get all irate about a $75 RRSP administration fee. Just pay it if your returns are good and your other expenses are low. People in the fund business tell you that clients happily pay out hundreds or even thousands in management fees without even noticing — but they fly into a rage if presented with a $25 bill for transferring an account.

The fund company or broker who's truly the cheapest may also be the one who nags you for a "nuisance fee" — but at least it's out in the open. By contrast, a fund that's dinging you for huge expenses each year may seem to be absorbing all of those annoying charges itself. But don't worry, you're paying.

Waiting until the Market Looks Better

Ignore this one if you're a psychic. But for the rest of us, attempting to divine the direction of the market is like trying to catch the wind. The movement of share prices is as intangible and random as the weather, or it may as well be.

The fund industry will tell you that "the time to invest is when you have the money." In other words, trying to jump on and off stocks is pointless. And, for once, the fund sellers' homilies are right on the mark. The evidence is overwhelming that market timing is pointless, so grit your teeth and invest. As they used to say in an annoying Irish lottery ad: "If you're not in, you can't win."

Index

A

ABC rules
  for Canadian equity funds, 163
  for global equity funds, 161
ACB (adjusted cost base), 311
account application form, 36–39
account statements, 21, 49–50
actively managed funds, 95, 159
  equity funds, 146
  ETFs vs., 212–213
  European funds, 169
  index funds vs., 212–213
adjusted cost base (ACB), 311
advisors
  asking for references, 322
  buying mutual funds from, 18
  churning, 329–330
  commissioned, 105–106, 111–113, 319–320
  experience of, 323
  fee-only, 106–107, 319–320
  holistic planning, 328
  income-splitting, 321–322
  interviewing, 319–323
  Investment Industry Regulatory Organization of Canada, 321
  lack of communication, 327
  limiting investment options, 328
  Mutual Funds Dealers Association of Canada, 321
  pet theories, 330
  poor performance, 325–326
  pushing for discretionary authority, 327
  pushing new products, 326
  salaried, 107–108
  sample client statement, 323
  switching firms frequently, 326–327
  tax deferral, 321–322
  training, 323
  unregistered investments, 329
Advocis membership, 113
age rule, bond funds, 198–199
AGF Global Select Fund, 153, 162
AIC Advantage fund, 152–153
all-in-one funds, 267–275
  advantages of, 271
  Canadian, 269
  CIBC Managed Balanced Portfolio, 274–275
  CIBC Managed Growth Portfolio, 271
  disadvantages of, 272–273
  global, 269
  management expense ratios, 270
  overview, 267
  rebalancing, 271–272
  researching before buying, 270–271
  risk categories
    conservative packages, 268
    growth packages, 269
    moderate packages, 268
  third-party funds, 273
Altamira, 131
annual compound returns, MRFP, 45
annual report on costs and compensation (ARCC), 51
annual reports, 50–51
annuitants, 261
apathetic investing, 332–333
Apple iPhone, 139
ARCC (annual report on costs and compensation), 51
Asian funds, 170
asset capture, 320
asset protection, seg funds, 261–262
Autorité des marchés financiers, 114
average, calculating, 23
average annual compound return, 13–14

B

back offices, 39

back-end load, 22, 110, 329
  in capital gains calculations, 311
  defined, 33
  discount brokers, 87–88
  Invesco, 117
  transaction slip, 40

balanced funds
  asset mix of, 180–181
  choosing, 186–188
  defined, 17
  Dynamic Global Yield Private Pool, 190
  fees and expenses, 184–185
  Fidelity Balanced Portfolio, 190
  fund manager performance, 185–186
  global balanced funds, 188–190
  income balanced fund, 191
  income trusts, 191
  Mellow Llama Fund, 186
  overview, 179–180
  PH&N Monthly Income, 188
  profitability of, 181–182
  RBC Balanced Fund, 183
  RBC Managed Payout Solution, 188
  real estate trusts, 191
  retiring with, 182
  returns, 182–183
  Scotia Canadian Balanced Fund, 188
  segregated funds, 189
  tactical balanced funds, 192–193
  Tasmanian Devil Fund, 186

balanced investors, 58, 65, 143–144, 158

banks
  actively managed funds, 95
  Big Five banks, 33
  Canadian Imperial Bank of Commerce,
    274–275
  disadvantages of, 96–98
  global equity funds, 99
  index funds, 95
  overview, 93–94

  PH&N Monthly Income, 101
  registered representatives, 94
  Renaissance International Equity Currency
    Neutral, 100
  TD Canadian Small Cap Equity, 101
  third-party funds, 99

Bell, Andrew, 59–60

Beutel Goodman, 131

Big Five banks, 33

bitcoin, 8

BlackBerry, 62, 139

blue-chip companies, 228, 230

BMO S&P/TSX Capped Composite Index ETF, 213

BMO Target Education Portfolios, 251

bond ETFs, 72–73

bond funds
  age rule, 198–199
  choosing, 200–201
  defined, 17
  deflation and, 197–198
  global
    diversification, 209
    Fidelity Investment Grade Total Bond, 210
    overview, 208–209
    RBC Global Bond, 210
  high-yield, 207–208
  index funds and, 203
  inflation and, 201–202
  interest rates and, 202
  long bonds, 203–204
  overview, 195–196
  short-term
    iShares Core Canadian Short Term Bond
      Index, 206
    money market funds vs., 205–206
    overview, 204–205
    PH&N Short Term Bond and Mortgage, 206
  stocks vs., 196–197, 199

bonds
  bond ETFs, 72–73
  defined, 8, 15–16, 72
  investing directly in, 73–74

book value, 50, 52

BSE SENSEX index, 167
buying mutual funds, 17–18
  banks
    actively managed funds, 95
    disadvantages of, 96–98
    global equity funds, 99
    index funds, 95
    overview, 93–94
    PH&N Monthly Income, 101
    registered representatives, 94
    Renaissance International Equity Currency
      Neutral, 100
    TD Canadian Small Cap Equity, 101
    third-party funds, 99
  direct sellers
    advantages of, 122–128
    Altamira, 131
    Beutel Goodman, 131
    Charles Schwab, 130
    disadvantages of, 128–130
    frequent trading, 125–128
    high minimum purchases, 121
    IG Wealth Management, 133–134
    investment advice, 123–124
    Leith Wheeler, 132
    Mawer, 132–133
    McLean Budden, 131
    overview, 119–121
    Pembroke Management, 132
    Phillips, Hager & North, 131
    profitability of using, 123
    Saxon Investment Management, 131
    Sceptre, 131
    Scudder, 130
    simplicity of using, 124–125
    Steadyhand Investment Management Ltd., 133
    Vanguard, 130
    when to choose, 122
  discount brokers, 18
    back-end-load, 88
    choosing, 88–90
    commissions, 86–87
    convenience of, 84
    defined, 82
    disadvantages of, 91
    front-load, 86
    as information resource, 85
    overview, 81–82
    setting up with, 83
    wide selection of options, 85
  fund companies, 18
  fund salespersons
    choosing, 115
    commissioned advisors, 105–106, 111–113
    fee transparency, 109–110
    fee-only financial planners, 106–107
    mutual fund classes, 116–117
    overview, 103–105
    qualifications, 113–114
    salaried advisors, 107–108
  load funds, 32–33
  no-load funds, 33–34
  online purchases, 18
  overview, 17–18
  professional advisors, 18
  reasons for, 19–27
  robo advisor, 92

C

CAD-hedged ETF, 213, 224
Canada Deposit Insurance Corp, 70
Canada Pension Plan (CPP), 54
Canadian Airlines, 59
Canadian equity funds
  ABC rules for, 163
  Canoe Equity Portfolio Class F, 163–164
  defined, 156–157
  equity categories, 162
  Fidelity True North Fund, 164
  PH&N Conservative Equity Income Series F, 164
Canadian fund packages, 269
Canadian Imperial Bank of Commerce (CIBC),
  274–275
Canadian Investment Funds Standards
  Committee, 21
Canadian Investment Regulatory Organization (CIRO),
  112, 114, 285
Canadian Securities Course, 114

Canadian Securities Institute (CSI), 114

CanadianFundWatch.com, 283

Canoe Equity Portfolio Class F, 163–164

capital appreciation, 13

capital gains
  defined, 11, 304
  dividend income vs., 11–12
  taxes, 310–312

capped indexes, 215–216

cashable GICs, 69

Castro, Anna, 101

Certified Financial Planner (CFP), 114

Charles Schwab, 130

churning, 329–330

CI Global Income & Growth fund, 45–48

CIBC (Canadian Imperial Bank of Commerce), 274–275

CIBC Canadian Equity Fund, 215–216

CIBC Managed Balanced Portfolio, 274–275

CIBC Managed Growth Portfolio, 271

CIBC Monthly Income, 236

CIRO (Canadian Investment Regulatory Organization), 112, 114, 285

closed-end funds, 9, 77

commissioned advisors, 319–320
  financial planners, 112
  insurance agents and brokers, 112–113
  overview, 105–106
  stockbrokers, 111–112

commodity supercycle, 175

confirmation (transaction) slips, 40

Connor, Clark & Lunn Investment Management, 101

conservative fund packages, 268

contributions
  RRSPs, 291–292
  TFSAs, 294–295

convertible GICs, 69

cost base, 311

CPP (Canada Pension Plan), 54

Craig, Michael, 101

cryptocurrency funds, 255

CSI (Canadian Securities Institute), 114

current yield, money market funds, 243

D

debt, 56–57, 105

Deckart, Christian, 161

deductions, 313

deferred sales charges (DSC), 33. *See also* back-end load

defined contribution plans, 56

deflation, 197–198

direct sellers
  advantages of, 122–128
  Altamira, 131
  Beutel Goodman, 131
  Charles Schwab, 130
  disadvantages of, 128–130
  frequent trading, 125–128
  high minimum purchases, 121
  IG Wealth Management, 133–134
  investment advice, 123–124
  Leith Wheeler, 132
  Mawer, 132–133
  McLean Budden, 131
  overview, 119–121
  Pembroke Management, 132
  Phillips, Hager & North, 131
  profitability of using, 123
  Saxon Investment Management, 131
  Sceptre, 131
  Scudder, 130
  simplicity of using, 124–125
  Steadyhand Investment Management Ltd., 133
  Vanguard, 130
  when to choose, 122

disadvantages, 96–98

discount brokers
  back-end-load, 88
  buying mutual funds from, 18
  choosing, 88–90
  commissions, 86–87
  convenience of, 84
  defined, 82
  disadvantages of, 91
  front-load, 86
  as information resource, 85

overview, 81–82
setting up with, 83
wide selection of options, 85
discretionary authority, 327
distributions
  capital gain distributions, 301, 310–312
  defined, 12, 292
  determining what fund has declared, 307–308
  dividend distributions, 301
  overview, 304
  paying out to fundholders, 304–306
  researching, 235
  taxes and, 214–215, 306–309
diversification, 23–24, 61, 63
  equity funds, 152
  global bonds, 209
  over-diversifying, 331–332
  under-diversifying, 332
dividend and income funds
  choosing, 235
  CIBC Monthly Income, 236
  growth companies, 230–231
  income trust funds, 237–238
  overview, 227–229
  preferred shares, 237
  slow-growing companies, 229–230
  taxes and, 232–234
  TD Monthly Income, 236
dividends
  capital gains vs., 11–12
  defined, 11, 304
documentation
  account application form, 36–39
  account statements, 49–50
  annual reports, 50–51
  book value, 52
  confirmation slip, 40
  management reports of fund performance
    annual compound returns, 45
    financial highlights, 45
    investment objectives, 44
    management expense ratio, 47
    management fees, 45
    net assets, 47
    past performance, 45
    portfolio breakdown, 47
    portfolio turnover rate, 48
    recent developments, 44
    related party transactions, 45
    results of operations, 44
    risk experience, 44
    top-25 holdings, 47
    year-by-year returns, 45–46
  overview, 35–36
  prospectus
    canceling mutual fund purchase, 43
    fees and expenses, 42–43
    investment objectives, 41–42
    overview, 40–41
    risks associated with investment, 41–42
dollar cost-averaging, 25
DSC (deferred sales charges), 33. *See also* back-end load
Dynamic Global Yield Private Pool, 190
Dynamic U.S. Strategic Yield Fund, 161–162

E

EAFE (Europe Australasia Far East) index, 221
effective yield, money market funds, 243
emergency fund, 57
emerging markets funds, 172–173
environmental, social and governance (ESG) funds,
    251–252
equity funds, 126
  actively managed funds, 146
  blue-chip winners, 149
  choosing, 147
  defined, 17
  diversification, 152
  fund managers, 151
  heirloom funds
    balanced investors, 158
    Canadian equity funds, 156–157, 162–164
    global equity funds, 156, 160–162
    growth investors, 158
    overview, 155–156
    savers, 157
    specialty funds vs., 157
    splitting money between, 158–160

equity funds *(continued)*

  industry groups, 148–149

  international equity funds, 159

  investing vs. gambling, 138–139

  investment styles, 143–144

  knowing when to sell, 152–153

  lessons learned from history, 144–146

  long-term view, 140, 152–153

  1980–2023, 145

  1987–1997, 144

  1992–2002, 145

  1997–2007, 145

  Nortel, 141–142

  overview, 137–153

  regional funds, 168–173

    Asian funds, 170

    emerging markets funds, 172–173

    European funds, 169

    Japanese funds, 170–171

    overview, 168–169

    U.S. funds, 171–172

  returns, 147

  reviewing past performance, 149–151

  sector funds

    financial services funds, 177

    overview, 174

    resource funds, 174–175

    science and technology funds, 176

  small/mid-cap funds, 166–168

  2008–2023, 145

escalating-rate GICs, 70

ESG (environmental, social and governance) funds, 251–252

ETFs. *See* exchange-traded funds

Euronext 100, 169

Europe Australasia Far East (EAFE) index, 221

European funds, 169

exchange-traded funds (ETFs), 28, 62, 75, 159

  actively managed funds vs., 212–213

  affordability, 213–214

  buying, 221–224

  evaluating performance, 218

  fitting into portfolio, 216–217

  mutual funds vs., 218–220

  overcoming salespeople's dislike of, 220–221

  overview, 211–212

  regulations for selling, 321

  risks, 215–216

  specialized, 224–225

  taxes, 312–313

  taxes and, 214–215

F

FAANG stocks, 171

F-class funds, 117

federal dividend tax credit, 308–309

fee transparency, 109–110

fee-only advisors, 106–107, 319–320

fees and expenses

  balanced funds, 184–185

  disclosing in prospectus, 42–43

  MRFP management fees, 45

  obsessing about insignificant fees, 334

  seg funds probate fees, 262

FHSA (first home savings account), 315

Fidelity, 312

Fidelity Balanced Portfolio, 190

Fidelity ClearPath funds, 250

Fidelity Investment Grade Total Bond, 210

Fidelity True North Fund, 164

Fijalkowski, Dagmara, 201

financial plan

  balanced investors, 58, 65

  Canada Pension Plan, 54

  diversification, 61

  financial priorities, 55–57

  growth investors, 58, 65–66

  Guaranteed Income Supplement, 55

  index funds, 62–63

  Old Age Security, 55

  overview, 53–54

  Quebec Pension Plan, 55

  RRSP loan, 60

  savers, 59, 64

  uncertainty of investing, 59–60

financial planners, 106–107, 112. *See also* advisors

Financial Post, 283

financial priorities, 55–57

financial services funds, 177

financial statements, 20–21, 50–51

Financial Times Stock Exchange 100 (FTSE), 169

first home savings account (FHSA), 315

First Investment Counsel Corp, 10

Fool and His Money, A: (Rothchild), 24

front-load (sales charge), 33, 86, 117

FT Wilshire 5000 Index, 222

FTSE (Financial Times Stock Exchange 100), 169

FTSE Canada Universe Bond Index, 196

fund companies, 18

fund managers, 8, 151, 185–186, 218–219

fund packages
  advantages of, 271
  Canadian, 269
  CIBC Managed Balanced Portfolio, 274–275
  CIBC Managed Growth Portfolio, 271
  disadvantages of, 272–273
  global, 269
  management expense ratios, 270
  overview, 267
  rebalancing, 271–272
  researching before buying, 270–271
  risk categories
    conservative packages, 268
    growth packages, 269
    moderate packages, 268
  third-party funds, 273

fund salespersons
  choosing, 115
  commissioned advisors, 105–106, 111–113
  fee transparency, 109–110
  fee-only financial planners, 106–107
  mutual fund classes, 116–117
  overview, 103–105
  qualifications
    Advocis membership, 113
    Autorité des marchés financiers, 114
    Canadian Securities Course, 114
    Canadian Securities Institute, 114
    Certified Financial Planner, 114
    CIRO, 114
    Institut québécois de planification financière, 114

Institute of Advanced Financial Planners membership, 114
    Registered Financial Planner, 114
  salaried advisors, 107–108

fund sponsor (management company), 8

Fundlibrary.com, 282

funds. *See also* equity funds; exchange-traded funds; index funds
  balanced funds
    asset mix of, 180–181
    choosing, 186–188
    Dynamic Global Yield Private Pool, 190
    Fidelity Balanced Portfolio, 190
    fund manager performance, 185–186
    global balanced funds, 188–190
    high fees and expenses, 184–185
    income balanced fund, 191
    income trusts, 191
    Mellow Llama Fund, 186
    overview, 179–180
    PH&N Monthly Income, 188
    profitability of, 181–182
    RBC Balanced Fund, 183
    RBC Managed Payout Solution, 188
    real estate trusts, 191
    retiring with, 182
    returns, 182–183
    Scotia Canadian Balanced Fund, 188
    segregated funds, 189
    tactical balanced funds, 192–193
    Tasmanian Devil Fund, 186
  bond funds
    age rule, 198–199
    choosing, 200–201
    deflation and, 197–198
    global, 208–210
    high-yield, 207–208
    index funds and, 203
    inflation and, 201–202
    long bonds, 203–204
    overview, 195–196
    short-term, 204–206
    stocks vs., 196–197
  cryptocurrency funds, 255

funds *(continued)*

dividend and income funds

choosing, 235

CIBC Monthly Income, 236

growth companies, 230–231

income trust funds, 237–238

overview, 227–229

preferred shares, 237

slow-growing companies, 229–230

taxes and, 232–234

TD Monthly Income, 236

environmental, social and governance (ESG) funds, 251–252

fund packages

advantages of, 271

CIBC Managed Balanced Portfolio, 274–275

CIBC Managed Growth Portfolio, 271

disadvantages of, 272–273

management expense ratios, 270

overview, 267

risk categories, 268–269

third-party funds, 273

heirloom equity funds, 155–164

income trusts, 77, 191, 237–238

infrastructure funds, 254

labour-sponsored funds, 252–254

money market funds

choosing, 245–248

current yield, 243

effective yield, 243

guaranteed investment certificates vs., 241

HISA funds, 245

overview, 239–240

segregated funds, 242

short-term bond funds, 244

segregated funds

asset protection, 261–262

choosing, 265–266

guarantee, 260–261

MLI Fidelity Canadian Asset Allocation GIF Fund, 265

overview, 257–258

passing on to heirs, 262–263

popularity of, 259

resetting value, 261

security, 258–259

survivorship bias, 264

target date funds, 250–251

ultra-specific mandates, 255

funds of funds. *See* fund packages

futures, 76

G

Genua, Tony, 162

Get Smarter About Money website, 285

GICs (guaranteed investment certificates), 16

benefits of, 70–71

cashable GICs, 69

convertible GICs, 69

escalating-rate GICs, 70

finding best rates, 70

index-linked GICs, 69

inflation and, 71–72

laddering, 70

money market funds vs., 241

overview, 68

global balanced funds, 188–190

global bonds

diversification, 209

Fidelity Investment Grade Total Bond, 210

overview, 208–209

RBC Global Bond, 210

global equity funds, 99

ABC rules for, 161

AGF Global Select fund, 162

defined, 156

Dynamic U.S. Strategic Yield, 161–162

Mawer Global Equity, 161

overview, 160

global fund packages, 269

Globefund.com, 280–281

government and industry organizations

Get Smarter About Money website, 285

Investment Funds Institute of Canada, 284

Mutual Fund Dealers Association of Canada, 285

System for Electronic Document Analysis and Retrieval, 285–286

growth companies, 230–231

growth fund packages, 269

growth investors, 58, 65–66, 143–144, 158

growth stocks, 214

guaranteed funds, 258. *See also* segregated funds

Guaranteed Income Supplement, 55

guaranteed investment certificates (GICs), 16

  benefits of, 70–71

  cashable GICs, 69

  convertible GICs, 69

  escalating-rate GICs, 70

  finding best rates, 70

  index-linked GICs, 69

  inflation and, 71–72

  laddering, 70

  money market funds vs., 241

  overview, 68

H

hedge funds, 77

heirloom funds

  balanced investors, 158

  Canadian equity funds

    Canoe Equity Portfolio Class F, 163–164

    defined, 156–157

    Fidelity True North Fund, 164

    overview, 162–163

    PH&N Conservative Equity Income Series F, 164

  global equity funds

    ABC rules for, 161

    AGF Global Select Fund, 162

    defined, 156

    Dynamic U.S. Strategic Yield, 161–162

    Mawer Global Equity, 161

    overview, 160

  growth investors, 158

  overview, 155–156

  savers, 157

  specialty funds vs., 157

  splitting money between, 158–160

high interest saving account (HISA) funds, 245

high-yield bond funds, 207–208

holistic planning, 328

holistic wealth planning, 320

I

IFIC (Investment Funds Institute of Canada), 26, 284

IG Wealth Management, 133–134, 272

IIROC (Investment Industry Regulatory Organization of Canada), 112, 285, 321

income balanced fund, 191

income trusts, 77, 191, 237–238

income funds. *See* dividend and income funds

income-splitting, 321–322

independents

  advantages of, 122–128

  Altamira, 131

  Beutel Goodman, 131

  Charles Schwab, 130

  disadvantages of, 128–130

  frequent trading, 125–128

  high minimum purchases, 121

  IG Wealth Management, 133–134

  investment advice, 123–124

  Leith Wheeler, 132

  Mawer, 132–133

  McLean Budden, 131

  overview, 119–121

  Pembroke Management, 132

  Phillips, Hager & North, 131

  profitability of using, 123

  Saxon Investment Management, 131

  Sceptre, 131

  Scudder, 130

  simplicity of using, 124–125

  Steadyhand Investment Management Ltd., 133

  Vanguard, 130

  when to choose, 122

index funds, 34, 62–63, 75, 95, 159

  actively managed funds vs., 212–213

  affordability, 213–214

  buying, 221–224

  defined, 28

  fitting into portfolio, 216–217

index funds *(continued)*
  overcoming salespeople's dislike of, 220–221
  overview, 211–212
  risks, 215–216
  specialized, 224–225
  taxes and, 214–215, 312–313
  tilted funds, 225
index-linked GICs, 69
inflation
  bond funds and, 201–202
  guaranteed investment certificate and, 71–72
  interest rates and, 64, 146, 183, 191, 201–202
informal trusts, 313–314
information resources
  balanced research, 288
  brokers and planners, 287
  fund company sites, 286–287
  government and industry organizations
    Get Smarter About Money website, 285
    Investment Funds Institute of Canada, 284
    Mutual Fund Dealers Association of Canada, 285
    System for Electronic Document Analysis and
      Retrieval, 285–286
  independent sources
    books and newspapers, 283–284
    CanadianFundWatch.com, 283
    Financial Post, 283
    Fundlibrary.com, 282
    Globefund.com, 22, 280–281
    Lipper Leaders, 283
    MoneySense.ca, 282
    Morningstar.ca, 21–22, 151, 281–282
  overview, 279
infrastructure funds, 254
Institut québécois de planification financière, 114
Institute of Advanced Financial Planners
    membership, 114
insurance agents and brokers, 112–113
interest rates
  bond funds and, 202
  bond prices and, 244
  bond yield and, 243
  high-yield funds, 207

HISA funds, 245
inflation and, 64, 146, 183, 191, 201–202
long-term funds and, 204
preferred shares, 237
strip bonds and, 74
international equity funds, 159
in-trust accounts, 313–314
Invesco, 117
investing
  gambling vs., 138–139
  investment styles, 143–144
investment advisors. *See* advisors
Investment Funds Institute of Canada (IFIC), 26, 284
Investment Industry Regulatory Organization of
    Canada (IIROC), 112, 285, 321
investment objectives, MRFP, 44
investors
  balanced investors, 58, 65
  common mistakes of
    apathetic investing, 332–333
    hanging on to bad investments, 333
    ignoring expenses, 333
    obsessing about insignificant fees, 334
    over-diversifying, 331–332
    poor tax planning, 334
    procrastination, 332
    trying to time the market, 334
    under-diversifying, 332
    withdrawing cash from RRSP, 333
  growth investors, 58, 65–66
  savers, 59, 64
iPhone, 139
iShares Canadian Real Return Bond Index ETF, 223
iShares Canadian Select Dividend Index ETF, 235
iShares Core Canadian Short Term Bond
    Index, 206
iShares Core Canadian Universe Bond Index ETF,
    203, 225
iShares Core S&P 500 Index ETF, 213, 224

J

Japanese funds, 170–171

K

Know Your Client (KYC) principle, 37–38
Know Your Product (KYP) requirement, 38

L

labour-sponsored funds, 252–254
Latin American funds, 173
Leckie, Roy, 100
Leffler, Edward, 10
Leith Wheeler, 132
life insurance, 57
limited partnerships, 77
Lipper Leaders, 283
load funds
  buying, 32
  overview, 31–32
  sales commissions, 32–33
long bonds, 203–204
low-load funds, 33
Lysakowski, Scott, 101

M

Mackenzie Global Dividend fund, 134
Mackenzie Mutual Fund Tax Guide, 312
Macquaker, Charles, 100
Madeiros, Christian, 101
Malkiel, Burton, 219
managed investment products, 77
management company (fund sponsor), 8
management expense ratios (MERs), 26, 116
  bond funds, 200
  fund packages, 270
  management reports of fund performance, 47
  money market funds, 247–248
management reports of fund performance (MRFP), 31, 287
  annual compound returns, 45
  financial highlights, 45
  investment objectives, 44
  management expense ratio, 47
  management fees, 45
  net assets, 47
  past performance, 45
  portfolio breakdown, 47
  portfolio turnover rate, 48
  recent developments, 44
  related party transactions, 45
  results of operations, 44
  risk experience, 44
  top-25 holdings, 47
  year-by-year returns, 45–46
Mawer Global Equity Fund, 161
Mawer Investment Management Ltd., 121, 132–133
McLean Budden, 131
median, defined, 23
Mellow Llama Fund, 186
MERs (management expense ratios), 26, 116
  bond funds, 200
  fund packages, 270
  management reports of fund performance, 47
  money market funds, 247–248
Mersch, Frank, 150
MFDA (Mutual Fund Dealers Association of Canada), 285, 321
MLI Fidelity Canadian Asset Allocation GIF Fund, 265
moderate fund packages, 268
money market funds
  choosing, 245–248
  current yield, 243
  defined, 17
  effective yield, 243
  guaranteed investment certificates vs., 241
  HISA funds, 245
  overview, 239–240
  segregated funds, 242
  short-term bond funds vs., 205–206, 244
MoneySense.ca, 282
Morningstar
  iShares Core Canadian Short Term Bond Index, 206
  Morningstar.ca, 21–22, 100–101, 281–282
  PH&N Short Term Bond and Mortgage, 206
  recommendations
    bank funds, 100–101
    bond funds, 201
    Canadian balanced funds, 188
    dividend and income funds, 236

Morningstar *(continued)*

   equity funds, 161–164

   global balanced funds, 190

   global bond funds, 210

   low-cost funds, 223

   short-term bond funds, 206

  survivorship bias, 182, 264

Moroz, Paul, 161

MRFP (management reports of fund performance), 31, 287

  annual compound returns, 45

  financial highlights, 45

  investment objectives, 44

  management expense ratio, 47

  management fees, 45

  net assets, 47

  past performance, 45

  portfolio breakdown, 47

  portfolio turnover rate, 48

  recent developments, 44

  related party transactions, 45

  results of operations, 44

  risk experience, 44

  top-25 holdings, 47

  year-by-year returns, 45–46

MSCI Emerging Markets Index, 172

MSCI world index, 222

Mutual Fund Dealers Association of Canada (MFDA), 285, 321

Mutual Fund Fee Calculator, 285

mutual funds

  balanced funds, 17

  bond funds, 17

  bonds, 8, 15–16

  buying

   discount brokers, 18

   fund companies, 18

   online purchases, 18

   overview, 17–18

   professional advisors, 18

  classes of, 116–117

  closed-end funds, 9

  defined, 8

  distribution, 12

  equity funds, 17

  ETFs vs., 218–220

  fund manager, 8

  management company, 8

  management expense ratio, 27–28

  money market funds, 17

  net asset value, 9

  net asset value per share, 9

  open-end funds, 9–10

  origin of, 10

  percentage return, 12

  performance reports, 30

  profitability of, 15

  profusion of products, 29

  prospectuses, 30–31

  returns

   capital gains vs. dividend income, 11–12

   as percentage of capital, 12–14

  stocks, 8

  stocks and shares, 15–16

  style drift, 28

  total assets, 8

  unitholders, 8

N

NerdWallet, 70

net asset value, 9

net asset value per share (NAVPS), 9, 21

net assets, MRFP, 47

Nippon Telegraph, 171

no-load fund companies. *See* independents

no-load funds, 10, 18, 33–34

Nortel, 62, 141–142, 215–216

O

Old Age Security, 55

online resources

  calculating fees, 27

  CanadianFundWatch.com, 283

  CDIC coverage, 71

  Cheat Sheet, 3

  discount brokers, 87

ETFs and index funds, 203
Financial Post, 283
Fundlibrary.com, 282
fund's past performance, 150
GIC rates, 70
Globefund.com, 22, 280–281
Lipper Leaders, 283
MoneySense.ca, 282
Morningstar.ca, 21–22, 151, 281–282
researching funds, 22
Stingy Investor Web site, 90
open-end funds, 9–10

P

Pallet Pallet, 59
pan-European index, 169
partnerships, 77
Pembroke Management, 132
pension adjustment, 291
percentage return, 12
PH&N Conservative Equity Income Series F, 164
PH&N Monthly Income, 101, 188
PH&N Short Term Bond and Mortgage, 206
Phillips, Hager & North, 131
pooled funds, 272
portfolio breakdown, MRFP, 47
portfolio turnover rate, MRFP, 48
preferred shares, 237
procrastination, 332
professional advisors. *See* advisors
profitability of mutual funds, 15
prospectus
    canceling mutual fund purchase, 43
    costs and fees, 42–43
    investment objectives, 41–42
    overview, 40–41
    risks associated with investment, 41–42

Q

Quebec Pension Plan, 55

R

Random Walk Down Wall Street, A (Malkiel), 219
Ratehub, 70
rational expectations theory, 165–166
RBC Balanced Fund, 183
RBC Global Bond, 210
RBC Managed Payout Solution, 188
RBC Select Balanced Portfolio, 36
Real Estate Investment Trusts (REITs), 238
real estate trusts, 191
rebalancing portfolio, 271–273
recent developments, MRFP, 44
redemption charge, 22, 110, 329
    in capital gains calculations, 311
    defined, 33
    discount brokers, 87–88
    Invesco, 117
    transaction slip, 40
regional equity funds
    Asian funds, 170
    emerging markets funds, 172–173
    European funds, 169
    Japanese funds, 170–171
    overview, 168–169
    U.S. funds, 171–172
registered education savings plans (RESPs), 314–315
Registered Financial Planner (RFP), 114
registered representatives, 94
registered retirement income fund (RRIF), 293–294
Registered Retirement Savings Plan (RRSP)
    account application form, 36–39
    asset mix, 301–302
    buying, 297–299
    capital gain distributions, 301
    contributions, 291–292
    converting to RRIF, 293–294
    defined, 101
    dividend funds and, 230, 233–234
    international investments, 300–301
    overview, 290
    RRSP loan, 60

Registered Retirement Savings Plan (RRSP) *(continued)*
  self-directed, 299–300
  tax-deferred income, 292–293
  TFSA vs., 296–297
  withdrawing cash from, 333
REITs (Real Estate Investment Trusts), 238
related party transactions, MRFP, 45
Renaissance International Equity Currency Neutral, 100
Research In Motion (RIM), 139
resource funds, 174–175
RESPs (registered education savings plans), 314–315
return of capital, 310
returns
  average annual compound return, 13–14
  balanced funds, 182–183
  capital gains vs. dividend income, 11–12
  equity funds, 147
  as percentage of capital, 12–14
RFP (Registered Financial Planner), 114
rights, 76
RIM (Research In Motion), 139
Riopelle, Sarah, 192–193, 201
risks associated with investment
  disclosing, 41–42
  ETFs, 215–216
  index funds, 215–216
  risk capacity, 38
  risk experience, 44
robo advisor, 92
Rothchild, John, 24
Rothery, Norman, 90
Royal Bank of Canada, 36
royalty trusts, 77
RRIF (registered retirement income fund), 293–294
RRSP (Registered Retirement Savings Plan)
  account application form, 36–39
  asset mix, 301–302
  buying, 297–299
  capital gain distributions, 301
  contributions, 291–292
  converting to RRIF, 293–294

  defined, 101
  dividend funds and, 230, 233–234
  international investments, 300–301
  overview, 290
  RRSP loan, 60
  self-directed, 299–300
  tax-deferred income, 292–293
  TFSA vs., 296–297
  withdrawing cash from, 333
Russell 3000 index, 172

S

S&P Canada Aggregate Bond Index, 196
S&P/TSX 60, 222
S&P/TSX Composite, 48–49, 142
salaried advisors, 107–108
sales channel, 221
sales charge, 33, 86, 117
sales commissions. *See also* commissioned advisors
  discount brokers, 86–87
  load funds, 32–33
savers, 59, 64, 143–144, 157
savings accounts. *See also* Registered Retirement Savings Plan
  first home savings account, 315
  registered education savings plans, 314–315
  tax-free savings account
    contributions, 294–295
    dividend funds and, 234
    investing in, 296
    overview, 294
    RRSP vs., 296–297
Saxon Investment Management, 131
Sceptre, 131
scholarship trusts, 314
science and technology funds, 176
Scotia Canadian Balanced Fund, 188
Scotia Selected Balanced Income Portfolio, 99–100
Scudder, 130
sector equity funds
  financial services funds, 177
  overview, 174

resource funds, 174–175

science and technology funds, 176

SEDAR (System for Electronic Document Analysis and Retrieval), 285–286

segregated funds (seg funds), 189, 242

  asset protection, 261–262

  beneficiaries, 261

  choosing, 265–266

  guarantee, 260–261

  MLI Fidelity Canadian Asset Allocation GIF Fund, 265

  overview, 257–258

  passing on to heirs, 262–263

  "pillow factor," 266

  popularity of, 259

  probate fees and, 262

  resetting value, 261

  security, 258–259

  survivorship bias, 264

self-directed RESPs, 319

self-directed RRSPs, 299–300

selling mutual funds, 27

Shopify Inc., 76

short-term bond funds, 244

  iShares Core Canadian Short Term Bond Index, 206

  money market funds vs., 205–206

  overview, 204–205

  PH&N Short Term Bond and Mortgage, 206

slow-growing companies, 229–230

small/mid-cap equity funds, 166–168

Solactive Broad Canadian TR Index, 196

specialty funds, 157

Steadyhand Investment Management Ltd., 133

Stingy Investor Web site, 90

stock market capitalization, 167

stockbrokers, 111–112

stocks

  bond funds vs., 196–197, 199

  buying individual stocks, 75–76

  defined, 8, 15–16

  overview, 74

strip bonds, 73–74

survivorship bias, 182, 264

System for Electronic Document Analysis and Retrieval (SEDAR), 285–286

T

T3 tax slip, 309

T5 tax slip, 309

tactical balanced funds, 192–193

target date funds, 250–251

Tasmanian Devil Fund, 186

tax deferral, 321–322

tax efficiency, 301–302

taxes

  capital gain distributions, 310–312

  deductions, 313

  dividend and income funds and, 232–234

  ETFs and, 214–215, 312–313

  exchanges, 309–310

  federal dividend tax credit, 308–309

  first home savings account, 315

  fund distributions, 304–312

  index funds, 214–215, 312–313

  informal trusts, 313–314

  in-trust accounts, 313–314

  portfolio rebalancing and, 272

  registered education savings plans, 314–315

  switching funds to avoid, 310

  tax slips, 309

  year-end fund purchases, 312

tax-free savings account (TFSA)

  contributions, 294–295

  dividend funds and, 234

  investing in, 296

  overview, 294

  RRSP vs., 296–297

T-bills (Treasure bill funds), 246

T-class funds, 117

TD Canadian Bond E class, 203

TD Canadian Index Class E, 223

TD Canadian Small Cap Equity, 101

TD Monthly Income, 236

TFSA (tax-free savings account)

  contributions, 294–295

  dividend funds and, 234

  investing in, 296

  overview, 294

  RRSP vs., 296–297

third-party funds, 99, 272, 273
tilted funds, 225
top-25 holdings, MRFP, 47
total assets, defined, 8
total expense ratio, 51
trailers, 130
transaction (confirmation) slips, 40
Treasure bill funds (T-bills), 246
Trimark Select Growth Fund, 156

U

ultra-specific mandates, 255
uncertainty of investing, 59–60
unit trusts, 77
unitholders, defined, 8
unregistered investments, 329
U.S. funds, 171–172

V

Vanguard, 130

W

Walter Scott & Partners, 101
warrants, 76

will, 57
wraps
    advantages of, 271
    Canadian, 269
    CIBC Managed Balanced Portfolio, 274–275
    CIBC Managed Growth Portfolio, 271
    disadvantages of, 272–273
    global, 269
    management expense ratios, 270
    overview, 267
    rebalancing, 271–272
    researching before buying, 270–271
    risk categories
        conservative packages, 268
        growth packages, 269
        moderate packages, 268
    third-party funds, 273

Y

year-by-year returns, MRFP, 45–46

About the Author

Bryan Borzykowski: Bryan is an award-winning business and investment journalist. He's written for the *New York Times*, CNBC, BBC, *Globe and Mail*, Financial Post, Wired, *Washington Post* and many other publications. Bryan is also the author of several Wiley books, including *The Canadian's Guide to Personal Finance for Singles* and *ETFs For Canadians For Dummies*, 2nd Edition among others. He also often appears on CTV News Channel, SiriusXM, and BNN Bloomberg. Bryan is currently the founder and editorial director of ALLCAPS Content, an agency that creates editorial-style content and communications for companies. He was also the president of the Society for Advancing Business Editing and Writing (SABEW), an international organization for business journalists and is currently the president of the *Canadian Jewish News*.

Andrew Bell: Andrew worked as an investment reporter and editor with The Globe and Mail for 12 years. He joined Business News Network as a reporter in 2001. Bell, an import from Dublin, Ireland, was the main compiler of "Stars & Dogs" in Saturday's Globe for 10 years. He has also taken to the stage, where he practises a demanding "method" that involves getting the audience and other performers as off-balance and upset as possible. He lives in Cabbagetown, Toronto, with his wife and daughter.

Matthew Elder: Matthew is a journalist and communications consultant specializing in personal finance. His 40-year career includes columnist and editor positions with *The Montreal Gazette and Financial Post*, where he coordinated those newspapers' coverage of investment funds. Matthew subsequently led development of content for Morningstar Canada. He went on to create Sensible Communications, which produces content for the financial-services industry.

Dedication

Bryan dedicates this book to his wife, three daughters, and even his two dogs. They are the reasons (motivationally but also literally — especially the dogs) why he gets up and goes to work every morning.

Author's Acknowledgments

Bryan is thrilled to once again work with the Wiley crew on this book. Thanks to Tracy Boggier and Elizabeth Stilwell for asking me to be part of this and Victoria Carmody for putting up with a few missed deadlines — but we made it, right? I'm also grateful for my old *Canadian Business* magazine editor, Michael McCullough, who helped me with some research and writing for this edition, and Mark Brown and Glynis Ratcliffe, my colleagues at ALLCAPS Content, for their ongoing support. Finally, but most importantly, I could not do any books or really anything without the support of my family.

Publisher's Acknowledgments

Acquisitions Editor: Elizabeth Stilwell

Development Editor and Project Manager: Victoria Carmody

Copy Editor: Jerelind Charles

Technical Editor: Donald Loney

Managing Editor: Sofia Malik

Production Editor: Tamilmani Varadharaj

Cover Image: © Yuichiro Chino/Getty Images